THE
IMPORTANCE OF
BEING URBAN

HISTORICAL STUDIES OF URBAN AMERICA

Edited by Lilia Fernández, Timothy J. Gilfoyle, Becky M. Nicolaides,
and Amanda I. Seligman
James R. Grossman, Editor Emeritus

RECENT TITLES IN THE SERIES

A complete list of series titles is available on the University of Chicago Press website.

THE IMPORTANCE OF BEING URBAN

Designing the Progressive
School District, 1890–1940

DAVID A. GAMSON

The University of Chicago Press
Chicago and London

The University of Chicago Press, Chicago 60637
The University of Chicago Press, Ltd., London
© 2019 by The University of Chicago
Published 2019
Printed in the United States of America

28 27 26 25 24 23 22 21 20 19   1 2 3 4 5

ISBN-13: 978-0-226-63454-8 (cloth)
ISBN-13: 978-0-226-63468-5 (e-book)
DOI: https://doi.org/10.7208/chicago/9780226634685.001.0001

Library of Congress Cataloging-in-Publication Data

Names: Gamson, David, author.
Title: The importance of being urban : designing the progressive
    school district, 1890–1940 / David A. Gamson.
Other titles: Historical studies of urban America.
Description: Chicago ; London : The University of Chicago Press, 2019. |
    Series: Historical studies of urban America
Identifiers: LCCN 2018056060 | ISBN 9780226634548 (cloth : alk. paper) |
    ISBN 9780226634685 (e-book)
Subjects: LCSH: Urban schools—United States. | School districts—
    United States.
Classification: LCC LC5131 .G35 2019 | DDC 370.9173/2—dc23
LC record available at https://lccn.loc.gov/2018056060

♾ This paper meets the requirements of ANSI/NISO Z39.48–1992
(Permanence of Paper).

To David Tyack (1930–2016),
the one best mentor,
and
Ian and Nancy Gamson,
the two best parents

CONTENTS

ACKNOWLEDGMENTS

As with any major production, a book such as this could not have been com- ix pleted without the assistance of numerous people, and I have encountered many generous souls throughout the course of my research and writing for this project.

Particularly worthy of mention are those diligent archivists, librarians, and school district employees—often unnamed and unknown—who have persisted in their stewardship of the primary source materials that are so highly valuable to historians. Without access to stashes of school board minutes, superintendent files, administrative memos, teacher materials, mimeographs, district bulletins, among many other types of sources, it would have been impossible to complete this study. The range of resources produced by Progressive Era school districts demonstrates the wide scope of their activities in the early twentieth century.

Deserving special recognition is the Seattle Public School Archives, a department of the school system that is a model for what an educational archive can be. Eleanor Teows was the head archivist during my research in Seattle, and I am deeply in her debt. She not only revealed the many sources available regarding the city's educational history but also, in so doing, made me aware of the existence of the types of documents I then located in other cities. The librarians of the University of Washington Special Collections also offered great assistance.

In Portland, Oregon, the staff at the Records Management Department of the Portland Public Schools, especially David Evans, accommodated a scholar in their offices so he could review school district files far older than those they regularly retrieve. The Portland Public Library, itself a product of the Progressive Era, stores a wide variety of press clippings and unpublished district reports. The Portland school district central office welcomed me in to study school board minutes.

Oakland, California, once had a wonderful district library stocked with professional development materials from past and present; alas, due to significant budget cuts stemming from a series of state and city financial crises, many of its holdings were either disposed of or warehoused and, thus, have not been within the reach of the researcher. Nevertheless, staff at the district central office kindly provided what they could from their files and cleared some desk space for me to work. The Oakland History Room in the Oakland Public Library thankfully houses a range of older district publications, and the main library retains some older city newspapers that are unavailable elsewhere. I thank Gary Yee for the time he took to familiarize me with the many dimensions of conducting research in Oakland.

The Denver Public Schools can be lauded for recognizing the precious nature of their older, handwritten school board minutes, symbolized by its decision to keep these large volumes locked in a vault, yet they remain available to the researcher. The Western History Room of the beautiful Denver Public Library supplemented district records with published and unpublished state and school materials. I was fortunate to have access to the Jesse H. Newlon Papers and the Archie L. Threlkeld Papers in the Penrose Library at the University of Denver, for they yielded unparalleled glimpses into the minds of significant individuals in this book.

Stanford University's Cubberley Education Library served as a crucial foundation for the origins of this study, and the outstanding staff, especially Kelly Roll, deserve credit for assisting my many quirky requests and questions. Cubberley Education Library houses a preeminent national collection of nineteenth- and twentieth-century school records and materials. Despite periodic threats to close the library or to dispatch with its archival material (a fate that befell some education collections at Teachers College, Columbia University, and the National Institute for Education), it remains a jewel for educational researchers.

The materials above were supplemented with assistance from librarians and interlibrary loan departments of universities across the country, and I am indebted to scores of library employees whom I shall never meet but without whom I could not have completed my work. Special acknowledgment is due to the interlibrary loan staff at my home institution of the Pennsylvania State University who have ardently tracked and located pamphlets, articles, bulletins, and the books necessary for my study.

I have been extremely lucky to work with exceptional scholars and mentors in my academic career to date. Larry Cuban first introduced me to the history of school reform and, as I pursued my research, provided me with consistent and solid guidance, just as he has so affably for many other scholars over the years. Milbrey McLaughlin first nurtured my interest in school district reform and remained tirelessly enthusiastic about my investigation. Carl Kaestle has been a model of a scholar and a mentor, and I cannot imagine pursuing my interest in twentieth-century reform without his support, encouragement, and marvelous instincts for historical questions and inquiry. I owe my deepest gratitude to the late David Tyack. A gracious scholar, a wise mentor, and fabulous teacher, David embodied the humane approach we should take with all whom we encounter both inside and outside the academy.

I was fortunate to gain financial support for key aspects of this study, allowing me time to investigate questions of district reform across the twentieth century. The Spencer Foundation offered invaluable assistance through a small grant and later with a National Academy of Education/Spencer Postdoctoral Fellowship. I was honored to receive an Advanced Studies Fellowship at Brown University funded by the William and Flora Hewlett Foundation and the Spencer Foundation. Under the direction of Carl Kaestle, the Advanced Studies Fellowship brought together a group of scholars who have contributed immeasurably to my intellectual growth, including Adam Nelson, Beth Rose, Katie McDermott, Doug Reed, Liz DeBray, Nora Gordon, Chris Lubienski, Kim Freeman, Marguerite Clark, James Patterson, Warren Simmons, Howard Chudacoff, Marion Orr, Wendy Schiller, and John Modell.

Colleagues in the History of Education Society have buttressed my work with emotional and intellectual support. I am especially grateful to Jack Dougherty, Hilary Moss, Judith Kafka, Heather Lewis, Bethany Rogers, Chuck Dorn, Karen Benjamin, John Spencer, Benita Blessing, Ben Justice, Sevan Terazian, and Dan Perlstein. A number of (slightly) more seasoned historians have offered guidance, suggestions, and encouragement throughout my career, among them, Jonathan Zimmerman, John Rury, Bill Reese, Wayne Urban, Kate Rousmaniere, Jeff Mirel, and Nancy Beadie.

The unparalleled professional staff at the University of Chicago Press have, from beginning to end, supported and challenged me. Robert Devens first saw promise in my project, but Tim Mennel deserves the credit for reigniting the project and for his persistence and enduring patience, as well as for his remarkably keen insights, prompts, suggestions, and a knack for knowing when and how to nudge authors (or, at least, this author). Amanda Seligman delivered incisive feedback on the full manuscript, pushing me to expand on core arguments, and I am indebted to all the other series editors who remained committed to this project: Lilia Fernández, Timothy J.

Gilfoyle, and Becky Nicolaides. Rachel Kelly Unger expertly supervised the manuscript submission process, and Yvonne Zipter served as an eagle-eyed copyeditor. As external reviewers of the manuscript, Barbara Beatty and Robert Johnston provided scrutiny, historiographic suggestions, and comments both conceptual and minute, all the while highlighting what they liked and that which needed overhaul. Of course, none of the individuals above could completely save me from myself and any remaining errors are all my own to claim.

Other friends and fellow travelers sustained me in the early days of my research: Seth Pollack, Ida Oberman, Jennifer O'Day, and Amy Gerstein. Kristin Hershbell Charles was there at the inception of this research topic, and I never would have made it through the early stages of this project had she not been there to offer an inexhaustible supply of support and encouragement. Friends I made in my early days at Penn State have remained so, despite my long periods of silence: Ralph Rodriguez, Mark Adams, Sean Reardon, James McCarthy, and Steve Thorne, among many others.

The College of Education at the Pennsylvania State University has provided important support through travel and research funding. During my first years at Penn State, the late Bill Boyd graciously offered time and advice on succeeding in academia and on matters related to my historical investigations. I have benefited enormously from a series of phenomenal research assistants at Penn State, especially graduate assistants Eric Cummings and Emily Hodge. (Emily read through the complete manuscript, offering perceptive suggestions and important edits.) John Jones, Christine Crain, Angel Zheng, and Jamie Schwartz also dug into a range of sources for me. Katie Dulaney indefatigably assisted with the preparation of the index.

As a sixth- through twelfth-grade history and social studies teacher in Minnesota I was, and continue to be, astonished by my many students who asked insistent, often incessant, questions about the nature of American society. Their ability to inquire thoughtfully about the past, to interrogate textbook history, to write with precision, and to discuss and debate issues of class and race provides a model of decorum that far outshines the behavior of far too many adults and American politicians.

Friends who lived foolishly close to my research sites amiably offered places to stay during my research sojourns. In Seattle, Neil Charney, Nancy Whittaker, and their daughters Charlotte and Ruby (along with a spate of mysteriously disappearing cats) offered me living quarters more times than I can count. When I needed to return to the San Francisco Bay Area, Sean Reardon carved out space for me as well time and camaraderie for much-needed libations. In Denver, Van Schoales kindly provided shelter.

This book also gives me a chance to reflect on those who helped me in my intellectual journey, especially at Bowdoin College where I first cut my analytic teeth with the help of Larry Lutchmansingh, Philip Uninsky, Roger Howell, and Kidder Smith. Bill Watterson has been an enormous intellectual influence, not the least of which is due to his poetry that reminds all authors "that the end of the book / is the last white page / you go on revising forever."* I would never have pursued the field of education had it not been for the masterful guidance of Anne Pierson and Paul Hazelton, both of whom helped me see how education can be explored through the lenses of the liberal arts.

My family deserves the most thanks of all. My parents and my brother Jonathan, sister-in-law Ellen, nephew Riley, and niece Elise also housed and fed me on numerous trips to the Pacific Northwest. My brother Andrew has mastered the ability to remain supportive while not asking too many questions about when that book will be finished. My parents, educators both, have served as inspirations. My mother, who started her career as an English and art teacher, has always been endlessly enthusiastic about learning. My father, an Australian transplant, taught American history for several decades to appreciative college students; I blame him for my inability to resist asking historical questions.

My sons, Elijah and Gabriel, are due much more than I can repay them for time lost to work on "the book" over the years when they would much rather that I had spent time with them. They are resilient and remarkable, clever and creative, joyful and kind. They will never know how much I appreciate their fortitude and compassion as they endure the life that comes with parents who are academics. It often feels unfair what we ask of them.

Finally, the amazing Kimberly Powell has managed to help sustain me and our children at the same time that she has forged her own remarkable career. She has demonstrated more patience than any spouse should have to and has endured far too many missed weekends and delayed holidays. Moreover, her grasp of theory consistently helps remind me of the deep thinking that must take place when engaging in the education of children, that we must avoid easy answers to complex phenomena, and that we must insist on fostering creativity in both our students and our teachers.

---

*William Collins Watterson, "Nightscape with Doves," *New Yorker* (February 9, 1987), 77.

INTRODUCTION

DISTRICT PROGRESSIVES
AND THE PROGRESSIVE SCHOOL DISTRICT

Why does the United States still have school districts? Do they serve a purpose that could not be carried out by schools, states, or other external agencies? Beginning in the 1960s, educational reformers began asking similar
questions, and they challenged, often fiercely, the traditional role played by
the American school district, arguing that this conventional educational institution had become dysfunctional, if not defunct. More recently, innovators
have sought to render the district essentially irrelevant or powerless through
charter schools, vouchers, cyber schools, or common academic standards
developed at the state or national levels. Bombarded by constant, widespread
reports of school "failure," Americans have come to harbor a level of distrust
of urban districts that has been hard to reverse.[1]

Yet despite the bleak view that many Americans have of the nation's city
schools, the urban school district was once considered to be among the great
democratic creations of the twentieth century. From the 1890s until the
Second World War, most prominent educational leaders and policy makers
depicted urban school systems as the cutting of school improvement and as
laboratories of progressive educational innovation, much in the same way
that municipal reformers of the era portrayed cities as experimental stations
for novel forms of governance. Scholars have lost sight of this earlier history,
in part, because of the piercing critiques of urban schools that emerged a
generation ago, views that have tended to persist ever since.[2]

The enduringly dour view of the American school district—whether accurate or not—masks a fascinating story about the role that school districts
have played in the nation's educational history. Progressives saw city school
systems as beacons of change and exemplars of coordinated, efficient, and
democratic reform. Unlike many Americans today, early twentieth-century
reformers had tremendous faith in the capacity of social institutions to correct the weaknesses of industrial society; indeed, large progressive districts

stood as one of the fundamental bulwarks against the perils of modern city life. The urban school district—or, as many contemporaries called it, the "city school system"—was the essential agent in successfully orchestrating educational change. Because it offered public education to children from a spectrum of social backgrounds and economic classes, reformers believed that the urban school district held the potential to deliver on the promise of equal educational opportunity. The progressive school district, its advocates asserted, offered the means for quelling class differences, fostering a tranquil industrial democracy, and ensuring the assimilation of immigrants. Progressive educational leaders argued that the urban school district could do what individual schools could never accomplish on their own—namely, provide the blend of expertise, breadth of scope, concentration of cultural resources, and supply of social services necessary to prepare students for life in an increasingly complex world.

The Importance of Being Urban looks anew at this Progressive Era institution, exploring why civic leaders, academics, muckraking journalists, educators, and administrators all agreed on the urgency of urban educational reform and why they believed that the newly designed "progressive school district" was singularly qualified to carry out comprehensive educational improvement. Through a comparative analysis of four western cities—Oakland, California; Denver, Colorado; Portland, Oregon; and Seattle, Washington—this book offers a novel perspective on education in the Progressive Era and on the role that urban school districts played in fostering widespread school reform and providing the kinds of educational opportunities that local leaders believed were best suited to American democracy. By investigating the design and development of "democratic" and "progressive" school systems between 1890 and 1940, the study offers a set of interrelated portraits of how educational leaders gathered and shared ideas, adopted and adapted innovations, and coordinated and implemented citywide reform.[3]

In order to pursue these larger themes, this study focuses on several core questions. First, what did it mean to be a progressive school district and why was the district considered the crucial unit for urban educational reform during the Progressive Era? Second, how did the progressive city school system embody the principles of democracy and provide "equal educational opportunity" for all its students? And, finally, how did urban politics and civic organizations influence the development of districts during these important years? In answering these questions, this book explores the concept of progressivism from an alternative perspective.

The historiography of the Progressive Era in the United States has a long and rich tradition, and as many scholars know, the search for a unifying definition of "progressivism" has proven vexing. The same quandary holds true for educational progressivism, and historians have had an analytic tendency to divide educational progressivism into multiple philosophical streams as a way to parse the period's complexity. In his classic study of the history of urban education, for example, David Tyack identified several categories of educational progressives that have served historians ever since; two of these groups—the administrative progressives and the pedagogical progressives—have garnered the most scholarly attention since the publication of Tyack's *The One Best System*. Other educational historians have also abandoned the effort to be analytically all-inclusive, examining progressivism from more compartmentalized perspectives with carefully bounded parameters. Some scholars, for instance, differentiate between scientists and radicals or among humanists, developmentalists, social efficiency experts, and social meliorists as a means of contending with the "vague, essentially undefinable, entity called progressive education." As a result, historians' conclusions about progressivism have thus varied widely, depending on the interpretive stance each takes.[4]

Yet a curious thing happened as I dove into a historical exploration of school districts and read through their archives, school board minutes, and committee reports. None of school districts under investigation fit neatly into the standard analytic categories. Some nationally prominent academic theorists unquestionably embodied the characteristics of social efficiency, just as other types of curricula clearly exemplified experimental pedagogical strategies. Nevertheless, deeper digging into local school system records revealed an intriguing pattern: district practices rarely conformed to the labels scholars have traditionally attached to various progressive ideologies, interest groups, and philosophies. What did this mean? The explanation advanced here is that educational progressivism looks strikingly different when analyzed from the perspective of urban school practitioners—the administrators and teachers given the daily responsibility of educating thousands of schoolchildren—than it does from the national level, that is, from the vantage point of widely known experts, academics, or curriculum theorists. In other words, when studying progressivism, the unit of analysis matters.

The unique quality of local educational progressivism becomes especially apparent when juxtaposing the independent actions of educational leaders in different cities. What at first seemed to be the idiosyncratic policies of particular districts instead turned out to be common practice, repeated across several cities. In place of the alleged philosophical rifts was a much more inclusive form of educational innovation. This "district progressivism," as I term it, was more pragmatic and less ideological than the versions of progressivism encountered in the historiography. Indeed, local educational leaders often combined practices that in retrospect appear contradictory and that historians depict as incompatible and irreconcilable, such as child-centered pedagogy and intelligence testing or administrative efficiency and "creative play." The main purpose here is not to quarrel with the standard analytic conceptions per se; indeed, they can be extremely useful in distilling the main intellectual and educational tendencies of the period—especially administrative and pedagogical progressivism—and offer helpful descriptors for identifying various predilections. Nonetheless, this book demonstrates that educational progressivism took on a distinctly different character as it was interpreted by local leaders at the district level, educators who quite consciously described themselves as builders of progressive urban school systems.[5]

The willful eclecticism of district progressives—those local leaders who embodied district progressivism—mirrored that of many municipal reformers of the time. Just as Cleveland's Frederic Howe "turned the world into a kind of lending library of practical, tested reform notions," urban school reformers scoured other cities and states for the most promising educational innovations. In 1915, for example, the president of Portland's school board argued that leaders in all types of organizations, be they industrial or educational, should remain vigilant for and open to new ideas. "Let a better way of doing a certain thing be reported in any part of the world," he declared, "and immediately the old method of performance is discarded and the new adopted."[6]

The appropriation of designs applied equally well to contemporary governance experiments at the municipal and state levels. At precisely the same time that Portland's school board president heralded the adoption of new methods, prominent progressive political theorists, such as Herbert Croly and Charles Beard, delighted at Oregon's experiments in direct democracy and institutional reorganization. Beard wrote that Oregon's reforms would receive approval from "the friends of democracy and friends of efficiency" across the nation.[7] Beard's intentional combination of efficiency and democracy—concepts that some scholars find perplexingly incongruous—captures one of the paradoxes of the Progressive Era. Consider, for example, the New York Bureau of Research's regular publication, *Efficient Citizen*, or the book title of the bureau's cofounder, William H. Allen: *Efficient Democracy*. Understanding how practices deemed efficient and democratic became intertwined helps illuminate the work of both municipal and school reformers.[8]

For their part, city school administrators and board members selected practices that seemed the most feasible solutions to pressing problems, implementing some of the initiatives advocated by leading national reformers and adapting others to suit their own purposes. The accumulation and mixing of philosophies and innovations was hardly confined to those experts determined to professionalize all forms of governance, whom some scholars have depicted as constituting the driving force behind significant municipal reform. Rather, we find the same merging of groups and goals among labor unions, worker collectives, teacher organizations, women's groups, moral reformers, and newspapers.

A school system did not become instantly progressive simply by introducing a jumble of new practices, and educators and scholars have often disagreed about what, precisely, it meant to be a progressive school district. So, how many districts were considered progressive? Lawrence Cremin, who saw evidence of progressivism in multiple school districts, was surprised by those who did not share his view of the movement as rather ubiquitous. How, he wondered, could the Progressive Era academic Harold Rugg include only four public school districts in his retrospective 1947 list of some three dozen "pioneering progressive ventures"? None of the four school systems Rugg named— Winnetka, Illinois; Bronxville, New York; Shaker Heights, Ohio; and Quincy, Massachusetts—could be considered urban schools districts, far from it. The first three were nested in tony suburbs. Quincy unquestionably garnered bona fide progressive credentials, but that was primarily during the short period 1875–80 when under the direction of Francis Parker. Cremin, contending that Rugg had a "limited view of progressive education," dismissed Rugg's tally as an inaccurate undercount. Rugg, it is true, was more interested in the exciting instructional practices that could be found in what he called "free-lance" progressive schools than he was in the tendencies of whole school districts. Nevertheless, despite Cremin's belief that the progressive districts flourished, scholars have been unable to identify many school districts that contained the kind of pedagogical experimentalism usually associated with progressivism. Whether Cremin or Rugg had a more discerning eye for progressive education matters less than the overall point that we simply do not know enough about what it meant to be a progressive school district.[9]

Scholars miss out on a crucial part of American social and political history if they overlook how progressives designed their urban school districts. In the 1910s and 1920s, the United States contained something on the order of a hundred fifty thousand school districts, and, although only a fraction of these would have been considered urban at the time, prominent experts implored districts of all sizes and locations to follow the model being established by city school systems. The urban districts analyzed herein exemplify how local educational leaders strove to become "progressive" and why they received attention and praise for doing so. Academic reformers and journalists from across the country commended each of these four cities for their implementation of innovations described as progressive, democratic, and scientific. Thus, if we are interested in why local leaders selected specific types of practices, how they customized reforms to fit their own urban environments, or how innovations diffused between and among cities, then Oakland, Denver, Seattle, and Portland yield ample evidence of what it meant to be a progressive school district.

These western cities also experienced substantial population and commercial expansion during the same years, albeit slightly later than the metropolitan centers of the East, and they saw themselves as belonging to the same reference group. In fact, in the self-assessments they conducted of their progress, they compared themselves to each other, not to districts in the East, and they regularly cited one another's statistics, scores, and financial data. Although they certainly scrutinized educational developments east of the Rockies, when they wanted to see how they measured up to similar systems, they placed their western sister cities on the scale. Consequently, they were simultaneously peers and rivals, believing at times that they vied for the educational supremacy of the West. This is not to argue that there was a particular form of western exceptionalism or to suggest that western school districts developed in a way that was fundamentally unlike those in other sections of the country; it is meant to show how these western educational leaders viewed their world.[10]

Despite commonalities, any investigation of urban reform must also recognize the unique personality of each of these cities; after all, in the late 1800s and early 1900s, civic identity was often directly connected to the reputation of the homegrown schools. Therefore, as a means of balancing the concurrent dramas of school reform and municipal politics, each city is given its own case study. The fates of these cities were often intertwined; therefore this book encompasses what might be considered a set of cumulative case studies that are independent yet interrelated. Consistency across cities is achieved by examining three school reforms common to (or at least considered by) all four cities: administrative reorganization, student classification (i.e., the "scientific" labeling of student abilities), and curriculum reform. As explained in more depth in chapter 2, these three reforms represent much of what was at the heart of Progressive Era educational innovation. Exploring how school leaders linked and implemented these three reforms allows for an underlying structure to the narrative, while it also preserves the unique story of each school system.[11]

Alongside some significant differences, the stories of these school districts also reveal some surprising similarities that challenge traditional narratives on progressivism. Educators or districts that at first blush appear to illustrate a clear example of, say, social efficiency, turn out to also have had some intriguing pedagogical proclivities. The reverse is also true: urban educators who seemed dedicated to pedagogical experimentation and aligned with the ideas of John Dewey sometimes adopted hard-edged efficiency reforms. In other words, we find numerous illustrations of the nuances and complexities contained with the phrase "progressive education" and the notion of "democratic schooling." Indeed, the very mutability of these two concepts helps explain why topics such as instructional freedom, equal opportunity, and democratic administration sparked tense and heated debates at major professional conferences and local school board meetings alike. Understanding the uneven use of the words "progressive" and "democratic" illuminates how it was that many school administrators convinced parents and communities to accept a version of "equal educational opportunity" that explicitly rejected the idea that all children should receive the same, or even similar, academic opportunities.

A careful tracing of these urban school reforms ultimately requires the extension of the traditional Progressive Era chronology beyond the standard bookend of World War I. Clearly, some significant social reforms of the larger progressive movement had peeled off or withered by the end of the Great War, prompting Jane Addams to complain that the 1920s constituted "a period of political and social sag."[12] Yet some historians have demonstrated that aspects of the movement nonetheless outlived the war. "Progressivism survived in the 1920s," says Arthur Link, "because several important elements of the movement remained either in full vigor or in only slightly diminished strength."[13] In the sphere of education, this reformist verve was on display well into the 1920s and 1930s. During these decades, a whole new diverse collection of educational innovations—reforms that leaders self-consciously labeled as progressive—were just beginning to flex their wings.

At the same time that urban school districts strove to be progressive, municipal reformers in those same cities attempted to modernize their governance systems by abolishing bossism, eliminating corruption, and developing new models of administration. They rewrote city charters to ease the way for more efficient forms of municipal government through new commission or city-manager plans. Observing the interactions of civic organizations and school reform groups deepens both the story and a comprehension of the era. Understanding the political backdrop to educational reforms is essential, of course, but it can be difficult to capture the political essence of politics in each city, especially over the rather long period of 1890–1940, just as it can be equally challenging to weave the most crucial political events into a narrative without elbowing out crucial educational shifts. Not all developments can be given equal weight, of course, presenting a challenge for both analysis and narrative.

Ultimately, the key to blending the educational and the political came through focusing on a set of years that persistently proved fascinating and unsettling throughout the research for this book: the stretch of time from roughly 1913 to 1918. The great educational turmoil and restlessness that bubbled up during the last decade of the nineteenth century and first decade of the twentieth eventually found its articulation in the plans, proposals, and publications issued after 1913. Moreover, much of what happens after 1918 is the ongoing effort to refine and implement these same plans. Broadening the scope to incorporate the period up through 1928, a year by which the essential character traits of each of these progressive districts had been established, captures the full-throated expression of educational progressivism. In other words, once the most vigorous reform activity began around 1913, most of the significant progressive educational change in these districts took place in the fifteen years that followed.

The pre– and post–World War I years have been of interest to American historians for a swath of reasons: progressive politics, Wilson's presidency, the women's suffrage movement, the rise of business elites, the shifting fortunes of labor, the battles against political machines, entry into the war and the reactionary period that followed, among many others. Furthermore, researchers examining the arts and sciences, everything from music and choreography to general relativity, have highlighted the significance of this time period for its explosion of experimentation and creative thought. Historians of education have addressed the progressive educational changes of the era, but they have traditionally treated them as a playing out of conflicts between rising professional power, civic elites, expertise, and bureaucratization and centralization.[14]

Many of the significant educational developments of this period were also locally influenced by the municipal leagues and taxpayer groups that popped up in the years 1913–28. Historians have been well aware these leagues and councils and how they contributed to the commercial, political, and economic maelstroms—and progress—that swept through cities around World War I, and they have studied the direct connections to municipal governance, but they have not always looked closely at the concomitant impact on other types of urban organizations. In this regard, education is often a kind of institutional outsider, primarily because of the unusual structural and political independence school districts traditionally strove to have from city hall.

The links between city schools and local civic groups matter in understanding progressive educational change because during the 1910s school boards and district leaders made some of the most consequential decisions about the nature of their educational policies, structures, and values. The texture of urban progressivism in each city differed depending on its particular mix of civic organizations and local political powers. Moreover, because these years were so politically tumultuous, the exact moment of innovation was also significant, almost as if the democratic dartboard of decision making was constantly spinning, but not slowing, until the mid-1920s. The precise timing that a dart of experimentation struck its target influenced the particular reforms that educational leaders in that city ultimately selected. In many cases, the distinctive shade of educational progressivism established in the 1910s and 1920s ultimately characterized the district for decades to come.[15]

Not all civic organizations that formed during the 1910s and 1920s qualify as progressive, of course, and a wide variety of publicly minded groups—some qualifying as more regressive—influenced policies during this period. Even if accounting for all types of formal and informal associations is impractical, some exerted more influence than others. Some cannot be ignored. The Ku Klux Klan, for example, asserted itself in many cities during the 1920s, western and otherwise, becoming, if only for a short span of years, a politically significant, disruptive, voice in urban and state politics. Oddly enough, some of the Klan's statements on schooling sounded remarkably similar to the progressive education tenets. Exactly how much influence the Klan had varied from state to state, but they were powerful enough to control some state legislatures and parade in many cities unharassed. If anything, the rise of the "Second Klan" in the 1920s serves to signal a discordant tone of racial and ethnic relations in the rapidly growing cities of the West.[16]

Some interpretive cautions and qualifications are in order. First, to say that city school systems were once considered beacons of change and exemplars of progressive and democratic reform in early twentieth-century America is, most certainly, not to suggest that urban districts offered a high-quality education to all students. Prominent school districts may have served some students well, but they underserved or failed many others, most often those in poor, working-class, immigrant, and minority communities. The fact that urban districts once attained a privileged place in American education has led some observers to depict the story of urban school districts in the twentieth century as one of exhilarating rise and precipitous decline. This study is, in part, an attempt to step away from that "rise and fall" tale of city school systems, at the same time that it seeks to avoid the pitfall of searching for the sources of contemporary problems in the policies of the past. Drifts toward presentism are hopefully countered by viewing democracy and school reform through the lens of the district progressives and by examining the viable alternatives that were available to them at the time.[17] Finally, this study seeks to distance itself from a penchant among educational researchers to retrospectively critique progressive educators as "antidemocratic"; instead, it endeavors to analyze the reasons why many progressives believed that their new practices, such as testing and tracking, epitomized democratic education.[18]

Using the district as the unit of analysis has some downsides. Superintendents, school board members, and other administrators (usually men) were most frequently the builders and decision-makers of progressive urban school systems, and therefore much of the evidence for this study comes from an administrative viewpoint. Whenever and wherever possible, that perspective is balanced by the views and voices of teachers (usually women), as well as those of community members and outside observers; these are culled from sources such as teacher magazines, local newsletters, union publications, conference addresses, education journals, newspapers, reports of local civic groups, and parents' letters and petitions.

———

In sum, this book offers several new perspectives on Progressive Era educational reform by arguing that educational progressivism manifested itself differently at the local level than the national level. This distinction can best be seen by examining how local district leaders—whom I call district progressives—accumulated and adopted a variety of educational reforms considered progressive. Usually administrators in the district, these district progressives recognized value in many of the progressive ideas and innovations advanced at the time by nationally prominent educators and sought to introduce these new practices in their own school systems. They were less concerned about the internal consistency of progressive ideas and philosophies because they were dedicated to successfully educating thousands of children in rapidly growing cities and they focused on identifying practical solutions to sets of pressing programs. District progressives simultaneously adopted curricula and instructional practices associated with Deweyan notions of pedagogy while they implemented intelligence tests and other reforms considered representative of social efficiency and scientific management. By looking across multiple urban school systems, it becomes clear that district progressivism was a common pattern, not simply representative of an isolated case or two. The heavy scholarly concentration on separate streams of progressivism has meant that researchers have failed to capture the full complexity of local practitioners working in urban school districts.

Chapter 1 asks: How did the path of American education become entwined with the fate of the American city, especially in ways that would have been inconceivable even to the most devoted and optimistic nineteenth-century school reformer? It explores why turn-of-the-century municipal reformers viewed cities as "the hope of democracy" and why they believed that public education, and—more specifically—the large urban school district, was an essential institution for safeguarding children from the "evils" of modern, industrialized society.

The second chapter focuses on the reform designs devised by national leaders in the realms of education improvement and municipal governance, providing more depth and detail on the innovations elites urged cities to adopt, and it offers a preliminary analysis of three main ideas that constituted the ideology of urban educational progressivism. Despite seeming inconsistencies across types of reforms, several tenets provided the conceptual foundation for the plans implemented in city school systems. District progressives saw their mission as instilling a new understanding of "true democracy," a goal they believed they could achieve through a threefold strategy: revision of district curricula, differentiation of children and practices, and reform of schools on a citywide scale. What did urban educators mean when they talked about progressivism? Many district progressives set out to rework the American social fabric through fundamental shifts in the way their city school systems operated; their ultimate goal was to alter how equal educational opportunity would be distributed to children of different social and economic backgrounds.

Chapter 3 traces the evolution of the modern city school system as it was understood by leaders in Oakland. Oakland has sometimes been seen as a quintessential administrative progressive school district because of its swift adoption of efficiency-oriented reforms after World War I. In this regard, the chapter devotes special attention to the superintendency of Fred Hunter (1917–28), an aggressive innovator with a national reputation as a leader who "democratized" his schools and received support from local urban elites. Although some district leaders evinced a limited view of the potential of children, others dedicated energy to broad pedagogical change, demonstrating previously unheralded qualities that contravene the standard narrative about district administrators as unimaginative central office bureaucrats uninterested in instructional practice.

The unconventional approach the Denver Public Schools took to including teachers in curriculum reform during the 1920s has led to a portrait of the city as an alternative to rigidly administered, top-down districts. Chapter 4 examines how Superintendent Jesse Newlon (1920–27) and his successor, A. L. Threlkeld (1927–37), crafted a district culture devoted to democratic teacher participation. Nevertheless, although Denver educators articulated a vision of democracy that appears distinct from that voiced by Oakland leaders, they also revealed some surprising similarities. Moreover, whether in spite of or due to the interweaving of multiple philosophies, the district's experiences with intelligence testing also led to unheralded critiques of testing and tracking practices that have been gone unrecognized.

Chapter 5 focuses on Portland, where school Superintendent Frank Rigler (1896–1913) designed a citywide curriculum that was so precise that on any given school day he believed he "could sit in his office and know on what page in each book" students were currently working throughout the city. Throughout most of his tenure, Rigler received praise for his curricular plans. Despite Portland's seemingly strong reputation, external evaluators were shocked when they surveyed the district in 1913, the same year a harsh municipal governance survey was also completed. Instead of finding a vibrant educational system, investigators encountered an organization in which teachers felt they had neither the responsibility nor the right "to depart from the rigidly uniform prescriptions of the course of study, reinforced by inspection from the central office." Rigler was replaced for a time by an ambitiously progressive school chief, but Portland demonstrated a penchant for fluctuating between different styles of educational leadership between 1913 and the 1930s, and the city offers an illustration of what happened when local leaders and school boards could neither firmly reject nor accept progressive plans and practices.

At first glance, Seattle, the subject of chapter 6, appeared to avoid much of the tumult experienced by other city school districts in the years before and during World War I, a stability symbolized by the remarkably long tenure of Superintendent Frank Cooper (1901–22). Historians describe Cooper as a pedagogical progressive due to his efforts to improve schooling through initiatives like creative play, project-based learning, and the replacement of traditional school desks with tables and chairs better suited to the atmosphere of a modern classroom. Yet the characterization of Seattle as a haven for Dewey-inspired practices is misleading; the district implemented a number of practices that represented rather hard-edged forms of administrative progressivism. For a time during the 1910s, the city boasted two socialist school board members, and the city holds some puzzles due to the kinds of practices they supported.

In addition to identifying some of the lessons that can be drawn only when these four districts are examined side by side, the final chapter explores some of the insights that emerge from a deep study of the decisions made and the innovations introduced by progressive educators in urban school districts. It also asks: What lessons might these school systems hold for school reform today? The United States still depends on its local school districts, large and small, to educate its children and to carry out most of the associated educational responsibilities throughout the nation. A better understanding of how these local units of democratic educational governance developed and how they selected among a range of instructional practices not only shatters some misconceptions but it can also can shed light on current American expectations for democratic education. What hidden curriculum does the progressive past hold for the precarious present and the possible future?

I

THE RACE FOR URBAN STATUS

14 There was nothing wrong with the American city that could not be fixed with what was right about the American city. At least that was how Progressive Era urban educators saw it. In a country that had long seen itself as quintessentially rural, the urban turn that accompanied the advent of the twentieth century was psychologically disruptive, especially as public figures increasingly linked the fate of cities to the fate of the nation. Educational reformers began to radiate an infectious faith that the urban school district was poised to usher in a new educational epoch. One of the true believers was Professor Ellwood P. Cubberley of Stanford University. In an era already characterized by vigorous social reform, Cubberley believed that the early twentieth-century city school system was on the vanguard of progressive educational innovation, perfectly situated to build a stronger, more democratic nation.[1]

In the minds of many progressives, the city became a novel instrument for social improvement and national uplift. "Nearly all of the important progress which has been made in education in America in the past quarter century has been made in our cities," proclaimed Cubberley in 1915. Urban school districts, he believed, were the true laboratories of progressive educational experimentation. "It is the cities which have perfected their administrative organization and developed an administrative machinery capable of handling educational business on a large scale," he wrote a year later. "It is in the cities, too, that the large problems of public school organization and administration have been worked out and the fundamental administrative principles we now follow have been established." Cubberley predicted that "the decade or decade and a half which is just ahead" would be a "great period of application for the principles now formulated." The city, it seemed, offered a fertile environment for realizing the dream of universal democratic education in the United States.[2]

Cubberley was hardly alone in his enthusiasm. "The school systems of our cities present one of the most inspiring aspects of our municipal advance," wrote historian Charles Beard in 1912, "and recent tendencies seem to show that we are on the eve of a new era." From the 1890s through the 1930s, civic leaders and academics heralded the rising status of the modern urban school system. Educators and laypeople alike pointed to a "new movement in education" and a "new science of education" that went hand in hand with the broader social reform and experimentation already afoot. Cities had serious problems to be sure—overcrowded housing, inadequate sanitation, and hazardous factories—but a new generation of public figures believed they also contained the resources and institutions necessary to address these problems. The city's advantages could be used to outweigh its disadvantages.[3]

The early decades of the twentieth century marked the ascendancy of the urban school district in America. If the urban moment in the history of American political progressivism was, as Daniel T. Rodgers has argued, "sliced thin enough to be sandwiched between the Populist revolt and Theodore Roosevelt's reformation of the presidency," then we might say that the urban moment in educational progressivism started later and lasted longer, ultimately persisting beyond most conventional types of urban progressivism.[4] The delayed onset of educational progressivism was especially characteristic of schooling in the metropolitan centers of the American West. Just as western educational leaders like Cubberley and his Stanford colleagues believed that urban school systems pointed the way to the future, other western municipal reformers and urban-minded politicians understood that, in turn, good schools symbolized strong cities. "There is no better constructive publicity for a city than to be known over the entire country as a city of good schools," one member of the Portland, Oregon, school board confidently stated in 1915.[5] Local leaders recognized that a strong city school system signaled the accumulation of civic and cultural capital. Whenever the editors of western newspapers like the *Portland Oregonian* highlighted "modern" developments across their city—modern shipbuilding, factories, bank buildings— they consistently praised urban schools for utilizing the "best modern methods" of instruction and for constructing educational facilities that ranked "high in comparison with those of other American cities of the same size."[6]

Urban leaders regularly took stock of their stature in relation to other comparable cities in their region, for they appreciated that perception was often more important than fact. Development of the urban West, historian Bradford Luckingham argues, depended on civic "boosterism"—an attitude of competitiveness combined with active promotion. "To neglect to boost growth and development for a city and its hinterland," he writes, "was to deny progress and risk decline and defeat." Cities succeeded, Luckingham says, not only because of natural advantages "but also because of aggressive, ambitious leaders who were intent on seeing their particular urban centers emerge as winners in the race for urban status."[7]

"There is an art of municipal as well as business advertisement," asserted the Denver Chamber of Commerce committee in 1915, "and it should be the continuing endeavor of all of us so to elevate Denver's name and fame as to assure, speedily and forever, its proper destiny as the inland metropolis of Western America." Aware of the vibrancy of this increasingly urban frontier, municipal leaders often connected urban health to school quality as an important path to future success. A certain amount of civic pride, combined with a clear sense of the value of robust educational indicators, contributed to the spirit of competition, especially in the swiftly growing cities of the West.[8]

While Denver dreamed of itself as the great inland metropolis, other cities envisioned coastal dominance. "Four cities," wrote Seattle school administrator Fred Ayer in 1924, "are now striving for the commercial supremacy of the west coast of the United States: Los Angeles, San Francisco, Portland, and Seattle. The story of the encouragement of railroads and steamship lines, of the creation of harbors and the building of docks, of the dredging of channels and the building of lighthouses, of the spanning of rivers and the digging of canals," noted Ayer, "is one that is familiar to commercial circles. Less familiar, but no less important," he said, "is the story of the aggressive utilization of the educational facilities of these western cities for the purposes of city building and the attraction of prospective residents."[9]

Ayer understood the importance municipally minded leaders placed on schools. In city after western city, urban planners folded improved school systems into their blueprints for comprehensive urban development. When Oakland hosted the 1923 National Education Association (NEA) annual meeting—an important national honor—Mayor Davie proudly proclaimed that his city was distinguished as having one of the "best-known school systems in the United States of America." He touted the achievements of the Oakland schools alongside other municipal accomplishments that made the city "progressive" and "attractive to the manufacturer seeking a western location." Oakland had recently completed a $5 million school construction program, he said, and was about to embark on another. The Oakland school system, Davie happily concluded, was "one of the most progressive" in the United States. These were all attributes he hoped would be sufficient to coax families and factories to his city.[10]

Spirited comparisons between cities became critical and commonplace for cities west of the Rocky Mountains as they competed for new inhabitants. Populations in the western urban centers skyrocketed in the fifty years after 1890 as the amount of farmable land began to shrink. Historian Walter Nugent

TABLE 1. Population Growth in the Four Cities, 1870–1950

Year	Oakland, CA	Denver, CO	Portland, OR	Seattle, WA
1870	10,500	4,759	8,293	1,107
1880	34,555	35,629	17,577	3,533
1890	48,682	106,713	46,385	42,837
1900	66,960	133,859	90,426	80,671
1910	150,174	213,381	207,214	237,194
1920	216,261	256,491	258,288	315,312
1930	284,063	287,861	301,815	365,583
1940	302,163	322,412	305,394	368,302
1950	383,200	415,760	373,105	466,110

Source: Campbell Gibson and Emily Lennon, "Table 22: Nativity of the Population for Urban Places Ever among the 50 Largest Urban Places since 1870: 1850 to 1990," U.S. Bureau of the Census, Population Division, internet release date March 9, 1999; last revised October 31, 2011, http://www.census.gov/population/www /documentation/twps0029/tab22.html.

pinpoints 1913 as the year after which farms and farm populations stopped expanding in the United States. By 1913, Nugent says, Frederick Turner's 1893 pronouncement about the close of the settlement frontier finally fit the facts. Along with the shift from farms to factories and rural life to urban life, says Nugent, came a significant "shift in lifestyles and worldviews, one that required decades to complete."[11] To immigrants, migrants, and progressives alike, the future of the West was increasingly metropolitan.[12]

The shifting demographics of the West had an immediate impact on cities and schools, as well as on innovation therein. In 1890, for example, Oakland's population was 46,682; by 1940, it had increased sixfold to 302,163. Portland and Seattle experienced very similar growth rates during the same years (see table 1). Meanwhile, Denver's population, already topping a hundred thousand by 1890, more than tripled over the following fifty years. Of course, many cities throughout the East and Midwest had simultaneous spikes in their populations, but western cities experienced some growing pains more acutely. Moreover, the great distances that many westerners had to travel to attend professional meetings not only limited their interactions with eastern counterparts but also curbed their contact with one another, and western school administrators began to demand recognition for the specific challenges they faced.

"The industrial and educational problems of the West" are unique, announced Salt Lake City's superintendent in 1912, and other educators concurred. "There are many problems, distinctively western in character, which ought to be thrashed out among our educational people," said the superintendent of schools in Berkeley, California. "The time is ripe for the formation of a great Western Teachers' Association to include all the Pacific Coast and Rocky Mountain States," declared the Salt Lake City school chief, who believed that such an organization would boost the "professional spirit and professional standards which, with us, are still altogether too crude." The Sacramento superintendent agreed, arguing that a new western educational association would form "a connecting link" between the state educational associations and the NEA, adding that "we will marvel at our own neglect in not establishing it sooner." This hint of cultural inferiority was commonplace among western educators up until World War I. Their solution, typically American, was to create new professional organizations that could serve as conduits for the dissemination of educational ideas.[13]

All in all, westerners believed that a regionally based educational association was a prerequisite to future success. Western superintendents had another motive for their flurry of activity around 1912: they intended their plans to reach a dramatic culmination in 1915, when two international expositions were to be held in California—the Panama-Pacific in San Francisco and the Panama-California in San Diego. If successful, these two fairs would offer western leaders an opportunity to brandish their accomplishments. "The West is one great new territory," one leader proclaimed, "educationally plastic, and with infinite possibilities for future growth."[14]

Educators became infected with the spirit of civic competitiveness as easily as had business leaders and politicians, recognizing the importance of the dynamic link between urban rivalry and school strength; indeed, they often exploited it. Superintendents published charts measuring the achievement of their students, placing them side by side with the results from other cities. The data for these comparisons took multiple forms, often student test scores, especially as the new technology of the standardized test became more widely available after 1910; but districts also published comparative tables of students' height, weight, sense of color, or spelling prowess—any evidence that demonstrated superiority, no matter how minute or seemingly insignificant, was used as an indicator of dominance or, at least, competitiveness.

Outsiders could also serve to intensify the competition. A. E. Winship, the peripatetic editor of the *Journal of Education* and a vigorous champion of public education who visited city school systems across the country, dashed off his impressions of local educational improvements as he went. Winship's assessments, printed as columns and editorials in the journal, elicited pride from locals or envy from rivals, thereby contributing to fresh cycles of civic competition. After a visit to Portland, Oregon, in 1914, for example, Winship proclaimed: "If left free to work out plans and realize ideals, Portland will give all other cities a lively race for first place."[15] The contenders in this race—according to reformers like Winship, Oakland's Davie or Seattle's Ayer—were not individual schools but the large urban school systems associated with rapidly growing American cities, districts that became increasingly connected to municipal identity.

One result of the collective western attention devoted to education was a rapid increase in school funding. Some estimates indicate that the West spent more per capita on education than any other region between 1880 and 1920.[16] In his 1920 comparative analysis of the "efficiency" of state school systems as they developed between 1890 and 1918, Leonard Ayres, director of education and statistics for the Russell Sage Foundation, was startled when his data indicated that the school systems of the western states had made the greatest progress of any region during this twenty-eight-year period (see fig. 1.1). The West's gain came at the East's loss: the average national rank of the eastern states had fallen from eleven to nineteen, while the western states, with an average rank of twenty-one in 1890, had moved up to thirteen by 1918.[17] Easterners began to take notice.

The relationship between municipal reformers, academics, and educational practitioners could be mutually reinforcing. Professors in schools of education praised innovative urban districts and designated them as models for smaller districts to emulate, often to the annoyance of hard-working rural educators. Local leaders in many city school systems enthusiastically implemented the designs developed by faculty at institutions such as Stanford, Harvard, Teachers College, or the University of Chicago, all the while effusing confidence in their ability to repair the perceived defects of nineteenth-century education. Business leaders and school boards lobbied locals for increased financial support, successfully raising funds through school taxes and school bonds. City social clubs helped pay for visiting lecturers who painted compelling portraits of progressive experiments being conducted in other cities. On the whole, progressives seeking school district change tapped into a momentum of municipal reform that helped sweep educational innovations along in a larger wave of social progress. However, definitions of what constituted "social progress" varied a great deal; therefore, deeper exploration of reformist tendencies is vital.

———

Students of history have long recognized the zeal of turn-of-the-century social critics and reformers, but standard textbook narratives of the Progressive Era often depict the more gruesome and revolting problems of city life.

RANKS OF STATES AS SHOWN BY INDEX NUMBERS FOR FOUR PERIODS

1890	1900	1910	1918
1 D. C.	1 Mass.	1 Wash.	1 Mont.
2 Mass.	2 N. Y.	2 Cal.	2 Cal.
3 Cal.	3 D. C.	3 D. C.	3 Ariz.
4 N. Y.	4 Cal.	4 Mass.	4 N. J.
5 R. I.	5 Conn.	5 Nev.	5 D. C.
6 Conn.	6 R. I.	6 N. J.	6 Wash.
7 Colo.	7 Nev.	7 Mont.	7 Iowa
8 N. J.	8 Colo.	8 N. Y.	8 Utah
9 Mont.	9 N. J.	9 Utah	9 Mass.
10 Penn.	10 Mont.	10 R. I.	10 Mich.
11 Nev.	11 Utah	11 Ill.	11 Conn.
12 Md.	12 Ohio	12 Conn.	12 Ohio
13 Ohio	13 Ill.	13 Colo.	13 N. Y.
14 Ariz.	14 Wash.	14 Ohio	14 Colo.
15 Ill.	15 Penn.	15 Ore.	15 N. D.
16 Mich.	16 Ind.	16 Penn.	16 Nev.
17 Wis.	17 Neb.	17 Ind.	17 Ind.
18 Iowa	18 Mich.	18 Ariz.	18 Idaho
19 N. H.	19 Md.	19 Mich.	19 Minn.
20 Wash.	20 Vt.	20 Idaho	20 Ore.
21 Kans.	21 Minn.	21 Minn.	21 Penn.
22 Wyo.	22 N. D.	22 Neb.	22 Neb.
23 Vt.	23 Iowa	23 Wis.	23 Hawaii
24 Maine	24 Wis.	24 Kans.	24 Ill.
25 Ind.	25 S. D.	25 Wyo.	25 Wyo.
26 Minn.	26 N. H.	26 S. D.	26 R. I.
27 Del.	27 Maine	27 N. D.	27 Kans.
28 Utah	28 Ore.	28 N. H.	28 C. Z.
29 Fla.	29 Wyo.	29 Vt.	29 S. D.
30 Ore.	30 Mo.	30 Iowa	30 N. H.
31 Neb.	31 Kans.	31 Maine	31 N. M.
32 S. D.	32 Ariz.	32 Mo.	32 Vt.
33 Mo.	33 Del.	33 Md.	33 Wis.
34 N. D.	34 Idaho	34 Del.	34 Mo.
35 Ky.	35 W. Va.	35 Okla.	35 Maine
36 Texas	36 Ky.	36 W. Va.	36 Okla.
37 Idaho	37 N. M.	37 Texas	37 Md.
38 Va.	38 Texas	38 N. M.	38 Del.
39 Miss.	39 Okla.	39 La.	39 Texas
40 W. Va.	40 Fla.	40 Ky.	40 Fla.
41 Tenn.	41 Tenn.	41 Va.	41 W. Va.
42 Ark.	42 Va.	42 Fla.	42 P. R.
43 La.	43 La.	43 Tenn.	43 Va.
44 Ala.	44 Ga.	44 Ga.	44 Tenn.
45 N. C.	45 Ark.	45 Ala.	45 Ky.
46 Ga.	46 Miss.	46 Ark.	46 La.
47 S. C.	47 S. C.	47 Miss.	47 Ga.
48 N. M.	48 Ala.	48 N. C.	48 N. C.
	49 N. C.	49 S. C.	49 Ala.
			50 Ark.
			51 Miss.
			52 S. C.

FIGURE 1.1. The efficiency of state school systems at four points in time between 1890 and 1918, as ranked by Ayres. (Leonard Ayres, *An Index Number for State School Systems* [New York: Russell Sage Foundation, 1920], 45.)

The Triangle Shirtwaist factory fire of 1911, smudged and weary child laborers, Upton Sinclair's sausage factories, and Jacob Riis's street children—these
are the images that populate the collective vision of Progressive Era America.
Therefore, it is often easy to overlook the boundless optimism many progressives had for the promise of urban institutions, especially for the role of
education in building a stronger society. At the same time that they decried
corruption, filth, and poverty, progressives also emphasized the vitality of
urban centers. Cities were the "hope of democracy" declared Frederic Howe,
adviser to Cleveland's reformist mayor Tom Johnson in 1906. "The modern
city marks an epoch in our civilization," he wrote. "Through it, a new society
has been created."[18] William Munro, professor of government at Harvard, told
his students that cities were becoming the "controlling factor" in American
life, and he reiterated Henry Drummond's aphorism, "He who makes the city
makes the world."[19]

Progressives thought that the city, problems and all, provided a unique
opportunity for working out the challenges of modern American democracy
in a new industrial age. Turn-of-the-century civic reformers, historian Paul
Boyer points out, sought to bring about "the fundamental restructuring of
the urban environment."[20] School reformers endeavored to accomplish no
less than the concomitant fundamental reorganization of the urban educational environment. The key to progress was to be as urban as possible.

DESIGNING OPTIMISM

Unlike women's suffrage, temperance, trade unionism, or governance reform,
education was a subject that usually united, rather than divided, most urban
reformers. The movement for the "new education," as many contemporaries called it, was replete with individuals holding remarkably diverse ideologies. For example, the urban muckraker Lincoln Steffens, who railed against
civic corruption and municipal "graftitis," softened his gaze when he turned
to the topic of schooling. In his autobiography he recalled how he had once
dreamed of transforming the dull and dusty education of his youth into a dramatically different kind of experience whereby "the students would be learning instead of the teacher teaching" and intellectual subjects would be so
vigorously debated that they ultimately would come to occupy the position
"that football holds in modern American universities."[21]

William Howard Taft, not long out of the White House, gave a 1915 address
to the NEA in which he wondered aloud if it might not be possible to introduce
standards of academic achievement in school systems throughout the country. Taft advocated for a kind of early educational accountability system—a

national examining body that, at the request of local communities, would evaluate a local school system and "report to the people who are paying the money for it what kind of a school system it is."[22] Scratch the surface of nearly anyone's thoughts on education, and you were bound to find a reform or two. Apparently unbeknownst to Taft, such evaluations were already in the works, as educational experts were in the midst of a school survey movement through which they conducted investigations of school districts across the country and prodded school systems to introduce new waves of reform.

Those who had faith in the possibility of tangible progress tended to have the view, as Charles Beard later put it, that the past had been "chaos, without order or design."[23] Twentieth-century reformers were buoyant with a belief that solutions to past chaos and contemporary social problems were all within reach. And why not? Developments across the nation continually confirmed educators' confidence in their power to handle large-scale projects and changes. Between 1890 and 1940, American optimism and accomplishments soared. Teddy Roosevelt ceremonially completed the Panama Canal (1914) and Charles Lindbergh crossed the Atlantic in a single flight (1927). Even during the Depression, new skyscrapers like the Chrysler Building (1930), the Empire State Building (1931), and the Rockefeller Center (1933), punctuated the urban skyline.

In the West, urban planners with plenty of space on hand built horizontally rather than vertically and disciples of the City Beautiful movement convinced municipal leaders to invest their public buildings with a certain exalted majesty. In fact, one of Oakland's first "skyscrapers" was its city hall, built in 1912. Both the San Francisco–Oakland Bay Bridge and the Golden Gate Bridge, opening in 1936 and 1937, respectively, proved that oceans—try as they might to extend their fingers inland—were no match for the dedicated engineers who learned to span inlets, bays, and sounds. New tunnels pierced previously impenetrable mountains, and the Hoover (1931–36) and Grand Coulee (1934–41) Dams demonstrated how Americans could "tame" their surroundings and transform them toward new uses. Progressive reformers turned their attention not only outward toward restructuring the natural environment but also inward toward reshaping human culture. From Teddy Roosevelt to Franklin Roosevelt, progressives had faith in both the power of public institutions to improve society and the precision of American scientists to refashion the physical world. Surely, if engineers could join oceans, span bays, control rivers, and bore through mountains, the seemingly simple task of improving schools should be swiftly accomplished.

The architect Daniel Burnham embodied the progressive spirit for the kind of large-scale projects that preoccupied many urban leaders. In one of his lectures, Burnham, who designed a city plan for Chicago and an ultimately unrealized plan for San Francisco, emphatically challenged his audience to think on a grand scale: "Make no little plans. They have no magic to stir men's blood and probably themselves will not be realized. Make big plans; aim high in hope and work, remembering that a noble logical diagram once recorded will never die, but long after we are gone, will be a living thing, asserting [itself] with growing intensity."[24] Urban school superintendents were the planners and engineers of their educational world, and they boldly proposed their own noble logical diagrams for the sweeping improvement of city school systems. Encouraging them in their design endeavors were progressive scholars from across the country, counting among their number not only professors in schools of education but also like-minded economists, psychologists, philosophers, and university presidents. Mixing science, rhetoric, and an indefatigable enthusiasm, these academy-based reformers set out to redraw the map of American education.

Faculty at elite universities promoted themselves as experts in the new science of education. Prominent reformers appointed to these institutions—such as Ellwood Cubberley and Lewis Terman at Stanford University; Franklin Bobbitt, Charles Judd, and (from 1894 to 1904) John Dewey at the University of Chicago; and George Strayer, William C. Bagley, Harold Rugg, George Counts, and (after 1904) John Dewey at Teachers College, Columbia University—worked individually and collectively to study and transform traditional American educational practices. Their comprehensive visions incorporated plans for administrative reorganization, pedagogical improvement, curriculum revision, physical plant expansion, and the enhancement of student health care. As these national reformers saw it, their task was to lay out the broad, fundamental principles that local practitioners could follow in designing specific plans for their own cities. Only periodically did these academics point out the wide gulf of differences between some of their ideas.

Educators had reason to be confident, for they lived during a time of phenomenal educational expansion. "As they looked about them," Lawrence Cremin explains, "they saw a school structure which was the envy of other nations—an elementary system which embraced the vast majority of America's children and a secondary system which enrolled more youngsters than any other secondary schools the world over. It is little wonder that they looked to the future with optimism, and that they painted a picture of educational struggles which had been waged and won, and enemies which had been routed and destroyed."[25]

Twenty-first-century Americans tend to hold an idealized view of the one-room schoolhouse, often harboring nostalgia for the nineteenth-century pedagogical past. Such wistfulness would have been unthinkable to progressives. To early twentieth-century educators, the one-room schoolhouse was hardly a quaint icon; rather, it was an obsolete and unwelcome holdover that reformers targeted for extinction. In Denver, for example, a 1923 superintendent's report proudly included a picture of a bulletin board covered in photographs of old one-room school houses from the region that had all recently been demolished or officially abandoned.[26] These dilapidated, often haphazard, constructions were replaced by newer, modern, architecturally imposing buildings. The large, cosmopolitan school, with its neoclassical or Romantic architectural style, represented access to a wide array of coursework and symbolized a turning point in American education.

In their lectures and writings progressive reformers argued that urban problems were, in fact, really unique opportunities, and they incorporated that same idea into a new generation of student textbooks, many of which they themselves wrote. The "modern industrial city is a new and complex creation," explained one 1926 social studies text, *The New Social Civics*. The shifting urban environment of the twentieth century resulted in unfamiliar conditions and novel sets of problems, and "new methods must be found to deal with them," said the book's two authors—D. E. Phillips and Jesse Newlon—who were city school leaders themselves. They thought it only natural to include a chapter titled "The City and City Problems" in their book. "Face your problem and solve it," they advised their young readers; the city "has brought evils and great problems, but we must remember that it has brought equally great blessings and still greater opportunities."[27]

In his courses at Stanford, Cubberley assigned John Spargo's *The Bitter Cry of the Children*, a muckraking attack on the misery and maladies facing urban children. Yet Cubberley saw the book not "as a shameful record for a democracy" but as a demonstration of "how much better our record was becoming year by year."[28] As reformers explained it, the challenges created by growing American cities were not enduring dilemmas but rather problems to be systematically solved. Too many accidents in crowded city streets? Teach children about safety. Too much vandalism or juvenile delinquency? Mandate classes in character education. Too many unhealthy children? Offer school-based medical services alongside lessons on health and hygiene.

"Anyone who gets discouraged by the difficulties encountered in forwarding a given local improvement," declared the Chicago sociologist Charles Zueblin in his 1916 edition of *American Municipal Progress*, "has only to scan the collective achievements of this young century to gain abundant courage and faith. Already this century has witnessed the first municipalized street railways and telephone in American cities," he said, along with "a national

epidemic of street paving and cleaning; the quadrupling of electric lighting service; . . . a successful crusade against dirt of all kinds—smoke, flies,
germs—and the diffusion of constructive provisions for health like baths,
laundries, comfort stations, milk stations, school nurses and open air schools."
Moreover, said Zueblin, the twentieth century's first fifteen years had resulted
in a "school curriculum [that gave] every child a complete education from
the kindergarten to the vocational course in school or university or shop."[29]
Whether through public health or public schooling, the expanding city provided the optimal setting for significant social reform. Municipal leaders
increasingly viewed school systems as the perfect partners in their compulsion for hygiene and order. If it was the city's duty to provide a complete education, then the schools could, in turn, help foster a stronger, if not a cleaner,
social environment.

The desire to improve the American city bubbled forth from multiple
wellsprings. Urban centers housed the full array of American political energy,
be it a cautious, middle-class desire for incremental improvement, the fierce
moralizing of conservative progressivism, or the biting, anti-capitalist rhetoric of labor unions. In effect, the city offered a new space for reimagining
an America fitted for the twentieth century. Harvard's Munro believed that
there was "no service more patriotic than that of helping to make [the city]
a better place for men to live."[30] Many reformers saw it as their duty to contribute to that patriotic service through the improvement of city schools.
For some, the task was to professionalize educational governance by root-
ing out civic corruption and squelching school board malfeasance. For others, classroom instruction offered the most enduring avenue for protecting
democracy. Patriotic education could take any number of forms, such as citizenship classes, new civics textbooks, or—as in the years immediately following World War I—anti-Bolshevist campaigns to cleanse the schools through
Americanization classes. Although such efforts might conceivably have provided fuel for ideological fires or multiple municipal conflicts, educational
reforms often harnessed a common energy that progressives directed toward
urban planning, economic growth, and civic competition.[31]

Outwitting the City

The anomalous expansion of cities, no matter how celebrated by urban boosters, nevertheless troubled educators who worried about the unique hazards
that the urban environment posed to growing children. The agrarian traditions that had once anchored country life had already begun to slip away,
sparking anxiety among many late nineteenth-century educators, who feared

the negative consequences that might befall pupils who were reared away from the natural world. For their part, university-based researchers called for investigations into the impact that urban influences had on the mental and emotional development of young pupils.

Enter a new educational expert: the psychologist. A scientific understanding of child development, experts argued, would yield school curriculum accurately tailored to the demands of the twentieth century. G. Stanley Hall, along with other educational psychologists, warned educators that they could no longer assume that urban-bred children carried the same experiential knowledge as their peers in rural communities. Already, teachers in city schools had begun to realize, as Hall put it, "that city life is unnatural and that those who grow up without knowing the country are defrauded of that without which childhood can never be complete or normal."[32] While it may be difficult to truly grasp the nature of this sentiment today, it was clearly a motivating factor that held a power over many progressives, including Dewey.

Building on research conducted in Germany, Hall was one of the first researchers to conduct "scientific" studies of children in the United States. In 1883, Hall set out to develop "an inventory of the contents of the minds of children" as they entered elementary school. Through the examination of textbooks and curricular materials, conversations with teachers, and pilot studies with children, he created a list of items, concepts, and objects that standard school books and teachers generally expected children would know as they arrived for their first day of school. Employing experienced kindergarten teachers as interviewers and researchers, Hall asked children if they had done things such as plant a seed (only 37 percent of city children had), observe a rainbow (35 percent), or witness a watchmaker at work (32 percent).[33]

The results of the study convinced Hall that city schools were foundering in dangerous cognitive waters. For example, 80 percent of city children did not know what a beehive was; 75.5 percent of the children could not identify what season it was when asked; 50 percent seemed to have no knowledge of frogs; and although a solid 81.5 percent said they knew what a cow was, some apparently thought that that it was about the size of a mouse. Here was clear evidence of urban deprivation, Hall concluded. Yet some findings might have suggested to Hall that young children simply vary a great deal in terms of their accumulated knowledge, no matter their background. For example, while 65 percent knew what a circle was, only 8 percent could identify a triangle; although 94 percent could point to their stomach, only 8.5 percent could point to their ribs.[34] Nonetheless, the results drove his thinking for years.

"There is next to nothing of pedagogic value," Hall ultimately concluded, "of which it is safe to assume [children have] at the outset of school-life." Convinced by the findings of his proto-school readiness inventories, Hall argued that, "on the whole, the material of the city is no doubt inferior in pedagogic value to country experience."[35] Teachers should be wary of "the danger of books and word-cram," he said. Hall's chief concern was that primary-school instructors would do irreparable harm to young children during their first years in school if they falsely assumed that their newest students knew more than they actually did. Teachers, he said, should begin by teaching with real-life objects for two to six months before they dared moved on to the abstractions contained in textbooks. Such was the peril of the city.[36]

The idea of the city as a negative, if not sinister, influence on children was a theme that persisted in educational thought throughout the early decades of the century, if not longer. Reformers detailed the ills of city schools, an approach that offered a strategic advantage, for the multiple flaws of the urban environment could then serve as a foil for the self-anointed saviors of progressivism as they offered their policy salves and new visions for the future. The city "robs children of their native interest in the normal activities of the natural world" and deprives them "of their natural rights to fresh air and sunshine, the beauty of the earth and splendor of the sky," argued art educator Henry Turner Bailey. What, he asked, could the city substitute in place of "those wholesome, fundamental, educational, character building activities of life in the country?" He had a ready answer: "It offers early familiarity with depravity and crime . . . dancing, automobile driving, the radio, craps, cards, pool and billiards, and the salacious magazines and super-heated novels and tales of adventure sold at the news-stands."[37] While dancing, driving, and radios seem much less of a threat today, Bailey's catalog of urban vice generally reflected the kinds of concerns that disturbed moral reformers of the period.

Despite the romantic portraits of rural life sometimes painted by men like Hall and Bailey, progressive critiques were not generally pastoral in attitude or narrowly moralistic in their tone. Neither were they usually overtly political, although the "politics" of urban educational progressivism is not easily characterized. Certainly, perspectives of a political or economic nature periodically popped up in their rhetoric, as when Bailey, sounding like a latter-day American William Blake, leveled a broadside at industrial capitalism. "The present social order," he said, "allows big business to crowd mills and factories so close together that they poison the air and load it with soot to such an extent that trees and shrubs, flowers and green grass die lingering deaths and children are stunted in body and warped in mind." Bailey's message was less a radical call for social transformation, however, than it was a plea to recognize the educational necessity of counteracting urban despair. "Progressive education," said Bailey, "means the determined effort to outwit these unfavorable conditions of modern life in industrial centers." By preemptively providing progressive education, the city could compensate for its own weaknesses by presenting the best it had to offer, whether through lectures, concerts, or masterpieces of art. Schools, said Bailey, opened up children's eyes to the cultural delights of the city: to architecture, sculpture, and painting.[38]

The City: Foster Parent of Democracy

Schools could never completely thwart all negative effects of urban life, of course, so urban progressives augmented their arguments that city school systems should sit at the center of American educational life. One significant, and ultimately successful, recasting of the rural-urban relationship was to reverse the logic in the notion that rural life was inherently more beneficial to children. Instead, urban boosters argued, the educational services, curricula, and instruction that city school systems provided far surpassed anything available in rural schools. If urban schools offered students a higher quality and a wider array of educational resources, so the thinking went, then city school districts would also foster and strengthen democracy. "The modern city is the offspring of the industrial revolution," explained Charles Zueblin in 1916, and "it is also the parent, or at least the foster parent, of democracy."[39]

Through efforts to transform the image of the city, urban educators and progressive reformers essentially turned Jefferson's notion of democracy on its head. They argued that urban society, not the traditional agrarian community, was the best incubator of democracy, a point they made with increasing frequency throughout the era. "If people have to live together, they have to work together," ultimately making them far more cooperative and interdependent, argued Zueblin. "The meditative rustics at the general store chew their cud and discuss abstract democracy," Zueblin mused, but city dwellers collectively learned "concrete democracy" by installing water and sewage systems under the streets that they then paved. "The compulsion of cooperation makes the city the laboratory of applied democracy," Zueblin proclaimed; "The people in the modern city thrive."[40]

The notion of applied democracy was an idea tailor-made for American public education, arming educators with convincing new rhetoric that schools provided an ideal mechanism for making tangible improvements to society. Phillips and Newlon stated it plainly in their civics book: "*It is our educational system that will make possible a future democracy* [italics in original]. . . . A properly educated people should be able to solve all difficulties that may arise."[41] Cleveland's Frederic Howe listed education as one of the essential weapons needed to combat modern problems. "The city," he wrote,

IS EVERY CHILD ENTITLED to an EQUAL
EDUCATIONAL OPPORTUNITY ?

I ATTEND A COUNTRY SCHOOL.
My school term is 7 months.
My teacher is paid $755 a year.
My teacher is a high-
   school graduate.
My teacher has taught
   one year.
My school-house has
   one room.
My school library con-
   tains 100 books.

I ATTEND A CITY SCHOOL.
My school term is 10 months.
My teacher is paid. $1968 a year.
My teacher is a college
   graduate.
My teacher has taught
   five years.
My school-house has
   24 rooms.
My school library contains
   5000 books.

FIGURE 1.2. The challenge of providing equal educational opportunity, as portrayed by the National Education Association in 1926. (National Education Association, "A Handbook of Major Educational Issues," *Research Bulletin of the National Education Association* 4, no. 4 [September 1926]: 210–11.)

"is to be the arena where the social and political forces that are coming to the fore will play . . . for with universal education, a free press, a free ballot, all contributing to the formation of definite political and social ideals, civilization is armed with powers such as she has never before enjoyed."[42] As we shall see, however, this utopian vision of universal access to education offered a sanitized view of politics.

In addition to their reversal of the logic of agrarian democracy, urban progressives also developed a new twist to the idea of educational equality. The notion of equal educational opportunity had been a staple of educational discussions ever since common school reformers sought to provide the majority of American children with something akin to a uniform curriculum. Nonetheless, the precise meaning of educational equality was rarely clearly defined. In the standard educational rhetoric, the explicit goals of democratic education were to create intelligent citizens and to provide free public schooling to all.[43]

The task of offering a good, basic education to all children proved remarkably difficult, however, due in part to evolving beliefs about what constituted an adequate curriculum and to shifting social and professional ideas about children's educational needs. Furthermore, the uneven distribution of educational resources across and within states presented a significant obstacle to educational equality. In the 1920s, NEA leaders blamed fiscal disparity for "the serious differences in educational opportunity" that existed in the nation. One NEA research bulletin asserted that only the *urban school* would provide the desired equality of educational opportunity to American students; rural schools could hardly offer anything comparable to the city school's multiple benefits (see fig. 1.2). Some rural districts were so poor, NEA reformers cautioned, "that even an excessively high tax rate fails to provide its children with an acceptable common school education."[44]

Badly impoverished school districts could not offer students essential educational opportunities. Therefore, NEA researchers warned, these financially depleted districts posed a serious threat to democracy. Not unlike Horace Mann half a century before them, progressive reformers raised the specter of an uneducated populace, though in tones somewhat more muted than Mann's admonitions of mass uprising. "Children in the poor district will soon be voting citizens, with as much voice in directing public affairs as those of the rich district," said one NEA bulletin. Communities that allowed "many of their children to grow into illiterate and ignorant adulthood" risked permitting ill-informed voters to "stifle progress" and nullify "intelligent ballot[s]." In contrast to this alarming vision of a destabilized democracy, stood the city school district, the kind of solid organization able to marshal the resources necessary for equal educational opportunity in the twentieth century.[45] Although the progressive depiction of the city school district as a social equalizer relied on an idealized portrait of urban education, it accurately represented an emerging ideology about the connections between municipal improvement, education, and democracy.

The progressive fascination with "applied democracy" also helps explain a propensity among reformers for combining broad, comprehensive plans with a microscopic inquisitiveness. When Frederic Howe described his own enthusiastic absorption in the intricate task of redrawing the urban environment, he characterized it as kind of a calling: "I studied cities as one might study art; I was interested in curbs, in sewers, in sky-lines."[46] District progressives burned with a similar passion for the minutiae of educational improvement. When contracted to conduct formal evaluations of specific school systems, as they increasingly were after 1910, educational surveyors often went well beyond matters curricular, offering expositions about the purchase of proper drinking fountains, the hazards of poor classroom ventilation, and their unfortunate encounters with fetid and filthy bathrooms.[47]

One assumption that the new educational scientists of the Progressive Era shared with their journalistic and muckraking contemporaries was the belief that facts and information, when based in investigative research and then shared publicly, would ultimately result in positive change. This assumption held firm in progressive thought for a remarkable number of years. A growing cadre of municipal experts stressed the need for developing uniform school district records and reports that revealed vital information to school communities; standardized reports also offered a convenient means for comparing statistics and programs across cities, which in turn led to more competitive boosterism.

In 1908, David Snedden and William H. Allen, working on behalf of the New York Committee on the Physical Welfare of School Children, fumed that few school district annual reports contained the kind of useful evidence necessary to successfully inform and operate a large city school system, thereby illustrating what they called "a striking phase of inefficiency in American municipal administration." In contrast, the authors heralded reports from the bureaus of immigration, census, and labor as examples of what they called "devices of efficient publicity." The goal, as Snedden and Allen saw it, should be to supply both outside experts and local administrators with useful statistical tables. Appropriate accounting methods, educators were told, would offer "the layman of average intelligence, but of more than average interest" the information needed to understand, and support, school improvement efforts. Educational data, made lucid and available to the public, were essential to the reform process, Snedden and Allen argued, precisely because these individuals of "average intelligence" were the citizens who usually sat on school boards and stood "between the taxpayers and the institutions."[48] In other words, school boards would serve either as the barriers or as the builders of the new education, and they needed access to accurate and precise information in order to craft their decisions.

Not all Progressive Era municipal problems and improvements were of equal complexity, of course. Building bridges, laying sewer lines, widening boulevards, and even standardizing disorganized administrative records could be executed with precision, but the education of children was another matter altogether. Then as now, teaching and learning have never been completely amenable to programmatic blueprints, no matter how carefully drafted or scientifically calculated. Educational problems, even when they seem perfectly clear, are rarely easily addressed or solved. What, then, did educational progressives see as the most pressing issues? A full appreciation of the solutions proposed by district progressives requires an understanding of the perceived weaknesses and defects.

PRESSING PROBLEMS AND PARTIAL SOLUTIONS

The educational problems identified at the beginning of the Progressive Era were really an amalgam of enduring dilemmas, accrued throughout the nineteenth century, mixed with the newer and quite vexing social conditions that accompanied increased immigration, industrialization, and urbanization.

Although educational historians have documented many of the challenges that faced turn-of-the-twentieth-century educators, some of the core concerns are worth a brief revisit, especially as they relate to school district development.

Throughout much of the nineteenth century, state educational leaders like Massachusetts's Horace Mann and Michigan's John Pierce issued warnings about weak curricula, shoddy teaching, inadequate textbooks, and slapdash educational facilities. Toward the end of that century, a new generation of reformers took on the business of school improvement with renewed energy and fresh ideas. But reformers of the early Progressive Era sometimes found the problems they confronted were, in fact, an outgrowth of the "successes" of the common school movement.

Mid-nineteenth-century public school advocates had stressed the need for enhanced staff professionalization, best achieved, they contended, through standardized pedagogical practices and teacher training programs that could overcome local shortcomings. Greater uniformity in curricula and student textbooks, common school leaders argued, would ensure at least a minimum amount of educational opportunity for all public school students. These nineteenth-century reformers believed—not necessarily unreasonably, given the unevenness of teaching and textbooks across districts and states—that emphasis on uniformity and standardization would pressure local districts to abandon outmoded practices, to boost the quality of their educational materials, and to raise the expectations they held for their teachers. When taken to extremes, however, as these reforms often were in city school systems during the 1880s and 1890s, educational uniformity could become stultifying, rigid, and inhumane.[49]

Such was the situation encountered by pediatrician Joseph Mayer Rice in 1891, when he conducted a medical inspection of elementary schools in New York City. To his dismay, Rice found a culture of schooling antithetical to healthy learning. Raising one of the first critical voices to publicly admonish urban schools for their callous instructional practices and for the kinds of physical hardships they foisted on their students, Rice vividly described classrooms that enforced silence and immobility in their students all while employing pedagogical techniques he characterized as "barbarous and absurd." Publishing his critique in the journal *Forum*, Rice decried the old-style "unscientific or mechanical" schools of New York, "still conducted on the antiquated notion that the function of the school consists primarily, if not entirely, in crowding into the memory of the child a certain number of cut-and-dried facts." The aim of instruction, asserted Rice, was consequently limited to "drilling facts into the minds of children, and to hearing them recite lessons that they have learned by heart from textbooks."[50]

Rice encountered administrators so preoccupied with efficiency and adherence to the prescribed curriculum that they relentlessly rebuked teachers who did not effectively use every minute throughout the day. The result was an atmosphere of anxious and hurried instruction. "By giving the child ready-made thoughts, the minutes required in thinking are saved," Rice lamented. "By giving the child ready-made definitions, the minutes required in formulating them are saved." Anything that was "of no measurable advantage to the child" was prohibited, he reported, "such as the movement of the head or a limb." When Rice asked if such physical immobility was truly necessary, one school principal curtly responded, "Why should they look behind them when the teacher is in front of them?"[51]

Gaining rapid fame for his initial exposé, Rice next undertook an investigation of school systems throughout the East and Midwest. Between January and June of 1892, Rice traveled to a total of thirty-six cities; in many, he found practices as equally distressing as those in New York. In Baltimore, Philadelphia, St. Louis, Minneapolis, and Chicago, Rice found school systems imbued with an attitude he characterized as the "cold, hard, and cruel struggle for results." In St. Louis, many teachers preferred to conduct stiff and formal recitations in which students, standing rigid and still, simply spouted the required answers. Too often, the teacher's responses merely consisted of saying: "Right," "Wrong," "Next," "Don't lean against the wall," and "Keep your toes on the line."[52] In some Chicago schools, students had been furnished with only one reading book, "so they were obliged to read the same book over and over again until the end of the term." Even when students had proper textbooks, they often served as sources to be memorized. "In several instances when a pupil stopped for a moment's reflection," Rice reported, "the teacher remarked abruptly, *'Don't stop to think, but tell me what you know.'*"[53]

In 1893, Rice published his collected essays in a book entitled *The Public-School System of the United States*. Most educators were unprepared for anything like Rice's assault. Up to this point in time, education had mostly been a local affair, and any significant problems, if they were noticed at all, had been discussed and dealt with among the smaller community of educators and parents. Harsh critiques of particular schools or districts penned by county supervisors often made their way into state annual reports, but rarely had anything like Rice's sustained and detailed attack on specific classroom practices been unveiled at a national level. "The light of science" had not yet entered these buildings, said Rice, and he felt it his mission to direct the glare in their direction.[54]

Many urban educators were outraged. How could Rice, never a teacher himself, have the temerity to pass judgment on public school professionals

who had spent their lives in education? Especially insulting was Rice's insin-
uation that education could be energized only through the know-how of
educational researchers from outside the school system. Teachers, retorted
one New York administrator, need hardly "wait until the advent of learning-
begrimed pedagogical 'experts' or science-bespattered psychologists before
feeling the electric waves of professional enthusiasm."[55] In another response,
New Yorker Henry Schneider asserted that Rice undermined his own cause
by rhetorically overstepping himself. "He relies upon an aroused and enlightened public opinion to remedy the evils he points out," Schneider said, "but
like most radical reformers, he goes too far and in his zeal forgets the only
means by which the improvement of our school can be attained." The "only
means" that Schneider had in mind, were the city's teachers, "those noble
men and women who have always striven and always will strive" to improve
the schools. "The teachers know the defects of our school system as well as, if
not better than Dr. Rice," Schneider said, and Rice would have done a greater
service if he had alerted the American people "that there is in our corps of
school officers sufficient genius and ability to regenerate our system and cast
off its defects."[56]

Whether sufficient regenerative "genius" truly existed in New York's
schools—or anywhere else—was very much an open question among progressives. Indeed, many municipal progressives relied on outside critiques
and legal actions to force reform on corrupt politicians, absentee landlords,
and greedy industrialists, but whether they were making improvements from
the inside out was another matter. Consciously or not, both Rice and his
detractors alighted on several enduring dilemmas that had long vexed institutional reformers. Could reform come from within the system or was external
pressure necessary? Who held the legitimacy to critique local school districts
and propose solutions? Schneider argued, for example, that the New York
school board "had long been engaged in proposing legislation" that would
eventually remedy many of the problems Rice had identified. Rice had done
an injustice to teachers who spent their careers seeking educational improvement, Schneider felt, and "who for years have borne the brunt of the battle,
quietly but none the less effectively, fighting successfully the forces of ignorance and apathy and the desolating influence of politics." Rice, Schneider
added, "forgets that in a republic we can not summarily root out evils."[57]

Robert Wiebe has argued that one "great casualty" of the Progressive Era
was the "island community," and he has traced how progressives, attempting to systematize solutions to urban problems, sought to create connections
to the larger world around them.[58] The consequences of this shift in focus,

from a local perspective to a national one, were dramatic. Throughout the nineteenth century, local school districts often contained no more than one or two schools. As in other spheres of public life at the turn of the century, however, local leaders found their traditional practices abruptly cast in comparison to those in other cities. The combined pressure of urban competition, external critiques, and calls for uniform records proved especially powerful, and educators often felt compelled to adopt practices that conformed to those in other cities. These pressures were rarely politically neutral.[59]

Many city school systems were also caught off guard by the sudden surge in students and by the urgent need for additional classrooms and teachers that resulted. Administrators found themselves adrift without clear plans for expansion or even the means to adapt to a swiftly changing situation. The result, in city after city, was a district-wide jumble of replicated practices, strident uniformity, and teachers strained to the breaking point, often because of the burden of institutionalized routines. At precisely the moment when many other municipal reforms were underway, the timing was perfect for progressives to pick up the cause of schooling. During the years between 1890 and 1910, in ever-growing numbers and in increasingly public outlets, politicians, journalists, academics, and even practitioners described the conditions of school buildings, the quality of instruction, and the state of the curriculum in terms that were rarely complimentary. Many accounts emulated the muckraking mood of the age, directing attention toward educational practices and social conditions that had long been out of public scrutiny.

Poverty Trumps Pedagogy

Another intrepid observer of the links between schooling and the urban environment was Jacob Riis. Rapidly gaining recognition in the 1890s for his photographic and journalistic exposés of poverty in New York, Riis argued that urban school reform was an essential step toward improving the lives of tenement children. Jails—not schools—he complained, often served as the primary educators of many children.[60] At first, Riis denounced a rather amorphous "system" for its failure to compel students to attend school as the law required, thus contributing, he said, to the problems of the street gypsies.[61] Over time Riis's gaze shifted, and he focused his formidable skills on more specific conditions in New York City's public schools. Throughout his school visits, Riis found eye-strainingly ill-lit schools filled with rank air, buildings overrun with rats, and classrooms packed with seventy or eighty children. He found evidence of extensive administrative corruption—symbolized, for example, by the appointment of a dead man (deceased more than a year) as a school board member in one ward. Some school buildings were virtual firetraps. An inspector described one Bronx school as no more than "a wooden shanty . . . heated by stoves . . . a regular tinder box."[62]

New York, of course, was unusual in terms of its size, but that novelty went unappreciated by the thousands of would-be students who were turned away from already overenrolled schools each year. Riis estimated that fifty thousand children roamed the streets because there was no room in the schools; the only defense that the school commissioners gave, he said, was "that they 'didn't know' there were so many."[63] For a time, New York symbolized the kinds of challenges that all cities faced—or would soon face. If it happened in New York, it was bound to happen elsewhere. Once the virulent critiques that pummeled New York commenced, few cities were safe from progressives set on fault-finding, and faults they found in East and West. Yet more so than in the nineteenth century, educators and non-educators alike began to search for the sources of school problems within larger social conditions.

"The problem of poverty in its relation to childhood and education is, to us in America, quite new," wrote John Spargo in his 1906 exposé of the impact of poverty on young children in New York City.[64] Robert Hunter's pioneering study *Poverty* had been published just two years earlier, alerting Americans— many apparently for the first time—to the graver consequences of urbanization and industrialization. Poverty was not new, even if industrial capitalism created new forms of impoverished conditions. Schools already felt the debilitating effects of poverty on a daily basis; and alongside specific school concerns, some progressives began to entertain the notion that social and economic conditions caused problematic student behavior and achievement. The connections between poverty and a pupil's school performance that today are well-demonstrated were by no means clear at the time. So, when William Maxwell, superintendent of the newly reorganized and centralized New York City public schools, declared in 1901 that hundreds of thousands of schoolchildren were unable to study or learn because they were underfed, Spargo undertook detailed observations of the potential connections.[65]

Spargo found many children too weak in mind and body to do the schoolwork required of them. One captain of a Salvation Army "Slum Post" described the children who arrived at his door as weak, famished, filthy, forlorn, and inexpressibly miserable. Packing pupils into already overstuffed schools would hardly solve the most serious problems, a situation that led Spargo to a central contradiction at the heart of turn-of-the-century urban education. "Regarding education as the only safe anchorage of a Democracy," he said, "we make it compulsory and boast that it is one of the fundamental principles of our econ-

omy that every child shall be given a certain amount of elementary instruction." However, the ideal of universal education was far from being realized,
and compulsory attendance, even when it worked, rarely addressed the spectrum of social ills facing children.[66]

Despite the widespread evidence Spargo found of student malnourish-
ment, many teachers and school principals obstinately refused to investigate or even acknowledge the veracity of these claims. One principal, whom
Spargo described as "a devoted believer in the theory of the survival of the
fittest and in the elimination of the weak by competition and struggle," said of
his students: "If you attempt to take hardship and suffering out of their lives
by smoothing the pathway of life for these children, you weaken their character, and, by so doing, you sin against the children themselves and, through
them, against society." Teachers often held similar beliefs, and some rebuffed
Spargo's request to ask their students when they had last eaten. When Spargo
asked one teacher to survey her class about the regularity of their meals, she
sent back a note: "Nobody underfed but the teacher."[67] Teachers and administrators frequently found that it was easier to push failing students out of
school than it was to improve teaching or to engage in tiresome battles with
school boards for additional resources.

The extant evidence from turn-of-the-century classroom observations
tends to confirm that the kinds of pedagogical concerns raised by Rice in
the 1890s persisted well into the twentieth century. Ten years after Rice's
first *Forum* articles, for example, journalist Adele Marie Shaw conducted
her own examination of public school systems at the behest of Walter Hines
Page, editor of the *World's Work*. Shaw's reports never received the same
kind of national attention as Rice's (perhaps because Americans were already
becoming inured to the "crisis" in education), yet she nonetheless captured
the types of stubborn shortcomings that endured in public school systems.

Shaw encountered one New York City geography lesson that was in "lum-
bering progress," and she described the class as a deadening repetition of
"bored question and perfunctory answer" enforced by "a resolute repres-
sion of any tendency to stray from the printed page." This school, she said,
"ignored absolutely any individuality in the pupils and fitted them for nothing more than a mechanical obedience to another's thinking." The teachers,
whom Shaw described as "harassed, visibly worn, harsh, and unkind," readily
barked at any students who dared depart from the lesson or who gratuitously
moved one of their limbs.[68] Was it not possible, another reformer asked in
1913, to "adapt education more to the child" and to "reach into the home and
console and protect and cooperate with him better than we do?" Education should fit the child's "psychology, their traditions, their environment or

inheritance."[69] Riis, Spargo, and Shaw, along with other sensitive observers, hoped for a new atmosphere within the schools, one that was as nurturing as it was relevant. They were all part of an emerging consensus.

Change was hardly simple, of course, no matter how clearly the problems were stated. Among other obstacles, reformers found themselves confronting a dogged sense of satisfaction about the state of American education. "Every man in the Middle West seems equally sure of the superiority of his own State's system, maintaining that it best fulfils the American ideal of free education," Shaw reported after her school visits.[70] This obstinate sense of superiority and complacency, smugness even, meant that school improvement measures often met with resistance.

Facts, Laggards, and Remedies

Around the turn of the century, however, the locus of educational debate began to shift, moving away from the continual castigations of the "old education"— although these critiques persisted for some time—and toward deliberate efforts at defining what the "new education" should look like. Whether this moment would be truly pivotal in the movement for progressive education depended on the willingness of local educators, academics, civic leaders, and politicians to address core matters of American education. Several fundamental concerns required attention, among them, the purposes of public schooling in a democracy, the knowledge that students should learn, and the types of assessment appropriate to American education. Some educators settled for shallower depths of inquiry, readily accepting practices provided by prominent reformers, especially those armed with instruments for scientific measurement. The enthusiastic adoption—or imposition—of efficiency-oriented reforms has been a leitmotif prominent within the historiography. But "efficiency" has too often served as an umbrella term that masks some of the more interesting clashes among seemingly liked-minded people.

Joseph Rice had encountered spirited opposition to his early educational critiques, but he was unprepared for the wrath he later incurred when he presented findings from his follow-up investigations. After his first round of school visits in the early 1890s, Rice had taken it on himself to investigate the amount of time and instructional attention devoted to the teaching of core subjects, such as spelling, arithmetic, and writing. Having conducted tests with children in nineteen city school systems, Rice presented his findings to the NEA Superintendents Department in 1897. His data demonstrated, he said, that children who had spent forty minutes a day for eight years studying spelling did not spell any better than children in the schools that devoted only ten minutes per day doing so.[71] Rice's findings flew in the face of accepted wisdom.

According to educational statistician Leonard Ayres, Rice's presentation threw the audience of superintendents into "consternation, dismay, and indignant protest." The resulting storm of "vigorously voiced opposition was directed, not against the methods and results of the investigation, but against the investigator who had pretended to measure the results of teaching spelling by testing the ability of children to spell."[72] "With striking unanimity," Ayres reported, "they voiced the conviction that any attempt to evaluate the teaching of spelling in terms of the ability of the pupils to spell was essentially impossible and based on a profound misconception of the function of education."[73]

The idea that students should be tested on the amount of knowledge and skills they acquire is so commonplace today (even if educators argue about the appropriate forms and frequency of testing) that it seems strange indeed that educators would be opposed to administering spelling tests in order to determine instructional effectiveness. However, nineteenth-century educators lived at a time when the theoretical paradigm of "faculty psychology" or "mental discipline" still held sway. Educators grounded in this tradition believed that the main justification for teaching *any* subject was not so much for the specific disciplinary content but for how the *process* of rigorous learning trained the mind. Most famously articulated by the Yale Report of 1828, the notion of mental discipline emphasized the importance of choosing the right curricular material and employing rote methods of learning. Such activity helped strengthen and organize the pupil's mind, thereby producing a better intellect. The hard work of memorization, concentration, and recitation was good for children, educators believed, because concerted mental effort fostered internalized habits of obedience, diligence, and speed.[74]

As educational psychologist David Berliner points out, educators who worked under the premise of faculty psychology saw "good teaching" as normative judgment, and therefore it was more valued than "effective" or "efficient teaching," terms that derive their meaning from empirical data. In other words, core questions of educational quality could not be decided by scientific investigation, at least according to many school leaders in 1897. By suggesting that education and its immediate outcomes could be measured, Rice, an outsider unschooled in the theory of faculty psychology, had done something that only a non-educator could have done at the time. In undertaking his investigations, Rice helped usher in the push for "scientific management" in education. With that said, when Rice used the phrase, he had in mind that the practice of education should be based on evidence not on the opinions of those who happened to run the schools. This was a different view of scientific management than that held by the disciples of Frederick Winslow Taylor, usually considered the father of scientific management.[75]

In recent decades, scholars have criticized scientific management for its abuses and misuses, and with good reason, for many of the ideas and practices spawned by scientific management were applied recklessly, inappropriately, and damagingly. Nevertheless, scholars sometimes overlook the accumulation of educational problems—especially those in large urban school districts—that the age of efficiency, at least in part, helped to correct. As influential researchers like Cubberley and Teachers College professor Edward L. Thorndike, among many others, began to spread the notion that education could be scientifically investigated, urban school leaders found it increasingly difficult to persist with pedagogical approaches that were patently ineffective, to dismiss out of hand publicly reported statistics of poor student achievement, or, for that matter, to sanction overtly harsh or unkind teacher behavior that showed little evidence of success. One need not be an apologist for scientific management to recognize that many conditions required correctives.[76]

Another urgent problem took its place alongside the already troubling conditions of inadequate buildings, instructional bullying, and wooden teaching.[77] In many cities, curiously large percentages of children appeared neither to be learning nor to be advancing from grade to grade, something that became more and more apparent as district central offices increasingly required their schools to submit uniform student attendance and achievement data.[78] Many urban school systems found themselves with an abundance of older children still stuck in the earlier grades. The surplus of "overage" students swiftly became a distressing national situation, especially in rapidly growing metropolitan areas because year after year more pupils began accumulating in the lower elementary grades, unable to pass their promotion exams. William Maxwell, the New York City school superintendent, was one of the first urban administrators to draw public attention to these concerns, when in 1904 he published city school figures showing that a full 39 percent of students were above the normal age for their grades. Maxwell's report sent a jolt through the educational world.[79]

The New York City–based Russell Sage Foundation was especially struck by Maxwell's findings. Interested in discovering the full extent the problem, the foundation enlisted the assistance of the new director of their Department of Education and Statistics, Leonard Ayres, who had spent the previous ten years as a teacher and school administrator in Puerto Rico (and was the same individual who witnessed and commented on the ungracious reception of Rice's 1897 NEA presentation). The foundation asked Ayres to address the following questions:

- How many children in our schools fail to make normal progress from grade to grade and why do they fail?
- How many children drop out of school before finishing the elementary course and why do they drop out?
- What are the facts and what are the remedies?

These were modern questions to be sure. Rarely had the lack of individual student advancement been seen as a systematic problem—nor had inquiries into the outcomes of the public schools been addressed so straightforwardly. Ayres began by using New York as a pilot site, then moved on to examine the school records of some thirty-one city school systems. In his published 1909 report, *Laggards in Our Schools*, Ayres estimated that just over one-third of the total elementary school population enrolled in the nation's city school systems was overage—an astonishing finding.[80] This was "not at all a problem concerning a few under-developed or feeble-minded children," Ayres said. "It is one affecting most intimately perhaps 6,000,000 children in the United States."[81]

"This falling back problem is called *retardation*," said Ayres, thereby coining a term that, although it was meant to be a simple analytic designation, ultimately became a popular pejorative epithet. The student who falls behind, Ayres said, "becomes discouraged through his lack of success and, when he has passed the compulsory attendance age, he leaves school." Ayers termed this dropping out process "elimination," as had Thorndike before him.[82] Ayres was especially concerned about students who had only reached the fifth or sixth grade, instead of the eighth, by the age of fourteen; these students rarely stayed in school long enough to graduate. "The educational importance of this fact is great," said Ayres. "We are apt to think of the common school course as representing the least amount of schooling that should be permitted to anyone," he explained. "But the fact remains that a large part of all our children are not completing it." How could it be that so many children had fallen behind or dropped out? Ayres offered a range of potential explanations: physical weaknesses, inefficient teaching, irregular attendance, unsuitable courses of study, the shifting of children between schools, or the fact that many children came from foreign countries.[83]

Whatever the causes, Ayres argued that current educational practices were unjust to the child and disastrous to the schools. Although at first glance

Ayres's report appeared to fault the standard school curriculum (or "course of study") of the day, its most significant conclusion implicitly blamed schoolchildren for the problem: most American students, Ayres stated, were simply incapable of learning the standard subject matter. The fact that so many children fell behind or abandoned schooling also proved to Ayres that "our courses of study as at present constituted are fitted not to the slow child or the average child but to the unusually bright one."[84] In making this statement, Ayres voiced a sentiment that was gathering credence at the time, especially as more and more children gained access to the public schools. After all, as discussed below, only roughly 69 percent of school-age children were officially enrolled during this period, suggesting that the Ayres's estimates may ultimately have been an undercount.

Although Ayres's data offered compelling evidence that "overageness" was a widespread problem, he was nevertheless stumped by the "great range in the percentages of retardation" he discovered among cities. In Medford, Massachusetts, for example, only 7.5 percent of children were behind grade, whereas in New York City and in Portland, Oregon, the percentage was closer to 30 percent. Worse yet were the numbers of overage students in Cincinnati, Ohio (58.7 percent), and Erie, Pennsylvania (60.1 percent). Some of the most distressing examples were in cities with de jure segregation. In Wilmington, Delaware, white schoolchildren had a 37.2 percent overage rate, whereas African American schools had a disturbing 62.8 percent. In Memphis, Tennessee, both populations fared poorly, but the 75.8 percent retardation rate of African American schoolchildren was by far the worst Ayres found; the white schools in Memphis reported a 51.3 rate.[85] Ayres did not comment on the huge disparities between black and white children. Nor did he mention race or the harmful effects of segregation, either in *Laggards* or in his other work on the comparative efficiency of school systems. Unfortunately, he was not alone in the tendency to ignore or overlook racist educational practices in the North or South; many educational progressives demonstrated the same obliviousness to the problems of racism at the same time that they forthrightly addressed other social problems in American cities.

Despite the surprising variation Ayres found across different cities, the evidence that gave him pause—although not for very long—was data regarding the differences between individual schools within the same city. Ayres provided examples of schools in New York City that differed by more that 35 percentage points in their "backwardness" rates. Most striking, however, were disparities between schools situated in the same neighborhoods and drawing on students "from the same racial and social classes." Even here, the spread was as wide as 21 percentage points. The differences were not due to the sex of the pupils, Ayres noted (at a time when some cities still operated separate boys and girls schools). "The difference then must be in the schools themselves," he deduced. In other words, Ayres decided that percentage of overage rates between schools simply constituted a reliable measure of school efficiency, but he did not explore the implications.[86]

If Ayres acknowledged that school quality was one clear cause of significant differences in overage rates—even when schools in the same city worked with similar student populations—why did he then presume that the *curriculum* was the problem? He might just as easily have concluded that better instruction was the key to school improvement. One likely explanation for his lack of attention to instruction is that so many other contemporary educational researchers and reformers, not the least of which was Thorndike, vociferously argued that the curriculum was ill-suited to the child. Thorndike never contended that teachers could teach the traditional disciplinary subjects more effectively.[87]

Laggards in Our Schools gained widespread attention, influencing practices in urban districts across the country. The study also offered some of the earliest, nationally available data on western city school systems. For example, Ayres reported the percentages of overage students in Los Angeles (38.3 percent) and in Portland, Oregon (30.7 percent). Yet what Ayres demonstrated perhaps most effectively was that America's urban schools, no matter their location, were all struggling with the same problem. *Laggards* led to multiple diagnoses and prescriptions for improvement; some were sound, many were not.

Across the country from Ayres's home base in New York, Frederic Burk, director of the State Normal School in San Francisco, worked with his teachers-in-training to pinpoint the sources of and the solutions to student elimination. Burk believed that the primary cause for student failure was patently obvious. "Very few people, big or little," he said, "readily stick to a thing at which they are not reasonably successful." Yet the graded system of the traditional school compelled children to persist whether they succeeded or not, for it "assumes that *all pupils*, during the school exercise, shall *pay exactly the same degree of attention, and shall reach comprehension by exactly the same mental process, and shall reach it simultaneously*" (emphasis in original).[88] Burk's remarks appeared in his short 1913 monograph, *Lock-Step Schooling and a Remedy*, a study that detailed dropout statistics, critiqued the standard urban system of age-graded schooling, and explained the successful remedies he had developed in San Francisco.

Burk characterized the curricular practice of enforced uniformity as "lock-step schooling," a phrase that captured the sentiment well enough to be frequently repeated by progressives as a pithy diagnostic description of nineteenth- and early twentieth-century educational problems. It was hard enough to teach one student, Burk explained, but "reflect a moment upon the assumption of the system that a teacher can and shall force *forty* pupils to put themselves in this unnatural state, *simultaneously, and maintain it for ten to forty minutes at a stretch, day in and day out.*" Burk's keenest observation was perhaps his most compassionate: "Learning in classes under this requirement of forced attention is one continual body-wriggling, brain-fagging, nerve-frazzling and soul-soddening struggle to yield a juiceless attention, to fight against distractions with yielding steps, and to suffer a racking fatigue that knows no tomorrow. There is no escape," Burk acknowledged, "except into the restful stupidity of chronic inattention."[89]

Perhaps better than anyone else at the time, save John Dewey, Burk identified what might be considered the great educational challenge of the twentieth century: Was it possible to teach all students, no matter their backgrounds or abilities, so that they ultimately all reached a common level of competence in core academic subjects? And if so, what kind of pedagogical practice and curricular content would be required to achieve this goal? "If there is a means to fall behind," Burk contended, "there should be a means to go ahead."[90] His solution was to "individualize" instruction so students could progress through curricular materials at his or her own pace. The individualized instruction approach that Burk created and modified through his work in San Francisco generated great enthusiasm among educators across the country, often inspiring school leaders to experiment in their own schools and districts.[91]

————

Taken together, the critiques of urban education delivered from the early 1890s through the mid-1910s offered a portrait of American schools as uninteresting, unsafe, and unsanitary. They told a story of capricious, sometimes vicious, authority, of poorly trained teachers, and of learning opportunities frittered away day after day. Many city schools appeared to undermine the grander goal of universal education by enforcing unreasonably strict codes of classroom behavior, by teaching abstract lessons rather than connecting learning to the tangibles of everyday life, by needlessly failing students who did not make an arbitrary standard, and by sanctioning an atmosphere that was all-too-often hostile toward immigrants, minorities, and the poorest urban children. Therefore, by 1910, it was hardly clear that urban school districts could solve their own problems.

CITY SCHOOL SYSTEMS AS THE ENGINES OF NATIONAL CHANGE

Although the nation was becoming increasingly urban, it was neither inevi-table nor obvious that the city school system would play a significant role in reshaping education for the twentieth century. In fact, even the keenest contemporary observer of late nineteenth-century America would have been unlikely to predict that the public school would evolve into the kind of core American social institution that it is today.

There are a number of reasons why public schooling in general, and urban schooling in particular, did not loom large in the American psyche. Nineteenth-century children, after all, spent much less of their lives in school than they do today. In 1890, for example, although the average official school year lasted approximately 135 days (about six months), the average number of days that an American child actually attended school was eighty-six (just over four months). Only 69 percent of eligible five- to seventeen-year-olds were enrolled in school, and of those enrolled, barely two-thirds showed up on any given school day. Most children who did go to school dropped out by age thirteen or fourteen, if not earlier, leaving only 5.6 percent of the nation's fourteen- to seventeen-year-olds enrolled in high school, and many of those students did not graduate.[92] National averages can be misleading, of course, for they blur important demographic and geographic variations. Nevertheless, one conclusion that can legitimately be drawn from these statistics is that few Americans had reason to believe that publicly supported schooling, whatever institutionalized form it might take, would become especially influential or widespread.

If the future path of schooling was uncertain, so was the nature of edu-cational authority and governance. Even though local districts held sway in the nineteenth century, Mann and other common school reformers believed that increasing centralization at the state level, not at the local level, was the solution to reinvigorating the "dormancy and deadness" of education in local communities.[93] Several decades later, and at the other end of the spectrum, many of Dewey's ideas seemed more directly applicable to small schools or to individual classrooms than to large urban school systems. How then did the path of American education become entwined with the fate of the American city, especially in ways that would have been inconceivable even to the most devoted and optimistic nineteenth-century school reformer?

Cities were part cause and part consequence of an increasingly complex American environment. Many progressives believed that one of the school's most important duties was to prepare American citizens, and to do so in a way that allowed young people to adapt to an increasingly multidimensional society. Referencing James Bryce's classic 1888 study, *The American Commonwealth*, New York's William Maxwell argued that the functions of the American citizen were "far more complicated, delicate, and difficult than the corresponding functions of the citizen of any European country."[94] Contemporaries believed, and historians have agreed, that the citizenship responsibilities of late nineteenth-century Americans were becoming increasingly arduous. Americans had more frequent elections; their political concerns and candidates were scattered across local, county, and state jurisdictions; and at the same time, traditional loyalties to political parties were breaking down.[95]

Heads of city school districts, along with urban-focused academics, were often on the frontlines in the battle for school reform, as any glance at the periodicals and conferences of the era attests. The annual addresses of the NEA's Department of Superintendence—the association's increasingly influential division devoted to the management and improvement of school districts—covered a spectrum of the topics that would soon come to dominate debate for decades to come. Indeed, a taste of the discussions at just the 1890 NEA annual meeting alone helps demonstrate the mix of educational opinions circulating at the time, while they also foreshadow many of the themes and tensions that would emerge in the half century to follow.

The 1890 NEA meeting held special significance due to several presentations that year on the topic of city school systems. Maxwell, who at the time was superintendent of the Brooklyn public schools and just beginning to take on a leadership role among fellow school superintendents, presented a paper lamenting the fact that thousands of children left school without attaining the minimum knowledge that he believed every citizen should possess. Maxwell argued that the state—not the district or the school—should determine "the subjects of study and their proper sequence" and that the state should set the minimum amount of time per week devoted to each subject.[96] Maxwell argued that school boards should relinquish control over the more serious details of public schooling, such as curricular matters, about which they had little knowledge.

The immediate responses to Maxwell's paper demonstrated how fiercely many city school superintendents retained their loyalty to local control. "Unnecessary and injurious" was how the school superintendent of Providence, Rhode Island, characterized Maxwell's push for centralized state authority. "Let us have the unity that comes from agreement upon approved principles and methods sanctioned by experience," he countered, "not that rigid uniformity that comes from external prescription."[97]

H. S. Jones, school superintendent in Erie, Pennsylvania, was particularly troubled by what he believed was Maxwell's assumption that the people of the United States were homogeneous. Far from it, he said; Erie was populated with immigrants from Germany, Ireland, Italy, and Poland. "One of the weaknesses of the public school system today," Jones argued, "is its stubborn tendency toward uniformity in courses of study, and methods of instruction and management." Jones contended that "elasticity, and even wide differences in systems," should be permitted, "especially in large cities." Flexibility should also be granted to teachers as well, he believed, for, too often, "city school systems bury expert talent under a grinding service in details that could as well be handled by persons of ordinary ability." The expert teacher, Jones concluded, "must be called from the tread-mill of routine and set at the solution of the hundreds of problems which stand as obstructions to genuine progress." Unless greater instructional freedom was allowed, he warned, teaching would be "driven into narrow, mechanical lines."[98] It was precisely this kind of rigid, mechanical teaching that Joseph Rice was about to uncover in school systems across the country.

Other discussants at Maxwell's NEA session raised even more concerns and questions, especially about school boards, which at the time controlled many of the day-to-day operations of the schools under their watch. Were school board members truly competent to make the most important and intricate educational decisions, meeting attendees asked, especially in cities facing rapid accumulations of new challenges? Should it be the school board, or district administrators, who prescribed the courses of study, determined the methods of instruction, and hired qualified teachers? "These duties involve a knowledge of education, its principles, history, and conditions, which few men possess who are not professional experts," argued the superintendent of the Cincinnati schools. "Real progress in school instruction in our cities for the past twenty years has been largely the result of the efficiency and authority of school superintendents," he added, a remark that undoubtedly elicited widespread head nodding among his assembled colleagues.[99] It was obvious to these men that the superintendency was a position of fundamental importance; yet *how much* power the superintendent should hold remained unspecified.

Several other sessions at that same 1890 NEA meeting raised pertinent questions that were both as timeless as they were urgent; at least the concerns were urgent to practitioners who saw enrollments in their schools spiking. How centralized should the school system be? Should the curriculum emphasize uniform lessons for all children or should subjects vary according to the backgrounds of students and their families? Should the superintendent be considered more of businessman than a scholar and pedagogue? Should administrators help teachers to become as skilled and creative as possible or should they command them to follow a mandated curriculum?

The very fact that the urban school district served as the subject of such vigorous debate confirmed its rising status. Many reformers began to believe that if national educational problems were to be worked out anywhere, it would be in city schools. After the turn of the century, cities became laboratories and models, the currency of reform interactions. Ambitious educators in smaller school systems understood that they should look to the larger cities for innovations and inspiration. When Charles Meek, the bold, young superintendent of the public schools of Boise, Idaho, discussed the development of educational programs in his own school system, he proudly listed the transformations to organization, facilities, and equipment, all of which stemmed from the school board's decision that "the time had arrived for the beginning of a modern city system." Meek boasted of the many innovations that Boise had adopted by 1913: additions to the high school and elementary curriculum, the upgrading of school facilities, and the hiring of new teachers and supervisors.[100] Given his confident description of Boise's advances, Meek clearly had an image in mind of what it meant to be a "modern city system."

Some optimistic social reformers began to view city schools as a kind of safeguard against the riptide of capitalism. The socialist economist Scott Nearing (who was soon to be fired from the University of Pennsylvania for his critique of the commercial causes of World War I) wrote in 1915 that the "civilized world, reorganized and reconstituted, rebuilt in all of its economic phases, demands a new teaching which shall relate men and women to the changed conditions of life. This is the new basis for education, this new foundation upon which must be erected a superstructure of educational opportunity for succeeding generations." If urbanization and industrialization came riddled with nefarious economic problems, perhaps urban schools promised novel solutions and possibilities for true democratic growth. Through the marshaling of resources and the provision of new services, the city school system might just hold the key to modern democratic renewal. Nearing saw Cincinnati as an example of a "great city school system," and he called for all educators to recognize the changes afoot and "to remodel the institutions of education in such a way that they shall meet the new needs of the new life."[101]

———

The first third of the twentieth century, proclaimed Superintendent Joseph Gwinn of San Francisco in 1933, was sure to stand out to future generations "as a golden age, in which the foundations were laid and processes developed and used that have lifted city school administration out of the casual and political toward the scientific and the democratic."[102] Gwinn's remarks, delivered in a speech on the occasion of Ellwood Cubberley's retirement as dean of the Stanford School of Education, captured a contemporary faith that the golden age of education was not some faded image from a remote past but was instead something that could be observed unfolding daily in the educational experiences of the progressive present. The blend of science and democracy, heralded by Gwinn, proved to be an especially potent mixture, for therein reformers saw new answers to the old challenge of creating an equal American society through the public schools.

By the second decade of the twentieth century, municipal reformers—who earlier might have ignored the public schools—began to include education as one of the essential components in an urban reform agenda. "The well-developed school systems, the great public libraries, the lecture courses, public concerts, botanical and other gardens, the means of recreation offered in the universally present public parks and playgrounds," wrote political scientist Frank Goodnow in 1910, "are all evidences of the change from the feeling of hopelessness with regard to the future of cities which was characteristic of the early part of the nineteenth century."[103] Schools played an especially important role in dispelling the old bleakness that clung to the nineteenth-century urban environment. "The public schoolhouse," said Zueblin, "has become a center of beauty and life, as well as of light in American municipalities."[104]

Cities also provided the flywheel for future educational reform. They had financial and cultural resources; they offered the capacity for the development of large, centralized school districts; and, as Cubberley explained, cities were able "to draw to the management of their school systems the keenest thinkers and most capable administrators engaged in educational work."[105] Zueblin offered a metaphor that captured a similar sentiment. "The city is a magnet and every added citizen becomes magnetized and tends to draw another," he said. "Public education draws a growing multitude to the city." The schoolhouses become, in Zueblin's phrasing, miraculous "palaces of learning."[106]

Miraculous or not, the city school district garnered a reputation as the primary site of serious school reform. Critics of the educational status quo had uncovered severe problems that demanded immediate attention, they had identified flawed practices in classrooms and boardrooms, and they had offered some tentative steps toward solutions. District progressives agreed that city schools served as the perfect laboratories for testing innovation. The large urban school system could attract the most prominent educators and offer the opportunity for citywide reform. Moreover, it was the agent of change preferred by muckrakers, educational experts, and municipal reformers. Perhaps most importantly, cities and their schools represented the best and brightest hope for the realization of applied democracy.

Nevertheless, it remained to be seen what kinds of specific plans could resolve the multiple problems of nineteenth-century schooling and yield the desired outcomes. How could city school systems fit themselves to a new age?

2

THE PLANS AND PRINCIPLES
OF DISTRICT PROGRESSIVISM

By 1916 a revolution had taken place in the hearts and minds of many American educational reformers. The revolution, however, yet remained to be carried out in the nation's public schools. The educational restlessness that had
begun simmering in the 1890s took a full generation to reach a steady boil,
and throughout the last decade of the nineteenth century and the first decade
of the twentieth, municipal reformers, academics, and city school superintendents persistently called for fundamental change. Despite general agreement on the set of problems facing schools, reformers continued to debate
what the future urban school district should look like. Even by 1910, educators in city school systems who considered themselves "progressive" had
accumulated little in the way of practical plans, consistent philosophies, or
common policy agendas around which they could unite and organize.

To those eager for rapid improvement, the pace of change seemed gla-
cial. Some observers blamed educators for dragging their feet, while reform-
minded educators tended to blame school boards or community members
for their lack of receptivity to innovation. Joseph Rice, who could claim
some responsibility for stirring up educational disenchantment in the 1890s,
argued that the cause of "lamentably slow progress" was not public resistance; he thought the responsibility for the sluggish pace of school improvement rested with professional educators and their lack of "practical programs
for progress."[1]

Close examination of local school records reveals that it was not until the
middle of the twentieth century's second decade that clear plans and proposals for what educational leaders began calling "progressive city school systems" started to emerge. In fact, educational progressivism reached a noticeable turning point in the mid-1910s, as evidenced by a series of sweeping
changes in school districts across the country. Nevertheless, once underway,
the educational transition was hardly smooth, and alterations to previous

practice were usually accompanied by some measure of disruption, especially at the local level. "No recent year," announced the *American School
Board Journal*, "has seen such wholesale changes in superintendencies and
other higher school positions as the present year—1913." During the previous
twelve months, reported the *American School Board Journal*, some sections
of the country had experienced "a perfect storm of unrest culminating in
wholesale resignations, dismissals, and new appointments."[2] Indeed, the cities examined in this book experienced significant conflict and rapid superintendent turnover during precisely this same period—events that appear idiosyncratic until the districts are observed side by side. The question that hung
over urban school districts was whether this turmoil could be harnessed and
repurposed for productive reform.

Chapter 1 detailed the educational and social problems that fueled reformers' concerns and focused their exuberant attention on the power of the progressive city to overcome the educational challenges they had inherited. A
next step is to examine the types of solutions leaders proposed for combating
those problems in the years after 1913 and to explore the larger ideas and principles that supported their reform efforts. Much of the ferment—both political and educational—that characterized these particular years resulted from
a series political clashes and educational debates, conflicts that ultimately
yielded sets of specific school reforms, proposed by leaders at the national
level and interpreted by school district leaders in Oakland, Denver, Portland,
and Seattle.[3]

Plans meant very little, however, if they did not meet the needs of districts. This chapter identifies some of the signature practices and innovations
district leaders encountered during this era, particularly those they might
have seen as potential solutions to their own particular problems. In order
to comprehend what educators meant when they talked about the progressive school district, it is necessary to explore the most significant educational
proposals that formed the national backdrop for urban improvement efforts,
especially those that emerged during the 1910s and 1920s. In addition, this
chapter asks: What kinds of underlying ideas formed the conceptual foundations for the initiatives that district progressive adopted?

Historians often depict the Progressive Era as coming to a close at the end
of World War I, and for a time, educational scholars followed suit. Far from
being a period in which progressivism lost momentum, the middle years of
the 1910s were a decisive period in the history of educational reform, a historical moment in which consequential characteristics of the four districts
studied here were determined. The history of progressive education, when
observed through the lens of urban school districts, shows how new core

progressive practices—those proposed at national conferences in major publications between 1913 and 1918—were implemented in the decade or two that followed, thereby requiring the extension of the traditional periodization of progressivism.[4]

As described in the chapters that follow, each urban district was embedded within a particular political milieu that could either ease or inhibit certain types of school reform. Therefore, the final section of this chapter briefly discusses some of the significant national municipal innovations that swept across the country at roughly the same time as these key educational reforms. Not only were the discussions, debates, and outcomes about these particular municipal initiatives important on their own, but the civic organizations that coalesced to support or oppose specific municipal initiatives also often persisted long enough to exert influence on the nature of school district reforms as well.

TURMOIL AND REFORM, 1913–18

The sense of educational disequilibrium was palpable in the pages of contemporary publications of the 1910s. The middle years of this decade constituted a unique moment of significant disruption and reinvention across several dimensions of American life. Indeed, historian Henry May has argued that the years between 1912 and 1917 were crucial pivotal years in American culture, marking the Victorian past from the modern present. He called them "the first years of our own time."[5] The full significance of this transition, in education and elsewhere, is easily overlooked if we focus on World War I as the traditional dénouement of American progressivism or if we look at change in only a single city. Many leading educators of the time sensed that something was afoot; even if it was not quite the radical transformation of American schooling that progressives like Scott Nearing or Frank Goodnow hoped for, it certainly appeared to be a productive release of latent energy. "At some point, if not an instantaneous upheaval, there must have been a notable quickening of the pace of change," May surmised, "a period when things began to move so fast that the past, from then on, looked static."[6] Certainly it seemed that way to citizens living in rapidly growing cities, and so it was with the educators who sensed a hastening of the American heartbeat and who began to speak of a new epoch in public schooling.[7]

The noticeable shift was evident by 1912 or 1913, when educational reformers, experiencing a sudden burst of self-assurance, confidently informed Americans that they had developed practical plans for educational progress and identified the essential ingredients necessary to create successful school districts. In 1913, Harvard professor Paul Hanus maintained that he could articulate detailed specifics on the desired "nature, scope, and limits" for city school systems.[8] Charles Meek of Boise, Idaho, had already outlined the innovations that constituted the modern school system by 1913. W. S. Deffenbaugh, a specialist in school administration at the U.S. Bureau of Education, went further still, boldly painting a portrait of the ideal progressive district in 1915, identifying the kinds of programs and positions that should be *expected* of all city schools and stressing the enhanced student services that could only be offered by the modern district. Every building would have light and airy classrooms, he said, along with an auditorium, a gymnasium, playgrounds, and school gardens; and each child would have access to psychologists, physicians, and nurses, all features that were fresh additions to the educational mission.[9]

Elmer Ellsworth Brown, chancellor of New York University, enumerated the educational achievements that had taken place between 1900 and 1915, including among them the expansion of educational access for all people, the extraordinary increase in high school attendance, the rewriting of pedagogical literature "in a more scientific and scholarly spirit," the revolutionary changes in vocational education, and the better and wider use of school buildings.[10] And Ellwood Cubberley, we recall, asserted in 1915 that the *fundamental administrative principles* for school systems had been established—it was simply the *application* of those plans and principles that remained to be carried out.[11]

Through a steady flow of reports, publications, and lectures, educational reformers increasingly expressed their widespread conviction that they had made swift, strong strides toward educational improvement. Reformers in national agencies, universities, and local districts issued a staggering profusion of designs for district-driven reform; many of these innovations were ultimately adopted, often remaining in place for years. The abundance of educational initiatives was as overwhelming as it was unprecedented, and these plans often combined a broadness of scope with a detailed precision that only added to the cognitive load of the local leaders and school boards sorting through them.[12] Meanwhile, publishers launched a whole host of new journals focusing on topics in education and urban policy, in part to help interested practitioners make sense of the cornucopia of municipal undertakings.

The narrow slice of time between, roughly, 1913 and 1918 (or, broadening it slightly, 1912 and 1919) constituted quite possibly the most productive period in twentieth-century educational thought, at least in terms of the publications, proposals, and plans that focused on the improvement of urban school systems. Even a partial list of the works published during this period illustrates the spectrum of the views and visions that would occupy the minds of educators for years. In 1913, Franklin Bobbitt published a lengthy article on instructional leadership, "The Supervision of City Schools."[13] This was also the same year that Frederic Burk laid out his individualized study plan in his the widely read critique, *The Lock-Step System,* and Edward L. Thorndike published his two-volume treatise *Educational Psychology* (1913–14), often characterized as redirecting the focus of psychological research for much of the century.

With his daughter, John Dewey wrote *Schools of Tomorrow* (1915), highlighting some of the most interesting pedagogical experiments taking place throughout the country at the time; then Dewey issued his own master work, *Democracy and Education,* the following year (1916). Ellwood Cubberley published his extraordinarily popular textbook on American school leadership, *Public School Administration* (1916), and Franklin Bobbitt followed up on his earlier work with a major educational statement in his book *The Curriculum* (1918). William H. Kilpatrick wrote his widely read essay "The Project Method" (1918), which sketched out the kinds of hands-on activities teachers could pursue in their classrooms. And during these years, Lewis Terman wrote *The Measurement of Intelligence* (1916), followed slightly later by *The Intelligence of School Children* (1919)—two of the most influential educational volumes in terms of redirecting American perceptions of children.

The mid-decade was also flush with new genres of educational literature: school district surveys, evaluations, and practitioner-oriented reports, many of which offered the kinds of concrete details and specific recommendations that practitioners could sink their teeth into. The survey of the Portland, Oregon, Public Schools, for example, written in 1913, was republished by the World Book Company in 1915, as publishers discovered the vibrant market for evaluations of urban school districts. The surveys of the systems of Butte, Montana (1914), Oakland (1915), Denver (1916), Cleveland (1916), Gary, Indiana (1916), and Salt Lake City (1917) received remarkably widespread attention and were also used as textbooks for courses in educational administration or as guidebooks for local school administrators. Not to be outdone, federal education agencies and national organizations also issued bulletins and reports that documented major progressive plans and programs.[14]

Within the span of just a few years, then, local practitioners suddenly had access to studies covering a remarkable range of new practices, fresh lines of educational thought, and novel recommendations for implementing those ideas in districts and schools. The quest for new information was at times accelerated by the requirement that superintendents keep themselves abreast of developments in other school districts, a stipulation often written directly into job descriptions and contracts by school boards. Evidence that local educators strove to translate innovations straight into their schools is demonstrated aplenty in the district records from many city school systems, including those examined here.[15] Yet not all plans and practices were cut from the same cloth, and this is why scholars have sought to distinguish between distinct strands of educational progressivism.[16] If it is true that progressive educational thought split into multiple streams, then it was here during the second decade of the century that those differences first surfaced.

Two books, both published in 1916 and exceedingly influential, help illustrate the emerging differences in how educators perceived the problems and the solutions of American education: Dewey's *Democracy and Education* and Cubberley's *Public School Administration*. Each author cared deeply about improving the quality of public schooling, about reinventing the role of education in democracy, and about creating environments in which well-trained teachers could better meet the needs of their students. Taken together, these two volumes articulated something like a set of competing educational gospels for the next twenty-five years. Both the men and their books remained influential for decades, and their names appeared regularly in the writings of educators across the country and throughout all levels of the school system.

The differences between Dewey's vision of education and Cubberley's are legion, and one clue to unraveling the puzzle of "district progressivism" is to understand how and why urban school leaders interpreted these works in the ways they ultimately did. Dewey's study remains a masterwork of American philosophy, an expression of Pragmatism translated into its consequences for schooling. Yet *Democracy and Education*—at least on its face—offered little in the way of practical advice to the overwhelmed district administrator struggling to improve day-to-day practices, revise curricula, supervise teachers, control expenses, find seats for students, and manage an expanding system of schools. Moreover, Dewey's ponderous prose could make the task of tangibly rendering his ideas into feasible reform strategies all the more difficult.[17] All the same, *Democracy and Education* was a staple of educational conversations and bibliographies, and it persistently symbolized a certain fundamental spirit within progressive education.

If Dewey offered a philosophical manifesto, Cubberley offered something more akin to an educational reform manual. *Public School Administration* was, quite literally, a textbook on the practical principles of educational administration, neatly divided into distinct chapters with titles such as "Organization of Boards for School Control," "Records and Reports," "Costs, Funds, and Accounting," and "Efficiency Experts; Testing Results." Cubberley's straightforward syntactic style, polished into digestible doses through nearly two decades of teaching educational administration courses at Stanford, was direct, detailed, and characteristically confident. These qualities also served to make Cubberley an extremely popular educational consultant (as it would be called today) and allowed him to design specific reform plans that were subsequently adopted by many school boards.

It is not only in retrospect that the years between 1913 and 1918 seem significant; educators at the time were equally aware of the monumental changes afoot. University of Chicago professor Charles Judd recounted one 1915 American Council of Education session that had featured a fierce debate about testing and measurement. According to Judd, the clash at this meeting constituted the last stand of "the forces of conservatism" against science-minded progressives. Judd viewed the battle as the culmination of the educational investigations and reformist agitation evident since the 1890s: "There can be no doubt as we look back on that council meeting that one of the revolutions in American education was accomplished by that discussion. Since that day tests and measures have gone quietly on their way, as conquerors should. Tests and measures are to be found in every progressive school in the land. The victory of 1915, slowly prepared during the preceding twenty years, was decisive."[18] According to the victorious proponents of the new education, the great swell of progressive energy had finally begun to yield evidence of results, albeit periodically couched, as above, in the language of academic imperialism.

PLANNING FOR REFORM

It was an exciting time to be an American educator. Although some ideas for municipal improvement had been imported from Europe, reformers liked to believe that their own solutions were characteristic of American democratic ingenuity.[19] It was during these years that educational policy makers outlined the structure of the school district as we tend to think of it today, much as other city planners designed new configurations of governance along with comprehensive blueprints for hospital districts, water districts, or sewage districts.[20] Contemporaries often preferred to use the phrase "city school system," instead of "school district," seeking to differentiate their modern incarnation from the nineteenth-century rural "district school," which they viewed as hopelessly ineffective and obsolete, as well as from small urban "ward" districts, which they believed were too chaotic and corrupt. By 1918, the evidence indicates, many—but certainly not all—reformers across the nation held similar conceptions about what constituted the ideal progressive school system: an urban school district, significantly transformed, one to which reformers bestowed an array of functions virtually unimaginable to educators just one generation earlier.[21]

Notwithstanding the significant differences among reformers of national prominence, the plans that many urban school districts—again, not individual schools—elected to implement usually exhibited some underlying consistencies, especially in their application of progressive ideas. District progressives were remarkably adept at stitching together practices that at times have appeared contradictory. Yet, to say school districts often blended multiple perspectives is not to argue that reformers' ideas and innovations generated no friction; local practitioner confusion about, and tensions between, the differing interpretations of progressive innovations produced some dramatic storylines. Nevertheless, because many educators, no matter their ideological predictions, found common ground on several important goals of educational progressivism, identifying the primary areas of consensus helps to provide a foundation for much of their work, even if early harmony later gave way to discord.

1. *Meeting the needs of the child.* Perhaps the most ambitious, if least specific, concept at the heart of progressive education—one held by almost every progressive educator—was the notion that American schools should "meet the needs of the child" or "adapt schools to the child."[22]

2. *Revised curriculum and updated instruction.* Most reformers agreed that the increasingly complex industrial base of the twentieth century required a dramatically revised school curriculum.[23]

3. *"Proper" organization, administration, and governance.* Many urban progressives, especially those administratively oriented in scope, believed that the superintendent should act as the head of the whole school system—as the chief executive of an efficient corporation—rather than allowing the school board to meddle in daily administrative decisions.

4. *Professionalized training.* By ensuring that teachers as well as administrators were properly trained for their new roles in modern and specialized school systems, progressives believed they could foster a new era in educational professionalism.

5. *New buildings and facilities.* In order to offer updated curricular materials, new teaching methods, and sanitary and safe facilities, districts depended on access to new resources, buildings, and classrooms.[24]

The components of district progressive plans described above were not intended to be disconnected items that could be selected according to whim. Rather, just as progressive municipal reformers viewed the city as a complete unit, district reformers believed that their innovations were interdependent and should be blended into a unified plan. The logic of interconnectedness was self-evident to urban progressives. Superintendents needed concentrated executive power—the type that would result from administrative reorganization—in order to make fundamental changes to the educational practices of their districts. Once district administrators had sufficient authority, they could hire and train stronger teachers, oversee new curriculum development programs, supervise innovative testing ventures, and promote and oversee school construction plans.

Herbert S. Weet, superintendent of the Rochester, New York, public schools, argued that the multifarious dimensions of district leadership could be made more cohesive by concentrating on the underlying principles that bound reform efforts together. The "complexity of any modern city-school system is such that its activities seem almost innumerable," he told an NEA audience, "and yet, for each activity there is, or should be, a well-defined aim or ideal."[25] If Weet's district drew on an underlying set of principles, what were they? Was there a coherent educational philosophy that served as the connective tissue binding multiple innovations together? District progressives rarely articulated clear statements of philosophy; yet an examination of educational reforms they advocated during this period reveals a common set of core beliefs that buttressed most of their improvement efforts.

THE PRINCIPLES OF DISTRICT PROGRESSIVISM

In his 1934 study, *Educational Administration as Social Policy*, Jesse Newlon, who served as Denver's school superintendent from 1920 to 1927, then as a Teachers College professor until his untimely death in 1941, set out to analyze the philosophies articulated in eighteen widely used educational administration textbooks. Newlon was worried that an overemphasis on "efficient management" in these volumes meant that too little attention was devoted to "critical thinking" and to "the social and economic responsibilities" of education. "It is significant," he declared, "that none of these books attempts to develop a philosophy of education or of educational administration or inquires deeply into larger purposes which administration is designed to serve. Even Cubberley," he continued, ". . . attempts in his works on administration no systematic development of a social theory of education though he says the superintendent 'must . . . relegate to their *proper place* in the educational scheme all of the details of organization, administration, and school supervision' [Newlon's emphasis]. . . . There is, of course, a philosophy implicit in these books in their treatment of specific matters," Newlon contended, "but it is a confused mixture of the prevailing laissez-faire social and economic philosophy and the philosophy of business efficiency, with a vague democracy and Christian idealism." As such, he concluded, "the superiority and adequacy of our political and economic institutions are assumed."[26] Newlon captured the blend of beliefs and lacunae superbly.

Many educational reformers of the period were unquestionably more fascinated by concrete designs than in core theories or fundamental philosophies.[27] Stanford's Jesse Sears once observed that his colleagues were often more interested in "problems and in plans" than in "the theory upon which the plans were based."[28] Many prominent educational figures were frankly distrustful of philosophy because it reached its judgments by, as statistician Karl Pearson phrased it, "some obscure process of internal cogitation." In his 1892 book, *The Grammar of Science*, Pearson, a student of Francis Galton, advocated for a rational, scientific approach to setting social policy. Society needed citizens, Pearson argued, who would base their judgments and decisions less on their feelings and emotions than on a clear knowledge of the facts. "It is because the so-called philosophical method does not, when different individuals approach the same range of facts, lead, like the scientific, to practical unanimity of judgment, that science, rather than philosophy, offers the better training for modern citizenship."[29] Of course, Pearson confuses personal opinion with substantive philosophical inquiry, which may explain why he later was one of the highly educated individuals of the time able to embrace eugenics.

The discomfort that the new professional educational experts—they liked to think of themselves as the leaders of a new "science of education"—felt toward educational philosophy is readily apparent in their befuddled responses to John Dewey. The behaviorist John B. Watson, for example, who had originally gone to the University of Chicago to study with Dewey before his interests turned toward experimental psychology, later admitted, "I never knew what [Dewey] was talking about and, unfortunately, I still don't."[30] Similarly, Edward Thorndike once confessed, "*I just cannot understand Dewey.*"[31] Perhaps no better illustration of the apparent inability of educational scientists to comprehend Dewey's ideas came in their bewilderment at Dewey's critique of the intelligence testing movement. Guy Whipple, among many other testing advocates, had insisted that intelligence tests, classification of students, differentiation of the curriculum, and individualized instruction plans provided students with "equal educational opportunity." So when writing a 1923 article discussing these reforms, Whipple paused to interject: "Just how Dr. John Dewey finds in the testing movement a threat against the individualism that he cherishes, I confess I am unable to see."[32]

It would be a mistake, of course, to assume that only those with innate philosophical predilections, or who demonstrated comfort with contemporary theory, were motivated by the transformative ideals of progressive education. Much like the urban reformers in historian Daniel Rodgers's *Atlantic Crossings*, many district progressives were not philosophically inclined, but they cared passionately about ideas. True, they were not intellectuals in the sense that they took the time to explore the deeper purposes of education or to consider the many serious implications or potential consequences of their reforms. Nevertheless, their public conversations bristled with an excitement about the possibilities that the "new education" held for children, for their schools, and for themselves. They were eager to put ideas into practice.

If the progressive educators who focused on the reform of city school systems did not always have a clear philosophy of their own, this did not mean that they were without thoughts, ideas, or ideology. At least three general principles—we might also consider them ideas, beliefs, or values—provided the conceptual foundation for the plans designed and implemented by the innovators and city superintendents who focused on urban school reform. First, district progressives uniformly announced a dedication to building a true *democracy*; second, they believed that both children and educational practices should be *differentiated*; and, third, reformers believed that they had to transform whole city school systems rather than targeting individual schools; in other words, change had to be *district wide*. Although many inspired educators worked to transform single schools, when district progressives thought about implementing public school reform, the change agent they looked to was the urban school district. These three principles—democracy, differentiation, and district-wide design—were mutually reinforcing and, collectively, they provided much of the motivating energy for district progressivism.

Democracy: True or False?

"We Americans approach . . . present-day problems in the spirit of democracy and with more than a century of schooling in democracy behind us," declared Columbia University president Nicholas Murray Butler in 1907. "But," he asked, "are we quite sure that we know what democracy means and implies?" Butler fretted that the nation lacked a clear-headed understanding of democracy, and he was determined to correct any misconceptions by offering something more cogent. "There is a democracy false and a democracy true," he said, and to "consider the true and false conceptions of democracy is to equip ourselves with the armor of sound and well-tested principle to meet the tasks and problems of tomorrow." Butler distinguished between liberty—true democracy—and what he saw as mistaken notions of equality—false democracy. Butler wanted Americans to slough off the false democratic notions that would bring every citizen "down to the level of the average." Neither could his view of democracy countenance the "doctrine of mediocrity." "Jealousy of power honestly gained and justly exercised, envy of attainment or of possession," Butler argued, "are characteristics of the mob, not the people."[33] Butler was alone neither in believing that the core principles of democracy required clear and forceful articulation nor in his fear of the mob.[34]

"The evils and shortcomings of democracy are many and call loudly for remedies and improvement," proclaimed an equally anxious Cubberley just two years later. "Whether we shall have remedies and improvements or not depends very largely on how the next generation is trained," he wrote, once again depicting schools as the corrective to obsolete notions: "The ideas taught in the school today become the actuating principles of democracy tomorrow."[35] Elite educators jumped at the opportunity to sculpt a new model of democratic education. Yet as Butler's invocation of "the mob" and Cubberley's concerns about "evils and shortcomings" demonstrate, progressive educators were also ready to rouse an older chimera that had bedeviled previous generations of Americans: the fear of misrule by the masses. "Obviously there are enough good people to guide the Ship of State, if they are put in command," explained psychologist H. H. Goddard, another reformer of the time. "The disturbing fear is that the masses . . . will take matters into their own hands."[36]

From the 1890s through the 1930s, discussions of democracy peppered scholarly and popular publications, proposals for urban reform, and the reports of local superintendents. Many Progressive Era educators and public figures were convinced that nineteenth-century notions of democracy had become dangerously outmoded and inaccurate. Speeches, reports, and bulletins of the period—and not only those delivered by educators—carried phrases such as "real government by and for the people," "real democracy," and "democratization of the schools." There was nothing necessarily novel about educators contemplating the relationship between popular government and education, of course. Thomas Jefferson, Noah Webster, and Horace Mann, among many others, had warned their fellow Americans of the dangers of an undereducated populace. For more than a century, public figures had argued that schooling offered the means for ensuring a stable democracy.[37] American education provided an alternative to the class system of Europe, because, as Mann famously said, education served as "the great equalizer of the conditions of men—the balance wheel of the social machinery."[38]

By the late nineteenth century, however, educators began to raise new concerns about democracy, and they questioned, with a particular urgency, how schools could best prepare young citizens for participation in the twentieth century. American democracy could be deliberately developed, many

Progressive Era reformers believed, not left to chance, and education was crucial to the crafting of this revised democracy. Schools, reconsidered under the light of a new democracy, would nurture avid patriots, avoid "mental waste" among students, insure efficiency in school systems, and fashion a more harmonious society. Once redefined and refined, a newly robust democratic society could, in turn, be used to strengthen schooling.

For his part, John Dewey believed that the standard argument about democratic schooling—that the role of the schools was to make good citizens—was superficial and merely a minor aspect of a larger and more important goal.[39] One thing that distinguished, and distanced, Dewey from his more efficiency-minded contemporaries was his unique ability to envision practices that would confront inequalities, not replicate them. He sought to develop a strain of thought consistent with education in the modern American republic. He was able to use philosophy to cut to the essence of educational activity. As we have seen, many administrative progressives developed a distaste for, even a distrust of, such scholarly philosophical inquiry, and their impatience with Dewey often increasingly undercut his influence.[40]

Some scholars have questioned how dedicated progressives actually were to fundamental tenets of democratic equality and have retrospectively critiqued progressives as patently "anti-democratic."[41] For example, researchers have argued that instead of fostering an environment that stressed an active and involved citizenry, educators and public officials were complicit with business leaders in crafting a system of social control that subordinated democratic principles to business efficiency. Rather than expanding the kinds of opportunities available to children, therefore, progressives may have helped to implement something closer to an industrial democracy suited to capitalist expansion through practices such as testing, tracking, and authoritarian supervision. The Progressive Era was riddled with contradictions, however, and progressive versions of democracy were more complex and prismatic than usually acknowledged.[42]

The versatile use of the notion of democracy becomes especially apparent when investigating the reforms and practices labeled democratic by national elites and district progressives. In fact, the surprising variety of ways in which democracy could be attached to disparate educational ideas and initiatives is one of the most intriguing conundrums of the era. For example, democracy served as the descriptive alternative to the "aristocratic" educational practices of the nineteenth century; and at the same time, democracy represented the twentieth-century expansion of educational access to previously unenrolled groups of students. The various types of school curricula that these new students should learn were all touted as democratic as well, even when the curricular goals were remarkably divergent for different groups of students. Democracy could also be applied to new coursework or to revised textbooks that focused on American history or civics.

The professional relationships in schools and districts also fell within the purview of democracy, as educators sought to clarify the proper balance between administrative authority and teacher autonomy. Democracy could refer to the local educational governance; after all, the locally elected school board had long symbolized democratic participation. Some leaders interpreted this to mean that professional and instructional freedom need not be conceded to teachers because the governance was already democratic. Despite that, many progressives subjected pedagogical methods to democratic reinvention. Some teachers believed—and others were simply told—that democratic schooling required new instructional practices that would allow students both to explore their own interests and to learn to the full extent of their abilities. Finally, democracy was regularly invoked when progressives focused on the goal of equal educational opportunity.

Democratic education, by the new way of thinking, did not entail providing the same education to all students. The nineteenth-century uniform curriculum for all students was the "older conception of democracy," explained Superintendent Joseph Gwinn of San Francisco, the erroneous belief "that equality meant the same." Outdated curricular conceptions had demanded "one school and one prescribed course of study for all children, bright and dull alike," said Gwinn, "whether American-born or foreign-born, college-bound or corn-field bound." Instead, a reinvigorated conception of true democracy for the twentieth-century meant "equal educational opportunities for all children of all the people."[43] Equal opportunity became the focus of progressive democracy, and, according to educational leaders, "opportunity" entailed discarding the obsolete practices of democratic schooling. Instead, practitioners should widen and diversify the once-uniform course of study as a way of meeting the many needs and abilities of different types of pupils. This shift, from *equal curriculum* to *equal opportunity*, marked one of the most important historical turning points in the conception of American democratic education. Here was the difference between true and false democracy.

Although their terms and descriptions varied, there were essentially two main points that reformers like Gwinn, Cubberley, and Butler wanted Americans to absorb. The first was that democratic education in the twentieth century had made (or should make) a sharp break from its own past. Modern and "practical men," as Cubberley and Gwinn liked to think of themselves, dismissed most objections to their twentieth-century revision of democracy as emanating from the kind of conservative schoolmaster who "clings tenaciously to the past." Cubberley often reminded his contemporaries that the schools of the past had "directed most of their training to satisfying the needs of the children of the well-to-do classes" while youth going into industry in the nineteenth century had been "forced to take what was provided the others, or to do without." In other words, the new-but-true democracy was more humane and egalitarian.[44]

The second point these modern and practical men liked to make was that only the progressive urban school district had the capacity to deliver on the promise of this new democratic educational frontier. "Our city schools will soon be forced to give up the exceedingly democratic idea that all are equal, and that our society is devoid of classes," Cubberley prophesized in 1909. Therefore, he said, educators should "begin a specialization of educational effort along many new lines in an attempt better to adapt the school to the needs of these many classes in the city life."[45] Despite the confidence with which people like Cubberley issued their pronouncements, not all skeptical voices were easily quelled.

"Obviously a society to which stratification into separate classes would be fatal, must see to it that intellectual opportunities are accessible to all on equable and easy terms," Dewey stated in *Democracy and Education*. This was a rebuttal to those who capitulated on the matter of social and economic class hierarchies and sanctioned distinct curricula for different groups of children. Dewey scolded educational leaders who had denounced "as undemocratic the attempts to give all children at public expense the fuller education which their own children enjoy as a matter of course."[46] Dewey had long recognized that the "world in which most of us live is a world in which everyone has a calling and an occupation, something to do. Some are managers and others are subordinates," he said. "But the great thing for one as for the other is that each shall have had the education which enables him to see within his daily work all there is in it of large and human significance."[47] The recognition that students would have different occupational futures did not imply, Dewey insisted, that some students should have limited access to education.

Instead of the foreshortened educational plan of efficiency-minded reformers with its acceptance of stratification as the status quo, Dewey offered a vision of democracy that was far broader and richer than that proposed by virtually any of his contemporaries, for it required an education that struggled against social inequalities. "It is the aim of progressive education to take part in correcting unfair privilege and unfair deprivation, not to perpetuate them." Differences of economic opportunity, Dewey avowed, should not "dictate what the future callings of individuals are to be."[48]

Historian Robert Westbrook has pointed out, however, that Dewey employed many of the same terms as the administrative progressives, such as "social efficiency" and "civic efficiency." Therefore, the differences between his views and those of his more efficiency-minded contemporaries were not always clear and ultimately resulted in a good deal of confusion.[49] To the superficial observer at the time, Dewey might have seemed more an ally than an adversary. To Dewey, democratic and progressive education would "prize freedom more than docility; initiative more than automatic skill; insight and understanding more than capacity to recite lessons or to execute tasks under the direction of others"—all things that district progressives thought they agreed with, which is why he was always included in the references of the materials that superintendents shared with their teachers.[50]

Other reformers and educators who, like Dewey, were cognizant of the hazards of unbridled industrialization, often raised alarm about the powerful undertow of urban industrial life. In 1916, Charles Zueblin warned that industrial dependence would become ever harsher in the urban environment, for cities generally contained enough surplus labor, he said, "to beat down the standard of living of the employed and to provide a dangerous fringe of irresponsibility about its industries. The employed workers," he lamented, "usually have very little voice in the management of their daily affairs and hence get no discipline to make them self-governing in public life." Women had it even harder, he acknowledged, for those employed in industry "are even less independent than men." Zueblin worried about the state of democracy, but for reasons vastly different than those voiced by Butler. To Zueblin, false democracy was attended by industrial oppression. "Three-hundred-and-sixty-four days of dependence," he said, "hardly make a free voter on election day."[51]

It was one thing to declare that schools should foster citizenship, but it was usually less obvious what kind of citizenship educators wanted to create. Historian Julie Reuben has documented how Progressive Era educators who championed new courses and textbooks in what they called the "new civics" or "community civics" strategically attempted to reinterpret American citizenship. Textbook authors made a conscious shift away from the nineteenth-century emphasis on political rights and active public participation toward a stance that stressed cooperation with government and authority. The transition reflected progressives' respect for expertise, Reuben observes, and their curriculum urged children to adopt appropriate behaviors such as obedience, dependence, and compliance. Because the educators who designed the new civics programs could not envision both an active citizenry and a strong state, Reuben argues, they encouraged students to look at citizenship in largely nonpolitical terms. Government would provide the necessary social services, and, in return, the students should fulfill their duty as citizens by cooperating with governmental agencies.[52]

Many district progressives came to believe that neither teachers nor parents—or other members of the local community, for that matter—need participate too actively in educational decision making; this was the proper domain of researchers and experts. If school districts were to be democratic, it was to be through the election of school boards; these boards then acted as the community stewards of education. In turn, school boards appointed superintendents who provided the necessary educational expertise. Superintendents served as the "leaders of educational thought in their communities," explained the authors of *The Beginning Superintendent* and, as such, they were "valiantly striving to clarify the idea of democracy and make it functional in the minds of the youth and the patrons of the school."[53] At the local level, the superintendent was just as essential to the interpretation and clarification of democratic principles as were the national experts for the country at large.

In sum, true democracy meant a reworking of the American social fabric. The traditional and anachronistic rule by aristocratic and "well-to-do" authorities would be replaced by a phalanx of experts in education, politics, and civic engineering. Educational opportunities would be distributed not according to some obsolete notion of equality whereby the same curriculum was delivered to all students in uniform allotments but according to the ability of the pupil through curricula tailored to different groups. Nonetheless, the education that most mattered was that provided to the children at the top of the ability scale.

To some progressives, it was only natural that educators create a rarified selection of coursework for bright pupils because they were the individuals who would ultimately occupy positions of power, authority, and influence in society. These select few would also ensure that the democratic mob did not take matters into their own hands. "In the long run," reasoned Thorndike in a revealing 1919 statement that is worth digesting, "it has paid the 'masses' to be ruled by intelligence. . . . What is true in science and government seems to hold good in general for manufacturing, trade, art, law, education, and religion. It seems entirely safe to predict that the world will get better treatment by trusting its fortunes to its 95- or 99-percentile intelligences than it would be by itself. The argument for democracy is not that it gives power to all men without distinction, but that it gives greater freedom for ability and character to attain power."[54] Democracy, therefore, was inexorably grafted to another major principle of district progressivism: differentiation.

Democratic Differentiation: Social Equality versus Intellectual Equality

"How can there be such a thing as social equality with this wide range of mental capacity?" Henry Herbert Goddard asked a Princeton University audience in 1919 as he relayed the results of recent intelligence tests.[55] "Can we hope to have a successful democracy," he asked, "where the average mentality is thirteen?" Goddard—director of research at the Training School for Feeble-minded Girls and Boys in Vineland, New Jersey, and one of the first popularizers of the Stanford-Binet Intelligence Scale in America—was troubled by intelligence testers' "discovery" that the IQ of the average American was thirteen.[56] He believed that the wide differences in intelligence test scores demonstrated that Americans could not possibly all be intellectually equal, and he worried that the intellectual deficiencies inherent in a vast array of the citizenry threatened democracy.

Goddard asserted that test results had political implications, as his biographer Leila Zenderland has shown, for they placed a grave responsibility on the small minority who possessed the intelligence necessary for leadership.[57] The intellectual elite, Goddard said, "must so work for the welfare of the masses as to command their respect and affection."[58] Many other educators accepted the "average IQ of thirteen" finding as scientific, a belief that consequently shook their faith in the future of democracy, but the specific implications were unclear. Goddard was happy to sketch out the consequences on their behalf. Democracy, Goddard argued, meant "that the people rule by selecting the wisest, most intelligent and most human to tell them what to do to be happy." Democracy was, at heart, a "method for arriving at a truly benevolent aristocracy."[59] Intelligence tests had provided evidence that the most serene democracy, if not the strongest educational system, would result when the innate individual differences between children were accepted and then used as the basis for engineering social progress.[60] Intelligence tests had done nothing of the sort, of course, but Goddard and other IQ enthusiasts stretched them far beyond their narrow use.

Differentiation was not merely a creation of test-wielding psychologists, however. It was as thoroughly interlaced with early twentieth-century urban ideology as was democracy. As Adna Ferrin Weber argued in his popular book, *The Growth of Cities in the Nineteenth Century* (1899): "The city is the spectroscope of society; it analyzes and sifts the population, separating and classifying the diverse elements. The entire progress of civilization is a process of differentiation, and the city is the greatest differentiator."[61] This notion of the city as the "great differentiator"—as the sifter and sorter of the diverse elements of urban society—appeared in a remarkable number of scholarly and popular publications of the time, and it illuminated the work of urban educators in grand historical relief. In fact, differentiation had already been established as an ardent principle among city school leaders. The 1890 NEA report of the commission titled "School Superintendence in Cities," for example, proudly opened with Herbert Spencer's assertion that "a differentiation of structure and a specialization of function is the law of all growth and progress."[62]

In practice, city school leaders employed the concept of differentiation along three main lines: they differentiated *children* (or as they preferred to put it, they "scientifically classified" them according to their abilities), they differentiated the *curriculum* to meet the needs of these now-sorted children, and they differentiated the *structures of schooling* to accommodate new courses of study and to provide for the proper placement of children (such as the junior high or the vocational high school).

Educators saw the urban school system as one of the most useful tools of differentiation. In *The New Social Civics*, for example, Jesse Newlon and D. E. Phillips quoted a proverb—"City gates stand open to the bad as well as to the good"—while explaining to their junior high school readers that complex urban environments would support many trades, professions, and specialists.[63] Urban progressives interpreted the statistics of swiftly growing school enrollments as a healthy indicator of the successful advances being made in modern education. However, despite the excitement of booming school attendance, many urban practitioners found themselves struggling to effectively educate the increasingly diverse student population that arrived at the school door. This unavoidable situation raised another question that was at the heart of progressivism—how could American schools best educate a wide array of schoolchildren, especially when those students did not all learn at the same rate or in the same ways? As we have seen, this was the question essentially posed by Frederic Burk and Leonard Ayres, and it presented one of the most serious challenges to educators in the twentieth century. Of course, for years educators had encountered students who could not thrive in school. The solution had usually been to fail these pupils and push them out of school. Educators generally assumed that pupils who failed or dropped out were simply not suited to rigorous academic work; these children would find apprenticeships or work in trades and industries that better fit their abilities. The general process of students failing out or dropping out of school was what Thorndike termed "elimination" in 1908.[64]

Advocates of the new education stressed that schools should be the institutions that offered struggling students alternative pathways, not some inexpert external agency. The weakest schoolchildren should be "salvaged," not eliminated, implored the authors of *The Beginning Superintendent*. The superintendent, they argued, should recognize that these children were a part of the rich "complexities of human life and society." It was the superintendent's duty to see in these "wriggling, yeasty, undiscovered children not only potential future bookworms, but potential musicians, poets, artists, artisans, merchants, engineers, politicians, orators, lawyers, doctors, tillers of the soil, housewives, fathers and mothers, leaders and followers."[65] Instead of wasting children's widespread talents and abandoning failing pupils to an uncertain fate in an unfriendly urban environment, schools should now accommodate the full spectrum of students' abilities and backgrounds, thereby helping them to pursue their intellectual or vocational destinies. The authors of *The Beginning Superintendent*, along with other progressives like Burk and Eliot, represented a humanitarian-intellectual impulse embedded within much new educational thinking. Still other progressives could sound remarkably similar in their rhetoric; yet they drew on other impulses.

Convinced that measuring variations in student ability would lead to more smoothly functioning schools, Stanford's Lewis Terman explained that "individual differences exist for all traits. . . . This is true," he said, "whether the trait in question is height, weight, strength, lung capacity, number of blood corpuscles, hearing, vision, intelligence, courage, conscientiousness, social adaptability, vanity, or any one of a hundred others."[66] Nothing was more natural than simply pointing out these innate deviations among human beings and then considering how we might consequently adapt social institutions to them, Terman believed. Mental endowment happened to be the most important determinant of individual academic performance, and therefore it was more useful in explaining poor achievement than were "irregular attendance, the use of a foreign language in the home, bad teeth, adenoids, malnutrition, etc.," though he offered no evidence for this claim[67]

Terman's explanation offered a validation to school leaders who had grown increasingly frustrated with the problem of "laggards." Here, finally, was an explanation that educators could embrace, especially as it absolved them of blame. In the eighteenth- and early nineteenth-centuries, as Daniel Calhoun demonstrates, parents often blamed teachers when their children did not learn; and in some cases, the educators blamed themselves. In the mid- to late nineteenth century, teachers tended to blame bad grades on student behavior or lack of effort; thus, corporal punishment or placing a child in a corner seemed fitting punishments. But "as middle-brow thought grew more biological during the nineteenth century," explains Calhoun, "the defensive teacher was likely to say that her pupils lacked the inherited qualities that make up the ability to learn." A few scholars have pointed out that the tendency to classify and separate children based on their apparent abilities began well before the introduction of intelligence testing. Those earlier practices become especially clear when examining turn-of-the-century urban school records. Thorndike and Terman simply offered newer, more refined ways to explain differences in student achievement. But their statements had punch.[68]

Making one of the most significant assertions of the era, Terman declared that test scores demonstrated that educators still striving to help failing students, "may as well abandon, once and for all, the effort to bring all children up to grade."[69] Terman's proclamation—asserting that schools should forgo efforts at extra tutoring or enhanced instruction—rippled through urban school districts more quickly, and with greater effect, than did most new educational ideas. No longer need administrators blame themselves or their teachers for the failures of those students who could not advance at a "normal" rate. The defects, Terman told them, lay hidden within the children themselves. Terman's conclusions were refuted at the time, but only by a few public figures, and his statements rapidly gained great traction among educators at a pivotal moment in the growth of urban school systems.

Stephen Jay Gould has written of the penchant for hierarchical ranking—what he calls "our propensity for ordering complex variation as a gradual ascending scale"—and of the deeper tendency within Western thought to assign numerical worth to individuals.[70] Thorndike, Terman, and Goddard, along with their many followers, did exactly that, created ascending scales of child traits and human attributes, whether applied to height, corpuscles, or intellectual capacities. Once differentiation had been established as a guiding principle in urban education, reformers found it easier to argue that schools, curricula, and structures should be differentiated to correspond to the needs of students as newly determined by educational science.[71] Terman went on to study the careers over fifteen hundred children whom he determined to be geniuses based on their scores on his IQ test—these "little geniuses" were later referred to as the "Termites."[72]

Unified Reform through District-Wide Design

By the mid-1920s, and keenly aware of the vibrant curricular and pedagogical innovations blossoming in small private schools and university-operated laboratory schools, Superintendent Jesse Newlon sought ways to spread inventive progressive practices across multiple schools of the same city, in this case Denver, where Newlon spent seven years as superintendent (1920–27). Could a large school district, urban school leaders wondered, ever be as progressive and creative as the experimental schools that seemed to dot the landscape of American education? "A large school system obviously cannot be given over entirely to detailed and extensive curricular experiments such as can be conducted in avowed experimental schools," lamented a circumspect Jesse Newlon in 1926.[73]

For all the activity and agitation about the need to reform public education, the truly exciting pedagogical developments of the 1920s seemed to be taking place in small independent schools, as prominent founders of highly regarded schools—such as the Dalton School and the Country and Day School—published books on their own experiences. In their own widely read account of progressive practices, *Schools of To-morrow*, John and Evelyn Dewey reported on a number of lively pedagogical experiments in individual schools but offered only a lone example of a progressive school district, the public schools of Gary, Indiana. Yet Gary had been created virtually from scratch, part of a new, and rapidly expanding, industrial center planned by the U.S. Steel Corporation. The challenge facing almost every other public school superintendent was to work with school systems already in operation, which entailed confronting an accretion of traditions, politics, and old quarrels that required quelling or rethinking.[74]

Still, most advocates of urban school improvement believed that the city school system was the appropriate unit for change. In their 1928 book, *Better Schools: A Survey of Progressive Education in American Public Schools*, Carleton Washburne and Myron Stearns celebrated cities that were pursuing district-wide progressive practices, such as Rochester, New York; Dayton, Ohio; and Winnetka, Illinois (Washburne was the superintendent of the Winnetka public schools from 1919 to 1945 and not shy about self-promotion). "Information and initiative get better schools," the authors wrote in a classic expression of the Progressive Era faith in the power of public disclosure. Their dramatic stories of urban school transformation functioned something like modern morality tales; most of the cities they documented tended to follow a formula: city school systems once considered "bad" were transformed into healthy progressive districts through the heroic efforts of individuals or dedicated community groups (not necessarily through the educators themselves).[75]

The change that truly mattered to the vast majority of educators was reform that could take place in public school systems, not small-scale innovations in isolated locations, no matter how enthralling. Despite his own remarks about "avowed experimental schools," Newlon was quick to add that he did not intend to minimize "the importance of curriculum-experimentation" within larger school districts. "Some of the most important present-day methods and procedures in education originated in public schools," he said, and his own experience in Denver demonstrated how city systems could harness the potential creativity of small educational experiments by designating certain schools within their districts specifically for that purpose, as Denver had done with its "curriculum school." This was the trump card that public school leaders learned to play against their progressive colleagues in single-school sites: large school districts offered advantages unavailable to students in individual schools or even in small school districts.[76]

"Only under some form of large-scale educational organization can many of the important supplemental educational advantages, such as proper grading and promotion, special instruction and supervision, special-type schools, and health supervision, be provided for at all," Cubberley argued in 1916. Diversity of educational offerings could only occur when schooling took place on a sufficiently grand scale, the kind of "superstructure of educational opportunity" that Scott Nearing had envisioned just the year before. Proponents of system-wide district design believed that the components of a district should change in a strategic order, a view that was repeatedly highlighted in administrative textbooks and published school surveys. District-wide design was thus not only a third principle of reform, but it also provided the platform for the realization of the other two principles of democratic education and differentiation, tenets that could only be fulfilled under conditions that offered large numbers of students a variety of educational programs and practices.[77]

At a time well before most educational policy makers could envision making change on a national, or even statewide, scale, the idea of leveraging significant change throughout a city school system proved a heady mix for reformers interested in widespread educational improvement. Large urban districts allowed for the coordination of numerous educational efforts: the selection, placement, and supervision of teachers; the specialization of instruction; the adaptation of the curriculum; and the oversight of building programs and business matters. The complexity of modern urban life could be matched by the sophistication of the modern city school system. It took cities with their substantial resources to offer the new programs, services, and curricula that could provide educational opportunities to each and every individual child, which in turn resulted in "freedom, elasticity, and variety among individuals." As Newlon and his colleagues explained it, urban districts thereby contributed to a "consequently richer democracy of real self-directing individuals who have had meted out to them by a public educational system the sort of education which the industrial and social state made necessary."[78]

DESIGNING THE PROGRESSIVE SCHOOL DISTRICT

The underlying educational principles of democracy, differentiation, and district-wide design are suggestive themes in and of themselves for the intellectual history of the Progressive Era. In terms of the social history of education, what matters is how district progressives translated these principles into specific innovations and how they distinguished between practical innovations and those that were unworkable, all at the same time that they maneuvered their way through local political contexts. Three types of popular progressive reforms—administrative reorganization, student classification, and curriculum reform—serve as illustrations of the ways in which practitioners adopted initiatives in Oakland, Denver, Portland, and Seattle. Each city system was unique, of course, and local leaders did not always implement reforms with fidelity to a specific model. Therefore, offering a brief discussion of what national reformers tended to have in mind when they proposed the local adoption of these three practices is essential.[79]

Administrative Reorganization

By the 1890s, urban superintendents had a tradition of grumbling about what they saw as the corruption, callousness, and incompetence of American city school boards, and many administrators believed it was time to pull the rug of smug responsibility from under them. "The board of education serves several purposes and none of them well," went one quip among NEA superintendents. Leaders like William Maxwell fumed that superintendents were essentially forced to kowtow to the whims of board members who often had little knowledge of, and even less interest in, the improvement of school affairs. Although the small rural school district was once considered the epitome of democratic localism, reformers asserted that the traditional nineteenth-century "district system," with its jurisdiction of just one or two schools, had become both inefficient and counterproductive to the goals of an industrialized nation. They had to be replaced by a new democratic institution fit for the twentieth century.[80]

Sometime after 1912, prominent urban-minded reformers began to reach consensus on what an alternative model for school district structure might look like, a plan that soon gained the label "reorganization." Stated most simply, reorganization referred to the structural rearrangement of administrative responsibilities within the standard public school system. Up to this point in time, the individual school board members of many city school systems had been organized into committees that handled much of the standard business we now think of as the domain of central office staff: buildings, repairs, finance, supplies, teachers, and so on (see figs. 2.1 and 3.1 for depictions of older systems). These board committees were too unwieldy and too easily corrupted, reformers argued, and they should be stripped of much of their authority. Moreover, the school superintendent was usually situated beneath the board committees in the command chain of the district and handled only the strictest of academic issues, such as curriculum writing or the supervision of instruction. Reorganization meant the complete realignment of the power relationships within a school system by removing school board members from managerial decision making and the oversight of daily activities. The new generation of school leaders sought to combine all major district functions under the direct authority of the superintendent, who would then be responsible for managing district finances, teacher hiring, curriculum development, and school construction and maintenance, along with the other duties that had traditionally been controlled by individual board members or board committees.

Administrative progressives were extremely adept at developing arguments that bolstered their reorganization efforts, often couching their ideas within the context of "the rise of human organization" and making their plans seem less like proposals and more like natural evolutionary laws. They connected their innovations directly to the efforts of other municipal reformers, arguing that, as with other social services, the increasing complexity of urban public schools required a more significant level of coordination than had ever been possible under the antiquated administrative practices of the past. Historians have demonstrated that educators drew increasingly on analogies to the business world to justify reorganization. As Franklin Bobbitt explained in 1913, for example: "Whether the organization be for commerce or for manufacture, philanthropy or education, transportation or government, it is coming to appear that the fundamental tasks of management, direction, and supervision are always about the same."[81]

Still, not just any structure would do. There were proper and improper ways of organizing the layers of responsibility and expertise, reformers believed. Here, too, progressive education also mirrored the changes taking place at the same time in other domains of civic life, especially in the area of municipal government. The main assumption at work in both spheres was that good management, well organized and with clearly defined lines of authority and responsibility, would lead directly to better schooling or governance, essentially to "public business" of any kind. At the same time, educators were also becoming increasing intrigued by the growing field of public relations, and they understood that successful reform and reorganization required clear communication and cogent illustrations of proposed administrative layouts.

One method for displaying their new administrative progressive ideas—an approach that quickly became immensely popular—was the crisply designed organizational chart. In his book *Public School Administration* (1916), Cubberley emphasized the importance of adopting new bureaucratic structures for the administration of city school systems. He did so first by presenting organization charts for "faulty" and "incorrect" forms of administrative structures (see fig. 2.1) then by offering counterexamples of exemplary diagrams, each illustrating the ideal district configurations for medium and large cities, as represented in figures 2.2 and 2.3. Thus conceived, the simple and straightforward version of educational structure provided districts with an easily translated, fail-safe recipe for district reorganization.[82]

Progressive Era urban reformers were enchanted by the aesthetic of the organizational chart. Not only did it stamp a semblance of order onto a traditionally chaotic administrative tangle, but it also visually represented the new spirit of efficiency, expertise, and scientific coordination sweeping across a country bent on modernization. Whether municipal reformers advocated for a city-manager or commission form of municipal governance, they argued that public organizations should model corporate structures, or they encouraged districts to centralize under the primary responsibility of a single superintendent. The organizational chart offered urban reformers an immensely useful tool for graphically articulating and spreading their vision.[83] The editors of the journal *American City*, for example, supplied civic leaders with a plethora of illustrations depicting restructured local governments, reinvigorated municipal water districts, or orderly systems of park management, all of which relied on the cohesion that came with a proper administrative alignment.

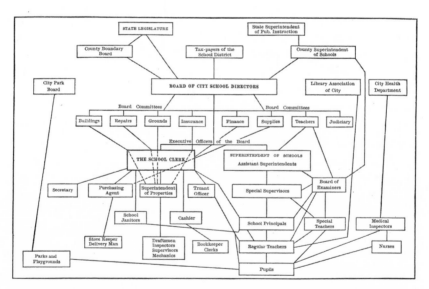

FIGURE 2.1. Cubberley's depiction of an incorrect form of school district organization, based on his 1913 survey of the Portland public schools. (Ellwood P. Cubberley, *Public School Administration* [Houghton Mifflin, 1916], 174–75.)

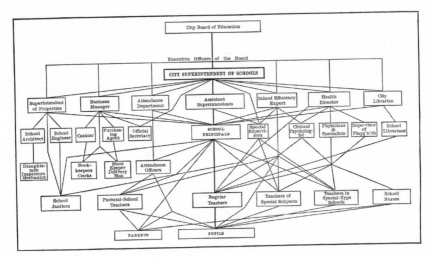

FIGURE 2.2. Cubberley's recommended organization chart for a large school district, 1916. (Ellwood P. Cubberley, *Public School Administration* [Boston: Houghton Mifflin, 1916], 172–73.)

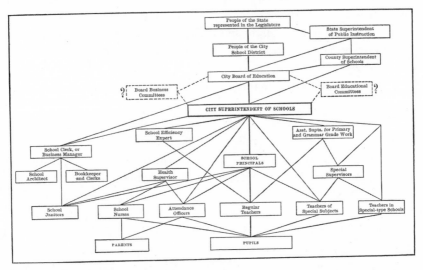

FIGURE 2.3. Cubberley's recommended organization chart for a medium-sized school district, 1916. (Ellwood P. Cubberley, *Public School Administration* [Boston: Houghton Mifflin, 1916], 170–71.)

The June 1915 issue of *American City* printed an organizational chart for the commissioner-manager form of municipal government that had been recommended by the National Municipal League. Reorganization was in the urban air. Many of these changes were consistent with the organizational revolution that was taking place across the country at the time.[84]

Cubberley was immensely talented at using organizational charts, intuitively understanding the power of the visual image and the specific example. Furthermore, offering both good and bad examples of administrative structure effectively doubled their persuasive impact. Many of the organizational charts Cubberley criticized came from cities he had studied or evaluated, and they often went hand in hand with the scathing narratives he delivered in his reports. In *Public School Administration*, his examples of defective practice came from San Francisco and from Portland, Oregon, a school system he had badly disparaged in a survey he produced just a few years earlier. Cubberley explained the organizational evils that would result from systems like Portland's that were not aligned according to his specifications: "Under such a form of educational organization the teaching force, due to lack of leadership and lack of central authority, is likely to be professionally unprogressive; the board of education . . . is almost certain to develop into a duplicate and conflicting board of superintendents; the school buildings are likely to be constructed and repaired in a costly and an unintelligent manner by the board of public works."[85] Cubberley adroitly concocted an organizational nightmare, one with which no ambitious school leader would want to be associated. Fear of external critiques was all the more true of school leaders in western cities who were already anxious about the status of their school systems. Cubberley's needling use of the phrase "professionally unprogressive"—imbued as it was with pejorative connotations—was also intended to taunt reluctant administrators into action.

School district reorganization is often considered the quintessential "administrative progressive" reform and therefore has served as something of an analytic marker for scholars distinguishing between progressives who focused on structural and administrative change and those more interested in improving curriculum and instruction.[86] With its line authority, specialization of function, embrace of corporate philosophy, and emphasis on efficiency, administrative reorganization has typified the kind of reform that historians argue offers clear evidence of the inappropriate appropriation of business values by educators.[87] Once the superintendent had been given greater authority to make district-wide decisions, then other "modern" educational practices—such as business-styled accounting practices, better record keeping, and, ultimately, intelligence testing—could be implemented more smoothly.[88]

Not all educators believed that these new notions of organization were healthy for school systems. While few openly rejected the goal of "efficiency"— certainly, educators rarely want to argue for *inefficiency*—some questioned whether administrative change was really the royal road to educational effectiveness.[89] John Dewey was troubled by the tendency to locate educational authority and decision making in an executive position. The solution to school problems, he felt, was "not to have one expert dictating educational methods and subject matter to a body of passive, recipient teachers, but the adoption of intellectual initiative, discussion, and decision throughout the entire school corps."[90] In making this case, Dewey voiced some of the tensions that had already begun to emerge between teachers, administrators, and school boards while he also foreshadowed the conflicts that would soon surface as teachers struggled for something more than a passive role in what was touted as democratic schooling. Although many administrators enthusiastically embraced reorganization, such was not always the case with school board members. After all, reorganization required school boards to relinquish much of the previous power they traditionally held over hiring, firing, requisitioning from local merchants, or contracting with other local businesses—powers that many board members were reluctant to surrender, due to motivations sincere or otherwise. The resulting reluctance and stonewalling that sometimes emerged has been missed by historians.

The process of reorganization rarely made room for the opinions of other community members, whether those of parents, labor unions, or civic clubs. Educational leaders liked to conjure up a scenario whereby citizens worked collectively to organize their city school systems, just as Charles Zueblin argued that a new concrete democracy would result from civic collaboration. Yet district reorganization was hardly a grassroots movement. The assumption among professionally trained educational administrators was that citizens would no more be allowed to install sewage pipes haphazardly, without the aid of civil engineers, than they would construct a curriculum or hire teachers without close supervision by educational specialists.

Classification of Students

The Progressive Era was a period of compulsive categorization, and the classification of students was the principle of differentiation applied directly to children. Nineteenth-century school leaders had discussed differences in academic performance between children; students exposed to exactly the same curriculum had long demonstrated variation in their capacities to learn or, more traditionally, to memorize and recite. Well before Leonard Ayres's *Laggards* made it a pressing national issue, thoughtful educators had recognized the challenges faced when some students fell behind. For a time, attention to the problem focused squarely on the system of age grading in public schools; once seen as an efficient way to group students, a number of educators came to view it as an approach that simply created other problems. For example, speaking at the 1893 NEA annual meeting, Ella Flagg Young addressed the issue of varied student achievement, arguing that "the main cause of the trouble is the monotonous routine, induced largely by the plan of keeping classes intact, and moving them from grade to grade at long and regular intervals of time."[91] Young envisioned two solutions. One was to allow students to be promoted from grade to grade much more frequently than once a year—in other words, some kind of flexible promotion plan. The other option was to establish "ungraded rooms," where struggling students could be given individual attention and then returned to their grade. Throughout the 1890s and well into the 1910s, locals experimented with both approaches, and numerous practitioners experienced success with ungraded rooms, but administrators often found it difficult to implement on a large scale. Popular publications and educational administration textbooks carried examples of various flexible promotion plans. No real consensus emerged.

G. Stanley Hall's 1883 study of urban and rural children was one of many important influences in prompting educational experts to seek explanations for discrepancies in student performance within the children themselves. In the 1890s, several universities across the country began to establish "child study" laboratories, modeled after the first such lab developed by Hall at Clark University.[92] Many educators predicted immense potential for the findings from more scientific studies of children. By 1918, educational psychologists believed they had developed a scientific system of intelligence testing that would allow students to be sorted according to their measured academic ability. The doctrine of innate individual differences was built on deep beliefs that yielded connections to confused evolutionary theories, eugenics, and discrimination based on race, religion, class, and national origin. Such beliefs had a dramatic impact on schooling practices and led to specific shifts in local policy making.

Well before the introduction of intelligence testing, many late nineteenth-century cities had developed different curricular tracks for high school students. Yet psychologists worked to create a more systematic approach to student classification, a process that gained momentum as some urban school systems began opening their own psychological clinics in the 1910s. The widespread use of IQ testing for sorting recruits in the First World War catapulted intelligence testing into the public mind and into the public schools. Although district psychological clinics had already begun using individual intelligence tests, the major innovation resulting from the war was the group form of the test—a standardized examination that could be administered in less than an hour, thereby theoretically giving district and schools an immediate tally of student academic abilities. The "intelligence quotient" (IQ) came from a deceptively simple, if rather arbitrary, formula: divide a subject's tested "mental age" (as scaled by Terman) by their chronological age. Students whose mental age exactly matched their chronological age would score a 1, or 100 in IQ terms, and would be considered of average intelligence. As used in schools, IQ testing served to reinforce and scientifically justify practices of differentiation already in place, albeit with some significant twists.

By the 1920s, the IQ test had become an icon of American psychology. It has been both praised and pilloried by scholars, teachers, and parents throughout the past century (at times IQ tests have been required by some districts and states and, at other times, been banned).[93] Consequently, it can be difficult to approach the historical study of IQ testing's impact on public schools with fresh eyes. To local educators in the Progressive Era, it is important to remember, the technology of the intelligence test was an unfamiliar, and potentially exciting, innovation. The rapid spread of intelligence testing as a popular topic at national conferences, in professional journals, and in graduate textbooks illustrates its hold on the imaginations of contemporary educators. Most district progressives were introduced to IQ testing as a scientifically reliable form of measurement; however, they were offered very little in the way of dispassionate or balanced analyses regarding the potential strengths and weaknesses of testing programs.

No one worked more tirelessly than Lewis Terman to translate the group army intelligence tests into a form that was both practical and palatable for public school consumption. Terman, a protégé of G. Stanley Hall, was a pioneer in developing intelligence tests even before the First World War and one of the strongest advocates of testing as a scientific solution to educational problems. Like many other experts of the day, Terman issued his pronouncements in books, textbooks, articles, speeches, and local surveys. A master salesman of his own ideas, Terman displayed his data on individual differences through charts, graphs, and tables. He provided annotated, bell-curved graphs of what the "mental-age distribution" should look like.[94]

Terman's graphs, like Cubberley's organizational charts, offered visual models that educators could easily comprehend and therefore follow and replicate in their own districts. However, unlike organizational charts, graphs of intelligence had a dramatic and enduring influence on cultural beliefs, representing what amounted to a static understanding of the nature of student academic ability. Terman's test results communicated the notion that the scientific distribution of intelligence should look roughly similar in each school district—the normal bell curve—thereby lending an air of inevitability to the results. "Intelligence tests have demonstrated the great extent and frequency of individual differences in the mental ability of unselected school children," wrote Terman, "and common sense tells us how necessary it is to take such differences into account in the framing of curricula and methods, in the classification of children for instruction, and in their educational and vocational guidance." Only rarely did skeptics point out that while intelligence testing may have had the air of science about it, these tests had never undergone any kind of thorough controlled experimentation that could reliably evaluate their practical utility in American schools.[95]

Terman's "commonsense" solution was straightforward: separate children into homogeneous groups for classroom instruction. Terman's primary assumption, one that he shared with an overwhelming number of educational psychologists and, later, with a majority of district progressives, was that children would be easier to teach—and more successfully taught—if they were separated into groups of students roughly comparable in ability. Of course, the systematic administration of group intelligence tests and the classification of students into multiple groups could only take place in schools and districts with sufficient numbers of pupils. Therefore, testing and tracking was also reliant on the development of large urban school systems, centrally controlled.

When districts were properly operated, educational psychologists asserted, the achievement of children should replicate Terman's bell curve. However, when pupils were taught in large heterogeneous groups and when the school curriculum did not meet the needs of students, as was the case with so many turn-of-the-century city school systems that reported large numbers of overage students, then the bell curve of achievement—or the promotion of students to the next grade level—would become unnaturally warped. Such was the case with districts that had not adapted their curricula to large numbers of their students. Cubberley offered figure 2.4 as an example of the results from one district where the course of study was unsuited to the needs and capacities of its students; nearly 25 percent of children were not making normal progress. These pupils, he said, were "being prepared to become failures in life. They remain in the lower grades, instead of passing on up, congesting these grades and interfering with the regular instruction of normal pupils; too large for their seats; often unfit associates for the smaller children." The result, he lamented, is "great human waste."[96]

At the heart of most progressive classification reforms was a severely narrowed conception of the child. The practice of intelligence testing not only drastically limited the definition of academic ability, but it also constricted educators' views of the promise and potential of the American child. The rhetorical tussle about whether, and how, schools should sort students into

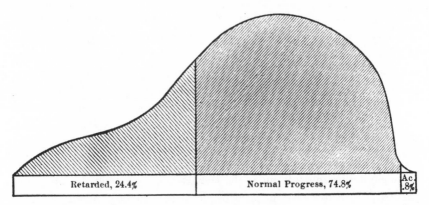

FIGURE 2.4. The promotional results of a poorly adjusted course of study, unsuited to students' needs and capacities (as envisioned by Terman and Cubberley). (Ellwood P. Cubberley, *Public School Administration* [Boston: Houghton Mifflin, 1916], 295.)

prospective career paths, based on ability or background, had already tumbled into the public sphere in the 1890s, especially after the 1893 report by the Committee of Ten (NEA's Committee on Secondary School Studies). Among other aims, the Committee of Ten was established to address the unevenness and inconsistencies of school curricula across the country. Originally intended to help colleges and high schools find greater clarity regarding high school requirements and college admissions expectations, the committee report ultimately argued for a strong academic curriculum for all students, whether they were bound for college or not. Other reformers soon scoffed at the notion of a common academic curriculum for all; intelligence tests, they contended, had demonstrated that a standardized curriculum was folly.

The intelligence that truly mattered to many psychologists of the era, like Thorndike and Goddard, was that exhibited by the small set of gifted students who would one day become the next generation of American political and social leaders. The idea that the nation's intellectually talented elite should receive the best education and hold the lion's share of the power was a theory that stretched back to Jefferson and was shared across the ideological spectrum by many progressives. Whether Thorndike's claim that in a democracy the masses should place their fortunes in the hands of society's "95- or 99-percentile intelligences" or W. E. B. DuBois's fervent hope that African Americans could trust in the social advance of their community's "talented tenth," many progressive reformers insisted that society would surge forward primarily through the success and guidance of its most capable members. That education for this select group should be of a caliber higher than that offered to the majority of American students almost went without saying.

Conflict about elite education only arose among educators when other reformers, equally capable and adamant, challenged the core assumptions of the scientific sorters. Charles Eliot, president of Harvard University, was suspicious of the extravagant claims of educators who wanted to limit access to the traditional academic disciplines. As chairman of the NEA's Committee of Ten, Eliot issued a report that argued *against* making distinctions between those students who were going to college and those who would move into the workforce after high school graduation. In the oft-cited language of the report: "Every subject which is taught at all in the secondary schools should be taught in the same way and to the same extent to every pupil *so long as he pursues it,* no matter what the probable destination of the pupil may be, or at what point his education should cease."[97]

G. Stanley Hall, for one, prickled at the Committee of Ten's recommendations. How could these men argue against the doctrine of modern science? "To refuse this concession to the wide range of individual differences is a specious delusion," Hall wrote in his 1904 study of adolescence. To force all students into "one mold would be wasteful, undemocratic, and pedagogically immoral." Certainly, the principle that students should pursue a college-preparatory curriculum, argued Hall, did "not apply to the great army of incapables, shading down to those who should be in schools for dullards or subnormal children."[98]

Eliot could not let Hall's critiques stand unanswered. He attacked Hall's assumption "that the incapables or abnormal children may properly be called a 'great army.' . . . The incapables," Eliot said, "are always but an insignificant proportion" of the school population. Hall's dismissive attitude toward American intellectual ability no doubt irked Eliot, for it was a theme that occupied him through much of his career. "It is a curious fact" Eliot had written in 1892, "that we Americans habitually underestimate the capacity of pupils at almost every stage of education from the primary school through the university." He rejected the notion that it was futile to educate the masses, responding that "we shall not know till we have tried what proportion of children are incapable of pursuing algebra, geometry, physics, and some foreign language by the time they are fourteen years of age."[99]

Opposed to the kind of premature predestination that seemed to preoccupy many American educators, Eliot used Hall's work in order to make a crucial point: "Thoughtful students of his *Psychology of Adolescence* will refuse to believe that the American public intends to have its children sorted before their teens into clerks, watchmakers, lithographers, telegraph operators, masons, teamsters, farm laborers, and so forth, and treated differently in their schools according to these prophecies of their appropriate life careers.

Who are to make these prophesies? Can parents? Can teachers? Can university presidents, or even professional students of childhood and adolescence?" Eliot added that he had seen hundreds of successful careers that no one—"not even the most intelligent and affectionate parent"—could have predicted. "I have always believed," he concluded, "that the individual child in a democratic society had a right to do his own prophesying about his own career, guided by his own ambitions and his own capacities, and abating his aspirations only under the irresistible pressure of adverse circumstances."[100]

One of the founders of the vocational guidance movement, Frank Parsons, saw vocational guidance as yet another progressive corrective to past practices. Writing in 1909, Parsons argued that vocational guidance was part and parcel of a "scientific method" for educating students. Parsons hoped to remove "drift," "chance," and "uninformed selection" from the process of choosing a vocation. "These vital problems should be solved in a careful, scientific way," he wrote, "with due regard to *each person's aptitudes, abilities, ambitions, resources, and limitations, and the relations of these elements to the conditions of success in different industries.*"[101] Parsons's use of the phrase "aptitudes, abilities, ambitions, resources, and limitations" signaled a theme that reverberated throughout the plans and promises of reformers for decades. The concept of identifying students' talents and abilities surfaced as essential features of the NEA's *Cardinal Principles of Secondary Education* of 1918, in publications of the National Society for the Study of Education, and in annual school district reports, as superintendents justified their new administrative and curricular practices to school patrons.[102] "Vocational guidance, properly conceived," explained the *Cardinal Principles* report, "organizes school work so that the pupil may be helped to discover his own capacities, aptitudes and interests," couching the process in terms of the child's decision, when it rarely was.[103]

The issues of intelligence, ability, tracking, and a child's potential have continued to generate spirited discussion throughout the past century. New scientific advances have sparked new assertions about intellectual ability even as educators have sought to restore equity to the ways in which school systems deliver education to poor and minority students, often by advocating for reforms that seek to undo the legacy of tracking established during the Progressive Era. One way that policy makers, then as now, shift the focus away from student ability is to look instead at the quality and types of curricula available to children. In the early twenty-first century, American policy makers have argued, not unlike educational leaders of the nineteenth century, that a common curriculum for all students will provide equal educational opportunity. The progressives, however, had something altogether different in mind.

Curriculum Reform

"The twentieth century has given us a new conception as to the function of the public school," announced the *NEA Research Bulletin* in 1925. "The people have clearly decreed," the bulletin declared, "that they expect the school to do far more than impart a few simple skills." To leaders at the NEA, the new requirements were straightforward: "Today, children of all mental and physical conditions knock at the school door and continue their attendance well up into the upper grades. They come by the thousands, speaking many languages, with varying customs, and diverse social and racial backgrounds. What does this mean in terms of the curriculum? It means that not one but many curricula must be created."[104] The idea that only *multiple curricula* would sufficiently address the challenges facing schools and schoolchildren captures an essential trait of district progressivism. Most urban educators believed that they could adequately adjust the school system and the school curriculum to meet the diverse needs and abilities of pupils, and they saw curricular reform, child classification, and administrative reorganization as working in unison.

The school curriculum has proven to be one of the most contentious features of American education. Even a quick scan of educational history reveals how frequently curricular disputes have popped up alongside, or as a consequence of, cultural, political, and religious tensions.[105] Curricular controversies are hardly a recent phenomenon. "We are met today in a period when the battle rages around the curriculum," Charles Judd declared in 1925. "The curriculum is a battle ground against conservatism," he said, referring to scholastic traditionalism, "because life is so full of important matters in this modern period that there is no room for instructional material which does not contribute positively and liberally to the equipment of the pupil for his life's work."[106] Although district progressives generally approved of the various new curricula developed and implemented during the Progressive Era, new instructional materials and practices sometimes found a less sympathetic public audience. Periodically, they encountered fierce critique or even withering parody.

Even before the turn of the century, some critics of "the new education" began voicing objections to the curricular additions that they derisively labeled "fads and frills." As early as 1904, for example, one educator lampooned what he saw as the fatuousness of new school subjects and ridiculed the awkward curricular marriages that resulted from grafting new curricular inventions to more traditional offerings. He depicted an imaginary day at a progressive school as follows:

Bird-calls, yawps, hoots, barks, cackles (anent nature study)—10 minutes; penmanship—5 minutes; effects of alcohol, narcotics, Washington pie, and strong
cigars—55 minutes; arithmetic—10 minutes; box-making, cutting, pasting, rip-
ping, painting, and kalsomining—45 minutes; geography—5 minutes.

"It will at once be seen that the old studies are included," he wryly concluded.[107] Despite the glee that satirists and cartoonists derived from skewer-
ing the more extreme forms of progressivism, a certain earnestness usually
characterized progressive deliberations about curricular matters.

The 1893 Committee of Ten report addressed substantive matters about
the nature of the American school curriculum, and it served as something of
a bridge between nineteenth- and twentieth-century views of the curriculum. Building off a question first asked by Herbert Spencer in 1859 ("What
Knowledge Is of Most Worth?"), the committee members essentially para-
phrased and repurposed the question, asking: What knowledge is of most
worth *in a democracy*? Eliot argued that the recommendations of the committee, stressing as they did a uniformly rigorous curriculum for all high
school students, were "sound and permanent educational principles, on
which alone a truly democratic school system can be based."[108] Two of the
committee's core queries have proven especially enduring: First, of what
kind of learning was the American student truly capable? And, second, how
could teaching of the traditional disciplines be improved so that these subjects would appeal to a broader range of students? As an initial response,
Eliot made a powerful assertion that has not been revisited as often as it
should by policy makers. "It seems to me probable," he wrote in 1892, "that
the proportion of grammar school children incapable of pursuing geometry,
algebra and a foreign language would turn out to be much smaller than we
now imagine."[109]

To consider the curricula of any school district is not simply to inquire
into required subject matter. When progressive reformers discussed curricular reform (or curriculum improvement or curriculum revision), they had
several things in mind, including the *content* of what was to be taught, the
pacing at which students should move through that content, the *differentiation* of subject matter designed to match student abilities, the *process* by
which educators created the new curricula, the *implementation* of new material, and finally, the *pedagogical methods* that should accompany certain types
of curricular content. All of these topics can be found scattered throughout
city school system records, demonstrating that the "curriculum" was never
unidimensional.

Today, as we read the publications, pronouncements, and plans of Progressive Era reformers it is possible to define differences in attitudes, ideologies, and approaches, as curriculum scholars have done. Yet, to city school educators of the time, these differences were less obvious and, frankly, often less important. Local leaders routinely mixed efficiency experts' publications with those written by more pedagogically minded thinkers when they offered their teachers lists of suggested curriculum readings.[110] Though it is important to recognize the philosophical differences embedded in various types of progressive curricula, it is equally necessary to consider whether district progressives implemented instructional materials with any kind of fidelity.[111]

One reason that local district progressives could so easily combine diverse approaches to curriculum development was because they found common agreement on at least three general directions that curricular reform should take. First, they believed that the curriculum should be tailored to the tastes and talents of their students. Second, progressives argued, almost unanimously, that the curriculum should be more "active," a term that implied, among other things, that teachers should strive to use instructional materials that engaged students more directly in their lessons than had the stale courses of the nineteenth century—by, for example, using real-world scenarios or problems. At the same time, an active curriculum had to be nimble enough to allow children's interests to help determine course content and to energize the direction and intensity of the learning process. Finally, progressives believed that curriculum development should no longer be a top-down process, whereby the superintendent, relying on the "cut-and-paste" method, selected and compiled curricular components and then presented them to his faculty as the final product.

The new vision of curriculum reform, at least as portrayed by the NEA in the then-and-now scenario depicted in figure 2.5 was that curriculum development should be a "cooperative" enterprise in which teachers, curriculum specialists, parents, and administrators worked together to build a new, more vital course of study.[112] Ultimately, this "cooperation" took many forms as it was introduced in school districts, from the active involvement of the teaching corps to a more rigidly controlled superintendent-driven process. Although the ideal image of broad stakeholder participation in curriculum construction was, no doubt, a convenient fiction in many districts, the illustration was possibly comforting to those teachers or parents not directly involved, for they could at least believe that they were somehow represented.

One particularly popular wave of curricular change, ultimately labeled the curriculum revision movement, rippled across city school systems in the

FIGURE 2.5. Curriculum construction in 1900 (*a*) and 1925 (*b*): cut and paste vs. pooling of leadership, as portrayed by the National Education Association. (National Education Association, "Keeping Pace with the Advancing Curriculum," *Research Bulletin of the National Education Association* 3, nos. 4–5 [September–November 1925]: 110–11.)

1920s and 1930s and continued to spread even into the 1940s and 1950s. Its advocates argued that curriculum revision would infuse the process of curriculum development with a democratic spirit by involving teachers more directly in the creation of course materials, in the experimental introduction of new curricula into classrooms, and in the final revision of the curricula based on teachers' results with their students.[113]

Reformers often expected the curriculum to accomplish multiple, but sometimes contradictory, functions. Progressive curriculum experts regularly claimed that the curriculum could strengthen democracy, foster citizenship, improve the mind, promote healthier lifestyles, train students for specific vocations, and help young people make more productive use of their leisure time. It is not surprising, then, that the scholarly depiction of the curriculum has been equally mixed. Historians studying the Progressive Era have described contemporary curricula variously as faddish, oppressive, watered-down, anti-intellectual, ideologically driven, vulgarly vocational, or unnecessarily elitist and abstract.[114]

Virtually every educational reformer had something to say about the curriculum and, as a consequence, the Progressive Era probably birthed more pages on curricular issues than on any other topic. Unlike organizational change or classification, curricular reform was less amenable to representation through models, charts, or other visual images—even if the *process* of subject-matter redesign could be depicted in a picture or diagram (note the chart in the upper corner of the right-side panel in fig. 2.5, which suggests an orderly structure for curriculum revision). It was as difficult then as it is now to capture the essence of what a powerful curricular lesson looks like in the hands of a gifted teacher. Still, city school systems attempted to adopt curricular reforms touted by recognized experts at the national meetings, and they sought to emulate the activities of other, seemingly more progressive schools or school districts. Organizations such as the NEA, the Progressive Education Association (PEA), and the National Society for the Study of Education, along with many subject-matter professional organizations, issued yearbooks, bulletins, and research studies on new practices across the country. These publications covered a range of practical matters, including how to modernize the traditional subjects like arithmetic and English; how to design, develop, and implement new district-wide courses of study adapted to students of different abilities; and how to create whole new content areas, such as vocational education, home economics, or "character" education. The modernization of the curriculum, reformers argued, would lead to a much more joyful learning experience for children (see, e.g., fig. 2.6).

FIGURE 2.6. The differences in teaching spelling in 1900 (*a*) and 1926 (*b*), as illustrated by the National Educational Association. (National Education Association, "A Handbook of Major Educational Issues," *Research Bulletin of the National Education Association* 4, no. 4 [September 1926]: 196–197.)

MUNICIPAL REFORMS OF THE ERA: THE COMMISSION PLAN
AND THE CITY-MANAGER PLAN

Nineteenth-century residents of American cities became exasperated with municipal corruption well before anyone promoted progressive education, and many civic groups had been trying for years to overhaul their local governments. Municipalities in the East were the first to confront powerful urban political machines such as William Marcy Tweed's Ring in New York or that of James McManes of Philadelphia. In the early 1890s, New Yorkers created the City Club of New York, which was dedicated to the development of "good government." When other cities established similar organizations, they collectively called for a meeting of like-minded groups, which materialized as the National Conference on Good Government in 1894. Delegates of more than forty-six urban reform associations from across the country made their way to that initial gathering, and the surge of interest led to the establishment of an annual event, resulting in the formation of the National Municipal League (NML). The NML quickly became the most influential national organization for municipal reform.[115]

From the annual meetings and publications of the NML poured forth a host of ideas and plans for reforming and strengthening American municipal governments. The first public proposal issued by the NML was the 1898 Model City Charter that recommended a strong-mayor plan of governance, intended to stem corruption and professionalize municipal affairs; and until events intervened to challenge that model, various cities promptly attempted changes based on this model. However, faith in the wisdom of the plan eroded rapidly in early 1900s after a cataclysmic hurricane swept over the island city of Galveston, Texas, in 1900, costing at least six thousand lives. The ensuing recovery debacle unmasked the deep failings of Galveston's extant municipal government, leading to the emergency creation of a governing commission composed of the city's most influential citizens to steer the rebuilding efforts. Galveston leaders ultimately formalized this "commission plan" of government, making it permanent and thereby drawing the attention of municipal reformers around the country.

The core idea of the commission plan was that it shifted power away from the strong-mayor approach, whereby a mayor had served as the municipal executive with the city council as the local legislative branch. The new plan still centralized power and authority but vested it in a small number of individuals (usually men) who had been elected at large (not by wards or districts) and who each took responsibility for one major department of city government (e.g., fire and police, finance and revenue, or waterworks and sewer, etc.). The commission plan was slow to take off after its initial creation in Galveston, but once it was adopted and more broadly promoted by Des Moines, Iowa, in 1908–9, the plan rapidly gained widespread attention and popularity, becoming something of a national sensation for municipal groups desperately looking for ways to solve a slew of urban problems. The commission plan's peak years came between 1910 and 1918, with the largest single-year adoptions by cities occurring in 1911 (72 adoptions that year), 1912 (38), and 1913 (64).[116]

As quickly as cities adopted the commission plan, however, they also began to recognize some of its significant limitations. In the meantime, the NML had been monitoring the progress of both the commission plan and the alternative plans of urban reform experimentation that other cities implemented simultaneously. One variation on the commission plan was known as the city-manager plan. As Harvard's William Munro explained in his 1916 textbook on municipal government: "The city-manager plan was devised to remedy ... two chief defects in the commission form of government, namely, the lack of concentration in administrative responsibility" and the tendency to put nonexperts, with no qualifications, in charge of the main municipal departments. In 1915, the NML revised its original Model City Charter, recommending, instead, the city-manager plan. In the years that followed, the city-manager plan overtook the commission plan in popularity. Just as the adoptions of the commission plan began to wane around 1918, the city-manager plan experienced its own surge in status, sustaining a steady adoption rate that lasted until about 1928.[117]

These years of harried municipal reform overlapped exactly with the period of turmoil evident in urban school districts in cities across the country. At precisely the moment that educational reformers drafted their detailed designs for school districts and began pushing for reorganization, municipal change swirled about them; and not just any type of change. Leaders and locals in all spheres of public life compared various formulas for balancing educational expertise with democratic governance. Highly active, civic-minded individuals traversed school board elections and NML meetings, infusing urban district discussions with new ideas and approaches. For example, in 1916 Cubberley inserted a brief discussion about the commission plan in *Public School Administration*. He recognized its potential but withheld an endorsement, cautioning that it was as of yet an experiment not completely proven.

One key notion that bound the commission and city-manager plans with progressive reformers' school district reorganization was the idea that public institutions should be run like businesses. As Charles Eliot put it when he was speaking to the Boston Economic Club: "Municipal government is pure

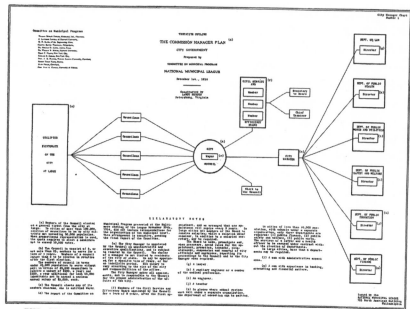

THE COMMISSION-MANAGER PLAN, AS RECOMMENDED BY THE COMMITTEE ON
MUNICIPAL PROGRAM OF THE NATIONAL MUNICIPAL LEAGUE

FIGURE 2.7. "The Commission-Manager Plan, as Recommended by the Committee on Municipal Program of the National Municipal League," approved December 1, 1914 (*American City* 12, no. 6 [June 1915]: 514.)

business and nothing else—absolutely nothing else."[118] Municipal reformers and educators were equally susceptible to visual representations of the stability that would arrive with the implementation of a new form of governance. Publications like *American City* reported on new advances in administrative structures, offering testimonials to the benefits of governance reform and reproducing plans issued by individual cities or by the National Municipal League, such as that in figure 2.7.

An array of civic groups usually had to work together to rewrite a city charter or to get a new municipal governance plan in place, often leading to temporary alignments of otherwise incongruous associations. Once implemented, however, initiatives could stray from their original goals and purposes, and local groups sometimes found themselves agitating for a shift to a city-manager plan or something else. Numerous local groups were usually involved in the initial push to hold elections and implement new municipal models, so confronting the reality of unexpected consequences could be fiscally and emotionally devastating. Civic groups often found it necessary to refortify and reenergize for a new round of activity. The initial alliances between associations often dissolved and new coalitions formed to take on a variety of other local challenges, movements, and crises.

———

City school systems launched themselves into these whirlwinds of municipal debates in the 1910s. The moment when any particular school innovation landed in a city mattered, especially in terms of who advocated for the reform, which mix of civic groups created alliances, and which organizations happened to hold the balance of power. As we shall see in all four cities examined in this book, the precise mix of these factors often made a significant difference. Administrative decisions mattered, particularly during the key years of 1913–18—and up through 1928.

The three common principles of the progressive education addressed here, along with their associated reforms, manifested themselves in cities across the country. In one way or another, school innovators struggled with concerns similar to those that occupied municipal reformers: How could democratic governance best be defined and practiced? Should authority be centralized or should schools and practitioners have more autonomy? Ought institutional decisions be made by executive offices or legislative branches? Did fundamental change require good candidates for office or would good structures solve the problem? Alongside these core questions rested other concerns that contemporaries regularly pondered, such as the nature of citizen participation, the role of women in twentieth-century society, the struggles between corporations and labor, balancing national reform organizations with the integrity of local communities, and how to smooth troubling divisions of class, race, and ethnicity. In what follows are four examples of how these questions were resolved.

3

EDUCATING EFFICIENT CITIZENS
IN OAKLAND, CALIFORNIA

96 Oakland was a city ascendant by the early 1920s. The economic and demographic shifts of the previous two decades resulted in a population spike, and Oakland's civic boosters envisioned the city as a contender in the competition to become the premiere city of the West Coast. Although the 1906 California earthquake devastated San Francisco, it carried opportunity to the city across the bay, along with an estimated 65,000 new residents. A large land annexation in 1909 added both more people and room for expansion, and the city's 1900 population of 66,960 more than doubled to 150,174 by 1910. "The Oakland of 1911 is a vigorous, energetic city," wrote one observer at the time, "imbued with a splendid civic spirit. It is a city confident of its own destiny—a city beginning to realize its prodigal natural endowments—a city that is determined to play its part in the great drama of events now shaping themselves on the shores of the Pacific."[1]

As San Francisco rebuilt and Los Angeles worked its way toward coastal prominence, Oakland had a number of factors nominating it as a foremost urban center. Oakland was a major hub of the transportation network of the West, the connecting point between rail, truck, and ocean shipping. Oakland served as the terminus for the transcontinental railroad, as an official seaport, and as a manufacturing center. In 1916, Charles Zueblin reported that the Oakland harbor commissioner was set on rivaling San Francisco by spending three million dollars in three years for municipal docks and a harbor railroad.[2] Two Oakland mayors dominated much of this period—Frank K. Mott from 1905 to 1915 and John Davie from 1915 to 1931—and both exemplified the urban vigor that leaders in many western municipalities hoped to project. Both mayors also worked aggressively, through whatever alliances or means necessary, to build a modern city. For example, Oakland City Hall, completed in 1912, was the city's first "skyscraper." Mayor Davie, hoping to make Oakland "the Detroit of the West," sought to transform the city into even more of a major manufacturing center during the 1920s.[3]

The enthusiasm of the urban builders, city planners, and industrialists matched the energy and optimism of school and social reformers. "The people of Oakland," declared the city's school superintendent Albert C. Barker in 1915, "believe in providing the best training possible for the city's future citizens." Such preparation entailed modifying "the curriculum of the past generation . . . to meet the needs of the present and the future."[4] When the mayor highlighted the accomplishments of the schools eight years later, he listed the attributes that made Oakland "attractive to the manufacturer seeking a western location." Oakland had recently completed a five-million-dollar school construction program, he said, and was about to embark on another. The school system, Davie boldly proclaimed, was "one of the most progressive" in the United States.[5] Outside observers concurred, praising the positive changes taking place for children; in 1915 the secretary of the California State Federation of Women's Clubs, thrilled by news of the city's New Century Club reformist activities creating playgrounds for children, wrote to its members: "How alive and progressive you are!"[6]

The Socialist Party's newspaper, *World*, saw the city's progress somewhat differently: "Oakland is a city controlled by several great corporations," the paper complained in 1909. "The Southern Pacific, the Western Pacific, the Traction [streetcar] Company, the Water Company, the Realty Syndicate—these are our lords and masters."[7] Indeed Oakland, like some other rapidly expanding cities of the time, had tried to shortcut its way to building necessary municipal resources by granting monopoly franchises to private corporations that, in turn, gained control over water, power, and rail. As a result, the Southern Pacific—the famous "octopus" of Frank Norris's novel of that title—controlled the wharf and access to jobs; even Oakland's main street had a dangerous rail line running down its center, an unmistakable symbol of corporate dominance. Public-service franchises formed alliances with the ward-based political machine overseen by Oakland political boss Mike Kelly, whose organization offered the kind of jobs and acculturation for ethnic minorities that were otherwise difficult to secure. The boosterism of both Mayor Davie and Superintendent Barker masked some of the deeper tensions that had begun to emerge within Oakland by 1915. During the mid-1910s and 1920s, new sets of actors pushed Oakland in multiple, and often opposing, directions of urban development and municipal reform, ultimately pitting the older political machine against a growing downtown business contingent that was bent on forming its own power structures.[8]

This chapter briefly explores educational development in Oakland during the 1890s and the first decade of the new century before giving special focus to the years between 1913 and 1928, a fifteen-year period during which the school system experienced some of its most consequential changes. By the late 1920s, outsiders had labeled Oakland one of the best school districts in the country, a reputation its administrators flaunted.[9] Oakland educators participated actively in national reform conversations, received praise from outside experts and visitors, and launched more than a few educators into positions of national prominence.[10]

If any school district of the period serves as a key to help decrypt the paradoxes of educational progressivism, Oakland is an excellent candidate. Some scholars view the city as an exemplar of California's role as the "implementation center" of softer educational progressivism and criticize its acquiescence in the face of the fuzzy pedagogical progressivism.[11] Others depict the district as tainted by its rigid scientism and its early role in the experimental use of intelligence testing, thereby treating the district as emblematic of quintessential administrative progressivism. One author, in an explicit attempt to overturn the popular myth that schools were better in the "good old days," even labels Progressive Era Oakland as an exemplar of "the bad old days," but this does nothing more than substitute new inaccuracies for old ones.[12] Nevertheless, the question remains: Why has Oakland evoked such contrasting portraits?

A close analysis of Oakland reveals the messier and more complex nature of district progressivism. For example, students of Oakland history have documented the pitched clashes that took place between and among the urban machine, large corporations, ethnic groups, labor unions, and a newer business elite. While some of these factions represented stronger power bases, they often acted through local municipal organizations to achieve specific ends. This was especially true of the downtown business elite who increasingly resisted the machinations and alliances between old corporations and the urban machine system. Although these power dynamics permanently shifted in the 1920s, significant structural inequalities, providing an opportunity for the rise of the Ku Klux Klan, one of whose members, Leon C. Francis, ran as a candidate for the Oakland school board in 1923. Francis was ultimately unsuccessful in his bid but not before gaining endorsements from civic groups such as the Redwood Improvement Association of East Oakland and the Christian Citizens' League.[13]

Of all of Oakland's school leaders during the Progressive Era, Fred Hunter—superintendent from 1917 to 1928—was undoubtedly the most energetic and high profile, a man who had a knack for publicity and capturing national attention. In fact, even Hunter's arrival in Oakland—along with the local groups that welcomed and opposed him—captures a particularly illustrative moment in Oakland's political history. Through Hunter's appointment, business elites sought to assert their power through institutions other than city hall, the schools being the most visible, and available, symbol of the time. The episode helps us to understand the interaction between civic groups, local politics and the resulting changes in progressive school policy as well as the complexities of school and municipal reform that traditional labels do not adequately explain.

DESIGNING DIFFERENCE: OAKLAND SCHOOLS
AND CHILDREN, 1893–1913

The American flag added a new star when California became the thirty-first state in the union in 1850, and just three years later, Oakland established its first public school. Ambitious young men in the West rarely viewed school teaching as an attractive career path, and in its earliest stages, local perception of school teachers was probably not unlike that of one Californian who said that men usually took teaching positions because they were "too lazy to work, hadn't the ability to gamble and . . . couldn't scrape a little on the fiddle."[14]

The career of John W. McClymonds, Oakland school superintendent from 1889 to 1913, represented a common transition from nineteenth- to twentieth-century educational practices. In 1893, he professed his hope that the nation's schools would develop "a truly American pedagogy," by delivering an equal education to all pupils.[15] Like other districts of the 1880s and early 1890s, Oakland educators consistently stressed to parents and patrons the importance of maintaining uniformity in the course of study (the district curriculum) for all students, asserting that this curricular consistency was the key to educational equality.[16] But as they approached the twentieth century, school leaders became increasingly concerned about the slow academic progress of certain individuals and groups of children.

Educators' disquiet about varied pupil progress led them to look for ways to define, explain, and address the differences they found among Oakland students. The result was an altered set of district policies not only concerning curriculum and instruction but also regarding the development of a new educational vision, one that entailed adding new functions and services to the core duties of the school system.

The adjustment of district purpose began with a search for an answer to a basic educational question: Why did students exposed to the same curriculum for the same amount of time perform so differently on tests of that material? The scores from student examinations were dramatically scattered and widespread. Starting in the early 1890s, McClymonds and other Oakland educators sought to uncover the sources of such difference: they surveyed the occupations and nationalities of pupils' parents; they initiated "scientific studies" on children in collaboration with the Child Study Laboratory at the newly established Stanford University; and they employed specialists to measure differences between children on an array of factors, from students' height and weight to their sense of color.[17] Early studies, however, led to few concrete solutions, and Oakland administrators looked at practices in other districts to see how they coped with similar problems.[18]

Concerns about student progress, or the lack thereof, pervaded all levels of the school system. In 1893, J. B. McChesney, the principal of Oakland High School, announced: "The High school will always contain two classes of students, those who wish to prepare for some higher institution of learning, and those who do not intend to prosecute their studies formally after leaving school. . . . It has always been my aim in the management of the high school," he said, "to offer to both classes the best opportunities possible. . . . It is high time that teachers and friends of educational movements see . . . that the best mental development of all youth is not in the same lines of activity." In the same year that the Committee of Ten issued its report arguing for uniformity in the high school curriculum, McChesney offered a strikingly prescient statement: "I trust the day is not far distant when Oakland will offer a system of differentiated schools to its citizens which shall be . . . the pride of the city." As early as the mid-1890s, then, Oakland had delineated differences in the academic ability of children and had begun to adjust programmatically in response.[19]

Teachers often had their own explanations for low academic performance and frequently came up with inventive solutions of their own. One deceptively simple, but effective, innovation in Oakland was designed to help struggling pupils before they dropped out of school; teachers established "ungraded rooms" where, as discussed briefly in the preceding chapter, they could assist those individual students who educators found had fallen behind due to a variety of reasons, usually unrelated to the school, including prolonged absence or truancy, illness at home, or frequent change of schools. Often the students who entered the ungraded rooms had been described by their classroom teachers as inattentive, diffident, flippant, melancholy, lazy, shiftless, untidy, or exceedingly trifling and troublesome. Yet in many of these cases, explained Ida Vandergaw, the teacher who established the first ungraded room in the district, the source of the academic problem could be identified as the student's inability to comprehend a core concept in one or two subjects as quickly as the rest of the class. "So he drags along, becoming more and more confused as the difficulties accumulate," she explained, and "as he does not understand the underlying principles of the subject, he does not reason, but guesses."[20]

The problem seemed rather straightforward to Vandergaw: a weak foundation in particular subject area explained student failure, and that lack of knowledge was usually due to some external factor, such as prolonged absence. "So we sometimes hear it said of a child, 'He has no head for mathematics,'" she explained, "or 'It seems impossible for him to learn grammar.' The only way to help that child," she continued, is to go back with him to the first principles of the subject in which he is deficient. In this class the teacher can make a study of each child's needs, and adapt her methods to his special requirements. It seems to me that the ungraded class is one good step toward solving the problem of how to make the system fit the child, instead of having the child fit the system.[21] Vandergaw articulated a primary goal of progressive education perfectly: make the system fit the child.

Starting with a single classroom in one school in 1897, the success of the ungraded room helped nudge it into other buildings, and by 1899, the program was in a total of six schools. The other teachers in Oakland's ungraded classrooms also reported multiple successes, while still acknowledging a handful of failed efforts. If we are looking for a reform that truly managed to fulfill the district progressive's faith that urban school systems could fit themselves to the individual schoolchild, the ungraded classroom serves as one clear example.[22] "The investment pays," concluded McClymonds, "it economizes the efforts of the regular teacher and it saves many pupils from being failures in school work." McClymonds hoped the ungraded rooms could help stem the numerous student failures and departures within the district.[23]

The turn of the century brought an invigorated interest in adapting the district to the differing needs of children, often because of the rapidly accelerating enrollment: the student population of 11,792 in 1900 nearly doubled to 22,589 by 1910. Just eight years later, the enrollment had reached 36,595.[24] Given their preexisting concerns about accommodating students, school administrators devoted an ever-increasing amount of attention to highlighting student differences.

Despite some experimentation with promotion plans, by 1910, Oakland administrators found that many students still lagged behind. No doubt influenced by Leonard Ayres's 1909 *Laggards in Our Schools*, McClymonds and other administrators began to chart these non-promotions, and the district collected detailed data on the number of children in each school who had failed their grade and who were therefore "retarded" or overage in their progress. When compiled, however, the numbers simply resulted in new puzzles. Some elementary schools had a school-wide overage rate of 4 percent while other schools had total rates of up to 50 percent, and some individual grades within these schools hit a rate of 100 percent.[25]

These were disturbing statistics of failure, and they seemed to call for a massive system-wide solution. Oakland administrators attributed the cause of overageness to a combination of factors (discussed below); but primarily they felt that the evidence clearly indicated that the district had to alter its curriculum: "It is more than likely that the course of study is too difficult in some of the grades," and the solution, McClymonds said, almost perfectly echoing Ayres, was to prepare a curriculum that would "appeal more directly to the interests of many of the children." Altering the type and difficulty of the curriculum was especially important for overage pupils who "should receive a training different than that given to the ordinary pupils."[26] Allowing students to fail year after year was fiscally unwise for any system, so acknowledging that some students should be trained to be self-supporting was in part a measure to restrain costs. It also meant a rather sharp reversal of educational ideology. In other words, by 1910 the district's chief leader, the same man who twenty years earlier had stressed the importance of district-wide uniformity in the curriculum, had flipped his strategy and argued instead for a new goal—that of a differentiated curriculum.[27] What we learn from a close examination of Oakland is that turn-of-the-century curriculum change was often a much slower and more deliberative process than has been recognized.[28]

By the time Superintendent McClymonds retired in 1913, he had overseen a full generation of educational change in Oakland. His twenty-three-year tenure paralleled the changing nature of schooling in turn-of-the-century America, demonstrating the evolution away from a type of Victorian education, with its focus on a strong, uniform curriculum, to a "modern" notion of schooling that emphasized the child's context and needs over a standard curriculum. "A generation ago the subject taught was of more importance than the child," he wrote in 1913, but now, he added, "the child is the central idea of the school."[29] In a valedictory statement, McClymonds recited his recent accomplishments. Oakland, he said, had extended "manual training in every school and to every child," had constructed play facilities and schools that would "put Oakland in the forerank of cities in the line of educational equipment," had developed a department of health and sanitation, and had created another department for the care of "subnormal" children.[30] McClymonds's tally demonstrated his concern that Oakland keep pace with other city school systems, while illustrating the powerful civic rivalry between urban school systems; so pressing was this sense of competition, in fact, that it emerged even in comparisons of playground equipment.

While his litany of reforms sounds akin to the checklist that progressives had been developing over the past twenty years, McClymonds's inventory was probably closer to a policy wish list than to practices underway, for many of these innovations were only just being introduced. Nevertheless, by the time of his departure in 1913, the school system had evolved from a collection of schools focused on transmitting a standard curriculum—as it had in the 1880s and early 1890s—into a full-fledged city system that sought to recognize the distinct needs and differing abilities of students across all schools.

THE SCHOOL SYSTEM OF AN "INTELLIGENT AND PROGRESSIVE CITY," 1913–17

The year 1913 was an important one for each city in this study. Although other urban school systems witnessed a "perfect storm of unrest" that year, resulting in a string of superintendent firings and resignations, the shift in Oakland from McClymonds to his successor was relatively peaceful. Each city in this study experienced a threshold moment when school administrators began to discuss the creation of "modern" schools and adoption of "progressive" practices. At a certain point in time within each district, educators made clear distinctions between old, outworn educational practices and the "new education." In Oakland, this shift came with the transition to a new superintendent in 1913. A. C. (Albert Charles) Barker, who had been an assistant superintendent under McClymonds, began by expressing his intention to alter "the traditional idea of education" and to observe the educational reforms taking place in other cities across the country. All of the new policies that Baker introduced into Oakland, he said, conformed "to the best modern practice."[31]

Barker had several things in mind when he referred to modern practice. First, he hoped for a new era of cooperation between researchers and school systems. When the NEA held its 1915 annual meeting in Oakland—an important recognition of the city's educational stature—Barker welcomed the audience of educators by arguing that one of the most important functions of the NEA should be "to evaluate the educational theories of the moment." Such an assessment could provide districts with sound practice and valuable assistance as they attempted to adapt "to the rapidly changing social, industrial, and economic needs of the times. I do not mean," he added, "that this body should be a clearing house for the fads of professional educators of 'merely national fame,' but that it shall give approval to the soundest educational opinion of the country."[32]

Barker hoped progressive educational research would entail conscientious experimentation, rather than a frenzied adoption of popular reforms, and thereby offers a glimpse of one possibility for educational research that might have existed outside of the Thorndike-Dewey dichotomy; in other words, rather than an excessive fixation on quantification and the rapid adoption of new reforms, we might have had a more measured and reflective stance toward pedagogical experimentation, something along the lines of what Dewey meant by scientific investigation.[33] Certainly, by 1915 many local school leaders across the country might already have felt overwhelmed by the flurry of reforms advocated at the national level. Barker's hope of distinguishing between "fad" and "sound opinion" suggests the frustration that many practitioners must have felt as they waded through the innovations that steadily accumulated at educational conferences. Nevertheless, as superintendent, Barker sought improvement that moved along several lines: the construction of new schools, the differentiation of the existing curriculum, the creation of new types of schools tailored to the needs of specific groups of students, the formation of a district research department, and the reorganization of the business department. To Barker, each area served as an essential component of the modern city school system.

New Schools and Services

Between 1910 and 1915, Oakland enrollments increased by 34 percent as waves of new students continued to flow into the schools. In the 1913–14 school year alone, fourteen new school buildings were completed. Oakland school leaders were immensely proud of the new structures erected in the early decades of the century. These buildings were far more handsome than their predecessors—Progressive Era architects borrowed freely from Mission, Italian Renaissance, and modern American styles, as photographs prominently featured in the annual reports attest. More importantly, these new schools sloughed off the flaws of older buildings by including new features for ensuring the health of students, such as the latest ventilation and lighting systems. They symbolized state-of-the-art approaches to education and displayed devices and designs that defined the modern school: auditoriums equipped with film projectors, neighborhood clubrooms, libraries, kindergartens, hospital rooms, principals' suites, teachers' lunchrooms, shining cafeterias, and "fully equipped" manual training and domestic science classrooms.[34] They were a physical embodiment of the modern faith in education.

Barker was usually less interested in organizational modernization than he was in curricular and programmatic change, but he targeted some administrative areas for reform, most likely as a way to remain aligned with some national shifts. In 1913, he reorganized the district's business department, and in 1914, he implemented a modern budget system based on a format recommended by the U.S. Commissioner of Education. Barker established a department of reference and research, a reform that was well-suited to Barker's inquisitive disposition while it also put Oakland in the forefront of the movement to establish district research departments.[35]

In 1913, Barker introduced yet another initiative to the school system, one that had only recently appeared on the educational scene: the junior high school. Despite its novelty, the junior high was not an untested construct. The purposes and practices of the junior high school were nevertheless the subject of spirited discussion among educators throughout the 1910s. As cities experimented with various forms, the outlines of a consensus began to emerge: the junior high should include grades seven, eight, and sometimes nine; it offered a way to introduce the traditional disciplines (or departments) of the high school into the lower grades; it focused on new pedagogical techniques suitable for adolescents; and it provided the possibility for the introduction of vocational or prevocational coursework for students as a preparation for more advanced studies in high school.[36]

In its early incarnation in Oakland, the junior high seemed something of an odd hybrid designed to fit competing needs in the district.[37] As Barker described it, the junior high school was an innovation that could embrace contrasting aims in education, offering a college-bound curriculum to non-college-bound students, at the same time that it allowed for some curricular, usually vocational, variation. The junior high in Oakland thus became a new organizational form through which it was possible to explore novel approaches to schooling, a way to adapt schooling to the needs of a diverse student population.[38] The connection between Oakland's junior high schools and the agenda of curricular differentiation soon became clear. Barker explained that the junior high would be coordinated with the elementary schools and the differentiated high schools so that students could prepare for the more rigorous academic atmosphere of the University High School (the district's college prep institution) or the manual training of Oakland's Vocational High School. Such curricular splits meant that decisions about the curricular path children would take often had to be made by the fifth grade. In other words, by 1915, the Oakland school system had created the differentiated group of high schools that the principal of Oakland High had, in 1893, envisioned might one day exist.[39]

Despite his adoption of several popular innovations, Barker continued to voice frustration at the character of Progressive Era educational reform. "We go on experimenting without controlled conditions," he said, "or looking hither and thither for the opinions of people who know no more than we do, or whose conditions are wholly different from ours." What Barker hoped to see was "real scientific investigation," he explained, "under expert direction and properly controlled conditions." Either the federal government or private foundations should aid in funding large-scale, controlled experimentation, he contended. This was not a message that found a ready and receptive audience among some other district progressives, many of whom believed the need for change was urgent, if only because mounting enrollments were forcing the issue.[40] Barker was not the only district progressive to propose alternative paths to what was becoming the emerging monoculture of educational science and psychology, yet these kinds of public ponderings were relatively rare.[41]

The Intrusion of Progressive Politics

No matter how compelling Barker's vision for educational research might have been, he had little opportunity to pursue it due to intervening financial and administrative concerns.[42] In 1915, Oakland experienced a mild recession, and concerned about escalating costs, the school board convened a meeting in early June 1915 to discuss expenses. The new buildings, innovations, and departments that the district had added since 1910 required substantial financial resources, and during the same period, the per capita cost of maintaining the schools based on the average daily attendance had increased 22 percent.

Much of the political and economic turmoil that had begun ten years earlier came to a head; as the public-service franchises began to lose some of their power, a group of local pro-business leaders was happy to assist in their demise. In 1905 representatives of the city's rapidly growing business community had formed the Oakland Chamber of Commerce to promote local economic growth, something the franchise monopolies had never shown any interest in facilitating. Members of this group, which included Mayor Mott, constituted Oakland's downtown business elite and included bankers, manufacturers, construction firms, and merchants small and large. They were eager to make Oakland a more dominant force on the West Coast.

Joseph R. Knowland served as the leader of the downtown elite, founding important social and civic organizations, including the Athens Athletic Club, an association around which much of Oakland high society ultimately orbited. Knowland was a U.S. Congressional Representative from 1904 until 1915, whereupon he left national politics and purchased the *Oakland Tribune*, allowing him to have an unparalleled voice in public affairs. Nevertheless, that voice did not give him immediate dominance, and he and his colleagues spent the next ten years strengthening their networks and trying to wrest control of the city from the franchise corporations and the Kelly machine. While Mott had been mayor, these local business leaders enjoyed a growing influence, as Mott was able to finesse relationships among the machine, the large corporations, and the business elite. When Mott chose not to seek reelection in 1915, the business elite put up a member of their own, Frank Bilger, hoping to fast-track their assent to power by securing the mayor's office.

Bilger was beaten by John Davie, marking an embarrassing failure for the Knowland group. Davie was comfortable working with both the Kelly machine and the franchise corporations and stymied the rise of the business elite, at least temporarily. A new city charter in 1910 created a commission form of municipal government in Oakland. Under Mott, the commission kept power somewhat decentralized, but once Davie took office, he allowed the franchises to consolidate their strength. As mayor, Davie put Oakland's commission government to good use. As one student of Oakland politics put it, "Far from being a victim of machine politicians, the commission structure, in Oakland and elsewhere, actually proved to be conducive to the machine style of politics." In 1916, the Davie-Kelly machine was able to pass an amendment to the charter, removing most of the restrictions on the franchise corporations.[43] Thereafter, the Knowland group began to forge new political coalitions, reaching out to national networks such as the National Municipal League and founding an Oakland version of the Good Government League.

A City School Survey

Due both to the mid-1910s recession and the profligacy of the commission government, Oakland's public coffers rapidly depleted. The school board sought out solutions to its escalating costs. Seeking to scrutinize educational programs and expenses, the board voted to employ Ellwood P. Cubberley of Stanford's School of Education, whom they considered "one of the foremost authorities on education administration in the United States." Cubberley's charge was to investigate "the reasons for the increased expense and to determine if it were possible to conduct the schools more economically without loss of efficiency." This, of course, was a question raised by many districts of the time.[44] The city school survey "movement," as it was later called, had begun just five years earlier, and Cubberley was among the most popular choices for conducting such surveys. Having a reformer of national prominence so close at hand must surely have felt like an educational advantage.

By contracting with Cubberley, the board had elected, in effect, to adopt yet another innovation.[45] For his part, Cubberley welcomed an opportunity to translate his general principles into specific recommendations for the Oakland schools. The resulting report offers an excellent example of how external experts urged local educators to accept their national designs for school improvement. The type of organization Cubberley recommended corresponded exactly with the administrative arrangements proposed in his Portland survey and that he was about to include in his 1916 textbook, *Public School Administration*.[46]

Cubberley advised the board to reorganize the district, asserting his notion that the superintendent should lead the whole school district and be held accountable for its success. This form of administration, he stated resolutely, was the method followed by all effective corporations. He commended the district for progress in several other areas, including the introduction of home economics and the commercial and technical courses that supplemented the more traditional "literary" and general science curricula. "It is good for the institutions of democracy that a larger and larger percentage of pupils should be attracted" to the schools, Cubberley reminded the board, and that the addition of more practical courses would help attract "all types of young people." Cubberley also urged the district to build even more junior high schools, thereby permitting "a differentiation of courses to meet different needs which is not now possible." And he offered a dozen comparative tables ranking Oakland in school spending and taxes against other cities in the West, East, and Midwest. Oakland emerged from these comparisons looking rather penurious; the district's administration was smaller than in other western cities, it paid its teachers less, and it had fewer departmental supervisors than most other cities its size.[47]

Rather than recommending a *reduction* in expenditures and services, as the school board's fiscal sentries undoubtedly hoped, Cubberley advocated an expanded and reorganized district, one that added personnel and programs. His report concluded that the increased costs could be skirted by abandoning all the new additions and "going back to the school system of ten or fifteen years ago. This, though," he astutely added, "no intelligent and progressive city is willing to do, and such action Oakland does not need to take." There was much still to be accomplished, Cubberley insisted, for the school district to become highly efficient and "if Oakland is to retain its current position of educational prominence. To stand still," he sternly cautioned, "even for a few years, means to drop toward the rear in the matter of public education." Cubberley's message was clear: nothing was worse than stagnation or the stigma of backwardness.[48]

It is unclear how much Cubberley's recommendations surprised the board, but they must have been unsettled. Nevertheless, despite the urgent tone of Cubberley' recommendations, the school board took no immediate action. Throughout the following year, the board commissioned even more focused inquiries into different dimensions of the district. During the 1910s, cities like Oakland and Berkeley made such common use of external experts for the purposes of municipal evaluation that one newspaper took to calling the process getting "experted."[49] Multiple recommendations made decision making more difficult, and the board made few advances toward the direction Cubberley had advised. In the years that followed, Barker successfully added some new programs, expanded the junior high school, and implemented forms of student classification. Nevertheless, in some of his public statements Barker aired his frustrations with the faddish recommendations made by educators of "merely national fame" who offered little in the way of a research base for their recommendations.[50]

Barker's resistance to seemingly simplistic efficiency measures demonstrated an intellectual tenacity that was becoming increasingly unusual, possibly serving as a model to some of those around him. His influence was perhaps best demonstrated by the willingness of his assistant superintendent to offer a rare critique of the efficiency movement. "I have no quarrel with the doctrine of efficiency that is everywhere stirring up a new interest in getting things done," Oakland assistant superintendent Lewis Avery told his NEA audience in 1915, "but only with its assumption of finality. In every quarter it has invaded," he said, "it seems to bring all back to a material basis and introduce a wholly materialistic spirit." The school system that fixated on efficiency would "prepare pupils for a certain niche in life" while it "unprepared them for others," and Avery called for a curriculum that would "promote the development of the individual rather than fit him to anything or for anything." Avery's stance illustrates the possibilities that existed within public school districts both for dissent and for the articulation of alternative views of progressivism.[51] However, Avery was far less vocal under his next superintendent.

Turning Point

Regardless of the innovations that Barker had brought to the district—or perhaps because of his resistance to other types of reform—some members of the Oakland school board grew increasingly dissatisfied with Barker's leadership. In the year and a half following Cubberley's survey, opposition to Barker slowly developed until the board erupted in conflict. Early in 1917, the *Oakland Tribune* reported an "open breach" in the school board. One board member accused three other members of engaging in "petty politics" and conspiring to remove Superintendent Barker from office.[52] Certainly, the results of the surveys the board had commissioned provided a convenient wedge to dislocate the superintendent. For his own part, Barker acknowledged that "certain members of the Board of Education are known to be opposed to my retention," and he announced that he would "refrain from becoming a party to any factional controversy." Therefore, he announced that he would not directly seek reappointment.[53]

Barker apparently meant that he would not actively campaign for reelection by the board, choosing to let the board work out its own conflict. Such a demure approach had worked for the Denver superintendent just the year before; he had allowed the Denver school board to debate itself to a conclusion and was then reappointed. The board members opposed to Barker immediately seized the opportunity, taking Barker's comments as capitulation. Despite the protests of two other board members and several community representatives, including members of the Central Labor Council, the board members in the majority quickly announced that they would initiate the search for a new superintendent. Moreover, they said they would look for an "outside man," a move that was still unusual at a time when most top administrators worked their way up through the system.[54]

Within a week of its reported breach and Barker's announcement, the Oakland board, eager to ensure the acquisition of a school chief who would guarantee Oakland's competitiveness in the national arena, appointed an advisory committee of "prominent educators and representative citizens." This committee, the board asserted, would serve to "eliminate politics entirely in the selection of a new superintendent" and would ensure that the "job shall seek the man, rather than the man seek the job." As constituted, the committee featured members of the growing downtown business elite along with top administrators from Bay Area institutions of higher education, ultimately including the presidents of the University of California, Mills College, and Stanford University, as well as Joseph King, president of the Oakland Chamber of Commerce; George Randolph, an executive with United Iron Works; and a Congregational minister. The sole labor representative, R. H. Wiand, quickly assessed that he had no chance of influencing the committee. He resigned so that he could run for the Oakland school board in upcoming elections. Wiand was swiftly replaced by Harrison S. Robinson, head of the Downtown Property Owner's Association and a close ally of the Knowland "machine."[55]

The firing of Barker and the creation of the advisory committee marked a transformative shift for the district. Once constituted, the district's advisory committee proceeded by taking two steps that revealed their intentions. First, they asked Professors Cubberley of Stanford and Alexis F. Lange of the University of California to provide reports on the "qualifications desirable for a school superintendent." Cubberley and Lange complied, quickly submitting their written recommendations. In fact, Cubberley provided what amounted to a condensed version of the main points expressed in his recently published *Public School Administration* and restated some of the recommendations he had made in his survey of the district two years earlier. Lange simply concurred with Cubberley's suggestions and cited several additional chapters from *Public School Administration* to which Oakland school leaders might look for guidance.[56] None of these recommendations were tailored to the Oakland context, they simply pointed the way to the adoption of a prefabricated blueprint.

In a second, and rather novel, move, the Oakland advisory committee contacted the school board of Cleveland, Ohio, about the procedure it had used earlier that same year to select its new superintendent, Frank Spaulding. Just a few years earlier, Spaulding had been contracted to help Cubberley with his survey of Portland, Oregon. Meanwhile, the Cleveland school board had commissioned a survey of its own school system, which yielded a massive twenty-three-volume report in 1916. As a consequence, Cleveland's superintendent search had received an unprecedented amount of national attention. As Spaulding later wrote in his autobiography, the Oakland advisory committee chair, President Wheeler of the University of California, contacted the Cleveland board requesting the "fullest information possible" about their superintendent search. The Cleveland school board's procedure, said Spaulding, "was universally approved and, in one case, immediately followed." That case was Oakland.[57]

Rather than simply adopting Cleveland's approach, however, the Oakland board also took direct advantage of its results by hiring Fred Hunter, one of Cleveland's top three candidates.[58] When reporting this story, Oakland newspapers announced that Hunter's near miss at the competitive Cleveland post placed him in "the foremost rank of public school superintendents."[59] After the board voted to hire Hunter, it immediately voted to enact Cubberley's reorganization plan for the district. All these decisions occurred remarkably rapidly, given that it was just over two months since the politicking on the board had begun.

Other developments demonstrated that the dispatching of Barker was as much a political move on the part of the downtown business elite as it was any kind of educational coup. First, at its meeting on April 2, 1917, the Chamber of Commerce adopted a resolution stating that its directors expressed "their hearty approval of the program of reorganization" (Cubberley's plan) adopted by the school board. Furthermore, they urged that the plan be "carried on diligently to a conclusion" and that Oakland district leaders should "give special attention to needs of a growing industrial and commercial community."[60] Oakland's labor papers protested fiercely with headlines that read "Protect the Schools from Political Intrigue" and its editors argued that "the people of Oakland have been most studiously and deceitfully fooled over the petty political plot of those members of the Board of Education who would wreck the department for their own personal end." The *Tri-City Labor Review* quoted Mayor Davie as being opposed to the supplanting of Barker and calling Hunter an "imported highbrow educator."[61]

Less than two weeks later, Knowland's *Oakland Tribune* placed a notice on the front page of its second section, emblazoned with the following statement: "We, the undersigned, being conversant and familiar with the recent plan of reorganization of the School Department, made by the Board of Education, do approve its action and do hereby endorse the appointment of Fred M. Hunter as superintendent of schools of the City of Oakland, and we do hereby further express our entire confidence in the judgment and integrity of the members of the Board of Education." The statement was signed by "a number of men prominent in the business and professional life of the city."[62] Here was the clearest evidence of the Knowland machine's effort to use the schools to stake out new political territory at a time when it had suffered defeat in other spheres.

The brashness of the move is perhaps paralleled only by the striking list of individuals who signed their names to the endorsement. In addition to Knowland, the catalog reads like a directory of what was later to be called the Good Government League as they formalized their public role. Included among them were a full tally of the city's notables: Harrison Robinson, who had been on the school board's recent advisory committee; Joseph King, president of the Chamber of Commerce; Albert Carter, a member of the Good Government League, who successfully ran against the Davie-Kelly machine for city council in 1921 and was elected to Congress in 1924; and H. C. Capwell, who was the owner of major Oakland department store and a founding member of the Chamber of Commerce.[63] Oakland's choice of Hunter also illustrates how members of the business elite supplanted lay involvement in educational governance in favor of forging direct links with nationally recognized educational "experts." In asserting that it had removed "politics entirely in the selection of a new superintendent," the board eliminated any opportunity for serious community input into the superintendent selection process.[64]

Superintendent Barker had been no provincial yokel, it should be noted, and under his watch, the city schools made strides toward many innovations considered progressive. Yet Barker's tenure in Oakland, from 1913 to 1917, overlapped with years of tremendous district turmoil and superintendent turnover, and it reflected events taking place across the country. Barker's ouster also opened the door to a new style of leadership and a new opportunity to craft a vision of district progressivism.

A DEMOCRATIZED PLAN FOR EDUCATION, 1917–28

When Mayor Davie proclaimed to the National Education Association in 1923 that his city was distinguished as having one of the most progressive and best-known school systems in the country, he credited the accomplishment "to the untiring efforts of our superintendent of schools, Mr. Fred M. Hunter."[65] By that time, Davie had put public disputes about the superintendency behind him and Hunter had already served six years as school chief and completed a one-year term as NEA president. During his eleven-year tenure in Oakland (1917–28) Hunter embraced innovations with unparalleled fervor. Within his first year, he introduced, among other reforms, a department of vocational guidance, a department of mental measurement (for IQ testing), a new budget and accounting system, an Americanization campaign, and separate courses for academically slower students.[66] Hunter's enthusiastic implementation of an array of efficiency-oriented measures, just the sort of robust changes applauded by the school board and the Oakland business community, would appear to clearly brand him as hard-nosed administrator. Nevertheless, he and other Oakland school leaders also undertook vigorous efforts to spread new, "active" forms of pedagogy throughout their schools. And Hunter consistently called for the development of "democratized" and "socialized" schools, ideas that had intellectual ties to reformers like Jane Addams and John Dewey.[67] If there were different sides to progressive education, which one was Hunter on?

"The most pronounced tendency in modern education," Hunter wrote when he moved to Oakland, "is expressed by the phrase, 'the democratization of the schools.'" What precisely Hunter meant by "democratization of the schools" is a central puzzle explored in the remainder of this chapter. The democratization concept was at the heart of Hunter's administration and he regularly identified it as a guiding principle for his transformation of the Oakland schools. Closer examination is required to determine how his views of democracy and democratic schooling corresponded to those articulated by

Dewey or Charles Eliot or H. H. Goddard. Whatever meaning Hunter had in mind, he ultimately implemented his vision of a progressive school system with such success that the district's structure and many of its practices persisted for decades.[68]

Like many western superintendents, Hunter had risen from modest beginnings. He began his career in education as nineteen-year-old teacher in rural Kansas. He later worked as a school principal and the director of evening schools at the Lincoln, Nebraska, YMCA before serving a series of brief terms as school superintendent in three small Nebraska towns. Then, between 1912 and 1917, as the superintendent of the Lincoln schools, Hunter worked out the ideas and innovations that gained him the attention of search committees in Cleveland and Oakland. At the time of his appointment to the Oakland post, he was completing a graduate degree at Teachers College, which the *Oakland Tribune* called "the foremost professional institution for the training of superintendents." In the same article, the paper described Hunter as a man of proven "managerial ability, of marked executive power," and a "student of civic and social problems."[69]

Hunter arrived in Oakland, therefore, with a reputation as a manager and an innovator.[70] He was already an active NEA participant and was consequently immersed in the language of contemporary reform. Indeed, Hunter's criticisms of the outdated "aristocratic" and "lock-step" system of education echoed the pronouncements of Cubberley and George Strayer at Teachers College, Columbia. The similarity was not coincidental: Strayer had served as Hunter's mentor at Teachers College. Members of the educational elite quickly recognized Hunter as a kindred spirit, for he was soon invited to participate in the exclusive Cleveland Conference, a regular gathering of education's national inner circle.[71] Thus, although he may have been an outsider in Oakland, Hunter was already an insider to the national network of educational heavy hitters.

In taking his new position, Hunter clearly had been given a mandate not only from the school board and Oakland's business elite but also from national leaders who carried a certain external legitimizing authority.[72] The board's decision to restructure assured Hunter an unprecedented amount of control over district affairs. Previously the Oakland school board (see fig. 3.1) had retained just the sort of "faulty" organization that Cubberley consistently criticized in his surveys and textbooks. Reorganization had both administrative and symbolic importance. As the official head of system-wide operations, Hunter instantly gained more power and more freedom to implement changes. The new district organizational chart—published in Hunter's first annual report—was a visual metaphor for the orderliness of administrative

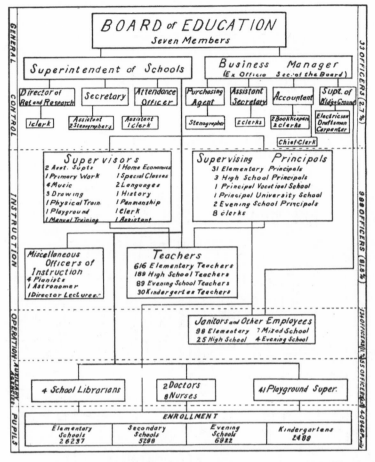

FIGURE 3.1. Oakland organization chart under Superintendent Barker, 1913–17. (Oakland Public Schools, *General Statistics of the Oakland Public Schools: General Report of the Superintendent of Schools, 1913–1917* [Oakland: Oakland Public Schools, 1917], 5.)

progressivism (see fig. 3.2). Throughout his tenure, Hunter emphasized how the new management structure led to the most productive and skillful teaching.[73] Reorganization provided the foundation for the coherent set of reforms that would follow. It is easy to overlook the dramatic shift in perspective this entailed, for the board's decision to reorganize signaled their acceptance of the idea that education was no longer a local affair, as did their selection of an outsider as superintendent. Moreover, reorganization required board members to relinquish some of their own power, a move that school boards in cities such as Portland and Seattle were unwilling to take.

ORGANIZATION CHART

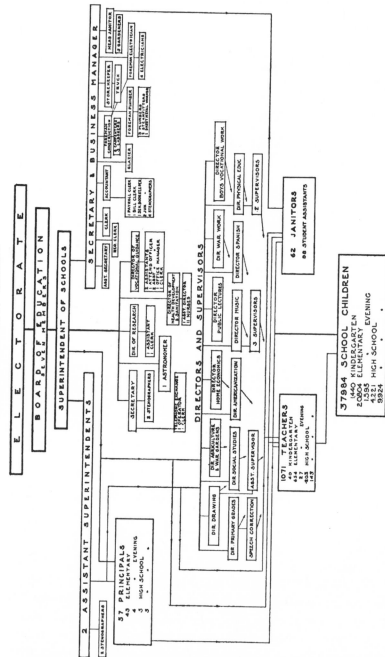

FIGURE 3.2. New Oakland organization chart under Hunter, 1918. (Oakland Public Schools, *Report of the Superintendent of Schools, 1917–18* [Oakland: Board of Education, 1919], 295.)

Hunter's understanding of democratic schooling was quite complicated— not complex in a philosophical sense; rather it is difficult to clearly summarize or identify a consistent line of thought. Confounding matters further, Hunter's verbal style was rather idiosyncratic, so his prose often obscured his intended meaning. Nevertheless, democratization held broad meaning for Hunter: it referred to the differentiation of the curriculum, the expansion of educational opportunities to increasing numbers of students, and the modifications he made to district structures so that the schools were properly adapted to diverse pupil needs. Democratization also implied a reconsideration of the role of the school district itself. In Hunter's mind, the democratic and progressive school entailed a comprehensive system of courses and services that could meet virtually all the needs of Oakland's rapidly growing student body. The district met these needs through the addition of vocational and technical schools, the creation of "cosmopolitan curriculums" for the large city high schools, the development of special classes for "defective" students, the wider use of the school plant for evening courses, and the expansion of the junior high school.[74]

Opening the schools to "all the children of all the people"—a motto that Hunter and many contemporaries frequently employed—was one of Hunter's primary goals, even if it required more educational resources. One vivid demonstration of the successful transition away from nineteenth-century aristocratic practices was the increasing popularity of the high school. Attendance in American high schools jumped from 202,963 in 1890 to 1,645,171 in 1918, an increase of 711 percent that far outstripped the total national population increase of 68 percent. Once seen as an elitist institution, resented by some American taxpayers, the public high school became the consummate symbol of progressive educational advance, for it broadened its course offerings to appeal to students of a diverse array of backgrounds.[75] The "trend toward real democracy," Hunter said, could be seen in cities like Los Angeles that had mustered a high school enrollment of twenty thousand students through the introduction of practical courses. Meanwhile, Oakland's high school enrollment hovered around four thousand at that point, and many Oakland students still dropped out before graduation.[76] This kind of ideal modern school system—one that stood for a concrete and "real democracy"—was just what Hunter sought to fashion in Oakland.

Hunter had worked out an agenda for his version of a progressive district during his five years in as school superintendent in Lincoln. In fact, many of the innovations he instituted in Oakland were reproductions of his Lincoln programs, with some additions, such as an Americanization campaign, classes in salesmanship, and what he referred to as "neighborhood schools."[77]

A District Progressive Agenda

Hunter began boldly. In what may have been the closest thing to a school district superintendent's educational manifesto, Fred Hunter published a 350-page annual report for 1917–18, bursting with research, statistics, graphs, statements of purpose, and descriptions of new programs and courses at the end of his first year. The annual report was in the process of becoming an important tool for public relations among school leaders of the time, and Hunter endeavored to use it as an instrument for image management both within the Oakland community and beyond, just as municipal reform experts, such as David Snedden and William H. Allen, had urged superintendents to do.[78] Soon superintendents adopted the practice of sending their reports to academics, universities, and their fellow school leaders in other districts in addition to sharing them with their own school boards.[79]

"Progress in a democracy," Hunter explained at one point, "cannot be permanent if carried on only by a few selected leaders." School programs, he said, often met utter failure because progressive leadership did not keep itself in touch with the public.[80] Hunter was determined to succeed, and his annual report served as a medium for communicating all facets of his reform agenda. Hunter believed that the results of Oakland's "scientific experimentation and investigation" offered a record of educational innovation to which other districts could look for inspiration if not admiration.[81] Thereafter, Hunter assiduously walked the thin line between keeping "in touch with the public" and attempting to manipulate it.

Hunter targeted almost every aspect of district operations for reinvigoration. He tallied all the activities and programs that he had introduced into the Oakland schools during his first year, and the list of programs itself is worthy of brief review, for it represents both the broad scope of his agenda and the boundless energy of the man. During the 1917–18 school year, Hunter reported, the district had added the following:

1. [A] Department of Vocational Guidance.
2. A Department of mental measurement as a basis of a system of promotions.
3. Budget system of accounting extended to the school units and departments of special instruction.
4. Continuation classes in upper elementary grades.
5. Part time classes in salesmanship.
6. A department of agriculture and home and school gardening.
7. Neighborhood schools.
8. A plan of curriculum development founded upon individual needs of pupils as studied by the teachers.

9.   A systematic plan of professional study and professional meetings.

10. Junior Chambers of Commerce in three high schools.

11. A Campaign of Americanization.

12. An organized system of patriotic and war work in the schools.

13. A policy of publicity through information distributed to all homes by school children.

14. Opportunity rooms for retarded pupils.

15. Special instruction in home-keeping for overgrown girls in industrial districts.[82]

Taken together, this catalog of initiatives essentially constituted much of Hunter's agenda for his eleven-year tenure in Oakland. Still, such a list did not constitute a coherent agenda, nor did it guarantee successful implementation, and few of these initiatives could be considered fully established programs by 1918. Yet it represented what district progressives believed should be included in their modern school systems, and it reveals a unique and specific perspective on the ways districts married pedagogical efforts and administrative mandates.

Hunter described the principles to which his practices adhered in his NEA speeches and in his Oakland superintendent reports.[83] Focusing on some of his doctrines offers a deeper glimpse into how Hunter and his central office staff proceeded with district-wide democratic reform. Hunter's principles might be best expressed as three sets of paired ideas: democratization and socialization, flexibility and adaptation, and efficiency and measurement. These concepts correlate rather well to the larger educational tenets described earlier as democracy, differentiation, and district-wide design.

The Socialization of the Oakland Schools

The concept of the "democratized" or "socialized" school (Hunter used the terms interchangeably) provided the primary foundation of Hunter's worldview. The notion that schooling should be socialized boasted a lineage from Addams and Dewey, but it was also adopted and expanded by numerous academics and practitioners, like Strayer, who displayed less precision in employing their terms. What to some educators represented the rich possibilities that the school could play as a force for social good and for humanizing the harshness of an industrialized system of production often became more static and less nuanced in the hands of large city school leaders.[84] What mattered to Hunter was the practical demonstration of socialization in his schools, such as classroom procedures motivated by "the activities of life."

including what became known as the "socialized recitation," another new practice that was especially popular around the First World War.

The socialized recitation, as described by people like Hunter and Strayer, emphasized the abolition of the nineteenth-century individual recitation by which an individual student "toed the line" and spouted memorized facts when prompted by a teacher. The socialized format was meant to engage groups of pupils in ways that took their interests into account. A flurry of textbooks appeared in the late 1910s and 1920s offering guidance on how to arrange classroom lessons based on this fresh approach. These volumes advocated a procedure that involved the teacher posing questions to a classroom full of children, rather than to an individual, whereupon the students responded. While socialized recitation may not have represented a significant pedagogical leap, it did involve the development of some additional student skills, given that teachers expected more than pat responses.[85]

Hunter provided examples of what he saw as potent examples of new classroom practices. One vignette involved a class of seventh graders who were studying the correlation between English and geography. Using a map of the state, the teacher challenged each student to choose a plot of land in which "a real estate investment might be considered desirable" and then to act as a salesperson endeavoring to sell the land to a classmate. Yet such classroom activities might easily serve to illustrate the kinds of pedagogy Dewey criticized as being "too trivial to be educative."[86] Nevertheless, it would be unfair to leave the impression that all coursework was thin on intellectual content. Indeed, careful examination of district curricula yields illustrations of several types of potentially powerful curricular ideas and practices.

Social studies was often described by progressive educators as more amenable to newer pedagogical techniques than some traditional subjects, which is perhaps why it served as the first curricular area to be completely overhauled and reissued to Oakland teachers. William John Cooper, the director of social studies, presented his teachers with a fresh 220-page course of study that represented a break from the standard, more rigid lesson plans of the day. A former Latin and history teacher, Cooper mixed strong historical content with novel approaches to teaching, including lively suggestions for solidly grounded classroom activities and references to the most recent research studies and pedagogical techniques. He encouraged teachers to choose from a range of instructional options, such as socialized recitations, rigorous investigations into historical content, dramatizations of major events, and projects oriented toward real social problems. When he came to the topic of Columbus, for example, he explained that the historical literature of recent decades had given rise to strikingly differing interpretations of the explorer, "extending from efforts to prove the great navigator worthy of canonization on the one hand to . . . attacks on his character and accomplishments on the other." In other words, Cooper prompted his teachers to engage their students in discussions that were potentially controversial (though he did not describe them as such) as well as in serious interpretive debates, something that teachers today often still find difficult to pull off. In other words, Cooper's curriculum challenges assumptions some scholars hold about the two dimensionality and low quality of curricula in progressive public schools.[87]

Cooper was also highly cognizant that teachers had "had drilled into them so long the idea that pupils must memorize facts set forth in a textbook." To address this problem, Cooper allowed multiple opportunities for teacher collaboration and professional development, and he sometimes modeled the newer pedagogical techniques himself. As such, Cooper provides a compelling example of the promise of progressive pedagogy, the kind that was possible when district progressives set out to fundamentally alter the staid practices of the past. Perhaps it is not surprising then that Cooper eventually left Oakland to become a superintendent in his own district. His talents were ultimately recognized at an even higher level when he was appointed as U.S. Commissioner of Education from 1929 to 1933.[88] He exemplifies the remarkable talent that could be found throughout city school systems during this era, even if that kind of creative pedagogical expression could not always be consistently expressed.

In their mingling of various pedagogical techniques, Oakland school leaders and teachers continued to merge ideas that now seem contradictory. For example, in the lists of recommended readings provided their teachers, Oakland administrators regularly included the somewhat doctrinaire writings of Strayer, the theoretical essays of Dewey, and the "project method" proposals of William H. Kilpatrick.[89] As a district progressive, Hunter was uninterested in divisions between contemporary theorists, because any "progressive" thinker could be an ally and any classroom practice that departed from the uniformity and the rigidity of the nineteenth century was to be embraced.

Another significant dimension of socialization entailed a whole new conception of the purpose of the city school system. The modern school district, Hunter firmly believed, should house new departments, divisions, and structures, each with a designated role in realizing larger district goals. Individual schools were no longer isolated but rather nested within a broader network of programs and agencies, all intended to guide and prepare students for productive roles in American society. Acting as the "community's chief social agent," as Hunter called it, the school district was the institution best suited to point students toward their futures.[90] Thus, when Hunter used the phrase "the socialized school," he also meant a *differentiated* city school system, one that adapted schools "to the needs and capacities of schoolchildren," that tossed aside "useless academic tradition," and that embraced the responsibility it now had to *all children*, "not merely to the normal or especially gifted."[91] In another important move, Hunter altered the scope of his programs by shifting from a focus on the individual student—"the needs of the child"—to specific *types* of children. Hunter insisted that Oakland courses of study should be developed to "meet the needs of groups of children representing as nearly as possible variations in natural tendency, natural ability, *economic conditions, and social inheritance*."[92] With this variation, Hunter, along with other district progressives, began to provide the same instructional treatment to whole neighborhoods and large sections of cities.

Flexibility, Adaptation, and Americanization

At a time when rising secondary school enrollments were a badge of school district success, Hunter, like other city school superintendents of the day, became increasingly troubled by the teenage dropout rate. Of the 1,920 Oakland students who started high school, only 598 remained three years later. Expanded vocational coursework was one avenue for holding students in high school through graduation, and one of Hunter's early initiatives was to create a system of vocational guidance.[93] "Nothing is more important in the development of an efficient people," said Hunter, "than the assignment of each to a career of a task [*sic*] in which he will be most effective and contribute best not only to his own happiness and development, but to the ultimate interests of the community, local and national, in which he lives." Not only would the guidance bureau ensure that each student was properly trained for a career and a place in the community, but it also served as the "connecting link" between school and the commercial world, paving a smooth pathway from childhood through maturity.[94]

In addition to high school dropouts, another major educational problem Hunter faced was the challenge of struggling students, especially younger pupils who failed to be promoted from grade to grade, sometimes several years in a row. These were the same "laggards" that Ayres had written about in 1909 and that Superintendent McClymonds had fretted over in Oakland in 1910. To Hunter, these overage students posed a threat not only to themselves but also to the efficiency of his school system and society as a whole. "In a rapidly growing and overcrowded system," Hunter wrote, perpetual student failure "is a serious problem. . . . These pupils," he warned, "become misfits and enter society unprepared for efficient productive living or for service to

their community and their fellow men."[95] Therefore, Hunter wanted to identify and target children before they reached high school through another
innovation that could offer programmatic flexibility: the junior high school.
Early in his tenure, Hunter further developed the few junior highs already
in the city, using them as an important component of his district-wide plan.
Such a system of schools, he said, provided every seventh-, eighth-, and
ninth-grade child in the city a junior high school within a mile and a half of
their home. (Until that point in time, many students in Oakland and elsewhere stayed in the elementary school through eighth or ninth grade.)

The junior high school ultimately served several significant goals in Oakland, playing a role that is easy to overlook. It offered an avenue for keeping
students in the system until they reached high schools, it created a mechanism for meeting the needs of different groups of students, and it provided
an entryway for Hunter's Americanization program, which expanded after
the end of World War I. During his first year, Hunter established committees of teachers and administrators to address several pressing issues in the
district. The Junior High Committee made several consequential recommendations that Hunter adopted in the years that followed. Essentially, the committee recommended that Oakland create two types of junior high schools.
The first would be modeled on the "cosmopolitan," college-preparatory high
school, offer a wide range of courses that would suit the needs of most of the
city's children, and be located in new buildings (each costing $250,000 to
$350,000), placed throughout the city.[96]

The second kind of junior high would serve the immigrant communities
living in West Oakland, the lower-income waterfront section of the city. "The
water-front districts and districts having a predominant foreign element
constitute a special problem," explained the committee, and they thought it
"unwise to divorce the seventh, eighth and ninth grades from the elementary grades in these districts peopled by our foreign Americans." Instead
of new buildings for these students, the committee reasoned, the existing
neighborhood elementary schools should be adapted so that the seventh,
eighth, and ninth grades are of the "junior high school type." The curricula
of the two types of junior highs should vary a good deal, asserted the committee; waterfront children "should have an opportunity to take three years
of pre-vocational and junior high school work applicable to their needs in
their home districts without transferring to another school at the end of the
sixth grade, as in the case of the other junior high schools." Not only were
academic courses curtailed but so were the electives from which they could
choose as well as the number of periods devoted to music, drawing, and
physical education.[97]

The junior high schools, as mentioned above, especially those "peopled by foreign students," also helped Hunter to realize another one of his goals: Americanization. Hunter was serious about citizenship training and what he called the "pressing problems of Americanization" in the "manufacturing and waterfront districts of Oakland." The waterfront district of West Oakland contained the largest number of foreign-born residents, and it was at "these thickly populated sections of the city" that he targeted his Americanization programs.[98] Americanization offered both a means for disseminating patriotism and a strategy for dealing with diversity. In October 1917, for example, the district gathered data from the schools about the "nativity" of pupils and their parents. This survey provided detailed information on the nationalities of the district's parents, on the percentages of national origin by school and by grade, and on the neighborhoods that had "a large foreign parentage."[99] Americanization spread to other schools as well, targeting neighborhood schools and focusing on civics, vocabulary, and hygiene, along with industrial and commercial courses.

The First World War revealed a fierce patriotic streak in Hunter that showed little sign of diminishing in the years that followed. Moreover, at this point in time, both sides of the San Francisco Bay experienced combative labor strikes, although labor's actions were much less successful in Oakland than in San Francisco. The Oakland business community often tied labor agitation to foreign nativity. As president of the NEA, Hunter cautioned that "our purposes as a nation are gravely threatened." On the one hand, Hunter raised fears of "the bolshevist invasion," claiming that the principles of representative government were being disregarded and that the U.S. government was held in disrespect. (He was apparently undisturbed by the excesses of the series of raids conducted by the U.S. Department of Justice to arrest suspected radical leftists known as the Palmer Raids.)[100] On the other hand, Hunter raised fear of "reactionaries," noting as evidence both the "power and wealth" that had accumulated in the United States after World War I and the disturbing repeal of social legislation. "Organizations are calling for the repeal of child-labor laws, the laws governing the working hours of women, the compulsory education laws, and the like."[101] Hunter perceived other threats to American democracy, including illiteracy, "the un-Americanized resident," "a crippled system of citizenship-training," and the "politician and demagogue." The schools, especially the socialized school, provided the bulwark against such threats. Hunter saw the public school as the "only agency for assuring a common understanding regarding democracy." The schoolroom, he said, employing one of his favorite phrases, was "the laboratory of democracy."[102]

Americanization served another citywide political purpose that is not often recognized by scholars. If the classic political machine was one of the traditional ways that ethnic minorities had been assimilated into communities in the late nineteenth and early twentieth centuries, what replaced it as a mechanism for acculturation once those bosses and their political machines began to disappear? One explanation is that schools took up this challenge. The "neighborhood school" concept—at least as developed by Hunter—was one systematic effort to supplant Oakland's Kelly-Davie machine at the same time that it could serve quell labor unrest. From this perspective, the creation of local schools designed to meet the specific neighborhood needs went beyond curricular tracking and served as a broader political substitute for the machine-driven socialization mechanisms. Hunter, after all, intended Oakland's schools to serve all ages, providing as it did evening classes for adults. The democratic school, argued Hunter, broadened the scope of the school "upward through mature life and downward to the nursery."[103] Certainly, this would have been a solution that received widespread support from Oakland's growing business elite.

Americanization was also linked to the application of another of Hunter's primary efficiency principles: measurement. "Mental Testing," wrote Oakland's Americanization committee while the country was still at war, "should be one of the regular practices of the Neighborhood School, at first for all failing pupils, and later for all pupils in the school." Hunter believed the socialized and democratized school system should solve the problem of student academic failure, which was most pronounced in the schools with a large percentage of foreign children.[104]

Measurement and Variation: Feeble Minds or Faulty Democracy?

"Scientific administration can achieve the ultimate purpose of the public school," Hunter explained, only when the school system had "systematic and well-established methods of measuring its own results." Therefore, every school system should include, "as an integral unit," a department of measurement. "The key to the whole situation," he said, "is the principle of measurement."[105]

Hunter's new mental measurement department had perhaps the most serious effects on Oakland children due to the way that administrators used the test results for district-wide student classification. In its earliest stages, "mental measurement" referred to multiple types of assessment, including achievement and intelligence testing, but it quickly became associated primarily with IQ tests. Hunter used the new department as another strategy for attacking the problem of failing, overage pupils. "The school system that is intelligently planning for the future," Hunter proclaimed, "will seek to eradicate with all its powers" the "expensive evil" of extensive failure and retardation. At one point, Hunter estimated that the problem of overageness was costing Oakland taxpayers at least $150,000 each year, due to the additional expenses required to educate children who repeated grades.[106] The junior high served as one avenue for addressing the problem of dropouts and struggling students, but it did nothing for younger children in elementary school.

Earlier in Oakland's history, practitioners like Ida Vandergaw had attempted to uncover the causes of failure and recognized that academic weaknesses were not always caused by lack of intellectual ability; thus, they had developed some successful strategies for bringing students back up to their grade level, such as the ungraded room. Although such practices were becoming passé by the mid- to late 1910s, as judged by the addresses given at national conferences, Oakland's 1917–18 annual report includes scattered committee statements revealing that local practitioners by no means saw intellectual capacity as the only, or even primary, cause for student failure. Indeed, the chairs of the district's study committees—such as the Failure and Promotion Committee, the Junior High Schools Committee, and even the Mental Measurement Committee—issued reports offering a wide variety of opinions about the reasons for failure and promotion. These included ill health, "disciplinary" issues, "environmental" problems, and "administrative" reasons—in fact one committee pointed out that problems of ill health had never been properly recorded and thus could be potentially be one of the primary causes of academic trouble. Although one committee included the ambiguous category of "mental condition" as a cause of failure, they were equally concerned with "irregular attendance" as a major source of school failure. After all, committee members stressed, on any given day Oakland only had a daily average attendance of 80 percent. "With one-fifth of our children absent from schools, we certainly must reckon this as one of the causes for retardation," one committee wryly concluded.[107]

Despite the evidence provided by his own faculty and staff about the multitude of potential sources for student failure, Hunter was completely uninterested in anything that was not cutting edge. Oakland's old measures for sorting students paled in comparison to the new practice of intelligence testing that emerged during and after the First World War. In Oakland and elsewhere, many district progressives believed testing held enormous potential for making schools more scientifically organized, democratic, and, indeed, more enjoyable for children. Scholars have since examined the biases and fallacies on which the intelligence testing movement was founded, and with hindsight, it is difficult to comprehend how progressive educators understood IQ testing as democratic.[108] Nonetheless, Oakland leaders summarily dismissed charges that intelligence tests—they often refer to the practice as mental testing—were problematic or undemocratic. Testing was Hunter's principle of measurement applied directly to children, and he insisted that testing offered the district a way to permanently shake off "lock-step" schooling. The older system of curricular uniformity had utterly failed, said Hunter. Such standardization had been the cause of large percentages of student elimination and retardation, Hunter contended, ignoring any evidence to the contrary. Testing would lead to curricular variation and flexibility.[109]

To establish his program of mental measurement, Hunter hired Virgil Dickson, a doctoral student of Lewis Terman's at Stanford. Whether by temperament or training, Dickson tackled his new job with the same unwavering confidence and energy that characterized both Hunter and Terman. As director of research for the Oakland schools, Dickson swiftly implemented a program of intelligence testing throughout the district. In the first half of 1918 alone, Dickson's department administered intelligence tests to over three thousand Oakland pupils. In his own section of the 1917–18 annual report, Dickson presented the resulting percentages of categories into which children fell: rapid, normal, slow, under age, at age, over age, under age and rapid, over age and slow. Moreover, he displayed the scores and classification categories through a set of colorful bell-curve-shaped graphs of which Terman most certainly would have been proud (see fig. 3.3).[110]

Even in the early stages of testing, Dickson seemed aware that testing might raise eyebrows, and he insisted that testing must be blended into everyday practice and treated as a "regular part of the school work." He cautioned that "segregations and promotions and placement of children should be made in a natural way and almost never mentioned as a result of a mental test." On the rare occasions that Dickson voiced any reservations about mental measurement, they usually focused on concerns that the tests might be improperly administered. He worried that teachers might muck up an otherwise pristine process or that some instructors were too eager to describe the work as "Hunting for Dummies" or "Feeble Minds"—not on any fundamental qualms about validity of the IQ scores themselves.[111] Dickson's verbalized apprehensions imply that the implementation of mental testing did not necessarily move as smoothly as its expert purveyors intended, even when there was little visible public protest.[112]

Dickson and Hunter swiftly broadened the testing program to include all schools and students in the city. This district-wide effort meant that virtually every Oakland teacher required training in the uses and purposes of testing,

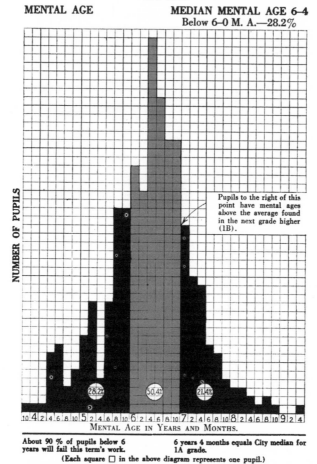

FIGURE 3.3. Tabulation of "mental age" results from Binet Intelligence Test given to Oakland first grade students, 1918. (Oakland Public Schools, *Report of the Superintendent of Schools, 1917–18* [Oakland: Board of Education, 1919], 214.)

and Dickson developed a strategy for educating teachers about the tests and their associated benefits. By mid-1918, Dickson had already given thirty-two addresses to gatherings of teachers and principals on subjects with titles like "Standard Tests in Classroom Work" and "Psychological Tests." He also taught university courses on testing to groups of teachers, principals, and supervisors during the school year and through summer school classes.[113]

Despite assertions by Hunter and Dickson that they proceeded cautiously with the program of intelligence testing, implementation was brisk. By the early 1920s, Dickson reported that he had given intelligence tests to over thirty thousand Oakland children. These tests proved "conclusively," he said, that the reason for student failure and retardation was mental inferiority in some 90 percent of the cases. Dickson was fond of stating that evidence had rapidly accumulated showing that mental age offered the *single best criterion* for decisions about student classification, while adding the lukewarm caution that it should never be the only criterion.[114]

Once the tests had been given throughout the school system, Hunter and Dickson saw the next step as the district-wide restructuring of instruction. "We have," explained Dickson, "adopted the policy, that the mental level of the child shall be taken as the point of departure" in determining proper student placement. The Oakland schools thereupon began to reorganize curricula and classes into "a three-track plan," adapted to student needs and arranged into a tiered system of coursework labeled as "accelerated, normal, and limited." Here, too, Dickson assured Oakland educators that other student factors had been taken into account when classifying pupils into their tracks, such as classroom accomplishment, age, interest, industry, health, and other considerations. Yet despite such assertions, Dickson could not resist the declaration that many of these factors had a direct relationship to proper placement by mental level. All students benefited from the new three-track arrangement, Dickson reported, maintaining that teachers invariably testified that pupils behaved better, worked better, and accomplished more than they had under the former system.[115] There is no evidence that the district ever conducted any kind of comprehensive evaluation of their massive curricular restructuring efforts, nor did they publish evidence that supported their larger claims; rather, they tended to rely on praise from other districts and academics. For example, Terman included Dickson's case study of Oakland in his 1922 edited volume, *Intelligence Testing and School Reorganization*, and he commended Oakland as representing the "leading methods of readjustment now being attempted in different parts of the country." The Oakland plan was an important model, Terman declared, because it affected "the entire school enrollment and the entire administrative system."[116]

Although Dickson periodically avowed devotion to democratic delegation of authority, there was never any doubt that the central administration designed and monitored the tracking plan carefully. "The adjustment of school curriculum to needs of pupils, the promotion and progress machinery, the causes of slow progress, the segregation of pupils into groups according to ability—all these are problems that must be attacked from the administrative angle," Dickson explained. "Teachers may see needs for readjustment and be anxious to make the necessary changes," he maintained, "but they are very helpless unless they have the co-operation of the administrative forces." The success of testing and tracking, he said, depended on teachers relinquishing their "individual standards" in favor of district mandates.[117] Evidence of conformity to the administration's plan suggests that schools found it desirable to cooperate. Or, as Dickson put it: "School after school has dropped into the general plan as the most natural way of working."[118]

Early advocates of intelligence testing knew they had to wage a battle on two fronts: the local and the national. In 1922, for example, Terman engaged in a series of public quarrels with Teachers College professor William C. Bagley and with author Walter Lippmann. Bagley contended that the testing movement was founded on psychological fallacies and that it was subversive of American ideals of democracy. The psychological "determinist," Bagley said, "proposes to chuck overboard the democratic ideal of education; to substitute a deceptive 'equity of opportunity' for a whole-hearted effort to bring the masses of our children up to a reasonable intellectual standard."[119] Terman shot back that Bagley held a "naïve view of democracy" and that his vision had been blurred by "the moist tears of sentiment." Bagley simply refused to face reality, insisted Terman, preferring instead to deliver "a waxed rhapsodic peroration on the miracles that skillful teachers work with morons and on the ultimate illumination of the world by gleams of light struck from dull minds."[120]

Ever the devoted Terman student, Dickson joined the fray with his own defense of intelligence testing and curricular tracking. "One frequently hears . . . ," he wrote, that any "scheme of classification" developed in the schools on the "basis of mentality" is "not democratic" or that the separation of students in schools is "undemocratic."[121] Oakland's system of testing and tracking, Dickson argued, was "more democratic than former systems because it offers to every child a freer opportunity to use his full capacity."[122] Democracy, Dickson carefully explained, "does not mean equality of achievement, but equality of opportunity for achievement."[123]

Some "idealists" mistakenly maintained, Dickson continued, that "through the educational process practically the same achievement is possible for all," and they erroneously believed that "every American youth has within him the power to become a Lincoln or an Edison." Yet the power of education was not unlimited, Dickson asserted; it could not develop and transform all children. "Who would argue," he asked, "that one who is an imbecile in early childhood can be changed to a genius in youth by being exposed to an ideal educational environment?" No, said Dickson, "true democracy" did not mean holding all students up to the same standards of attainment, it meant recognizing the differences between children and understanding that each child had a "place to fill." Therefore, Dickson reasoned, it would both "undemocratic" and "educationally wrong" *not* to give students such tests.[124] In taking his stance, Dickson not only captured the same line of reasoning about the dangers of false democracy that had animated the writings of Nicholas Murray Butler among others, but he also catapulted newer interpretations of testing, intellectual abilities, and true democracy into the ongoing discussions of district administrators who were looking to reform their school systems.

Other Segregations

In the early 1920s, Oakland experienced another demographic boom, this time in East Oakland, the section of the city that had been annexed in 1909. Between 1921 and 1924, 12,823 new single-family houses were built in Oakland, and almost 85 percent of those were in East Oakland. Many of the families who moved into these homes were white, native-born middle-class Protestants who had yet to be assimilated into the civic institutions of the city. The rapid growth of this group threatened traditional power bases while it also opened possibilities for new political affiliations. During these same years, Oakland, along with a number of other areas in the urban West, witnessed a surge of virulent racist agitation, most visible in the rise of the Ku Klux Klan (KKK). As historian Chris Rhomberg points out, this particular historical moment in Oakland provided the context for the political mobilization of group identity and for the rise of an urban social movement, led by the Ku Klux Klan. By 1924, the Oakland chapter of the Klan had at least two thousand members, and they claimed additional supporters numbering in the thousands.[125]

Racial and ethnic tensions flared with increasing intensity in Oakland, often sparked by pressures for housing and jobs as the city's immigrant and minority populations grew. The shipyard boom that Oakland had experienced during the war ended by 1922, fostering additional economic distress. Perhaps more than any other group at the time, the KKK voiced the discontent of white Oaklanders who felt disenfranchised by the extant municipal authorities and by the downtown business elite. In fact, the way the Klan described its goals often mimicked the rhetoric of other civic reformers of the day. For example, the Oakland chapter of the KKK announced that it was dedicated to "keep[ing] closer check upon public officials" and to preventing "laxity in the discharging of the duties of public offices." The Klan did not often play an open role in school affairs, although portions of their platform frequently included statements of strong support for public schools, embedded within its larger ideological outlook. One KKK flyer described the Klan mission with the proclamation: "Uphold white supremacy / Oppose entangling European alliances / Encouragement of and belief in the free public schools . . . AMERICANIZATION OF ALL!" Declarations of support for public schools were common among almost all Klan organizations of the 1920s.[126]

Many Klan officials became active in politics, officially or unofficially. At a time when fraternal societies were a common part of the grassroots political landscape, many Klan members saw no contradictions in belonging to the KKK and many other civic organizations, often serving as official officers. In fact, Klan leaders also established the East Bay Club as a parallel civic offshoot of their local order. Leon Francis, president of the East Bay Club, was the one open Klan member who ran for school board in 1923, although he fared rather poorly, receiving just 4,701 votes out of the total 38,988 cast in his precinct.[127] Despite being with some opposition, they also seem to have been accepted by many community members, even participating in some major public events. For instance, when their permit to parade in Oakland was revoked in 1924, they simply joined the Fourth of July parade in neighboring Richmond. A crowd of some fifty thousand witnessed the men and women of the KKK march by, dressed in their full regalia.[128]

The Klan's public presence in Oakland began to fade in 1925—due both to conflicts with the Atlanta-based national organization and to legal pressure from then district attorney Earl Warren—many of the leaders of the Oakland KKK remained politically active in the years to come. Moreover, the racial and ethnic enmity represented by the Klan continued to ripple throughout the city before and after their demise. Of course, racial mistrust was hardly manufactured solely by the Klan.

In the late nineteenth and early twentieth centuries, Chinese immigrants experienced rounds of vituperative attacks as nativist fury unleashed itself in states along the Pacific coast. One example of white resentment erupted between Oakland butcher shops in 1919 and 1920, as white union butchers bitterly vented their frustrations on the pages of the *Union Labor Record* about the low prices charged by Chinese butcher shops. Several issues of the *Labor Record* published vicious caricatures of the "Chinese threat," often depicting the "Oriental Menace" as inhuman and monstrous. One illustration portrayed an oversized "Oriental" hand sprouting long, sharp fingernails that raked across white Oakland merchants. The paper complained about the "Dark Methods" employed by Chinese butchers, which included "low wages," "long hours," and "inferior products."[129] Some of the animus was directed at local white proprietors of markets who sold "Oriental handled meat." The ongoing clashes continued throughout the early and mid-1920s, at least as represented by the pages of the union newspaper.[130] Racial tensions did not emerge solely around low prices in the marketplace.

In 1925, a Chinese mission was established in the Fruitvale neighborhood of East Oakland—the institution served as a home for orphaned Chinese American girls. Approximately eighteen of these girls attended the local Oakland public schools. In September 1926, parents of white children in John Swett Elementary, one of the schools serving East Oakland, erupted in protest. During the previous academic year, white and Chinese students in the school had been separated in different classrooms, but, due to overcrowding, the district opted to blend children into integrated rooms for the new school year. Distressed by this development, members of the Beulah Summit Improvement Club in East Oakland called an urgent meeting, and after some anxious discussion, the assembled parents voted to take their children out of school until the school district returned the Chinese American girls to separate classrooms. The next morning, approximately seventy-five children (out of a total enrollment of 110) remained at home; their parents proclaimed that they were "on strike." Superintendent Hunter, they insisted, had promised that their children would never be mixed into the same classrooms as Chinese students.[131]

Declaring that there was "no racial segregation in any Oakland school," Hunter contended that he never promised to separate the students into different classrooms on a permanent basis. He urged the parents to send their children back to school, but the strike continued into October, and the school board received protests from the United Parlor, Native Sons of the Golden State, an organization of Chinese American citizens. The United Parlor labeled the segregation "humiliating," and its executive secretary sent a letter to the school board asserting that "the movement for the segregation of children of Chinese descent into a separate school is born solely of an un-American race prejudice." Most of the girls of Chinese descent were American citizens, he said, and "to subject them to segregation would have a tendency to engender in them a feeling of resentment inimical to . . . their development into good American citizens."[132]

At the same time, the parents of the Beulah Summit Improvement Club would not back down. They also voted to petition the school board for a separate Oakland "Oriental School" and to suggest to the board that "all Chinese students in other schools would be compelled to attend this school." The strike was called off only after Hunter quietly agreed that any families of the "striking children" who so desired could have their children transferred to other schools. Though they accepted the agreement, members of the Beluah Summit group said they were determined to agitate for the creation of completely separate schools for Chinese and white students in the future. Although the papers announced that the "race war" was over, it was clear that some of the white parents had not given up the fight.[133]

Oakland had included racial covenants in its municipal plans as early as 1909. When new housing developments sprung up in the expanding sections of the city during the 1910s and 1920s, real estate brochures offered guarantees to prospective buyers, stating, for instance, that "no member of the African or Asiatic Races will be permitted to hold title or rental."[134] These restrictions were not tested often, but when they were, white neighbors attempted to enforce them through violence or other means. In 1924, when Sidney Deering, an African American restaurant owner, purchased a home in Piedmont, an exclusive area within Oakland, protesters smashed windows of the house, and the city quickly presented Deering with an ultimatum: sell the home to the city for $8,000 or it would start condemnation proceedings on the property.[135] One black newspaper publisher recalled other examples of black homebuyers in the early 1920s. In one case, he said, "the white people wanted to kill him because he moved into a white district. So we worked for him to watch over him for a period of twenty-four hours for about three or four months. After then things kind of quieted down." Nevertheless, the threats served their purpose. In 1930, African Americans accounted for 2.6 percent of the population of Oakland, but in East Oakland, it was less than 0.7 percent.[136] The housing segregation of the early decades of the century created the school segregation of the middle decades of the century, as more and more minority families moved to Oakland during the second shipyard boom of World War II.

INSTRUCTION AND LEADERSHIP

The day-to-day routines of Progressive Era teachers and administrators have been difficult to document through traditional historical sources. Therefore, many studies of urban education have tended to view all early twentieth-century district administrators in the same light: they were top-down autocrats who issued executive fiats and were disconnected from classrooms and instructional practices. In recent decades, education policy researchers have attributed many of the current problems in large school districts to the traditional hierarchical nature of the Progressive Era school system, with its specialization of tasks, line authority, and complex organizational structure. However, it is possible that not all progressive school districts conformed to these latter-day assumptions. In fact, evidence from Oakland complicates the standard view of administrative practices. Thanks to a 1922 thesis written by Einar Jacobsen, an Oakland administrator, we have an insider's depiction of district practices from the 1921–22 school year. Jacobsen documented all the visits made to individual schools in the district during the year by central office staff, including Hunter, his two deputy superintendents (Virgil Dickson and Lloyd Barzee), and his two assistant superintendents (E. Morris Cox and Lewis B. Avery).

Hunter visited all fifty-one of the Oakland schools at least once during the year and often more (sometimes up to eight separate trips), amounting to a total of 146 school visits. He generally spent about an hour in each school and his meetings with individual teachers averaged roughly twenty-two minutes. By Jacobsen's estimation, Hunter conducted some 659 separate face-to-face interactions during the year. The large numbers of schools meant that the assistant and deputy superintendents were just as busy, although they each had responsibility for a smaller subset of schools. Assistant superintendent Cox offers a representative example. He made 116 school visits, met with a total of 492 personnel (principals and teachers), and spent a total of 143.75 hours in the schools for the year. This would have meant that each Oakland administrator spent roughly three to four hours each week visiting schools. To put that in perspective, each leader devoted a full month of their working year inside schools and classrooms.[137]

Beyond simple time logged in schools, the content and quality of the interactions between teachers and administrators was what truly mattered. Jacobsen reported that the visits of 1921–22 focused specifically on the new districtwide curricular materials being used that year. Superintendents gave each teacher an opportunity to "express freely" her opinion of the new curriculum and to describe whether the new instructional materials worked successfully with her students. Jacobsen acknowledged that it was hard to measure the results of these kinds of personal contacts.[138] Nevertheless, the fact that administrators spent such a significant amount of time in schools and classrooms challenges preconceptions about the history of educational leadership. More specifically, it forces researchers to question whether progressive district administrators were always patently uninterested in instruction and generally far removed from classrooms. Certainly, curricular and instructional changes occupied the minds of both teachers and administrators throughout the era.

Oakland administrators tended to report that their curricular objectives were swiftly being realized through the revision program and via other initiatives designed to help socialize instruction. However, some classroom teachers voiced a much more nuanced view. One long-time practitioner who vividly articulated the challenges of making substantial instructional change was

Ida Vandergaw, a veteran supervisor of the primary grades and the instructor who had initiated the district's ungraded classrooms in the 1890s. "Many of us in the Oakland Schools, the majority," she said in 1926, "have acquainted ourselves with the theories underlying modern progressive educational ideals and methods." In an indication that she was thoroughly fluent in the rhetoric of progressivism, she continued, "we admit that we should train children for effective happy living in a democracy; we agree that each child should be given that which meets individual needs. We have been told that to secure our objective there must be on the part of the student whole-hearted, purposeful activity in a social situation." Vandergaw continued: "But, and here's the rub, how shall we secure this inner urge that 'defines the end, guides pursuit, and supplies the drive?' How shall we secure the maximum amount of 'pupil participation in purposes, plans, profits, processes?' How shall we develop leadership, and the ideals of service? How shall children's interests be made the basis for activities of large educational value? With the rest of the progressive educational world we know the theory, but we are not sure of the technique [or] method."[139]

It is refreshing to find, amid the rhetoric of measurement, of efficiency, and of swift success, a glimpse of honest contemplation. While superintendents like Hunter may have exuded confidence about the rapid and robust implementation of innovation, the practitioners working with these instructional reforms remind us that making change at the classroom level was no straightforward task. Hunter may have hoped to fill his classrooms with the best progressive ideas, but as Vandergaw demonstrates, grand curricular notions proved much more difficult to put in place than organizational charts, intelligence tests, or ability groups. Nevertheless, she tried.

Vandergaw's desire to formulate practical instructional methods for implementing progressive ideas ultimately expressed itself through an inclusive, district-wide approach to tackling this challenge. Working with the district's professional librarian, she vowed to "capitalize on the experience of the teaching force." She asked teachers "who had thoughtfully experimented with the project method" (note the modifier, "thoughtfully") to write up accounts of their successes with students. She ultimately collected over one hundred and fifty written descriptions of the work teachers had done with students from kindergarten through high school, and, along with photographs taken of different phases of student projects, the examples were displayed in the district's professional library.[140]

By 1927, Hunter was itching for new career challenges, first considering the presidency of the University of Nebraska and then the position of chancellor of the University of Denver, a post he was offered and accepted in 1928. Hunter wrote to a friend expressing how difficult had been the decision to leave Oakland just "when every item of the program was as completely in hand as is now the case."[141] Hunter remained active in the NEA for several years, and he hoped to collaborate on teacher training with district administrators in Denver, but his influence in elementary and secondary educational issues waned, especially as the Great Depression began to absorb much of his energy and attention at the university.

On Hunter's departure, the Oakland school board elected Assistant Superintendent Willard Givens as the new superintendent, a position he kept until 1935. Givens was a natural choice. By 1929, he had developed an organizational chart for the district that was even more elaborate than Hunter's.[142]

———

Oakland is an ideal school district for exploring the different strains of educational progressivism that intertwined themselves in the city schools during the era. The city offers evidence of how a remarkably wide variety of plans influenced the approaches that district progressives used to manage schools, revise curricula, and develop new instructional practices. Superintendent Hunter demonstrated a strong predilection for adopting as many new reforms as possible, including the use of intelligence tests to classify children and the adoption of new curricular methods intended to engage students in active learning by employing the social recitation, project method, or role playing of historical events. Hunter viewed all of these as appropriate measures urgently required to meet the needs of the child and adapt schooling to fit the academic abilities of different types of students. In so doing, Oakland leaders attempted to blend different visions of progressivism in ways that confound some previous analytic perspectives.

Taking a slightly longer view of Oakland—looking at its development from the 1890s through the 1920s—also demonstrates that the district employed a variety of strategies for educating different kinds of children, especially those children who had difficulty learning or keeping up with their grades. Efforts to differentiate children had begun in the 1890s and were not necessarily solely the product of the scientific management of the 1910s but rather of deeper tendencies to identify the sources of student failure. These investigations led to experimentation with various types of curricular tracks, especially at the high school level. In general, the practices that developed in relation to conceptions of differentiation were the product of a slow evolution of ideas and institutions.

Perhaps more importantly, from the 1890s into the 1910s teachers collected solid evidence demonstrating that that many children were not falling behind because of lack of intellectual ability but often due, instead, to a whole range of other reasons that included poverty, illness, prolonged absence from school, problems at home, and so forth. The work with students in the ungraded classrooms opened a window of opportunity for pursuing other explanations of low student achievement, but that window slammed shut once Hunter and Dickson began their tenure. Thereafter, all efforts in Oakland must ultimately be viewed in light of the kinds of explicit strategies used by leaders like Dickson, who sought to deliberately flip notions of democratic education. After 1917, school practices designed to meet the needs of students' futures were determined by the scores of intelligence tests and decisions about future career prospects that were made early in a pupil's academic life.

Yet Oakland also yields evidence that muddies the waters of easy interpretation. Most notably, curriculum supervisors such as William Cooper and Ida Vandergaw revealed a remarkable capacity to comprehend the inherent complexities of progressive practice and found inventive ways to deploy that understanding. Vandergaw's work with multiple teachers from numerous schools in developing practical approaches to the project method was motivated not by a mandate from the central office. Rather, it was an example of the collaborative work possible among teachers and knowledgeable supervisors as they explored the potential for brand new instructional approaches—and this just a few years after Kilpatrick had first proposed the idea. Moreover, the great deal of time that Hunter and his deputy and assistant superintendents spent in schools disrupts standard notions of administrative obliviousness to classroom concerns, indicating a deeper awareness of instructional practices and more familiarity with the day-to-day concerns of teachers and principals than is usually imagined. That said, the exact nature of those discussions is difficult to know with certainty.

Despite attention to enhanced educational practices, the lines of innovation were constrained by the segregation, ethnocentrism, and racism prevalent in the Oakland community. It is clear that the children living in the "thickly settled" neighborhoods, as Hunter described them, were given a narrower set of choices than were other students. Those sections of the city were identified as suitable locations for Americanization and vocational education. The alignment of political power that cleared the way for the reorganization of the district administrative structure also allowed Hunter to wield sufficient power to make decisions about the futures of thousands of students. Reforms designed to democratize and Americanize the district's students (and parents) were tightly linked to the efforts of the Oakland downtown business community to control the radicalism of the population, combat the political machine, and consolidate its power.

Was the kind of power that Hunter was able to grasp in Oakland anomalous, or can it be found in other districts as well? What about those districts like Denver that have been seen as alternatives to strong central control?

4

PIONEERING PRACTICE IN THE PUBLIC
SCHOOLS OF DENVER, COLORADO

The Progressive Era was, among other things, an age of imitation. Reformers, educators, and municipal leaders looked to other cities and countries
for fresh examples of governance and design. In 1911, Frederic C. Howe—
the Cleveland reformer who saw cities as the hope of democracy—departed
on a two-and-a-half-month tour to study the architectural designs and city
management of thirty European cities. Accompanying him on this European
expedition was a group of businessmen and mayors, among them Denver's
Mayor Robert Speer and the muckraker Lincoln Steffens. Speer learned
more than any of the other attendees, Steffens reported, for he looked at the
cities of Europe "like a painter seeing a paintable landscape" and returned to
Denver armed with private insight and public plans.[1]

Speer was not only Denver's mayor but he was also boss of the city's powerful political machine. Colorado's energetic progressive reformers cast him
as a villain and worked for years to unseat him, so it is surprising to learn
that Steffens praised Speer as an example of a progressive mayor who "set his
city going in the right direction." This unlikely pair makes more sense when
placed in the turbid context of Progressive Era urban politics. Although
Speer was a political boss, most scholars agree that Speer had a "deep sense
of civic patriotism." His philosophy of government was to be "progressive
along conservative lines" and to push for improvement at the lowest possible
cost.[2] One method for doing so was to "borrow freely" the reforms instituted
in other cities.[3] Speer opted to copy a grand "city beautiful" plan, bringing in
an urban planner from St. Louis to redesign the city by adding new parks and
wide boulevards. Between 1904 and 1912, Speer more than doubled the acre-
age of Denver's parks, many of which abutted school grounds. Where some
citizens saw new buildings, broad thoroughfares, and expanses of green, others saw evidence of Boss Speer's graft and favoritism.[4] In other words, Denver serves as an idea progressive city for study.

For decades, boosters, builders, and businessmen alike operated as Denver's civic soothsayers predicted the city's national rise. In the 1870s, for example, William Gilpin preordained Denver as the nation's future greatest city due to its "pre-eminently cosmopolitan" geographic position. Denver was the place where "the vast arena of the Pacific" would meet the Atlantic world as "the zodiac of nations closes its circle." Others may have been less hyperbolic in their praise, but the early twentieth century witnessed multiple statements of faith that Denver would assume a leadership role in the increasingly urban West.[5]

Educational writers, such as A. E. Winship of the *Journal of Education*, also acted as boosters of specific city school systems and publicists of progressive innovations. Highlighting Denver's dominant role in the Rocky Mountain region in 1926, Winship described Denver as an example of progressivism with a pioneer spirit. It escaped both "the conventionality of the traditional East" and the "individuality" of the West. Most impressive was Denver's course of study, constructed through a district-wide curriculum revision program; Winship called it a "scientific masterpiece," "the most complete, the most democratically constructed, the best balanced, and the most sane of any that has been created."[6]

If Oakland gained national recognition for its testing and classification practices in the 1920s, Denver captured attention for a decidedly different version of progressive reform. Arguing that classroom teachers must be more than mere "mechanics," Superintendent Jesse Newlon and his deputy A. L. Threlkeld developed a comprehensive curriculum revision program that sought "to secure the cooperation of the teachers in making the courses of study which they are to teach."[7] Denver was not the only district that utilized teachers in the curriculum revision process, but it was one of the first to do so on a broad scale and to develop a permanent institutional structure that ensured the continued active participation of teachers in ongoing curriculum development.[8] Denver's success in engaging teachers in the revision process and in leveraging the resulting teacher expertise has been touted as a rare case of system-wide change.[9] Denver's purportedly less autocratic approach has served as an alternative to districts viewed as rigidly authoritarian.[10] But what did a "democratically constructed" curriculum mean in practice and did it differ dramatically from a course of study that was more traditionally designed? Did members of the school system craft a district-wide curriculum that avoided the harsher dimensions of Americanization and IQ testing, all the while promoting the inclusion of students in classroom activities? How was democratic education defined in Denver? Although the case of Denver provides a perspective on Progressive Era change different from that of

Oakland, evidence from Denver also reveals that the two school systems bore some striking resemblances in the ways that school leaders conceptualized change, interacted with the national template of reform, and envisioned the role of the school district.

Given its appreciation for democratic leadership, was Denver somehow inoculated against the more extreme forms of social efficiency? From the 1890s through the 1910s, Denver experienced municipal reform, battles over of corruption, and counterreactions to reforms—often simultaneously—and some of the side effects spilled over into school politics. Denver offers a particularly interesting example of how using the additional perspective of municipal groups helps us better understand the strange bedfellows and surprising outcomes of the era. Moreover, it shows how school leaders could benefit by the previous groundwork carried out by earlier civic coalitions.

DESPOTISM WITH A GLOVED HAND

Denver began as not much more than a small mining camp in 1858 but quickly blossomed into a bustling frontier town due to the Pike's Peak Gold Rush. Its first public school was constructed in 1873, and much initial development of the Denver school system was managed by its curmudgeonly superintendent, Aaron Gove, who held office for thirty years and belonged to a species of superintendent soon to be extinct—the Victorian system builder—at a time when a sole individual could almost single-handedly preside over a full district.

Gove, a Civil War veteran, was born and raised in New England and became Denver superintendent in 1874, retaining the post for a full thirty years.[11] He supervised the growth of the Denver schools from what he called a "primitive" system of two buildings, twenty-five teachers, and a thousand students into a comparatively vast urban district, housing twenty schools, 254 teachers, and over twelve thousand students by the turn of the century. Due as much to his longevity and experience as to his sharp tongue, Gove achieved a national repute, regularly attending NEA meetings, and he was once considered as a serious candidate for the New York City superintendency.[12]

Gove characterized himself as a practical man who put stock in the "weight of experience, rather than of theory." His convictions about the role of the superintendent and the duties of teachers at times set him at odds with his contemporaries, especially those who emphasized the pedagogical dimension of school leadership. For example, in the 1890 NEA session on the leadership duties of superintendents of city school systems (discussed in chap. 1), Gove dismissed the notion that the superintendent should be primarily an educator, scolding the superintendent of Providence, Rhode Island, for suggesting that the function of the superintendent should be confined to "strictly pedagogical" responsibilities. "As every Western man can realize," Gove retorted with Rocky Mountain bravado, the "direct duties" of a superintendent properly included the oversight of school taxes, schoolhouse construction, and relations of the administration to the industrial and commercial communities.[13]

Gove was untroubled by the danger of the superintendent functioning as a businessman. Such a danger might be true in "the old cities of New England," he needled his eastern colleagues, "further west another statement seems to me nearer truth: The personal and public danger with the superintendent is that he be incompetent intelligently to participate in the business affairs of the corporation, whose executive officer he is or should be."[14] He thus foreshadowed a faith in business and efficiency that would come to characterize many school leaders as the century unfolded. Gove had cozy relations with his board members, many of who were business leaders and, like Gove, members of other civic organizations, such as the Freemasons, the Denver Athletic Club, and the State Historical and Natural History Society.[15] In addition to demonstrating that business values found their way into schools well before the 1910s, Gove's views also disrupt the popular nostalgic notion that nineteenth-century educators focused exclusively on academic content.

When Gove discussed pedagogy, he took a no-nonsense approach to emphasizing the essentials. Gove expected his teachers to demonstrate the same kind of "severe application to tasks" that he required of students, and his ideas on authority and pedagogy were closely related to his views on democracy.[16] In one infamous 1904 address to the NEA, Gove bristled at the efforts to form a teachers union and targeted Margaret Haley, president of the National Federation of Teachers. Haley wanted schools to stimulate citizens' civic responsibility, and she challenged school districts to give teachers greater autonomy. Haley simultaneously opposed the creep of commercialism and the "industrial ideal," as she labeled social efficiency, into the schools. "Freedom of activity directed by freed intelligence is the ideal of democracy," she proclaimed.[17] Revolted by such talk, Gove countered that teachers should be given little independence in carrying out their assigned duties. Why should they? After all, he said, teaching was an activity to be directed from above, comparable to "the turning out of work by an industrial establishment."[18]

Gove warned of a "dangerous sentiment" growing throughout the country: the belief that the public school system should be a democratic institution. "This is a false conception of true democracy," he exclaimed, articulating the same cautions about flawed definitions of democracy as those made by Columbia University's Nicholas Murray Butler around the same time (indeed, it was Butler who corresponded with Gove about the New York superintendency position). The local boards of education, not the teachers, asserted Gove, were the representative bodies of democracy; they made the laws and took responsibility for their actions. Gove's conception of urban educational leadership was of the superintendent as autocrat; in fact, in Denver he rarely gave his administrative subordinates the opportunity to speak. Such leadership need not be overbearing, Gove believed; after all, he once remarked, the superintendent's "despotism can be wielded with a gloved hand."[19]

Gove retired in 1904, bequeathing an organization that had been modeled on his own idiosyncratic philosophy of educational autocracy and a system that had dramatically expanded beyond a handful of buildings and teachers. After a 1904 district consolidation, Denver's school population jumped again, and Gove's Victorian school system—one in which little responsibility was delegated to teachers or even to other administrators—began to sag under the weight of multiple new demands. By 1910, with an enrollment of forty thousand (up from the twelve thousand when Gove had departed) and under the direction of Charles Chadsey, the Denver school system made a concerted break with its educational past and sprouted an array of new departments and programs that district leaders began to describe as "modern" and "progressive."[20]

DYNAMIC TO THE CORE: THE DENVER SYSTEM, 1907–12

"What are the specific forms through which the city school of today differs from the mechanically perfect yet lamentably rigid school system of the past?" Superintendent Chadsey asked his Denver audience in 1911.[21] At the same time that Mayor Speer transplanted European design ideas into Denver, Chadsey, school superintendent from 1907 to 1912, introduced innovations he had collected at national educational conferences. Chadsey was able to rattle off a mental checklist of the types of reforms that elevated the modern school system above its obsolete ancestor: better equipment, advances in architectural construction, more intelligently organized courses of study, progress in curriculum and textbook development, enhanced professional preparation of teachers, the "elimination of politics," improved business and educational administration, and a small school board with an educational expert as superintendent.[22]

Chadsey's superintendency in Denver illustrates a turning point toward "modern" schooling apparent in Oakland around the same time. If the threshold moment of the transition toward "progressive" practices came in Oakland around 1913, evidence of a shift in reform discourse emerged in Denver around 1910 or 1911. An 1892 graduate of Stanford University who received a PhD from Teachers College in 1897, Chadsey's background yielded him a broad national knowledge base and the kind of professional connections that proved invaluable for his work at the local level.[23] In fact, after heading the Denver system, Chadsey went on to fill highly prized superintendent posts in Detroit and then Chicago. In his history of the Detroit Public Schools, Jeffrey Mirel depicts Chadsey as the "very model of a modern urban superintendent."[24] Denver was Chadsey's first superintendency and it was here that he worked out some of his foundational ideas on a system-wide scale.

Beyond a Multiple of Individual Schools

Perhaps more so than many of his fellow superintendents, Chadsey seemed to anticipate the dramatic effects that new social conditions would have on the character of American education.[25] He marveled, for example, at the increasing complexity of the nation's public school systems, a shift that would require novel responses. In previous decades, said Chadsey, no one questioned that the role of the elementary school was simple and well defined and that its aim should be to provide training in the "so-called fundamentals of learning." All other activities and preparations for life were previously met outside of the public school system. But school leaders had begun to recognize, he said in 1910, that "the duty of the school [was] to provide some form of suitable training for almost every conceivable kind of activity."[26]

Chadsey's conception of the school district as a "system" emerged out of this expansion of scope and responsibilities. "Originally," Chadsey reflected, "the city school system was merely a multiple of individual schools" and administration of "whatever school system existed was very largely a matter of routine business and disciplinary control." The development of the "modern school system," said Chadsey, had occurred alongside "the general industrial expansion of the country and the increasing complexity of business and social life." This modern school system, he said, "widens yearly its sphere of usefulness and attempts courageously the solution of every problem"—a perfect encapsulation of what many progressive leaders had been calling for.[27] During his first few years as superintendent, Chadsey embodied the optimism characteristic of district progressives, introducing the types of innovations into the system that he felt addressed modern problems. In additional to those already mentioned, he hired medical inspectors and nurses, built new schools with more spacious classrooms, introduced manual training into the schools, and created special schools for children of differing abilities.[28]

Chadsey acknowledged that the administration of such a system was no longer a simple matter. Indeed, a typical school system was rapidly becoming an organization "difficult to describe or even to appreciate."[29] The proliferation of programs during his tenure presented numerous management challenges and caught many practitioners off guard. Despite his interest in modernization, Chadsey was not emboldened to innovate capriciously—quite the opposite. "A large city school system cannot, in the very nature of the case, afford to be a pioneer in the matter of radical experiments," he wrote in 1910. Rather, the big urban school district was compelled to observe developments in other systems and "to adopt only those things which offer a reasonable promise" of improving the conditions they displaced.[30]

Adjusting the System to the Students

One of the first challenges Chadsey confronted in responding to students' "needs and demands" was that of students who had fallen academically behind and therefore were overage for their grade level. Citing the two works that had recently raised overageness as a national problem—Leonard Ayres's *Laggards in Our Schools* (1909) and E. L. Thorndike's *Elimination of Pupils from School* (1908)—Chadsey explained in his own 1909 annual report that student failure was a problem "for every school system in the country." Compulsory education, he said, had added "an element which was not formerly found in the schools": students who did not "respond to the ordinary school impetus," usually meaning, again, children from immigrant families, minority families, or families whose members had not previously attended school. Chadsey attributed these variations in school experiences to the tremendous differences found in Denver's urban homes.[31]

Chadsey developed several strategies for attacking and alleviating wide variations in achievement. In the early phase of his superintendency, he urged an approach somewhat similar to that offered by a few of his contemporaries elsewhere, including Ida Vandergaw, in Oakland, by designing programs to help lagging students return to their grade level. Chadsey felt that student failure was not necessarily due to lack of intellectual capacity. "Experiments in other cities," he explained (without citing specific examples), "have shown that a large percentage of these pupils can, under such special conditions, make more than normal progress."[32] Given that up to one-third of students in urban systems were below grade level, this was no small challenge.

In 1910, Chadsey's central office staff conducted its own citywide study of student failure and set up special classes for educating children found to be academically behind. In these schools the customary curricular requirements were set aside, Chadsey explained, and he directed each teacher "to study the individuality of the pupils under his charge and to determine, if possible, the reasons why such children are retarded." If the primary problem was that the pupil was simply deficient in knowledge of a specific subject like arithmetic, the student would be placed with other pupils experiencing similar difficulties. Special attention was then given to the student's work in order "to strengthen his powers so as to enable him to reenter into the work of the grade composed of children more nearly his age." Thus, many students who fell behind because of inability to attend school regularly or to illness or other "environmental" difficulties were given special tutoring and specific educational opportunities until they could return to their grade—not an unimpressive accomplishment, especially as it embodied what so many progressives hoped to do: fit the school to the children.[33]

In sum, rather than simply responding to failure with intensified student classification, Chadsey and his teachers developed a number of district-wide strategies through which "the child of any environment, heredity, aptitude, or limitation may secure that which is for him the most effective training." It is essential to put Denver's efforts at returning students to grade level in perspective. Unlike many educators of the era—G. Stanley Hall and H. H. Goddard, for instance—who estimated that there remained large numbers of "undiagnosed retarded" students in every city, Chadsey felt that there was only a "small number [in Denver] who have fallen behind on account of mental inefficiency."[34]

In 1912, Chadsey moved to the superintendency in Detroit; his successor, William Smiley, was a Massachusetts native, who, as a student at Harvard College, had been befriended by President Charles Eliot. Smiley had arrived in Denver in 1882 and taught Latin and Greek at Denver's East High School; Aaron Gove appointed him as the high school's principal in 1892. Any plans Smiley might have had for the school district were interrupted, however, when the city of Denver became embroiled in fiscal and political controversy.[35]

PEDAGOGY AND POLITICS, 1912–20

The political struggles that ensued in Denver between, roughly, 1910 and 1916 initially had little to do with the schools but ultimately had significant, if serendipitous, consequences for the district in the decades that followed. Chadsey's superintendency had overlapped with a time of intense political activity of Denver's municipal reformers, in part due to Mayor Speer's dominating control of the city. Speer used many of the standard boss's strategies to retain power: manipulation of elections, close relationships with public-service corporations, and cooperation between law enforcement and the establishments of gambling, saloons, and prostitution. Reform efforts—some focused on vice, others on fiscal corruption—coalesced around the need for Speer's ouster. For years, the mayor and his many backers in the broader business community were able to outmaneuver groups bent on civic cleansing, even as Speer helped the Denver Tramway Company and the Denver Gas and Electric Company secure new twenty-year franchises in 1906.

Not until the municipal elections of 1910 did reformers gain any traction against Speer, this time through victories of their Citizens Party candidates. The victors announced that a commission government would be their next goal. The commission plan was still receiving grand accolades, and many cities sought to adopt it quickly. In fact, even though the Denver Chamber of Commerce was split over whether to support the plan, its own special committee recommended that if Denver wanted to assume its proper destiny as the great inland metropolis, then "nothing will contribute more immediately and conspicuously than the adoption of this thoroughly modern, efficient, business-like and popular plan of government."[36] For his part, Speer argued that the commission plan was antithetical to the kinds of efficient municipal governments that made the cities of Europe—those he had recently toured with Howe and Steffens—the "best governed" in the world.[37]

Despite strong opposition to the commission plan, reformers achieved their goal when voters approved a commission charter in February 1913. The initial elections for the five commissioner positions yielded men with both professional and political experience, a potentially vibrant mix of petit bourgeoisie, experienced civil servants, and representatives of the large business community. This was just the kind of array of talent that many commission reformers often hoped for: the commissioner of property was a former print shop proprietor; of public safety, a former sheriff; of finance, an investment broker; of public health and welfare, a physician who was formerly a public health officer; and of public works, the former city engineer.[38]

Members of the elite business community who had backed Speer were not ready to capitulate, however, and they formed the Colorado Taxpayers Protective League after the adoption of the new charter. Administrative problems with the new governing commissioners, however, popped up immediately without any help from the league. Despite the wealth of collective experience the new commissioners had, none had run the kind of government agencies over which they now had authority. And, as with many new commissions of the era, there was little in the way of guidance or direction, and no particular central policy to follow; all of this allowed for a leadership vacuum to appear. In the meantime, the Taxpayers Protective League continually badgered the beleaguered commissioners; as one scholar put it: "They constantly peered over the shoulders of the commissioners, tried to dictate budgeting policies, and generally harassed the commissioner to the point of distraction."[39]

Municipal expenses, rather than taking the expected drop, skyrocketed. The increased expense was due, in part, to the five commissioner's individual hiring practices and to their lack of coordination. Within a year of the establishment of the new Denver Commission, the Taxpayers Protective League invited the Bureau of Municipal Research of New York, the organization that William H. Allen had cofounded, to survey and assess Denver's finances, the conditions of each of the five departments, and the Commission Charter itself.[40] Even though the bureau had written favorably of the plan just two years earlier, their survey pointed out multiple new deficiencies.[41] Before long, Denver power brokers had arranged for a new charter, and in 1916, the city reverted to the strong-mayor form of municipal governance. As the *Denver Times* put it: "The return of Mr. Speer may mean 'one man' power, but that is better than no-man power."[42]

The schools did not escape the related turmoil unscathed. The year 1915 was particularly turbulent. In January 1915, Benjamin Hilliard, a member of the school board who was about to launch a successful campaign to enter the U.S. Congress, raised concerns about the efficiency of the school system. "The large cities and all lesser municipalities are officered by too many people and the systems are honeycombed with useless and unnecessary employees, Hilliard asserted.[43] Amid continued fiscal concern, the school board forced Smiley to resign, and in June 1915, Hilliard orchestrated the firing of 150 teachers from the system, an episode that one teacher later remembered as "the awful orgy" during which time "the entire school system was wrecked."[44]

Once again, Colorado Taxpayers Protective League saw an opportunity to directly influence public affairs. Pleased with the results of the Municipal Bureau of Research survey, the league demanded a similar investigation of the school system. That said, the precise origin of the survey request is somewhat unclear. Its origin has been traced to both the board and the Taxpayers Protective League, and Denver newspapers attributed the commissioning of the survey to the league. Nevertheless, the league and the school board eventually split the cost of the survey.[45]

Good Management and Modern Plumbing

The resulting survey of the Denver Public Schools was of the same genre as Cubberley's administrative study of Oakland, but the scope of the evaluation was much more comprehensive and thus more akin to the recent survey by Municipal Research Bureau or that conducted by Cubberley of Portland in 1913. As published in 1916, the Denver survey exceeded five hundred pages and examined nearly every element of the school system. The survey was headed by the University of Chicago's Franklin Bobbitt, best known at the time for his work on curriculum construction and his increasing alignment with social efficiency measures. Bobbitt enlisted other members of the "educational elite" to assist, including Lewis Terman of Stanford University and Charles Judd of the University of Chicago, among several others. Few aspects of the system escaped their attention.[46]

The Denver survey demonstrated the expansive reach of progressive reformers and their broad agreement about the methods districts should use to achieve system-wide improvement in areas such as curriculum, instruction, and administrative organization. Bobbitt and Judd both expressed grave concerns about the quality of Denver's curriculum and instructional practices. "The pupils are underworked, and the teachers are overworked," complained Bobbitt, voicing an almost timeless educational concern. Sounding every bit the pedagogical progressive, Bobbitt suggested that the "burden of effort" should be shifted from the teacher to the student to make learning more self-directed. Education, he said, should be made "experimental instead of being merely fact-learning."[47]

Bobbitt was nevertheless an administrator at heart. In his section on the management of the Denver schools, Bobbitt employed charts comparing the similarities between a manufacturing corporation and a "school corporation" that both employed twelve hundred people. Bobbitt recommended that Denver school leaders reorganize the district using a corporate structure as their model. "The people of the district need to understand," he wrote, "that there is not one set of principles of business management applicable to a business corporation and another different set applicable to the school corporation." Both were subject to the same laws, he said: "What brings success to the one will bring success to the other."[48]

If the survey as a whole served as an example of Progressive Era comprehensiveness, Terman's report on buildings and medical inspection illustrated the compulsive attention to detail that often characterized surveys of the time. Terman fastidiously cataloged his concerns about the condition of Denver schools: most schoolrooms were poorly lit; the heating systems were "primitive," the ventilation systems carried "dusty and parched" air into the classrooms; and many schools were surrounded by playgrounds "hardly wider than an alley." Terman was also surprised to find "that the medieval feather duster still holds sway in some of the school buildings of a progressive city," and he was disgusted to discover that bathrooms were "usually dark, often cold, and sometimes foul-smelling."[49]

Students and teachers who experienced the daily indignities of inadequate and unsanitary facilities no doubt welcomed these publicly reported observations. Terman's sharp rhetoric could be quite effective, whether turned on adversaries, on children who performed poorly on intelligence tests, or on unappealing school conditions. It is useful to remember that the social reformist streak in his version of scientism often yielded significant tangible benefits for educators and students alike.

The survey also instigated a clash between national visions and local politics. Although the editors of the *Elementary School Journal* praised the published version of the survey, two members of the school board—Ben B. Jones and Clarkson N. Guyer—strongly opposed the recommendations.[50] Especially perturbed by Bobbitt's outline for administrative reorganization, Jones and Guyer balked at an externally produced vision of school reform, especially given that the plan would also remove some of their power and authority. Bobbitt's plan, they argued, was "revolutionary" for it turned the management of the schools over to an "outsider" in the person of the super-intendent and called for "too great a centralization of power in the hands of one man." Consequently, they asserted, the reforms were "undemocratic."[51] Bobbitt attempted to address the criticisms of the survey, but board members became deadlocked. Ultimately, the board contacted Ellwood Cubberley as a kind of external mediator for resolving the standoff. Despite their other disagreements, the board apparently could agree that Cubberley would pro-vide an "unbiased" review of the recommendations.

Cubberley steadfastly supported the recommendations of the survey team. The plan was not "revolutionary," Cubberley carefully explained to Denver leaders; rather, it was "evolutionary," for it followed "the best lines of evolution in city school control" and, he added, it had already been "adopted by a number of our more progressive cities." Neither was the plan undem-ocratic. "If it is," he chided the stalwart board members, "we need to get a new conception of democracy as speedily as possible. Democracy ought to mean the greatest good for the greatest number" and should not necessar-ily mean that "many persons should work at any one problem." The superin-tendent was the proper person to focus on school matters and should by no means be considered an "outsider." Such a notion was harmfully misleading. The correct view, Cubberley asserted, was one that held that the superinten-dent should be of "national rather than a local character," an argument he also pushed in Oakland and elsewhere. Schools should no longer be seen as a "local industry," because education was far grander than the interests of any single town or city. In this regard, city school systems were the "experimental stations" of the larger educational movement.[52]

Cubberley nominally approved Bobbitt's administrative reorganization plan, and he included a visual representation of what he believed Denver's district organizational structure would have looked like as it existed in 1913.

This older form of organization (as depicted in fig. 4.1) was "seriously defective," Cubberley said, administration was inefficient, any progress was undoubtedly slow, and the system lacked any "authority to remedy bad conditions." One of the main flaws was the role played by the six school board committees, which Cubberley described as: "virtually half a dozen different school boards, each working more or less independently at parts of the educational problem, each exercising both legislative and executive functions, and each attempting many things which it is not only foolish for a . . . lay board to attempt, but things which lay boards cannot possibly be very competent to handle." Consequently, the individuals who should lead the district—the superintendent and his executive officers—were reduced to servings as mere "clerks and servants to the different board committees."[53]

Thereupon, Cubberley produced a new organizational design, one that laid out how he envisioned Denver could be reorganized should the school board accept the survey's recommendations (fig. 4.2). "The dominating characteristics of the new rules are the centralization of authority in the hands of an executive officer who may be held responsible for results," said Cubberley, "and a great simplification of business and educational procedure." School board members were sure to find relief under the new plan, he insisted, for

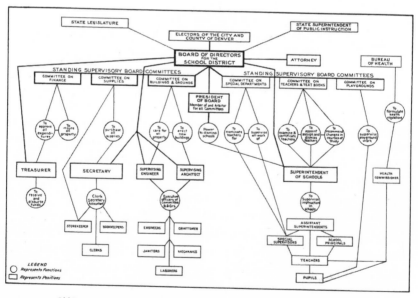

FIGURE 4.1. Old Denver organizational chart, 1913. (Ellwood P. Cubberley, "Supplemental Report on the Organization and Administration of School District Number One in the City and County of Denver," in *Report of the School Survey of School District Number One in the City and County of Denver* [Denver: School Survey Committee, 1916], between pages 14–15.)

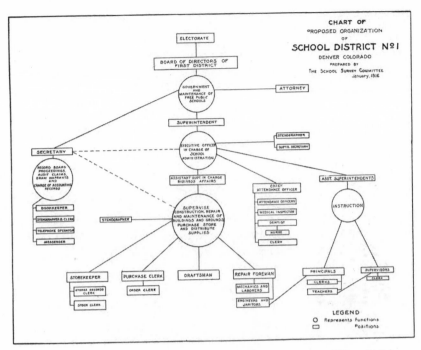

FIGURE 4.2. Denver reorganization as proposed by Bobbitt Survey Committee, 1916. (Ellwood P. Cubberley, "Supplemental Report on the Organization and Administration of School District Number One in the City and County of Denver," in *Report of the School Survey of School District Number One in the City and County of Denver* [Denver: School Survey Committee, 1916], between pages 12–13.)

"the vast amount of energy which the board formerly spent on administrative details is now saved for the larger and more important, and usually neglected problems."[54] After Cubberley submitted his supplementary report, a majority of the school board voted to reorganize its administration in accordance with Cubberley's model.[55]

After the Survey

School board politics did not cease with the conclusion of the survey. The sudden death of one school board member opened a new opportunity for Jones and Guyer to challenge the recommendations of the survey yet again. In the months that followed, the merits of the district reorganization plan were perpetually reargued as the board remained deadlocked. One public meeting featured a face-off between representatives of the Taxpayers Protective League and supporters of Jones and Guyer. A major point of contention remained the issue of "one-man power" conferred by the new bylaws on the superintendent. "Do we want to place so much responsibility on one man?" asked a spokesman for the Jones-Guyer contingent, asserting that "no living human being can shoulder the burden of such work." A Denver school principal was ready with a rejoinder, countering that "we're behind the times in this matter of centralizing the executive activities in one man. It is done in Chicago, in the states of Ohio, Indiana, Kentucky, in hundreds of progressive places East and West."[56]

Denver's practitioners clearly had a stake in this fight. One exasperated supervisor explained that there were far too many "incompetent teachers in the schools, placed there under the old system of favoritism." Worse still, he contended, he had witnessed janitors hurling abuse and profanity at school principals with impunity. One custodian had done just that before declaring, "Mr. So-and-So of the board gave me my job: just see if you can fire me." Some school supplies purchased by the school board were inferior, continued the supervisor, such as "a carload of penmanship paper" that was virtually unusable, because "it was bought by two board members who didn't know what they were doing." Not until June 1916 did the stalemate cease, due only to the intervention of the district court by ruling on the appropriate process to replace the deceased board member. Thereafter, the reorganization plan was finally and formally approved.[57]

Not coincidentally, the debate about the proper type of school governance for the public schools echoed the contemporaneous disputes waged between some of the same city leaders and civic groups about the proper nature of Denver's municipal government. The same issues of executive powers and ideologies were involved. Nevertheless, resolution of the district's organizational structure did not ease tensions. In 1917, just one year after the survey, Superintendent Smiley's replacement, Carlos Cole, endured an attack from within the board. Cantankerous board member Hilliard led the assault, charging that, among other failings, Cole had a "meddlesome tongue," that he had "shirked responsibility," and that he had accomplished little during his tenure.[58]

By this time, however, the Colorado Taxpayers Protective League— originally organized to address municipal fiscal concerns—had coalesced around a common frustration that the school board had taken little action in implementing any of the other significant changes recommended by the survey, even after the new bylaws were in place. The taxpayers league banded together with the Civic and Commercial Association, an organization that represented the city's major corporate interests, such as railroads and mining. Together these groups developed their own slate of school board candidates, raising some $75,000 in the process. These were the same groups that had aligned to regain mayoral control of governance and to reelect Speer in

1916, and their political savvy was further demonstrated by the activities that followed.[59]

Working in collaboration with the PTA, the Taxpayers Protective League obtained a mailing list of eligible voters. To each school district constituent, they sent each a brief written analysis of the school board situation, whereupon the PTA followed up with a door-to-door campaign. The league and the PTA urged other local groups to join their cause, eventually gaining the support of twenty-two of Denver's civic organizations. This coalition then approached the state legislature—which regulated the size of local school boards—and successfully lobbied for two additional seats to be added to the Denver board. Finally, members of the coalition even transported voters to the polls on election day. Given the widespread support, the three Taxpayers Protective League candidates—Lucius Hallett, Charles Schneck, and Frank Taylor—won decisively.[60]

After the election, Superintendent Cole managed to retain his position, but on his death in 1920, the board began the search for a new superintendent; this time, they looked for an "outsider," a national figure who could help reinvigorate the school system.

RECONSTRUCTION AND REVISION, 1920–27

Demonstrating their new commitment to look beyond the limits of local talent for a new chief administrator, the Denver school board unanimously chose Jesse Newlon, a young superintendent who had already gained a national reputation for reform. Newlon was a native of Indiana and had begun his career as a teacher in a one-room schoolhouse while still a student at Indiana University. Newlon's talents quickly landed him a principalship, and by 1914 he had earned a master's degree in educational administration from Teachers College, Columbia University. Newlon was active in the NEA and published in national educational journals as early as 1917.[61]

Newlon was well aware of some of the challenges facing him in Denver, including the low teacher morale, as his correspondence with some of his former mentors and his colleagues demonstrates. In fact, he wrote to one friend that "I am going to try to work cooperatively with the Denver force. By that method, I hope we can solve the problems." He wrote a similar letter to his Teachers College mentor Professor Fred Englehart, saying that "if we can work cooperatively [and] if we can have the assistance and advice of my many friends at Teacher's College, we can work out our problems."[62] Throughout his time in Denver, Newlon kept up a regular correspondence with his former faculty members.

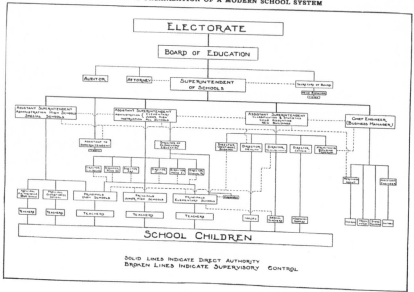

FIGURE 4.3. School district organization chart in Denver under Superintendent Newlon (1923), as recommended by the National Education Association in 1926. (National Education Association, "A Handbook of Major Educational Issues," *Research Bulletin of the National Education Association* 4, no. 4 [September 1926], 192–93.)

Newlon characterized his first few years in Denver as a time of "reconstruction and rehabilitation," describing his primary task as making up for time lost during the First World War and for the poor state of the school system at the time of his arrival. Little had changed in the four years since the Bobbitt survey, and given how long the district had drifted under the old school board, curriculum and instruction were not his first priorities.[63] In fact, Newlon acknowledged that he devoted much of his attention to administrative matters during the first phase of his Denver superintendency. He praised the district organizational structure he had inherited, even publishing an organizational chart in his annual report (fig. 4.3) that bore an extremely strong resemblance to Cubberley's 1916, but he continued to tweak the administration he had acquired while adding other innovations. A number of these reforms echoed the recommendations that Bobbitt's survey team had made several years earlier.[64]

Much of the change Newlon forged in Denver conformed to what historians have described as characteristic of administrative progressive or of the social efficiency movement. For example, he expanded the differentiation of the curriculum and implemented intelligence testing, designed, he said, to improve the classification of students for the purposes of instruction. The district's IQ testing program was coordinated by a new division for research, the Department of Classification and Statistics, which Newlon described as having made a significant contribution "to the effectiveness of the school system."[65] Newlon also contended that the introduction of intelligence tests had enabled Denver educators to classify pupils according to their "mental capacities." Denver educators had begun to sort students in the 1910s, Newlon explained, but during the first few years of his own tenure the work has been reorganized, extended, and made more effective—achievements of which he was clearly proud.[66]

Taken together, Newlon's innovations, such as administrative reorganization, intelligence testing, and differentiated coursework were remarkably similar to the types of reforms taking place in Oakland during the same period. Indeed, it is no exaggeration to assert that he expanded and intensified some of the corporate-style aspects of the system he had inherited. In effect, then, during the early 1920s, Newlon fashioned a school district that increasingly reflected the administrative progressive template of reform.

Given Newlon's national reputation for democratic reform—and bearing in mind that he is depicted by historians as one of the era's few "dissenters" to the cult of business values—how do we explain that educational progress in Oakland and Denver looked so similar? The evidence suggests several reasons for the resemblance. As a new superintendent, Newlon transported to Denver the educational ideas of his previous administrative experiences, just as Fred Hunter had carried ideas to Oakland from his tenure as superintendent in Lincoln, Nebraska. In fact, a revealing detail of Newlon's background that will surprise most educational historians is that, like Hunter, Newlon's previous experience had *also* been in Lincoln, Nebraska. Newlon had been principal of the Lincoln High School while Hunter was Lincoln superintendent, and when Hunter left in 1917 for his new position in Oakland, he recommended Newlon as his successor. As Lincoln's superintendent, Newlon preserved most of Hunter's programs.[67] The two men were friends and remained so long after their Lincoln relationship had ended. They maintained a regular correspondence throughout the next twenty years, sharing educational ideas, career advice, professional gossip, and even diets prescribed by their doctors (both men struggled with weight problems).[68] As superintendent in Lincoln, Newlon retained the use of intelligence testing for measuring student ability and the differentiation of the curriculum. Thus, Newlon and Hunter—a pair previously seen as progressive opposites—harbored similar ideals about how a progressive school district should be organized and sustained.[69]

Newlon made use of Hunter's advice in accepting his post in Denver as well. When Newlon received the job offer from the Denver school board,

Hunter counseled him: "Insist on a contract that really makes you superintendent." After all, Hunter had successfully taken that approach in Oakland.[70] Newlon followed Hunter's lead and stipulated that he would accept the position on the condition that the superintendent was considered sole head of the school district and that the school board was treated as a legislative, not an executive, body. In essence, Newlon benefited both from Hunter's experience and from the definitions of educational democracy that Cubberley had laid down in his pronouncements on Denver's organizational structure. Before his arrival, Newlon also asked for and received an assurance of traveling expenses and a salary of $8,000 for the first year, $9,000 for the second year, and $10,000 for the third, a large amount for the day.[71]

In addition to his experience in Lincoln with Hunter, Newlon's educational attitudes also were formed by his experiences at Teachers College, where he, like Hunter, was mentored and befriended by George Strayer, the renowned purveyor of scorecards for measuring the efficiency of school systems. However, unlike Hunter, Newlon was perhaps equally influenced by William Heard Kilpatrick, a noted disciple of Dewey's. Newlon's early writings and policies were tinged with views similar to those of Strayer and Hunter on differentiation and democracy.[72] For example, Newlon saw no contradiction in a school offering a curriculum adapted to the social or economic background of its student. "It is perfectly natural and proper," he wrote in 1917, that "industrial and commercial" courses be emphasized in the working-class and immigrant sections of Lincoln. Meanwhile, he said, the McKinley school—located more centrally and enrolling Lincoln's middle-class children—should offer "a liberal arts curriculum for [this] accelerated group of students who are destined for college preparatory courses . . . and after high school for the colleges, and eventually for leadership in the business, professional and social life of the community."[73] Such statements align closely with the declarations made by Hunter in his annual reports as he distinguished between Oakland neighborhoods and differentiated junior high curricula. Newlon did not think it unusual that social and economic class should determine the curricular and career prospects of students.

In Denver, Newlon concentrated on the creation of "comprehensive" secondary schools rather than on offering all students comparable experiences through curricular uniformity. Neighborhood elementary and junior high schools, he believed, should be aligned with larger comprehensive high schools. To Newlon, democratic schooling entailed creating a kind of common space for the education of children during their adolescent years, and the secondary school was the appropriate stage for the mixing of students of different backgrounds, abilities, and futures. This vision of the common high school was essential to Newlon's early views on democracy. Progressive educators had only recently won a pitched battle over the role and direction that American secondary education should take. Many educators believed the comprehensive high school represented a great victory, considering that the National Association of Manufacturers had pushed for much more rigid tracking through the creation of completely separate industrial schools.[74]

"It is a dangerous thing," Newlon wrote—not long after the fierce debates about the wisdom of splitting the American schools into two systems, one for vocational students and one for the academically oriented—"to accentuate the social stratification of our society by separating in our secondary schools the boys and girls who are . . . destined to occupy leading places in our social and industrial life from the boys and girls who will be artisans and will fill subordinate positions in the commercial and industrial life of our nation." The comprehensive high school, as Newlon saw it, offered an essential setting for social interaction. "It is very important," he explained, "that the leaders of democracy should rub elbows with the rank and file of democracy in some of the courses of the high school."[75] Public schools, therefore, need not offer the same education to all students, but they should provide them with common learning environments. In other words, *personal proximity* served democratic goals better than *curricular parity*. The notion of "leaders and followers" threaded itself throughout Newlon's superintendency in Denver. It was not until his tenure at Teachers College in the 1930s that Newlon began to fundamentally change his views on some of these matters.

As superintendent, Newlon continued to lean on his professional and intellectual connections to members of the educational elite. By 1920, he had been invited to join the exclusive Cleveland Conference, taking up membership alongside the ranks of Cubberley, Strayer, Terman, Bobbitt, Judd, Hunter, Kilpatrick, and H. B. Wilson, superintendent of the Berkeley, California, schools. When Newlon sought a director to take charge of Denver's new Department of Classification and Statistics, he relied on recommendations from both Strayer and Terman.[76] He took Strayer's advice again when he hired A. L. Threlkeld as his assistant superintendent.[77] Threlkeld had done graduate work at the University of Wisconsin and the University of Chicago as well as at Teachers College, where he attracted the attention of Strayer. Threlkeld was a wise choice for Denver; he quickly became instrumental in the development of the curriculum revision project.

The fact that four of Newlon's Cleveland Conference colleagues—Bobbitt, Terman, Judd, and Cubberley—had been involved with the 1916 Denver survey undoubtedly reinforced Newlon's use of the survey as a starting point when he began to reform and reinvigorate the district. Indeed, it might well have been uncomfortable for him not to do so. As a member of the NEA, Newlon demonstrated a continued commitment to his administratively minded friends.[78] And while he was president of the NEA, the association disseminated research bulletins advocating precisely the kind of administrative organizational structure that existed in Denver. In fact, the chart reproduced in the *NEA Research Bulletin* is exactly the same version that Newlon included in his 1923 Denver annual report; the sole difference being that the word "Denver," which had preceded "School Children" toward the bottom of the chart, had been deleted (fig. 4.3).

Bringing Democracy

Even before Newlon had arrived in Denver and assayed his new situation, he swiftly cottoned on to the low teacher morale throughout the system, much of which stemmed from lingering resentment about the rash of sudden teacher firings in 1915. Years of underfunding had also sapped energy from the whole district. One source of deep frustration for every teacher in the city was a salary that was markedly insufficient by the standards of the day. As the *Denver Teacher's Journal* summarized the situation on Newlon's arrival, the schools were run down, there was lack of coordination among the teachers, and the paltry salaries meant that the district could not attract talented instructors. Yet there remained, said the journal, a core of committed teachers who were sustained by "a real missionary spirit" but who were forced to live a "hand-to-mouth" existence.[79]

After the 1915 firings, some teachers had formed a local union affiliated with the American Federation of Labor, but the Denver teaching corps remained divided between the previously existing Grade School Teachers' Association and the High School Teachers Association. Not only was bad pay a major cause of discontent, but a significant differential between the salaries paid to teachers in the elementary schools versus the high schools created additional discord as well. The disparity was aggravated even further when a male teacher, hired into the elementary grades, received a higher salary than his female colleagues. Moreover, the introduction of the junior high school led to even more infighting about which organization could claim these new teachers. To make matters worse, in 1917, when the elementary school teachers asked for a $700 reduction in the gap in the salaries earned by each group, the school board responded with a castigating $200 reduction in elementary school teachers' pay instead.[80]

Few superintendents would enjoy walking into this kind of district atmosphere. However, one of the initiatives for which Newlon had been known in Lincoln was his successful introduction of a single salary scale—a plan whereby teachers with comparable education and experience are compensated equally, whether they are stationed in the elementary, the junior high, or the high schools. Aware of Newlon's earlier success, the grade school teachers went directly to the new superintendent to ask for his assistance. Rather than propose his own plan, Newlon urged the elementary teachers to first meet together, establish some key principles, and then to collaborate directly with the High School Teachers Association. A united front, he suggested, would be much more successful in dealing with the school board. In the meantime, Newlon formed his own committee of principals and faculty leaders to conduct research on salary plans across the country. The elementary and high school teachers were able to come to agreement swiftly, whereupon they were also joined by Newlon's team of administrators, two school board members, and a committee from the Chamber of Commerce. When presented to the full school board, the plan readily passed, making Denver the first large city in the country to adopt a single salary plan, and it had done so with widespread support throughout the system and the city.[81]

The salary plan received attention from the NEA and gained a great deal of national praise. Oakland's Hunter called it the "best salary schedule in the United States." Beyond boosting both morale and living standards for the teachers, the plan yielded other significant benefits. Since the new salary formula rewarded teachers for pursuing further education and professional growth, the enrollment of teachers taking summer and extension courses jumped into the hundreds, and the number of college graduates teaching in the Denver schools doubled between 1921 and 1925. Moreover, because elementary school teachers no longer felt that the only way to advance their careers was to switch to teaching at the high school level, the plan helped keep experienced and ambitious instructors in the elementary grades.[82]

Most importantly, Newlon's finessing of the whole salary episode showed his faith in the classroom teacher and demonstrated the value he placed on their active participation in important matters of district policy, especially those that directly affected their own professional destinies. Newlon soon verified that belief again when he undertook a campaign to raise five million dollars for a district building program. Because a large bond issue (designed to raise funds for new buildings) had failed in 1919, just before Newlon's arrival, the school board scoffed at the likelihood that another large building campaign would succeed. Rising to the challenge, Newlon forged a coalition of board members, principals, teachers, the PTA, and the press, a strategy that ultimately led to successful passage of a new bond issue. After passage, Newlon went one step further still, creating committees of teachers to assist architects in planning the buildings and classrooms, based on his belief that teachers best knew the needs of daily classroom operation. Eventually, individual school plans were coordinated by committees of teachers. As a result, teachers reportedly felt a great deal of ownership over the process and their new classrooms.[83]

Designing the Democratic School System, 1922–27

The participation of teachers in designing salary schedules and reviewing classroom blueprints are not the types of activities that generally receive accolades as significant progressive innovations. However, the kinds of professional collaborations that Newlon fostered in Denver may well have done more to establish egalitarian relationships in the district than most commonplace contemporary statements about the need for democratic leadership in a progressive school system. Throughout the rest of his career, Newlon focused on the vital role that teachers could play in district affairs, and he persistently articulated the notion that genuine involvement and cooperation of teachers in district activities was essential. "If we are to have a democratic school," he wrote, "we must have a democratic organization of the faculty, and, in my opinion, the faculty must participate in determining the policy of the school if the maximum of efficiency is to be obtained, whether it be in teaching, in administration, or in curriculum making."[84]

Historical evidence of meaningful democratic engagement in progressive school systems can prove difficult to identify, so historians have retained a healthy skepticism about claims made by district leadership. Thus, Newlon's characterization of his work merits attention, given the unique ways he drew links and set limits, between different actors in the school district. A democratic organization placed special responsibilities—even limits—on school leaders, Newlon believed. Administrators, he said, "ought to be big enough to accede, in some instances, to the judgment of their faculties when it is contrary to their own." This conception of district democracy signaled a departure from the standard thought of the day. "If we are to have democratic schools, taught and administered in a democratic way, with socialized instruction," he wrote while still in Lincoln, "we cannot have cut and dried programs handed down by administrators to faculties."[85] Such language suggests that, even before he implemented teacher-oriented reforms in Denver, Newlon had begun to think outside the somewhat narrower conceptual confines of two of his two mentors, Strayer and Hunter.

Direct engagement with the curriculum, Newlon contended, was the "best kind of professional study for teachers." When teachers had worked together for two or three years improving the curriculum—when they had debated curricular issues on committees and in faculty meetings and had "evolved and adopted" a curriculum—Newlon said, "that group of teachers will teach better and with more understanding and sympathy than they could ever otherwise teach." In developing his ideas on democratic roles for teachers, Newlon said that he drew on research conducted by H. B. Wilson, superintendent in Topeka, Kansas, who was soon to become the new superintendent in Berkeley, California, and who was already a member of the Cleveland Conference.[86] The confidence Newlon expressed early in his career about the collaborative work of teachers soon developed into an enduring conviction that served as the foundation for his work in Denver.

Scholars have noted that many Progressive Era administrators who praised and implemented "teacher involvement" often maintained strong administrative control and included teachers in curriculum revision only symbolically.[87] Therefore, the form of direct teacher engagement that Newlon fostered in his Denver curriculum revision program is noteworthy for the demonstrably genuine measure of respect it gave to teachers. The specifics of Denver's curriculum revision strategy, it should be noted, did not spring forth from Newlon's mind fully hatched. Rather, it was only after his first two years in Denver that Newlon initiated development on his curriculum revision project, using the early experiences of the program to guide his approach. It took some three years before he had refined his strategy enough to warrant broad implementation of the program and still several years more before the results of the program became fully clear.

The initial stages of Denver's curriculum revision program were rather modest and informal. With the advent of the 1922–23 school year, and once administrative matters were made more orderly, Newlon and Threlkeld enthusiastically devoted more attention to "purely educational advancement" by concentrating on curriculum revision. As Threlkeld later described it, the two men had originally articulated "no definite plan of procedure" during the first year of the program. The committees that had been appointed, he said, did what they could in the sparse after-school hours without much direction or assistance. "They were advised simply to read extensively in the literature of their several fields" (such an approach was reminiscent of the teacher "study groups" that proliferated throughout districts earlier in the century, sometimes inspiring but not necessarily directed toward practical application).[88] The result was that many committees did a great deal of reading but made little headway on revising the curriculum. Neither Newlon nor Threlkeld expressed much satisfaction with the results of the program's first year. They recognized that weary teachers, working nights, weekends, and holidays, and without clear direction, were unable to make significant steps forward.[89]

Convinced that a "more effective organization would be necessary if a thorough-going program of curriculum revision were to be carried out," Newlon and Threlkeld altered their strategy. They proposed to the school board that it provide substantial funding to support a more structured revision program, one that would include teacher-release time as well as the assistance of outside curriculum specialists. In making his case, Newlon combined his belief in the value of teacher collaboration with his fluency in the language of efficiency. "Curriculum-making is a first consideration in the successful administration of any school system," he explained to the board. And because curriculum development was directly related to instruction, he said, all appropriations, therefore, were ultimately for the purpose of instruction. Newlon reasoned that it would be "extremely wasteful and short sighted for a community to spend large sums of money on its schools and at the same time fail to concentrate in an effective way on the problem of making appropriate courses of study."[90]

The rhetoric of efficiency served Newlon well in convincing the board of the soundness of his proposal. He shrewdly presented his case in terms of the savings that would result rather than focusing on the expense incurred. "If ten percent of the teacher's time is spent on nonessentials and misplaced materials in courses of study," Newlon argued, "it actually represents an annual loss to the Denver taxpayers of $478,000 on the basis of the present budget." According to such logic, the district would reap benefits far greater than the $30,500 Newlon had requested if the curriculum were improved and streamlined. Beyond strict monetary justifications, Newlon raised concerns about the dangers of "mental waste" that resulted from an inadequate curriculum. Education, he argued, must raise each child up to her "maximum capacity." Such individual improvement could not be accomplished through the status quo; "by teaching such poorly selected lists of words . . . that pupils do not learn how to spell"; through programs that failed "to develop habits of accuracy, industry, and sound thinking, because materials of study have not been properly adjusted to the needs of the pupil"; or by having pupils, who varied widely in mental capacity, "studying the same subject in the same class" (a nod to differentiation).[91] When addressing the public and the school board, Newlon used social efficiency—not the doctrine of democracy—as the legitimizing philosophy for the promotion of his program.

Newlon and Threlkeld certainly recognized that Denver citizens might not see the urgency for curriculum revision. The importance of curriculum reform was "difficult for the public mind to grasp," they acknowledged, because so many of the phases were "intangible." In the years following World War I, when many school administrators were cautious about proposing additional spending on seeming "fads and frills," Newlon and Threlkeld held firm to their conviction that significant expenditure on the curriculum was vital.[92] Referring to the district's recent building campaign, the two men reasoned that Denver could ill afford to "spend millions of dollars upon school buildings and upon school teachers," only to find that an outdated and uncoordinated curriculum made it "impossible to realize effectively upon this large investment." Threlkeld put it more bluntly: "Modern buildings without modern programs of studies would be stupid."[93] The board agreed, readily approving the request for additional funding.

Denver's curriculum revision quickly became a joint effort between Newlon and Threlkeld, with Threlkeld serving as the primary author of some of the most significant monographs and articles about the revision process. As the two administrators crafted Denver's system of curriculum revision, they also articulated three principles that provided the guiding foundation for the program. More so than the arguments about efficiency, these three principles formed the core of the revision program during the years that followed. It was this set of principles that truly set Denver apart from most of its contemporaries. Newlon and Threlkeld argued, first, that participation of local teachers— "the professional corps"—should be the basis for the entire program of curriculum revision. No curriculum would be successful that had not "evolved to some extent out of the thinking of the teachers who are to apply it." Second, district administrators should not be absent from the process; they had an important role to play in coordinating, directing, and supervising the revision program. Third, Newlon and Threlkeld stressed that the "most advanced educational thought" should be incorporated into the content of the new Denver curriculum. "Any course of study put into operation in Denver," they wrote, "should represent the last word of investigation in its particular field."[94]

The Inclusion of Denver Teachers in Curriculum Revision

Newlon's profound faith in the classroom teacher is one of the main factors that explains the success of the Denver revision program.[95] After the board allotted money to the revision process, Newlon used over half the amount to hire substitutes who temporarily replaced the classroom teachers assigned to revision committees. "Curriculum revision is fundamental to all else," wrote Threlkeld, "and certainly it should not be done at odd times; especially it should not be done by those who have used up their best energies by teaching a full day in the classroom." Newlon and Threlkeld wanted alert and focused professionals who engaged energetically in curriculum development and who felt that their work was "anything but a side issue."[96]

The high regard for teachers that Newlon and Threlkeld exuded, as well as their understanding of the realities of intradistrict and interpersonal politics, was also evident in the decisions they made about the constitution of the revision committees. The classroom teacher was the starting point of the committees, said Threlkeld, and all committees were constituted so as to offer the "maximum inducement" for teachers to become engaged in committee deliberations. Newlon and Threlkeld acknowledged that teachers might be reluctant to speak if the committees were "presided over by administrative officers, whose aggressiveness has been highly developed by the nature of their work." To circumvent the danger of administrator domination, Newlon did not generally assign principals or other supervisors to the curricular committees. Subject-matter committees were made up almost exclusively of teachers, with a teacher appointed as committee chair; in all, the district had forty-five committees, a large undertaking.[97]

Another illustration of the district's novel approach to working with teachers was its utilization of outside experts. Threlkeld was especially exasperated by educational theorists who believed that "a curriculum revision program should be carried on single-handed by specialists and handed over to teachers to teach." Such an approach, he believed, would result in little real benefit. "Teachers no doubt can be presented with course of study and trained to be excellent reproducers of the work of others," he said, "but in this situation we could not look upon our teachers as sources of new thinking, which is necessary to progress."[98]

The core belief that teachers were sources of *original thought* also meant that district leaders allowed for a certain amount of variation in the methods and approaches that teachers could take in using the new courses of study in their classrooms. In fact, Newlon and Threlkeld noted, rather matter-of-factly, the final courses of study revealed differences in both approach and philosophy. The "force of tradition" was stronger in some fields, they explained, while in other fields the committees had the benefit of more extensive research. Thus, some subjects took a problem-based approach while others remained more traditional pedagogically. "It is our belief," the two men concluded, "that this variety is more desirable than the rigid uniformity that is produced by a pattern set by the administrative staff."[99]

Coordination and Supervision of Committees

Newlon and Threlkeld's second main tenet, that the curriculum revision program required local coordination and administration, demonstrated once more how they used organizational structure to buttress their more pedagogically oriented reforms. Scholars have devoted more attention to the pedagogically progressive characteristics of Denver than to its administrative philosophy, but grasping the administrative dimension of the program is critical to a full understanding of the district.[100] As developed by Newlon and Threlkeld, local coordination had at least a few main features. It was essential, they believed, to have one person in direct charge of the program; and since curriculum revision entered "into the whole life of a school system," this director should be "one with administrative duties covering the entire system."[101] Only a Denver administrator with sufficient authority was in a "proper position to weigh all values in making decisions and recommending policies of procedure." During the second and third years of the revision program, Newlon delegated this responsibility to Threlkeld. Then in 1925, Newlon asked the board to establish a permanent Department of Curriculum Revision with a full-time director in charge. Newlon hired Arthur K. Loomis as the new department's director. Loomis had recently completed his doctorate at Teachers College under the supervision of George Strayer, meaning that Strayer's influence endured to some degree during the development of the curriculum revision program.[102]

Another dimension of local organizational focus was the use of Denver-based university curriculum specialists. These experts served as coordinators and advisers to the specific subject-matter committees working in their academic field. The subject-matter committees in any given discipline—one committee from each subject area appointed from the elementary, junior high, and senior high school levels—were placed under the leadership of one of these specialists, often faculty members from the Colorado State Teachers College or the University of Colorado. Such an arrangement, said Threlkeld, combined "coordination and unity with maximum freedom of expression"—a potent blend of efficiency, progressive creativity, and expertise in subject matter.[103]

In addition to the sharing of subject-specific knowledge across grades, coordination through the university curriculum specialists also allowed committees to compare their work with one another. Often, Threlkeld said, one committee took "a more progressive point of view" than the others and therefore had created a curriculum that depended more heavily on new instructional practices such as the project method. The work of these more progressive committees could then be used by district leaders and the specialists to positively influence the more traditional tendencies of other committees, providing what Threlkeld called a "natural entering wedge for progress."[104] In this way, administrators leveraged the achievement of the more advanced teachers and created an additional strategic device for spreading innovation throughout the school system.

A final component of the local administration of the revision program involved the use of achievement tests to evaluate the effectiveness of the new courses of study. Initially, district administrators used commercially available standardized tests. They examined students a first time under the old courses of study and then a second time after they had been instructed using the revised curriculum. Newlon and Threlkeld soon realized, however, that externally developed examinations could not measure the full impact of the new curriculum (a challenge that persists in American schools today). Therefore, Newlon and Threlkeld called on the district's Department of Tests and Measurements to develop new assessments that were more closely aligned with the new courses of study. Working together with the teacher committees and the specialists in charge of committee supervision, the director of measurements prepared a series of tests for each of the new curricula, based on "what the courses actually assign." The purpose, explained Threlkeld, was to offer a "definite means of evaluating the effectiveness of content and method," as well as to provide individual classroom teachers with a means for analyzing their own work (the results of which are discussed further below).[105]

Incorporation of the "Most Advanced Educational Thought"

The third main principle of curriculum revision was that the most advanced educational research should be employed in Denver's efforts at school reform. Newlon and Threlkeld felt that much of the initial work could be accomplished through the local organization. However, at some point in the work of each committee, Threlkeld explained, it was "extremely helpful" to have an external expert comment on the work. District leaders met this need by inviting to Denver one of the "leading research specialists in the country" to work with committees. Here again, Denver diverged from standard practice. These national experts, Threlkeld explained, did not come for the usual "general lectures or general discussions," too often the approach to professional development. Instead, these specialists were invited at a time when the committee itself had already identified specific problems, when they were able to state their issues and concerns clearly, and when they had definite questions to ask. Even before their arrival, these curriculum specialists were informed about the progress of the committees, and once in Denver, they usually remained in Denver for several days. Afterward, they corresponded with the committees until the new course of study was ready for printing. This strategy, explained Threlkeld and Newlon, offered the opportunity for the "local staff to capitalize [on] the research work which has been carried on in many of our colleges, universities, and experimental schools."[106]

Between 1923 and 1928, over thirty-five nationally prominent curriculum specialists visited Denver, many of them coming on several occasions. These targeted sessions would also have served to preserve resources, as the district spent money on outside consultation only when necessary. Among the visitors were some of the best-known educators of the day from the Lincoln School and Teachers College, the University of Chicago, and Harvard University, as well as practitioners from a range of city school systems including Rochester, New York, Shaker Heights, Ohio, and Pittsburgh, Pennsylvania.[107] This kind of cross-fertilization with other progressive school districts and advice from national reformers created effective opportunities for the introduction of new practices, theories, and pedagogical techniques.

The ultimate goal of the Denver revision project had always been the development of a new and improved course of study; Newlon and Threlkeld often stressed that teacher professional growth was in many ways more important than the final curricular product. Although they emphasized the role that outside specialists could play in stimulating the thinking and growth of teachers, Newlon and Threlkeld's esteem for teachers also meant that the opinions of the teachers sometimes trumped the stance of the experts, a rather remarkable attitude for the day. "A body of teachers who are teaching courses which they have worked out under guidance," said Threlkeld, "will do better teaching even with courses that may not be the last word in every particular from every point of view of the expert if these teachers have worked them out and are earnestly trying to find out better ways."[108]

The Impact and Outcomes of Denver Curriculum Revision, 1925–37

By all accounts, teachers felt incredibly empowered by the expanded opportunities the district offered them. Some Denver teachers became active on a national stage as a result of the revision process. For example, one Denver instructor, Marie Murphy, gave a 1924 talk to the National League of Teachers, in which she detailed how teachers were included as the "most important factor" in the revision of curricula. Denver had shrugged off the outdated procedures of the past whereby a few administrative officers planned all instruction and the classroom teacher's role had been that of "obediently following the dictated course of study."[109]

Denver curriculum revision, she said, now offered teachers an avenue for professional training, and as a result, they became "ardent students of educational problems," especially in their own subject areas. They became familiar with the research, experimentation, and ongoing investigations in their own particular field. "The curricula of any school system must be dynamic;

it must be progressive," Murphy concluded. "Our participation in curriculum revision has meant progress, growth, and leadership."[110] Other teachers reflected Murphy's sentiments, even finding themselves treated as celebrities at national meetings for their pioneering work on curriculum construction.[111] Newlon regularly brought contingents of Denver administrators and teachers with him to each year's NEA annual meeting, reinforcing the professional growth of the district's efforts at home.[112]

By 1927, district administrators considered the first round of revision practically complete. Nonetheless, Newlon and Threlkeld asserted that curriculum revision had to be a "continuous" process, a stance that ultimately became another key goal of the program. One approach to making it continuous was through regular evaluation of the outcomes of the program. Loomis's department of curriculum revision undertook self-assessment through two means: system-wide tests and teacher questionnaires. Denver leaders used a range of examinations to assess the district-wide educational impact of their new courses of study. Because Newlon, like most urban superintendents of the time, was concerned about how Denver students measured up to pupils in other city school systems, the district also administered a battery of externally developed standardized achievement tests. These assessments included the commercially available Iowa High School Content Examination, the Stanford Achievement Test, the Woody-McCall Test in Mixed Fundamentals, and the Thorndike-McCall Reading Test.[113]

The results of the standardized achievement tests were encouraging: 60 percent of students in twelfth grade scored above the national mean in English, mathematics, science, and social science; ninth graders scored close to the norm in most subjects; and sixth graders were above the norm in reading, arithmetic, science, and language usage but lagged in spelling, history, and literature. These scores marked a victory for Denver, primarily because the tests uncovered no serious knowledge deficits that could be attributed to the curriculum revision program, which was essentially still an experiment. Furthermore, when Denver leaders compared the 1928 test scores to those given in 1924, the results showed consistent gains across all subjects.[114] Given the additional benefits of curriculum revision, such as increased teacher growth and participation, Denver leaders felt great pride in what they had accomplished.

External measures were one thing, but Denver leaders also wanted to determine how students were learning according to the district's own internal academic standards, so Newlon directed Loomis to design customized subject area assessments specifically aligned with the new courses of study. The outcomes of these examinations were also generally positive with some qualifications. For example, the tests of ninth graders demonstrated that the results were satisfactory in English language arts but unsatisfactory in mathematics, particularly in problem solving (a perennial challenge for educators). Sixth-grade students showed gains in all areas of arithmetic: arithmetic fundamentals, fractions, and problem solving. These tests—given in 1925, 1926, and 1928—demonstrated consistent student improvement from year to year.[115]

Newlon, Threlkeld, and Loomis also wanted feedback from those who had been most intimately involved with the project. Therefore, during the 1927–28 school year, Loomis conducted a district-wide evaluation that involved 750 classroom teachers in the appraisal of thirty-four new courses of study.[116] Loomis published detailed accounts of teacher feedback throughout the 1928–29 academic year in the *Denver Public Schools Bulletin*, and new district publication. The findings demonstrated that teachers generally expressed enthusiasm for the revision process and satisfaction with its preliminary results. More specifically, the program appeared to be strongest in laying out broad student learning goals, in allowing teachers to act on their own initiative in selecting pedagogical methods and materials, and in providing offerings for the brightest students.

The areas in which teachers rated the new courses of study as inadequate were not necessarily surprising. One of the major goals of progressive education all along had been to include students as active participants in the learning process, but this was also an aim that presented some of the biggest pedagogical challenges. The Loomis evaluation showed that improvement was needed specifically in terms of including pupils in initiating plans to reach their learning goals, in providing guidance to carry out those plans, and in enlisting student participation in judging their own results. The other area of weakness had to do with the adaptation of the course of study to students of "limited ability" and, in some cases, average ability. A related issue focused on the necessity of training new teachers for remedial instruction. Curricular and instructional adaptation for students perceived as having differing abilities was a persistent challenge for Denver administrators and teachers, illustrating what a thorny problem in achievement remained throughout the 1920s even though separate courses of study had been specifically designed for students labeled as "slow learners."[117]

Despite qualms local leaders may have had about some specific elements of their revision efforts, outside observers were less troubled by such matters. Denver received an unprecedented amount of positive attention for its curricular work. Despite his penchant for hyperbole, A. E. Winship was on the mark when he described the popularity of Denver's curriculum. Both Franklin Bobbitt and William H. Kilpatrick used the Denver courses of study in their own classes, demonstrating that Denver's curricular material appealed to progressives of very different stripes.[118] Moreover, although district progressives adopted and adapted ideas advocated by nationally prominent reformers, the reverse could also be true. Indeed, Denver's work serves as proof that the sharing of innovations and ideas could flow in two directions between universities and school districts. V. T. Thayer, a professor at Ohio State University, predicted that the work of Denver revision committees would "stimulate progressive educational thinking in the country at large," which was not necessarily an exaggeration.[119]

By 1926, Denver had sold over twelve thousand copies of its courses of study and another thousand of the research monograph that recounted the specific steps of the revision process. National attention catapulted Denver into prominence, and the receipts from the sales of monographs and courses of study provided unexpected financial resources for additional curriculum and teacher activity in the district. When Newlon was president of the NEA in 1925, the association established the "Cooperative Plan of Curriculum Revision of the NEA" designed "to assist school systems to work cooperatively in curriculum revision." Meanwhile, the *NEA Research Bulletin*, along with other journals of the time, devoted full issues to the topic of curriculum reform and revision, wherein Denver's work always figured prominently.[120]

The popularity of the Denver curriculum monographs, however, points to one of the great ironies of the revision program's success. Rather than adopting the *process* of curriculum revision that Newlon and Threlkeld argued was the primary benefit of their program, many school districts that purchased the courses of study from Denver simply used them as ready-made curricula. Estimates of the numbers of school districts engaged in some kind of collaborative curriculum revision program in the mid-1920s ranged from two hundred to a thousand but these tallies are likely more speculative than accurate. Some educators felt compelled to point out that the districts gaining the most attention for their curriculum revision work were often located in the West and Midwest. "The East is too traditional and too tight with its money," explained one Colorado academic involved in Denver's revision program; "it gives up established practices slowly and doesn't invest readily in reform."[121]

Conundrums of District-Wide Democratic Change

Reforming the many schools within a large urban school district represented one of the most significant challenges for district progressives. Newlon was keenly aware that some of his contemporaries were making pedagogical advances in experimental schools and in university laboratory schools. He and Threlkeld pointed to the Lincoln School of Teachers College as an example of the type of laboratory school in which it was feasible to carry out an "entirely experimental curriculum." But these kinds of innovations could only be successful in "a single public school or a very small public school system." They understood that they had to employ different strategies if they hoped to transform a whole district. "The schools ought to be progressive, they ought to go as far as possible in basing courses on sound educational theory and research, but it is frequently impossible to go the whole distance at one time. . . . The inertia to be overcome is too great," they explained, "to say nothing of the practical difficulties involved and the folly of subjecting large numbers of pupils and teachers to the hazards of an entirely experimental curriculum."[122]

Denver's curriculum revision program was designed, in part, to overcome barriers to district-wide change. From Newlon and Threlkeld's perspective, the large public school system needed a different operating logic than smaller schools or school systems. Looked at in terms of district-wide reform, the principles of Denver's curriculum revision program were intended both to spark teacher growth and to diffuse a culture of change throughout the city schools. Both Newlon and Threlkeld found that the teachers who most quickly improved their instruction were those who had worked on the creation of the curriculum. Not all teachers were involved in the curriculum project, however, and the two men worried that more conservative teachers who were "unfamiliar and unsympathetic with the new point of view in teaching . . . might fail almost completely if asked to undertake a course of study embodying all of the modern thought." Therefore, they said, administrators of large districts were sometimes justified in accepting and implementing a course of study "which does not go as far in the embodiment of the results of research as the administration thinks it should go."[123] Reformers who pushed too far, too fast, were likely to foster no change at all.

Although Newlon and Threlkeld stressed the value of teacher professional development that emerged from curriculum revision, one outcome of the program they may not have fully appreciated was the shift apparent in their own thinking. The two men began to articulate views of democracy distinct from that of many other district progressives. They went much further than most to avoid issuing curricular mandates from above. "Education dealing with life itself can never be so thoroughly mechanized as to make it possible to furnish a classroom mechanic with recipes and specific methods of procedure appropriate to every situation," they asserted. "Especially is this true in a democracy."[124] In his own reflections, Threlkeld criticized "intellectual snobs" who argued that "the great mass of teachers are incapable of any original thinking and that we will have the best results if we make of them mere reproducers of the thoughts of others." Such thinking, said Threlkeld, countenanced the "docile compliance" of the mass of teachers with the curricular "mandates of the few." Educational leaders more democratic in their philosophy of life, he said, "will take the view that we shall evolve at the top the highest possible type of specialist only by the cumulative effect of large numbers thinking." If curriculum development was going to be intelligent and enlightened, argued Threlkeld, "it must represent the thinking of the large numbers who make it up."[125]

Newlon and Threlkeld's views on democracy, however, did not imply that their revision effort should be thrown open to the popular opinions of teachers or to pedagogy by consensus. The role for expertise and leadership was essential. "The policy of delegating entirely to teachers the making of curricula," they wrote in 1926, "would be as fallacious as was the policy of leaving the teachers entirely out of this process, and would likewise fail to take account of the indispensable contribution that must be made by research and by specialists who, by devoting their lives to the study of teaching in particular subjects, become authorities in their fields."[126] The two men always asserted that teachers and their contributions remained vital for success: "Any educational philosophy which implies that the teachers are not to think for themselves but are merely to take orders from a few at the top is entirely antithetical to the spirit of democracy, which is the dominant spirit of America."[127]

Much the same relationship that existed between experts and teachers should also be replicated between teachers and students. "The Denver classroom teacher is regarded as an intelligent director or leader of boys and girls," Newlon and Threlkeld maintained.[128] Yet, despite their vocabulary of classroom democracy, Denver's curriculum revision program did not necessarily mean the creation of new forms of democratic schooling for the students themselves, even though district teachers sought to incorporate students in the learning process. As we have seen, Denver educators employed the practices of child classification and curricular differentiation that were decidedly not Deweyan in pedagogical terms. Still, the Denver annual reports and the comments made by teachers in Loomis's survey illustrate that differentiation between students was both a common concern and a standard practice within the district, even if Newlon devoted nowhere near the attention to IQ testing and tracking that Hunter and Dickson did in Oakland. Denver curriculum revision was founded on the fundamental belief that teachers needed to be actively engaged in curricular activity, but this same philosophy of engagement was not equally applied to students. True, Denver educators used such pedagogically progressive concepts as the "project method" and employed "the life situation criterion" in the selection of subject matter and activities. Yet, as the education researcher Gary Peltier observed in his study of Newlon's superintendency, "for all the child-centered orientation of both of these men and the curriculum program, the student was not listed as a force that affected instruction in the schools."[129] In this light, then, it is perhaps not surprising that educational historian Larry Cuban found little evidence of student-centered instruction in Denver.[130] Teachers, not students, were the primary targets of Denver's reform efforts.

In 1927, Newlon received an offer from Teachers College to become the new director of the Lincoln School, the very school that he had identified as the kind of experimental site that would be so difficult to emulate in a large urban school system like Denver's. Although Newlon professed "mental anguish" in trying to decide whether to take the offer, it would have been difficult for him to turn down. Teachers College was still very much at the center of the progressive educational universe in 1927, and the Lincoln School was at the center of the Teachers College approach to pedagogical experimentation. Newlon had maintained intellectual and emotional ties to Teachers College faculty, and the fact that Teachers College selected Newlon to run their flagship experimental school also demonstrated the high regard with which leading academics viewed the curriculum revision work that he and Threlkeld had undertaken in Denver.

TEACHERS, LEARNERS, AND EXPERTS, 1927–37

Given the collaborative nature of the working relationship between Newlon and Threlkeld, it is not surprising that there were few hiccups when Threlkeld took the reigns as the new Denver superintendent in 1927, and he ultimately remained in the post for a full decade. The district hardly remained stagnant, and what distinguishes the work of Threlkeld and his colleagues in the late 1920s and early 1930s is their continued intellectual growth.

Attempting to find new means for communicating with his professional corps, Threlkeld established the *Denver Public Schools Bulletin*, an organ he viewed as essential to keeping Denver teachers up to date. The bulletin was similar to that initiated by Hunter in Oakland and to other regular publications of the era that were becoming increasingly prevalent in urban progressive school districts. Rather than use the bulletin as many districts did—merely a way to report standard news items or extended quotes from prominent educators around the country—Threlkeld, Loomis, and Charles Greene, Denver's new director of research, effectively employed it to report on their own ongoing research findings within the district.[131] Threlkeld was never a simple custodian of Newlon's system, and he persistently pushed on the boundaries of practice during his tenure and cultivated his own thinking on the implications of democracy for progressive schooling. Moreover, district administrators began to question, even challenge, some of their previous assumptions about student ability and classification, although not in ways that resulted in fundamental change to Denver's classification or curricular practices.

"No greater stupidity has been exhibited in any of our discussions of education," Threlkeld told an audience in 1928, than the belief "that it is feasible to develop by exclusive and isolated systems" the training of elite leaders "while at the same time the masses, who must necessarily be the foundation of all of our social structure, are kept in ignorance. It is as if the best plant could be grown in the most barren soil." Threlkeld saw the education of the masses and the education of leaders as phases of the same process. Is it not true, he asked, that individuals with great potential can find maximum stimulation only in a society in which everyone else is also developing to the full extent of their powers?[132]

As an illustration of his point, Threlkeld pointed to Thomas Edison. The choice of Edison was delightfully appropriate, for just a few years earlier, Oakland's testing expert, Virgil Dickson, had used Edison to make the opposite point: that it was useless to try to elevate the quality of education for all students in the hopes that one might become an Edison.[133] "Anyone knows upon a moment's consideration," Threlkeld argued, "that without the help of lesser lights in tens of thousands of science laboratories throughout the world past and present, there would be no such tremendous culmination of scientific contribution from any one person, no matter what his native ability, as we have from Thomas A. Edison." In other words, only through millions of people learning, thinking, and working together could native genius truly reach its greatest achievements; and the same applied to all fields of intellectual activity. "Obviously," Threlkeld concluded, "in a society in which only ten thousand people are questioning, inquiring, arguing, thinking, there is not the possibility for the potential leader of intelligence that there is in a society where ten million or one hundred million people are thinking for themselves."[134] Despite Threlkeld's faith that his statements were clear, obvious, and logical, such insights remained rare at the time and—as the example of Dickson demonstrates—many prominent administrators thought exactly the reverse. Nevertheless, despite Threlkeld's objections to many of the standard beliefs of the late 1920s, his reflections did not necessarily result in immediate changes in district policy.

"Is classification a benefit or an evil?" asked Denver's director of research Charles E. Greene in 1931. "Does it promote ideals of democracy or develop snobs? . . . Does the intelligence test really predict ability to do school work?" Normally, these types of forthright questions would have been unusual for a city school administrator to ask at the time, but they demonstrated the kind of open questioning that was made possible, perhaps even encouraged, by Threlkeld's philosophical deliberations on democracy and the district's experience with the curriculum revision program. Moreover, Greene explained, after some ten years' experience with classification, a handful of academics had begun attacking "so-called homogeneous grouping." Greene sought to use evidence collected in Denver schools to investigate the potential implications for the district and its students.[135]

With remarkable directness, Greene identified the inherent contradictions within the notion of student classification. For example, he relayed the new findings of researchers like Percival Symonds, an associate professor of education at Teachers College, who found surprisingly wide discrepancies in achievement and intelligence test scores. Symonds showed that the same twelve-year-old student might vary as much as between 1.8 years and 4.1 years in her achievement scores in different classes.[136] The following year, Greene's assistant director of research, Guy Fox, published data from three-years' worth of intelligence testing in Denver, using both the Terman IQ test and the Otis IQ test. The Denver norms for each of these tests were considerably different: 106.5 for the Terman test; 99.53 for the Otis. Fox found that even larger inconsistencies emerged when these tests were used for student placement.[137]

Despite the irregularities of test results that Greene and Fox revealed, Denver school leaders had been using intelligence tests as a means of classifying students for a full decade. Greene reported, for example, that in the 1931–32 school year alone the district's research department administered over 83,000 tests, a figure that included some 32,703 group mental tests.[138] Therefore, reversing course, or even altering it, would have presented significant challenges to district practices that had long been structured on the ideology of classification, even to a system as open to reform as Denver.

In the original research cited by Greene, Symonds had recognized that practitioners could not reconsider student grouping without rethinking fundamental theories of education. To overturn standard practices would have once again placed district progressives in the awkward position of needing quick and practical policy alternatives. "When classification on the present plan is condemned," Greene acknowledged, "the problem rises immediately as to what basis should be used—for classification there must be in the larger schools." Even if Greene was unable to imagine the possibility of large schools without any kind of classification, he could admit that criticisms of classification had validity; but much more careful experimentation would be needed, he believed, before classification could be fully evaluated and either discarded or improved. "Until some better scheme of classification is presented, we should use the present plan with reservations and recognize that individual differences still abound within groups. . . . The problem of adapting methods of instruction and content remains the chief concern of those engaged in education."[139] Indeed, we might say, it remains so today.

———

What does Denver reveal about the nature of urban schooling and the hopes for democratic education during the Progressive Era? From Aaron Gove's admonitions about the dangers of falsely conceived democratic sentiments, through Cubberley's assertions about democracy implying "the greatest good for the greatest number," to Newlon and Threlkeld's warning that treating teachers as mere classroom mechanics was "antithetical to the spirit of democracy," Denver offers a full spectrum of district progressive thought on democracy. Perhaps more so than any other urban district of the era, Denver demonstrated the prismatic qualities of democratic education as interpreted by urban school leaders. The city revealed a central paradox inherent in the operation of Progressive Era school systems: perhaps a hierarchically structured corporate district with one-man rule was a necessary precondition for the democratic treatment of teachers and the implementation of many other reforms.

Without the intervention of civic organizations bent on fostering a more businesslike school board, Denver may never have offered the fertile terrain for robust renewal that Newlon found on his arrival. The crafting of a more equitable and professionalized atmosphere for teachers would likely have occurred only with the free hand for leadership that Newlon was bestowed by the change of board bylaws. There is, of course, a monumental irony in the notion that the types of pedagogical and curricular reforms that Denver pursued required precisely the types of administrative leadership that scholars have seen as incompatible, even unfriendly, to deeper, more substantive reforms of pedagogical progressivism.

A related irony is that the curriculum revision process—so carefully crafted by Newlon and Threlkeld—was often bypassed by the other school districts that simply purchased the Denver courses of study rather than embarking on a revision process of their own. Few districts of the era would have been able to marshal the types of financial resources needed to embark on such a district-wide reform effort, even those that found themselves in better shape than the hand-to-mouth condition that characterized Denver by the late 1910s. Still, Denver's achievements serve to remind American taxpayers—then and now—that significant improvement often requires serious investment.

Denver holds other insights for scholars and practitioners. The window of opportunity for considering alternative causes of student failure that opened in Oakland also appeared in Denver during the same years. In his experimentation with ungraded classrooms, Charles Chadsey likewise revealed similar findings: that with proper instruction, many pupils who had fallen behind could be returned to their grades. Student's ability to do schoolwork need not be predetermined. Yet Denver, like so many other districts, ultimately yielded to the temptations of intelligence testing. Still, it is rare indeed to find the kind of candid appraisal regarding the flaws of IQ testing made by district central office administrators, even if they had to acknowledge their own limitations in conceptualizing novel systems were difficult to develop or even conceptualize. Nevertheless, although Denver may have found ways to unshackle teachers from dull routines and mandates from above, those liberating effects may not have reached down to redeem students whose future prospects may well have been narrowed by the use of intelligence testing. In the generations that followed, the lack of imagination in creating new systems for working with students would become deeply detrimental for poor and minority students.

In 1916, Cubberley convinced the Denver school board that democracy did not mean that "many persons should work at any one problem," but Newlon and Threlkeld ultimately demonstrated that, in fact, some kinds of educational challenges actually must be addressed by many people deliberately putting their minds together. By 1928, Threlkeld used the insights he gleaned from the collaborative work of his teachers to propose another vision of democratic education: one in which millions of minds learned, grew, and worked together to create a better future.

5

COMPETING VISIONS FOR A PROGRESSIVE PORTLAND, OREGON

PORTLAND: CITY BEAUTIFUL TOO

180 After enjoying a generation of dominance in the Pacific Northwest, Portland businessmen looked nervously at the younger cities of Puget Sound. In 1897, while Portland still staggered from the financial panic of 1893, Seattle began its boom as the staging point for the Klondike gold rush. Portland's identity had long been based on its claim as the "natural metropolis" of the Pacific Northwest, but city leaders worried their reputation was endangered. The Portland *Oregonian* was therefore delighted when it could announce in 1900 that recent census findings demonstrated that Seattle had fallen ten thousand short of Portland's population. Throughout the next decade the *Oregonian* continued to assert that Portland was "more than holding its lead." The 1905 Lewis and Clark Centennial Exposition held in Portland provided a perfect opportunity for the city to parade itself as an industrial and scientific "school of progress," all the while advertising its attractiveness as a site for investment and relocation. The exposition allowed Portlanders to begin the twentieth century with a flourish of self-congratulation, at the same time that it gave them the chance to redesign key sectors of their city and its park system.[1]

Portland's erstwhile reputation in the historiography as staid and conservative has been overturned by more recent scholarship, putting the myth of Portland's monolithic culture of conventionalism to rest. In fact, Portland was home to some of the most progressive political struggles of the day. The city served as the base for both the national movement for direct democracy and the "Oregon System" of direct legislation. More importantly, a series of near-radical political reforms were supported not only by working-class parties alone but also by coalitions that had formed between laborers and Portland's liberal middle class.[2] That said, the conservative elements of the predominantly white, Protestant city did not simply disappear, and some of the most interesting national political tensions of the era can be found in local debates about the cultural institutions deemed central to Portland's sense of identity. For example, during and after World War I, much of Portland's educational work took place against the backdrop of a generally conservative atmosphere, evidenced by the initial success of a 1922 KKK-backed school bill that required all Oregon children of school age to attend *public* schools. The new law essentially outlawed private schools, and its advocates believed it would help eradicate ideological and ethnic pluralism, primarily through squashing the kind of *religious* pluralism symbolized by the growth of the Catholic school system. Although the Oregon school law was overturned by the Supreme Court in 1925, historians have traditionally seen its passage as the last gasp of a virulent, though waning, form of nativism.[3]

One consequence of the competing political tendencies within Portland's communities was the unfurling of dramatically different educational visions for the schools. The path that resulted was a switchback of alternating programs that demonstrated core divisions within the coalitions of groups that supported public education in Portland. During the mid-1910s, for example, the Portland schools experienced a swell of bold and daring educational experimentation, marking Portland as a potential demonstration site for the transformation of an American urban school system from its "dead" traditionalism to full-fledged progressivism. Other educators took notice. "The Pacific Coast is supremely interesting from any point of view," wrote the indefatigably enthusiastic *Journal of Education* editor A. E. Winship after a 1915 visit to Portland. "Its newness, its vitality, its freedom from the tyranny of tradition, its relation to the whole Pacific, to all of Asia, and to all Alaska make it a world all its own." Still, he claimed, Portland was the most conservative of all the major cities along the western seaboard, "as evidenced by the fact that fewer extreme experiments have been tried." Yet with his contrarian knack for optimism, Winship added that this consequently meant that fewer reforms had been "ruthlessly destroyed in their youth."[4]

Yet some of Winship's praise of Portland was premature. As of 1915, these new programs had hardly yet become institutionalized, despite the apparent enthusiasm of outsiders. More importantly, Portland chose not to implement some of the core progressive reforms that became fundamental to other city school systems. In Oakland and Denver, for example, the successful adoption of administrative reorganization meant that the balance of policy and decision-making power shifted away from board committees and toward the kind of professional educational leadership that national reformers, like Ellwood Cubberley and Lewis Terman, urged districts to accept. Historians have long characterized the Progressive Era as a period during which Americans embraced the transition toward expertise. Yet what about districts that refused to accept this shift?

As with Oakland and Denver, civic groups became engaged in political contests for school board representation and in wide-ranging conversations about the nature and direction of leadership necessary in a democracy. The whiplash changes on display in Portland raised one additional question: Whom do we trust in a democracy to run the public schools?

In the early twentieth century, Portland was thirty-six hours by train from San Francisco and just over six hours from Seattle. Educational innovations often spread back and forth between urban school districts as regularly as the itinerant experts who commuted between conferences, lectures, and their home universities. Throughout the first several decades of the twentieth century, new instructional ideas cascaded through the Portland Public Schools. The activity began in earnest after Portland leaders engaged a team of external surveyors to evaluate the school system in 1913.

The resulting report delivered a withering critique of the schools. Completed two years before Cubberley's Oakland survey and three years before Franklin Bobbitt's Denver survey, the Portland study was one of the first comprehensive school surveys, and it swiftly became a "classic" of survey literature. It was also one of the harshest public evaluations of the era and not only delivered a stiff jolt to the system but also reached a large audience outside the district, especially after it was turned into a textbook for courses in educational leadership.

Whether the disparagement of Portland was justified ultimately became of secondary importance to a board more concerned about local finances than national reputation, and four years after the 1913 report, the school board commissioned a second survey to determine the success the district had experienced in responding to the first survey. These two early surveys provide a glimpse of how educational leaders in Portland in the years before World War I proceeded with plans to create a school system that balanced outside innovations with internal needs. Unlike Oakland, however, the school board chose not to reorganize along the lines recommended by these surveys; the district thereby offers a distinct perspective on what it meant to be a progressive school system. What kinds of district foundations did educators continue to build for the next twenty years?[5] This chapter traces the Portland school system as it weathered the external forces of educational change and as four superintendents, each with his own distinct vision for Portland education, sought to design a modern urban school district.

RIGIDITY AND THE "RIGLER SYSTEM," 1896–1913

Frank Rigler, Portland's superintendent from 1896 to 1913, left a deep imprint on the city's public schools by a system that proved remarkably resilient in

the years that followed. Born in Pennsylvania in 1855, Rigler attended Philadelphia's illustrious public Central High School. His first job was in Philadelphia's department of city engineering, but he soon turned to teaching and
took his first administrative position as vice principal of the Philadelphia
Boys' Grammar School. In 1879, after only one year at this administrative
post, Rigler moved west to Oregon in the hope of curing an enduring throat
ailment, and he served brief terms as the superintendent in Polk County and
in Walla Walla, Washington. The Portland school board appointed him as
principal of Portland High School in 1894 and then as superintendent in 1896.

   With Rigler as its chief strategist, the district was operated, or at least
planned, with military precision. "In trying to put his ideas across, he used
good salesmanship, psychologically applied," explained one history of the
Portland schools, "but often with considerable pressure as well." The teachers were regularly convened for consultations, discussion, and advice, but the
culture of the district was such that they usually "found it desirable to cooperate."[6] Rigler retained almost complete control of the instructional activities
of the district. "So definitely was the work laid out," recollected one administrator who worked under Rigler, "so thoroughly did he impress his manner
of teaching upon his corps of teachers, that it was said that at any time of any
day in the term, he could sit in his office and know on what page in each book
work was being done at the time in every school in the city."[7]

   Like Aaron Gove, Denver's superintendent around the same time,
Rigler made it clear that he was no advocate of pedagogical innovation. "I
am not aware that our schools have any (approved) features that were not
to be found a generation ago," sniffed Rigler on assuming his superintendency
in 1896. "The friends of our schools who are apprehensive that the schools
have become too modern are needlessly alarmed," he assured board members and school patrons who might worry about creeping educational experimentation.[8] By Rigler's way of thinking, progress was not defined by updated
teaching methods; instead, he focused on fine-tuning a growing bureaucracy
and on improving an instructional program that he felt simply needed ever
stronger supervision. His suspicion of "modern" practices did not appear to
isolate him from the educational community outside Portland. He was a supporter of the NEA, serving as its Oregon director, and he actively promoted
the State Teachers' Association, spending a term as its president. The path he
chose to pursue in Portland was informed by these broader contacts, even as
he pursued his own version of educational progress.

   Over the course of seventeen years, Rigler, the onetime engineer, designed
a school system that was a vast urban mechanism. Despite his stated icon-
oclasm, he was not uninterested in reforms taking place elsewhere, and he
traveled east on at least one occasion to visit industrial trade schools, returning

to recommend the establishment of such a school in Portland. The board concurred, opening the School of Trades in 1908; the school, Rigler wrote, was "organized to meet the demand that is felt in the industrial world for more skilled mechanics, and to give greater opportunity to the young man who wants to learn a trade." So successful was this school that the district opened an industrial school for girls a year later. In all, Rigler opened three new high schools during his tenure, two of them intended to meet the perceived needs of modern commercial and industrial demands.[9] This was Rigler's approach to fitting the school to the child and his reaction to the increasing popularity of high schools, especially in a rapidly growing city like Portland.

Classification and Curriculum under Rigler

Beyond vocational education, the classification of children was an essential part of Rigler's district plan and one for which he became well known. Around the turn of the century, Rigler developed a system that reformulated the curriculum into a series of specific steps that students were required to take for advancement and promotion. The plan was a response to the same challenges facing Oakland and Denver as those districts struggled to accommodate relentless enrollment increases. Portland's average daily attendance, for example, jumped from 10,387 in 1902 to 23,712 by 1912. Rigler saw his plan as a no-nonsense approach to allowing children to "progress at whatever rate is found suitable to their powers," gloating in 1910 that his new system proved highly superior to the "very defective plan" it had replaced. Moreover, he argued, Portland's approach to classification was better than programs developed in Batavia, New York, and Cambridge, Massachusetts, two cities whose student promotion plans had also gained national attention for unconventional approaches to fostering student progress through the grades. At the time, the graded system of schooling was increasingly lambasted for its rigidity and inflexibility by prominent educators like Chicago's Ella Flagg Young and William T. Harris, the U.S. commissioner of education and former superintendent of the St. Louis schools.[10]

What made Rigler's approach distinctive was its subdivision of the school system's curricular content into fifty-four distinct units. He explained that the average student should be expected to complete all fifty-four units over the course of eight school years. Most students would cover roughly six units a year, but slower or faster students might take more or less time accordingly. Students were grouped homogeneously according to their abilities (as determined by their teacher or principal), allowing individual students to excel in some subjects while moving more steadily in others. The premise of his promotion system was that it permitted students to progress at different rates, while it also offered teachers the freedom to instruct according the needs of their classes.[11]

Rigler was proud of his plan and believed it provided curricular flexibility and individual attention as needed. He had reason to think his plan meritorious, for William T. Harris once praised it by declaring that "Mr. Rigler's system of classifying children into faster and more backward classes in the public schools is the sanest and most scientific that I have ever seen."[12] Superintendents and academics across the country regularly mentioned the "Portland plan" as one viable approach to classifying children.[13]

Although Rigler often hovered over the curricular details of the district, he seemed less inclined to concern himself with dull administrative duties or to scrutinize financial matters; in truth, he was given little authority to do so. E. H. Whitney, an administrator who worked under Rigler, once complained that there was little standardization of equipment throughout the district. Whitney's frustration stemmed from the fact that Portland adhered to a more traditional system of district administration, one that was often used in urban school systems in the late nineteenth century. To the casual observer, this conventional arrangement may seem like a mundane matter, but it became the crux of many a progressive argument.[14]

The predicament caused by the older district governance system is well illustrated by the organizational chart that Cubberley diagrammed to demonstrate the fundamental flaws of the Portland school district in his 1913 survey (fig. 2.1).[15] The school system was administered by the board through eight separate committees, each focused on a different area of general concern—such as buildings, repairs, finance, teachers, and so forth. Under this management scheme, Whitney explained, board members quite literally "carried requisitions in their pockets" and whenever a particular item or school supply was needed, a board member would give the school principal or janitor a completed requisition form which they would then take to a local merchant of the board member's choice "and the item was procured at a retail price."[16] The cozier methods that worked in a smaller district soon became cumbersome, if not emblematic of favoritism or municipal corruption.

The district's nineteenth-century administrative system began to fray under the pressure as enrollments began to increase rapidly after the turn of the century. National reforms had been slow to make inroads into Portland, so it may have been with reluctant resignation that the board approved the centralization of business matters in 1908 and, two years later, approved a Bureau of Properties and a Bureau of Purchases (however, these bureaus are not included in Cubberley's chart, indicating that they may never have become fully operational). The expansion of the district also affected Rigler, who would have been satisfied to continue as the sole educational administrator with narrow line authority over strict curricular and pedagogical matters. It was the board, not the superintendent himself, who decided an assistant superintendent was a necessary addition to the district hierarchy; and in 1907, the board created the position and appointed Daniel A. Grout, one of Portland's school principals, to the post.[17]

Taken together, the increased enrollment, new buildings, additional teachers, and new features of the system nudged school costs upward. Such fiscal escalation troubled a school board that proudly considered itself penurious. In fact, expenses far outstripped the growth in the student population: While school enrollments more than doubled between 1902 and 1912, school costs increased nearly sixfold. Outside of the school board, other civic organizations raised questions about expenditures. Determined to discover if their money was well spent, a group of citizens pressed the school board to commission a survey of the district to evaluate if Portland schools were being operated at "the highest pitch of efficiency."[18] The system that Rigler had so carefully constructed did not survive the study.

The 1913 Survey

The accepted narrative on the impetus for the Portland survey has been that the school board requested the survey of its own accord. However, the idea for the survey was first proposed by members of a community meeting in December 1912. At that point in time, Portland taxpayers still held an annual school meeting that met separately from the school board. The 1912 gathering sparked questions about school costs, educational programs, school buildings, methods of administration, and systems of accounting, along with other matters. Frustrated both at the increasing costs of the Portland schools and with the lack of available information about district's educational programs, the assembled taxpayers passed several resolutions that called for a wide-ranging survey of the city school system. At a special meeting held in January 1913, the school board gave formal approval to a citizens' committee to move forward with the survey, although not without some initial protest.[19]

The push for a school survey overlapped with another significant event in the city's history: a survey of Portland's municipal governance system conducted by the New York Bureau of Municipal Research, an investigative agency founded in 1907 that was rapidly gaining attention for its muckraking reports. In early 1913, the publisher of the *Oregon Journal* became interested in establishing a local bureau of municipal research to serve as a watchdog over the city's governance, and he assembled a committee of prominent Portland citizens to look into the creation of such an organization. One of the leaders pressing for investigations into both city and school governance and expenses was Richard W. Montague, a well-known Portland lawyer. Montague was a keen observer of urban reform, a key player in multiple urban improvement efforts, and a regular participant at National Municipal League annual meetings. He was also appointed as the head of the Portland taxpayers' committee that pressured the school board to allocate money for the school survey. Therefore, as in Denver, the twin movements for school reform and municipal cleansing shared leaders and language.[20]

Convinced that the Portland school investigation would best be conducted by "professional school men," Montague canvassed educational experts from across the country about the most qualified evaluators. The committee eventually settled on a survey team headed by Ellwood Cubberley, who, in turn, contracted additional assistance from Lewis Terman of Stanford University, Edward Elliot of the University of Wisconsin, Fletcher Dresslar of Peabody College for Teachers, Superintendent J. H. Francis of Los Angeles, and Frank Spaulding, superintendent of the Newton, Massachusetts, public schools; each of these men wrote a section of the resulting report.[21] The Portland survey was completed at a time when these same individuals were among a group of nationally known educators engaged in redefining American schooling. Thus, the investigation gave them a unique opportunity to enumerate the precise failings of schools of the past and to envision plans for the school district of the future. The survey catapulted many of Cubberley's most influential ideas, along with those of his colleagues, into the national spotlight.

In his vivid section on the problems of instructional practices in Portland's schools, Newton superintendent Spaulding pounced on the flaws he detected in the district. The atmosphere of the school system, "rigidly centralized, mechanical and mechanically administered," he declared, "is quite manifest in all the classroom work of the grammar grades [and] in the attitude of principals, teachers, and pupils." Rather than encountering a system in which each classroom teacher decided the rate of student progress, as Rigler had asserted, Spaulding found an atmosphere of restrictive uniformity and was astonished at the "noticeable absence of any feeling of educational responsibility" among practitioners. Portland teachers, wrote Spaulding, "are convinced that many of their efforts are futile, that much that they are attempting is of little or no value to their pupils; but what can they do about it? They have no responsibility, no right, to depart from the rigidly uniform prescriptions of the course of study, reinforced by inspection from the central office, and by the important term examinations."[22] The central weakness was Rigler's curriculum, which Spaulding described as "vivisected with mechanical accuracy into fifty-four dead pieces."[23]

Spaulding was astonished to find 264 pupils, ranging in age from eleven to eighteen, sitting side by side in the same classrooms with 112 children under eight years of age. Such a situation had occurred, he explained, due to the district's faulty classification system, a scheme that had somehow determined that all 376 of these pupils were alike, because "they all measure up to third grade work." Knowledge of the conventional elementary subjects was a useful criterion by which to determine appropriate classification and instruction, Spaulding acknowledged, but "nowhere and never should this be the only factor considered." He was equally troubled by what he saw as too much emphasis placed on testing "academic," "bookish," and overly "abstract" knowledge, a hallmark of the nineteenth-century learning tasks that educational progressives sought to replace. It was unusual for one city school superintendent to be so critical of another at this point in time, but Spaulding's acerbic tone might be explained in part by the fact that the Portland survey was conducted just four years after Leonard Ayres published *Laggards in our Schools*, and progressive educators were itching for change.[24]

Cubberley painted an equally grim picture in his chapters on district administration, identifying an array of flaws in the system and likely surprising board members expecting a sober analysis of expenditures. The school board retained far too much control over the details of school administration, making the superintendent "entirely too little of a leader; entirely too much of an office clerk," Cubberley complained. "The present method of conducting the education work of the district is not only wasteful of the time of the [board members], and wholly unnecessary from an educational or business point of view, but it has a depressing effect on the school system as a whole."[25]

In general, Cubberley felt, the whole school district "seemed to be more of a system of inspection and reporting than a system of helpful educational leadership," which thereby led to an organization that suffered "from too many rules and too little personal initiative." As judged by "the light of good administrative principles," Cubberley continued, the district both "gave the impression of lacking self-reliance, and of being weak from over-direction from above." This "fundamental weakness" of district administration, one that Cubberley reported witnessing in a number of schools, "seemed to pervade the whole supervisory system, and to extend from the top downward."[26] In short, Portland's public school system was a victim of the "village methods" inherited from its past: it was simply not urban enough and not sufficiently modern.

Stanford's Lewis Terman—who, we may recall, referred to the problems of Portland in the Denver survey (written just a few years later)—was troubled both by Rigler's classification scheme and by the school system's inattention to health matters. Terman was hardly opposed to classification, far from it. What galled him about Portland was the type of classification, in that it did not distinguish between children based on their abilities. Although Terman's views were not fully formed as of 1913, Rigler's system did not appear to conform to proper notions of scientific classification. Therefore, in Terman's mind, it was not classification at all.[27]

In addition to the survey team's comments, the investigation provided a rare opportunity for parents, community members, and teachers to voice their concerns about defects in the system and the conduct of school administrators. Some parents confirmed the dreary picture that Cubberley and Spaulding had drawn of the district; others raised grievances about specific leaders in the system. One angry parent, referring to Assistant Superintendent Grout, wrote: "Grout is a cold-blooded, cowardly, unsympathetic man and knows only intimidation and coercion as a means of controlling teachers. His elimination from the service is the first great step in reform." This same parent also complained about the treatment her own children had received when Grout had been their principal:

Grout is a machine man and when principal of Ladd school knew not how to control either pupils or teachers except by force and intimidation. My children were then afraid of him and the teachers. They were made to march with eyes forward and necks stiff. . . . Any child who broke the military precision of the ranks was given the "rabbit hold." This was a shake given by pressing the thumb and forefingers against the child's neck and if the pressure was hard enough it would cause the child to collapse. One child treated that way before the other children kept all cowed.[28]

Another parent fumed: "No language at my command would enable me to adequately express the educational weakness of our high schools. Our children are graduated from them with their initiative destroyed; without high ideals of purpose or life." Other parents, and at least one teacher, also proclaimed that they were deeply disturbed by the current state of the system.[29]

Although the survey report did not directly address parents' concerns, it did offer a number of solutions to Portland's problems, what its authors described as the "way out." Cubberley included organizational diagrams of the current structure of the Portland system as it existed in 1913 (fig. 2.1)—a structure that he said demonstrated a lack of coordination—and a proposed version (fig. 2.2) that he stated would provide the correct type of "unified educational organization."[30] Spaulding made a number of recommendations designed to resurrect the curriculum and introduce lively activity into the classroom. Placement of students must be determined, he wrote, *not* on "what a pupil *has* learned, but [on] what he *most needs to learn.*" The first and foremost step in determining needs, Spaulding believed, was through "an appreciative understanding of the capacities, interests, [and] possibilities" of each one of Portland's schoolchildren.[31] The task of determining children's capacities, interests, and possibilities assumed the creation of a new constellation of features within the modern urban school system; in fact, it necessitated a new conception of the nature of the school system itself. No individual teacher could completely grasp the full extent of student needs, Spaulding explained, nor could a small group of educators. Rather, the task of determining the needs of students was "the great responsibility of the nine hundred teachers, principals, supervisors and superintendents" who staffed the Portland school system. Education was no longer the province of the lone classroom teacher or of the individual school: properly conceived, it was the domain of the large urban school district outfitted with an array of programs, schools, and services.[32]

In a nutshell, here was the challenge facing urban educators at the time. The problem with Rigler's scheme, according to Spaulding and other likeminded progressives, was that it structured itself around an already reified curriculum rather than focusing on children. In other words, while Rigler viewed the curriculum as unalterable, district progressives believed that the child's abilities represented the unchanging constant.

Worried about the sort of criticism he would receive as a result of the survey, a nervous Rigler began doing what came naturally to him: he made demands of his subordinates. The superintendent contacted principals about Spaulding's visits to the schools, inquiring: "Which teachers did he visit? How long did he spend with each? What was the subject recited or discussed in each room?" Presented with information about Rigler's prying, the school board was forced to issue a statement that no one in the district was to "interfere in any way with the work of the survey."[33] Rigler's influence was waning.

The Portland survey sketched out other dimensions of the progressive school district in far more detail than had Cubberley's report on Oakland, and in doing so it foreshadowed the comprehensive study that would soon be conducted in Denver as well as the multivolume survey that would emerge from the investigation of the Cleveland public schools in 1916. Taken as a whole, the Portland survey offered a remarkable statement on what the modern progressive school district should look like, a portrait that, as of 1913, reformers were still creating. Fletcher Dresslar described the types of modern build-ings Portland should construct, and Los Angeles superintendent J. H. Francis laid out suggestions for vocational studies and synthesized the other sets of recommendations into a comprehensive plan for district reorganization. In a moment of unusual candor, Francis—another district progressive—warned Portland educational leaders that they should expect to face local opposition if they adopted the surveyors' plans. "Every new movement for the improve-ment of our educational system," he cautioned, encountered opposition from the "selfish" or from those who simply "do not understand." Francis insisted that when such community opposition manifested itself, it was the school leader's duty to "turn a deaf ear."[34] In other words, it was the district progres-sive's responsibility to stop community concern from blunting innovation.

The Portland survey reached an audience far beyond Portland. Like sev-eral other surveys of the period, the report was published by the World Book Company in their School Efficiency Series, giving other districts, along with future teachers and administrators, a textbook they could use as a guide for future work. Stanford professor Jesse Sears said that the survey presented a vision of the schools "as one complex and united enterprise of the people of Portland."[35] Even contemporary figures who might have been expected to recoil from efficiency-oriented measurement activities applauded the survey. The liberal intellectual Randolph Bourne praised the survey in the *New Republic*, saying that it represented "a new achievement in educational thinking" and would spell the "last of the old system and the promise of the school of tomorrow."[36] George Strayer of Teachers College, who himself soon became an indefatigable surveyor, found much to value in the survey, but he also worried that the "hypercritical attitude" of Spaulding's section on instruction might result only in local resentment.[37]

The tenor of the report would have been jarring, but the timing of the sur-vey influenced its unrelenting language. Recall that the chair of the original survey committee was Richard Montague, who was instrumental in com-missioning the New York Municipal Research Bureau to conduct Portland's local governance survey; that study also took place in the spring of 1913. The bureau's report was also described as shocking, sparking widespread outcry throughout the city. The bureau began publishing sections of its findings in April, and Spaulding's visit to the district—April 7–24—overlapped exactly with the release of some of these preliminary reports.[38] Although the simul-taneity of these events was likely a coincidence, their co-occurrence strongly suggests that Spaulding's language—as well as Cubberley's and that of other members of the school survey team—was likely influenced by the bureau's trenchant critique and forceful rhetoric.

Even a brief comparison of the two reports shows some of the similarities. "Not only is the budget making procedure illogical and conducive to secretive methods," wrote the bureau about Portland's Budget and Finance Office, "but the estimate forms are inefficient for administrative purposes." Other statements were similar: "Not only has the public not been adequately informed . . . but even the Council itself in passing appropriations has labored largely in the dark."[39] Given the attention that the bureau's reports attracted in Portland, it is difficult to imagine that Cubberley and Spaulding were not influenced by the muscularity of the bureau's prose. Gauging the public's startled response to the flaws of public governance, the school surveyors likely saw an opportunity to accomplish something similar in education.

As a result of the school survey, Rigler, certainly aware that he was about to be labeled "unprogressive," resigned even before the final report of the survey committee was issued.[40] The school board offered the vacant superintendency to Lewis R. Alderman, the Oregon state superintendent of instruction. Alderman stepped down from his state-level post in order to take the step up into the job of a city school chief, a position that brought with it greater prestige and a higher salary. Alderman had gained a reputation as an active and creative educational leader, and his challenge in Portland was to breathe fresh air into a stagnant system.[41]

ALDERMAN AGONISTES, 1913–18

Alderman was everything that Rigler was not. He was the first Portland superintendent to be born in Oregon, but he was also the first district administrator not to have worked his way up through the city school system. He was an innovator, an experimenter, and a creative spirit.[42] He carried with him to Portland an open-mindedness and a progressive energy that local leaders must have hoped would lift the critical cloud hanging over the system after the survey. Alderman quickly implemented a number of initiatives, and it was in this context that the education journalist Winship wrote that "Superintendent Alderman bids fair to do for Portland what he did for Oregon, and if he does, all aspirations will be achieved." City school leaders and citizens hoped to make Portland "the best city educationally in the country."[43]

While it seems unlikely that a significant turnaround of any large district could be orchestrated within in a year, Alderman found community support for the introduction of some innovations. In fact, just one year after the survey yet another municipal organization, this time the Oregon Civic League, published a condensed summary of its recommendations, along with a list of changes already implemented by the district (and to which the group amended a list of the errors that the survey team had committed). Recognizing that some of the practices that the schools had altered since the survey were admittedly minor, the league acknowledged that the survey team's major recommendations required passage of new statutes by the state legislature (the language of which had been characteristically proposed by Cubberley himself), indicating that the school board may not have had the autonomy to redistribute its own power. However, when the Civic League offered a summary of the "salient points" of the proposed legislation, it left out the provisions that would have required the most significant organizational restructuring—such as removing power from individual school board members—thereby leaving the district's structural relationships in place.[44]

Portland proceeded differently after the results of its survey than some of its contemporaries. Unlike the steps taken by the Denver school board some months after its own survey, or for that matter the decisions made belatedly in Oakland, Portland school board members did not target substantive administrative and organizational change. Such inaction might appear somewhat surprising, especially given the ongoing national notoriety the city suffered. Cubberley only added salt to their wounded pride when he published Portland's organizational chart as an example of "an incorrect form of educational organization" in his highly popular 1916 *Public School Administration* (fig. 2.1), gravely cautioning that teachers would surely become "professionally unprogressive" should the status quo persist.[45] In fact, it took another fourteen years before the district chose to reorganize administratively.

One explanation for the board member's aversion to reorganization was the reluctance to relinquish their traditional powers. Reorganization according to the survey plan would have meant handing over control of hiring decisions and purchasing, along with many other powers, to the superintendent. Some school board members in Denver fought the same battle to retain their authority just three years later, albeit with different results. Although he did not discuss it much, Alderman would likely have welcomed the centralization of power that accompanied reorganization, given the constraints under which he continued to operate. In fact, he later grumbled that the board had never even given him the freedom even to choose his own assistant superintendents.[46] It is useful to keep in mind that Alderman began his tenure in Portland at roughly the same time that A. C. Barker took the reins of the superintendency in Oakland. Both men operated under the older system of governance whereby the school board members and board committees had much more authority over district matters than did the superintendent. Neither man had the power or autonomy that both Hunter and Newlon would enjoy just a few years later.

Despite some organizational limitations, however, Alderman developed a unique district vision once he was appointed. As did many of his contemporaries, he believed his approach was undeniably progressive, yet it also presented an alternative version of the progressive school district than those developed in either Oakland or Denver. Alderman's agenda was predicated on a slightly different understanding of the city school system. While he instituted some programmatic elements that were common in other districts, Alderman also selected some curricular and structural changes that were variations on other popular progressive themes.

As explained by the Oregon Civic League pamphlet, Alderman had introduced some initial changes intended to address the recommendations of the survey, especially those targeting the problematic academic "abstractions" identified by Spaulding. He quickly initiated development on a new course of study, soon reporting that in arithmetic the teachers now worked with pupils to "make many concrete problems of their own, which are more real to them than the ordinary book problems." In English, he said, teachers stressed written composition and oral composition, giving less time to technical grammar. Using a discourse similar to Spaulding's, Alderman explained that educators in the Portland schools had "tried to discover the bent of the individual child, believing that by working along the line of the child's interest we can best help him."[47] The new district-wide curriculum aimed "to correlate closely the work of the schools with the life of this community."[48] Alderman enumerated other district innovations in his 1914 annual report, describing a new plan to keep teachers with their students for two years, the introduction of foreign languages into the elementary schools, and the creation of a pupils' vacation employment bureau. All these changes fit the list of progressive reforms, the type recommended by the survey, and therefore represented efforts to depart from the Rigler system.

Beyond easing the stifling curriculum, Alderman attempted to invigorate the stale atmosphere that surveyors had reported Portland teachers found oppressive. Easing pressure on teachers meant that Alderman also had to relax constraints on school principals in order to allow them more autonomy. The "teachers have been allowed a great deal of freedom," Alderman said, as had principals. In fact, as local populations grew, each principal had the responsibility to fit his school to the particular needs of its neighborhood, although Alderman did not always elaborate on the specifics of how principals gave their schools "distinct individuality" or even on how he changed the teaching environment. Spaulding had recommended the addition of kindergartens, and Alderman complied, inaugurating several during his tenure. One architectural innovation of which Alderman was particularly proud—for both its economy and its fire safety—was the one-story elementary school-house, a Portland "reform" that merited an article in *Ladies' Home Journal*.[49] Furthermore, despite the glowing descriptions Rigler had provided about them, Alderman found the trade schools in deplorable condition on his arrival. He later recalled with pride how he persuaded Simon Benson, a local lumber magnate, to donate $100,000 toward the construction of a new vocational school, to be called the Benson Polytechnic High School.[50]

Alderman also took heed of the recommendations made by Spaulding and Terman about the need to better classify Portland schoolchildren, and he introduced several approaches prevalent in other districts before World War I. Yet, although Alderman adopted both the language of classification, his practices were often less unyielding. "Children should be treated as individuals and not as averages," wrote Alderman, referring to how the district organized ungraded rooms into which were put "the unfits"—those children above or below grade. These ungraded rooms were similar to those in Oakland and Denver in that students were helped to learn at their own pace, but the goal in Portland was not to return students to their own classrooms. Instead, Portland children stayed in these rooms, some advancing two or three years in the space of one, while others worked more slowly. One boy, a native of Russia, reportedly finished all the grade schoolwork in two years.[51]

A man motivated by ideas who savored new instructional practices and developments in other cities, Alderman hoped his teachers would become inspired too. He began a teacher exchange program after his first year in Portland. "We hope that this plan will stimulate an interest on the part of all teachers to be eligible for exchange," he said, "and that it will bring to us the best ideas from the cities where our people teach," announcing with pleasure that Chicago had joined the exchange program in 1915.[52] Alderman enthusiastically highlighted new ideas and innovations in his new *School Bulletin*, a regular newsletter he established for communicating district initiatives to teachers and principals. The bulletin allowed him to discuss changes he was considering for Portland or to elaborate on reforms he had already implemented. For example, he had previously initiated elsewhere in Oregon a system for giving students credit for work they had done outside of school in music, applied arts, construction, homemaking, and agriculture, and he introduced a similar program in Portland high schools for music studied under accredited schools, for bookkeeping in small downtown businesses, and even for "home tasks" in some schools.[53]

Alderman tried out other experimental ideas—small and large—with gusto. He started "practice stores" in schools with donations from local merchants, he initiated school excursions to local industries, he began a museum education program, with a former teacher acting as docent, and he began a program in "visual education," another novel effort to enliven classroom teaching through the use of color images projected on a screen—in other words, slides, of which he had purchased two thousand. The Portland schools started a curricular program in nature study—directed by the appropriately named Mr. Weed—allowing children to listen to lectures about birds and to build birdhouses in their shop classes, and with help from university faculty, to construct flytraps, designed to make Portland a "flyless city."[54]

Alderman frequently publicized positive comments made about his efforts by outside observers. Superintendent Francis of Los Angeles, who had been a member of the survey team, declared in 1914 that "Portland had made more progress during the last year than any other city in the United States."[55] In 1915, Winship's *Journal of Education* carried another detailed and flattering portrait of reforms taking place in the Portland schools. "Educationally," wrote Winship, "Portland is no longer conservative but refreshingly, sanely progressive. No city has done more by way of efficiency in the last two years than has Portland," adding that the schools had done "nothing new for the sake of doing something new." When Cubberley directed a survey of the Salt Lake City schools, Alderman reproduced comparative financial tables from the report that favorably portrayed Portland when measured alongside cities such as San Francisco, Denver, and Seattle.[56]

Alderman also fanned the flames of urban competitiveness. At one NEA annual meeting, for example, he entered into a contest with Superintendents Cole of Denver and Cooper of Seattle "to see which of the three school systems could enroll the largest percentage of grammar graduates in high schools." Their challenge came at moment when urban districts began taking more pride in the expansion of their secondary schools and when one measure of progressive success turned on the percentages of students who districts could see through high school. Alderman used one of his innovations— the plan whereby grammar school teachers stayed with their students for multiple years as they progressed through the grades—as a means for improving the numbers of students who continued on to high school. Portland won the competition, and Alderman credited the success in large part to his innovation.[57]

The Strength of Individual Schools

"There is no better constructive publicity for a city than to be known over the entire country as a city of good schools" declared one glowing school board member in 1915, stirred by the praise Portland had been receiving.[58]

The *Oregonian*, the voice of the Portland establishment, commended the schools both for utilizing the "best modern methods" of instruction and for educational facilities that ranked "high in comparison with those of other American cities of the same size."[59] These strokes of approval from insiders and outsiders alike were no doubt soothing to a district still recovering from the national disgrace of a witheringly brutal school survey. Still, Alderman's contention that the district's stuffy atmosphere had improved, that the curriculum had been modified, and that new progressive programs had been fully and successfully implemented cannot be taken at face value, nor did it demonstrate that the district had yet undergone any kind of fundamental transformation.

One core idea that motivated Alderman was that the district's role was to foster the unique culture of each school within the system. "The strength of the whole school system, the value of the system to the people, lies in the *strength of the individual schools*," Alderman wrote in 1917. "And I say 'individual' in this connection," he continued, "with perhaps an added phase of meaning. I mean that the school to be successful must develop individuality." Alderman was glad of the "distinctive school pride" that he saw blossoming in the schools. He related with pleasure a "heated controversy" he had overheard between two first-grade girls who lived in different parts of the district; each girl contended that hers was the finest school in the city. Each was right, Alderman added; every child should feel that his or her school was the very best. "I should deplore it greatly," he said, "if every school plant in Portland were exactly the same, if every principal had the same ideas of administration, if every teacher were asked to do her work according to a uniform plan."[60]

To Alderman, a network of vibrant schools allowed for the kind of progressive development that seemed difficult to foster in large urban school districts, a challenge that became increasingly clear after Dewey published *Schools of Tomorrow* with his daughter in 1915, highlighting the vigorous activity possible in small schools under an inspired educator.[61] Therefore, Alderman's initiative to foster school individuality offered an alternative approach to creating a progressive school district than that taken in either Oakland or Denver. It was simply a way to capture another type of progressive spirit.

In showering new innovations down on the system, Alderman hoped that teachers and administrators at each school site would experience and adopt practices that inspired them. "To progress we must change," he told Portland educators. "We must have courage, we must venture out beyond the well-sounded depths."[62] Alderman's own attempt to hazard the depths was to borrow an organizational innovation from another district and adapt it to his own purposes in Portland, an approach he called his "two-group plan."

The Two-Group Plan

"A comparison of subjects taught in the elementary schools now with those that were taught thirty or forty years ago," said Alderman in 1917, "shows that the people have tried to enrich the course of study in keeping with the needs of the children. To the six or seven subjects of the old-time school," he continued, "have been added about ten more—civics, current events, hygiene, 'nature study,' drawing, music, sewing, cooking, manual training, and physical training or organized play." Despite the accumulation of subject matter, he cautioned, "no reorganization of the school has taken place so as to make them fit in." Alderman understood that the expansion of the curriculum had created acute challenges for many elementary school teachers, some of whom were required to teach more than a dozen subjects. Not many superintendents took the time to acknowledge the instructional weight added by the accretion of new material. At this point in time, the standard approach in most districts was to employ a subject-area supervisor who worked with elementary teachers. Therefore, as Alderman explained it, large school systems employed supervisors for nearly every subject, be it music, sewing, arithmetic, or play, "and each supervisor exacts a certain amount of time from every teacher." So not only was the teacher burdened by the preparation of so many subjects, but a great deal of time was also devoted to meetings with subject area supervisors. In trying to accommodate the needs of all their urban students, teachers' found their time was being completely taken up, without a resulting improvement in instruction. "She often feels that hers is a hopeless task," Alderman lamented.[63]

The two-group plan, as Alderman envisioned it, provided a solution to this problem brought on by the accumulation of new coursework. "It is not that the subjects are too many for the child; he needs them every one, especially when he is hemmed in by the limitations of city life," Alderman explained. The real problem was that there were too many subjects for the teacher. The task of adapting the school to the child was neither straightforward nor simple, as so many progressives quickly found. One main challenge was to reconfigure schooling in such a way that it operated more smoothly for educators. As we have seen, Alderman expected to see professional growth in his teachers, and he especially hoped to foster improvement in the district's instructional practices. Alderman reflected that instruction in the past had consisted almost entirely of hearing recitations. "Hearing recitations," he succinctly stated, "is not teaching."[64]

Alderman had good reason to worry about overtaxed teachers. In 1915, Grace DeGraff, a principal and president of the Portland League of Teachers Associations gave a fiery address in support of teacher tenure laws in which she masterfully articulated the plight of the modern practitioner. "The grade teacher has been told that she should better prepare herself for her work," DeGraff explained. "So she has taken advantage of everything offered." DeGraff continued:

> She has been told that she must know every subject well enough to teach it; that she must dress better; must take lecture courses and reading-circle work; that she must read and must travel; must have a library; must mingle with the parents; must conduct literary societies and debating clubs; must teach Sunday school; do church work; be a social worker; . . . give up her lunch period to take care of . . . pupils; buy supplies not furnished by the district and incidentally must be an expert instructor in twelve or fifteen subjects. . . . She has furthered school policies without having a part in shaping them. . . . From long training the teacher has learned to carry out orders and this has led to a servility that must be abolished if you wish the most competent teachers.[65]

DeGraff was one of those rare educators, like Ida Vandergaw of Oakland, who managed to capture and clearly depict the dilemma of teaching in a period caught between two pedagogical worlds: the uniformity of the late-nineteenth century and the flexibility of progressive practices. All the while, teachers worked within school districts attempting to transform themselves.

Alderman was not deaf to the concerns of strong and dedicated educators like DeGraff, and his solution was the two-group plan, a variation of the platoon school developed by William Wirt in Gary, Indiana.[66] As he explained it to his teachers, the plan was to organize the elementary school so that teachers would have two groups of twenty-five pupils each for the four fundamental studies—reading, language, arithmetic, and geography (with history and civics alternating). While one group was in her classroom, the other twenty-five of her pupils would work with another teacher, engaged in penmanship, spelling, nature study work, supervised play, manual training, sewing, cooking or another "special subject." All the "modern subjects," declared Alderman, were encompassed within the plan, including foreign language, literature, current events, music, drawing, and physical culture. The two-group arrangement allowed for new types of teaching as well, due to the classification of pupils by age, subject, interests, and needs. "The best feature about this plan," wrote Alderman, was that it gave more time for the teachers to work with students during the supervised study periods "as individuals not as averages," in a remark that echoed comments by Spaulding.[67]

In a 1917 NEA address, Alderman elaborated on his plan, explaining that the Portland two-group plan differed from the Gary plan "in many ways." He did not simply want to imitate Gary's approach, and he enumerated the differences between that plan and his, including his plan to have teachers progress through the grades with their students.[68] Principals of the three Portland schools implementing the plan reported a number of advantages, according to Alderman. Among the other improvements Alderman related, the plan reduced the number of subjects assigned to each teacher; required fewer supervisors and no additional teachers; prepared students for high school; broadened students' experience; and provided flexibility. Students who needed extra work in arithmetic or English could receive it. In his annual report, Alderman published graphs demonstrating that the work of students in the two-group schools was superior to that of students in Portland's traditional schools.[69] The two-group plan "succeeded beyond our hopes," concluded Alderman.[70]

By 1917, the two-group program had been fully implemented in four schools involving 160 teachers, and Alderman began to introduce the reform into another twenty-seven schools. Other Portland leaders seemed proud of the experiment as well. "Superintendent Alderman has taken a step, along with many other superintendents of progressive cities," wrote the *Oregonian*, "toward a new plan of reorganization to take care adequately of the increased number of studies that have been added to the curriculum in recent years."[71]

Despite the accolades given Wirt's Gary plan by Dewey and the many district leaders who experimented with the plan—historians have been skeptical about the progressive characteristics attributed to it. In their study of the Gary Public Schools, for example, Ronald Cohen and Raymond Mohl argue that Wirt's platoon school concept exemplified the paradoxes inherent within progressive education. They portray the platoon plan as an awkward attempt to forcibly join an efficiency-minded agenda to a more humane and democratic social progressivism. The authors quote one reformer from 1912 who stated that the Gary plan was "the most efficient, the most democratic public school system in this country." Cohen and Mohl go on to insist that this progressive reformer made that remark "without recognizing the irony of his statement."[72] Yet here is the crucial point about district progressives: they perceived no contradiction whatsoever between efficiency and democracy—not because they were naive but because they firmly believed the two ideas were compatible. It is only historians, writing decades later, who impose the inconsistency. Alderman also held the conviction that progressivism entwined multiple goals. He viewed his version of the Gary plan as satisfying all the essential educational aims of the era: providing freedom to the individual school; offering an adapted, flexible, and personalized education to the individual child; focusing and modernizing pedagogy; and doing so without incurring additional expense.

Not only did the two-group plan have a progressive pedigree, but it also served as an umbrella for many of the other initiatives that Alderman introduced into the district, one of the benefits of the plan being that it required fewer changes from "the customary program."[73] By overlaying newer reforms onto older structures, Alderman attempted to be both creative and consistent. In doing so, he served to illustrate a point made by his contemporaries about the Gary plan. One reviewer of Randolph Bourne's favorable study of the Gary schools perceptively suggested that systems might be more likely to graft elements of the Gary plan onto their schools than to transplant the system whole.[74] Portland's version of the two-group plan was most certainly an instance of this kind of grafting. Enamored with many progressive ideas, Alderman was more interested in borrowing practices that could energize his system than he was in replicating any one model of school reform with fidelity. In other words, he exemplified district progressivism.

Despite seeming success with some of his innovations, political controversy dogged Alderman, starting around 1916. Early that year, and again at the behest of community groups, a self-appointed committee set out to administer its own series of tests to Portland students as a way to offer an independent assessment of school quality. This episode of community-driven educational accountability ultimately became a back-and-forth saga involving newspapers and civic groups. Nevertheless, the initial assessments found that Portland children who were tested in grammar, spelling, history, geography, and arithmetic received scores that averaged a disappointing 46.2 percent correct. Alderman and other school officials challenged the accuracy and appropriateness of the tests, pointing out that many of the tests were completely misaligned, testing pupils on material they had not yet learned. Thereafter, a second committee was formed, this time at the request of the *Oregonian*. The newspaper editor selected a committee made up of the presidents of five civic organizations. The results of the second round were better: the students' average was 72.76 percent, not as high as Alderman had hoped, but it at least these scores silence those who claimed the Portland schools were failing.[75]

In March 1916, not long after the conclusion of the testing debacle, the school board met to consider whether Alderman's contract should be renewed for another three years. The *Portland Telegram*, a paper prone to yellow journalism, reported that this particular meeting became "one of the wildest and most sensational school board meetings ever held in Portland." The board debate exposed bitter internal feuds between its members and revealed growing opposition to Alderman. The school board voted to extend Alderman's contract, but for just one year. The *Telegram* used the opportunity to publish articles on community discontent (and no doubt raise readership), claiming at one point that Alderman made "the public schools experimental stations for the trying out of political schemes and educational high-speed theories."[76] Although the *Telegram* may have gotten some of its claims wrong, it was not misguided in regard to Alderman's use of the Portland's schools as experimental stations. That is precisely what district progressives did: try out popular reforms at the local level. How else to transform American education? Moreover, there is no indication that Alderman was insincere in his efforts to improve the Portland schools. Nevertheless, in 1917 the board had decided it was time for a second external survey of their system.

The Resurvey

Portland's economy was in the midst of a painful downturn in 1917 when the school board, this time with the support of the Chamber of Commerce, authorized a second survey of Portland Public Schools in order to determine their "advance or retrogression since the survey of 1913." The board chose to employ a lone individual to conduct this survey, superintendent of Houston Public Schools P. W. Horn. The "resurvey," as Horn called it, struck a different tone than had Cubberley's original team, perhaps as a response to the 1913 survey's "hypercritical" nature. No paean to the practices of scientific management, Horn's survey called on its audience to bear in mind the evolutionary nature of school reform, remarking "that there are many things about a school system which can never be definitely measured or stated with mathematical accuracy."[77]

Horn framed the essential questions that constituted the task before him: "Have the public schools of Portland gone forward or backward since 1913?" Of the one hundred and fifty recommendations in the original survey, he asked, how many had been put into effect? Which of the remaining ones should still be followed? It was not his goal, Horn asserted, to ascertain whether the Portland schools had reached their full measure of efficiency, for no school system ever reached its full efficiency.[78] Horn's resurvey provided a more positive portrait of the Portland schools. He praised the district for giving more responsibility to school principals and more freedom to teachers as well as for developing a curriculum that was less abstract. He also commended the district for a number of its new practices: awarding students school credits for work done at home, planting school gardens, rapidly increasing the high school enrollment, establishing ungraded rooms in twelve schools, and introducing kindergartens. And, although he still saw room for improvement, Horn found that the work in the fundamental subjects of reading, writing, arithmetic, spelling, and composition had improved considerably.[79]

Horn was particularly intrigued by the two-group plan. "Every school system perhaps owes it to the cause of education to make certain experiments along educational lines," he said, and "to make its due contribution to the sum total of knowledge on the subject of education." Horn saw the two-group plan as Portland's contribution to progressive experimentation.[80] Yet Horn also issued cautions about the potential hazards of spreading the two-group plan too quickly or too widely within the district. Foreshadowing the lessons of policy analysis learned later in the century, he remarked that if the school principal and teachers were not in sympathy with the innovation, implementation would be difficult and "the plan would be bound to fail."[81]

Despite the gains Portland had made in the four years since the original survey, Horn was alarmed that very few of the recommendations dealing with administration and organization had been carried out. Specifically, he expressed surprise that the administration had not been restructured according to Cubberley's organizational diagram. Meanwhile, the school board still concerned itself with petty matters of administration. In regard to the curriculum that Spaulding had so devastatingly described as "vivisected with mechanical accuracy into fifty-four dead pieces," Horn noted that the course of study—complete with its fifty-four curricular units—remained in print. He added, however, that he thought their rigidity "and hence their power for evil has been lost."[82]

Horn highlighted recommendations from the previous survey that had not been put into effect, but that he thought should be, including the reorganization of the district with the superintendent as the official head.[83] Then Horn added his own eighteen recommendations, some of which he hoped would help improve the system-wide problem of distrust that still hung over the district. An "efficiency expert," he said, should be employed by the district "whose chief duty it will be to apply the standard scientific tests to the work being done in the various schools." District research offices, as we have seen in Oakland and Denver, were becoming popular at the time, in part as one strategy for protecting the school system from future external surveys.[84]

Horn's survey received far less attention than had its 1913 predecessor, perhaps due to his muted language and his mixed vision of progressive education. Perhaps more importantly, it did little to calm tensions in the district, and conflicts flared throughout the rest of 1917 and into the next year.

A Return to Normalcy

Portlanders awoke on the morning of July 6, 1918, to read in the *Oregonian* that their superintendent had been "deposed" by the school board the night

before. In a surprise action, three of the five board members voted to officially remove Alderman as the administrative head of the school district.
Two individuals, newly elected to the board, joined with one incumbent
member to vote Alderman out of office. Alderman was demoted to the position of "superintendent of war work," and Daniel Grout, assistant superintendent under both Rigler and Alderman, was appointed as acting superintendent. The board remained steadfast in its decision over the following weeks,
despite sharp criticism by the *Oregon Journal*, the outrage of school patrons
who blasted the board for its "star chamber" tactics, the particularly strong
objections of one board member (who had visited Denver during its own
school board scuffle just two years earlier).[85]

Alderman's progressive innovations had caused divisions within the board,
but it may have been more than just that. As noted by two Works Progress
Administration historians some years later, "Alderman was hardly a man to
keep his talents under a bushel," and the superintendent's demeanor appears
to have been something of a factor in fostering antagonism toward both him
and his initiatives.[86] Although some board members had previously voiced
criticism of Alderman's administration, many city leaders seemed surprised
at the swiftness of the board's action. Horn's survey did not appear to damage
the district sufficiently to warrant Alderman's departure. Discord within the
system contributed to the board's decision, but other factors combined to create trouble for Alderman and his reforms. Portland experienced a recession
between 1913 and 1917, which led to significant pressures on the schools for
frugality.[87] This despite the fact Portland was hardly extravagant: the *Oregon
Voter* reported in 1918 Portland ranked twentieth out of thirty large cities for
per capita spending on education.[88]

Although the 1913 turnover between Rigler and Alderman happened in a
year of the "perfect storm" of administrative departures, by 1918 many districts, including Portland, Oakland, and Denver, were still very much in the
throes of the turmoil unleashed during those crucial middle years of the century's second decade. Although there is little direct evidence, Grout appears
to have been working behind the scenes to undermine Alderman. The First
World War also set a context in which Alderman's progressive initiatives
seemed out of sync with the general concern for the military effort and need
for fiscal prudence.

Alderman contemplated legal action against the school board, but eventually decided to relent. The editors of the *Oregon Journal* stated with resignation: "The *Journal* thought that Mr. Alderman ought not to have been
removed. In common with many it thinks so still. But Mr. Grout is superintendent now, and a believer in orderly affairs, this paper holds that his admin-

istration ought to be supported and his hands strengthened for the work that is ahead."[89]

After the board had voted to depose him, but before he had decided to submit to their decision, Alderman stated that he would "make every effort to have the present plan of organization so changed" so that when his successor had been chosen he would be permitted to name his own assistant superintendents. Based on his personal experiences, Alderman said, allowing the superintendent to hire his own subordinates would make for "greater harmony and insure better results in school administration."[90] Alderman's remarks were clearly directed at his assistant superintendent, Daniel Grout, who had also served in the same position under Rigler. All the same, it was Grout to whom the board next turned to lead the Portland schools, at least on an "acting superintendent" basis. In July 1918, Alderman was relieved of the superintendency and assigned to supervise war activities in the Portland schools.

AMERICANIZING DEMOCRACY, 1918–25

The board's decision to retain Grout as acting superintendent meant, in effect, a repudiation of Alderman's agenda and a concomitant desire to return to a more familiar state of pre-progressivism. Nevertheless, the board's confidence in Grout was hardly resounding. Some board members were not enthusiastic about his candidacy, even though seniority rights had entitled him to succeed Rigler. Plenty of public dissatisfaction with Grout persisted in the community as well. Indeed, when a rumor surfaced that the school board was about to appoint Grout as permanent superintendent in early 1919, several representatives of Portland civic groups appeared before the school board urgently asking them not to take such an action. If anyone was to be selected as superintendent, pleaded the group, it should be someone who had "the undivided support of all factions," adding that if such a consensus choice could be identified the "task of administering the affairs of the schools would not be so difficult."[91]

School board members expressed surprise at the haste with which the civic groups had rallied themselves, and the board assured them that no decision was imminent. However, intentionally or not, the board also revealed some of the serious challenges it faced. One board member explained that he had already visited the East Coast several times inquiring into qualifications of school leaders available for Portland's superintendency position and that he would likely need to go again. Another admitted that an "eminent educator" had recently come to him with the statement that "the laws governing the schools here [in Portland] were not what they should be and that he would not accept the superintendency under any consideration."[92] These rebukes from outsiders say a great deal about why the board was unable to find a suitable candidate; perhaps more significantly, they illustrate the rapidly shifting nature of the relationships between boards and superintendents. In short, by 1919, superintendent candidates were no longer willing to accept positions in cities where the boards held so much power.

The atmosphere within the board was hardly conducive to robust civic collegiality, according to the *Oregon Voter*, a magazine that provided information on legislators, ballots, and a variety of political initiatives. The *Voter* often reported on the ongoing strife in the board, and it described the difficulties of finding qualified candidates who were willing to run. The *Voter* suggested that local self-made business owner William F. Woodward, someone who was well respected by Portland's labor community, would be an ideal school board candidate, for he had taken "an active, aggressive and intelligent interest in school affairs and is eminently qualified." However, it added, even Woodward's "courage falters when he contemplates the grief of getting into the mess, and he declines." The *Voter* lamented that "scores of other leading citizens have been approached but turn from the suggestions with horror equal to that for an appointment as ambassador to a leper island."[93]

In April 1919, Portland civic clubs again attempted an intervention into what the *Oregon Voter* called the "rotten mess" of school board affairs. This time, the organizations convened for the purpose of "investigating all charges of inefficiency against the school administration, studying all problems of school policy, and outlining a definite school program satisfactory to the parents and people of Portland." The civic clubs sent out a hundred letters to Portland citizens representing a wide variety of community groups, including the Chamber of Commerce, Woman's Club, Oregon Civic League, Progressive Business Men's Club, Taxpayers' League, and Rotary Club.[94] Although little appears to have come of this effort, civic groups clearly evidenced a persistent dissatisfaction with the Portland schools, its school board, and its administrative leadership. Nevertheless, after unsuccessful searches for other candidates in the East, and after Grout had served a year as acting superintendent, the board eventually elected him as the new superintendent in 1919.

Grout had been in Portland since 1890, serving as principal in several schools from 1896 until 1907, when the board elected him as Rigler's assistant superintendent.[95] For students of vibrant progressive school reform, Grout's schools are not the place to look. His list of innovative achievements was hardly extensive, nor would it have been, even if contemporary events had not created an atmosphere unconducive to experimentation. During Grout's first year, World War I absorbed a good deal of attention, and the influenza epidemic closed the schools for five weeks (one January 1918 issue of the *School Bulletin* featured a diagram of a gauze mask that could be cut out and used as a pattern for fashioning a real one).[96] Furthermore, Grout seemed more interested in preserving or reintroducing characteristics of Rigler's regime than in introducing new programs. Throughout Grout's tenure, several of the standard characteristics of the district expanded or intensified without essentially changing in nature. Among these, Portland added new schools, increased teacher salaries after years of stagnation, and increased its offerings in vocational education.

Unlike his predecessor, or many of his counterparts in other city school systems, Grout did not fill his annual reports with grand rhetoric or bold visions. Grout was not one to claim that either he or his school system was progressive, perhaps an attitudinal carryover from his time spent working under the self-professed anti-progressive Frank Rigler. Therefore, it must have been with some joy that he included, in one 1920 *School Bulletin*, several lengthy quotes from Stuart Courtis's critique of the school curriculum in Gary, Indiana: "The general conclusion of the author is that the product of classroom teaching of the fundamentals is, at Gary, poor in quality and inadequate in amount; it approximates in character the product of the poorer conventional schools, and reveals in no particular the slightest indication that it has been affected either favorably or unfavorably by the enriched curriculum, or other special features of the Gary schools."[97] That Alderman had implemented a version of the Gary plan in Portland would have only increased Grout's glee at highlighting the flaws of this highly touted progressive district.

Still, Grout did not want to be viewed as completely regressive, and several of his innovations mirrored reforms implemented in other progressive school systems. Among these were the development of "democratic teacher committees," the creation of a district research bureau, which directed the adoption of intelligence testing, and the establishment of a program of Americanization.[98] The first effort, the establishment of teacher committees, was intended to inject the kind of teacher participation that was becoming a standard feature of many urban districts at the time, primarily through two means: the revision of the curriculum and the "democratic" selection of textbooks through a system of teacher committees. Neither of these programs, however, made any significant contribution to teacher autonomy or to professionalization within the district. Of course, all of Grout's initiatives, not coincidentally, took place within a conservative political swing in Portland and at a point in time when a "crusade for Americanization" temporarily gripped the city (as it did so elsewhere) and when the Ku Klux Klan gained a surprising and sudden popularity in Oregon.

As historian John Higham has demonstrated, Americanization received its primary impetus not from educators but from civic groups that exemplified the nation's widely divergent views of immigrants. One tendency emphasized a more humanitarian approach, exemplified by social settlements like Jane Addams's Hull-House, which sought to facilitate the social integration of new immigrants. A dramatically different perception of immigration, initiated by the new patriotic hereditary societies and led by the Daughters of the American Revolution, built on nationalist anxieties and fostered a more militant nationalism, which demanded conformity and obedience to American laws and traditions.[99] The Americanization efforts in Portland were clearly of the second variety.

"Our public school system is the proper medium for making patriotic American citizens," Grout exclaimed in 1918. "In the past," he cautioned, "we have thought ourselves absolutely secure from radical ideas which tend to destroy all good government, but recently we have awakened to the fact that this nation as well as other nations are threatened by an element which is working for the destruction of the fundamentals of good government." Sounding much like Fred Hunter in Oakland, Grout worked on the assumption that "the security and permanence of our government depend upon how effectively patriotic instruction is given in the schools." Therefore, it was with great urgency that he set about creating a district-wide Americanization program that would "make clear the meaning of patriotism" and "glorify the high qualities of courage, endurance, devotion and self-sacrifice" that were the hallmarks of America.[100]

The man Grout chose to lead the school program was M. L. Pratt, an individual who was skilled at adopting the rhetoric of Americanization, especially the dogmatic style characteristic of the Daughters of the American Revolution. Pratt readily adopted the attitude expressed by many patriotic societies that loyalty essentially equaled willing submissiveness. The Portland chapter of the Daughters of the American Revolution repeatedly emphasized that Americans should be "taught obedience to law, which is the groundwork of true citizenship," and Pratt dutifully listed "Obedience to Law" as one of his program's main objectives.[101] Portland's *School Bulletin* approvingly reprinted a course titled "American Ideals and Citizenship" from the *Seattle School Bulletin* that was meant to supplement standards lessons in American history. Among the topics listed were "Beginnings of Anglo-Saxon Ideals of Liberty," and "Establishment of a Conservative Democracy," illustrating a clear nativist streak.[102] Eventually, work in the Portland schools was coordinated directly with the Portland Americanization Council, a civic group (of which Grout was a charter member) that launched a city-wide Americanization survey designed both "to ascertain the number of foreign born and native illiterates in the city."[103] Grout insisted that the Americanization program was necessary to counteract the effects of (unnamed) "radical elements."[104]

The competing political tendencies in Portland raise questions about the direct connections between broader political proclivities and school practices. Because many groups supported "progressive" causes, school reforms cannot always be associated with specific political parties or local civic groups. In the case of Grout's Americanization programs, the links with conservatism are a bit clearer. For example, in addition to their association with the Daughters of the American Revolution, he and Pratt expressed a special affinity for the American Defense Society, a nationalist organization that urged schools to ban the teaching of German.[105] This did not mean, however, that Alderman had necessarily gained traction among Portland's more liberal-leaning groups. In fact, in 1918, the two newly elected members of the school board who helped depose Alderman had both been strongly backed by Portland labor organizations.

The political alliances and divisions of Progressive Era Portland make it challenging to easily connect the dots between individuals, ideologies, and policies, as many of the major conflicts of the era demonstrate. For example, in 1922 the Scottish Rite Masons proposed a statewide compulsory school bill, using Oregon's direct legislation system to place an initiative on the ballot that would require all children between the ages of eight and sixteen to attend the public schools. The bill was strongly backed by the Ku Klux Klan. By the early 1920s, the KKK had become active in Portland, as it had in Oakland. And more so than in California, the Klan gained a strong political foothold throughout the state of Oregon.

Some of the bill's advocates championed the effort as a democratic approach to leveling an unequal society. One of the bill's staunchest supporters was William F. Woodward, the individual whom the *Oregon Voter* had identified as an ideal school board candidate. In 1920, Woodward consented to running for school board and was easily elected. Woodward became a fierce defender of the public schools, so much so that he argued for the merits of the school bill, treating it as something of a rebuttal to the "damning" and "hostile criticism" he felt was too frequently and unfairly directed at the Portland schools. Moreover, Woodward saw the school bill as an egalitarian measure, serving as a social and political response to an elitist attitude whereby members of Portland's wealthy establishment chose to "sequester" their children away into private schools, separating them from the "common herd."[106]

In a widely reported public debate about the school bill, Woodward gave an address in support of the compulsory school initiative. The public school, he declared, is the only institution in the nation that "draws unto itself every child without regard to birth, creed, race or affiliation." The schools, he believed, served both as a concrete demonstration of "true equality under our law" and as a symbol of toleration. Public education took people from all nations of the world and wove them "into the fabric of a democracy." The real "menace to our people," Woodward contended, would be the creation of a land of conflicting groups, segmented according to narrow religious beliefs. He concluded with a vision of what the public schools could do: "I say within the school house and on the public school playground rests today the only pure democracy under the sun."[107]

William D. Wheelwright, a former president of the Portland Chamber of Commerce, spoke in opposition to the bill. Wheelwright argued that the bill was hardly a democratic measure. Rather, he said, it was conceived in "insincerity and supported by untruthfulness." After all, Wheelwright stated, it was "a matter of common knowledge that the bill is aimed primarily at the parochial schools of the Roman Catholic Church." The group that wrote the bill was not responding to any real danger but only to a "figment of its own imagination," something demonstrated by the fact that it could only be supported by "hysterical appeals to spurious patriotism." And far from being egalitarian, direct legislation of this type represented instead a "wanton interference with the rights of the citizen" and "a tyranny that takes us back to medievalism." Oregon was in no jeopardy whatsoever from the "trifling proportion" of children educated in private and parochial schools. "It is however in great peril," Wheelwright cautioned, "from a comparatively small number of fanatics who wish to curtail the liberties of their fellow citizens." Finally, he concluded, the bill was "clearly unconstitutional."[108]

The *Oregon Voter* published transcripts of the addresses given by Woodward and Wheelwright. Printed squarely in the middle of the *Voter's* coverage was a large, two-page advertisement from the Portland Committee of Citizens and Taxpayers. The ad warned readers that "the so-called Compulsory Education Bill, if enacted by the people, will increase taxes more than a million dollars a year," because an additional fourteen thousand children would suddenly be added to the rolls of the public schools. Oregon industries and agriculture would be especially burdened, asserted the taxpayer committee, arguing that "unless the farmer can find tax relief neither he nor the state can prosper." Among the signatories of the taxpayer committee were William Wheelwright and Richard Montague. Once again, the paths of municipal reformers crossed. The school bill was approved by the Oregon electorate in November 1922, passing with a statewide margin of 115,506 to 103,685. The victory was not long lived. Opponents of the bill immediately challenged its constitutionality. The case made its way through the courts until in 1925 the U.S. Supreme Court found—in *Sisters of the Holy Names v. Pierce*—that the law was unconstitutional, the majority asserting that the state had no right to "standardize its children."[109]

According to Higham, the bill "was perhaps the last and certainly one of the most severe Americanization laws."[110] This perspective makes sense in the context of Grout's increasing attention to Americanization coursework. But the school bill was not primarily a curricular matter. In fact, it was not really school reform at all. It did nothing to improve teaching or transform coursework. Instead, some of the bill's advocates simply attempted to use the public school as a cudgel against threats to their way of life, which is why some observers have treated the bill as a pure form of nativist prejudice. Others, like Woodward, may have had more idealistic and egalitarian goals, but the bill contained no assurances of greater tolerance or equality.

In his incisive analysis of Progressive Era Portland, Robert Johnston argues that it is overly simplistic to view the triumph of the school bill as pure bigotry. Many of the bill's proponents were not primarily anti-Catholic, he points out; instead, they "spoke powerfully to concerns about the power of the elites and the prospects for equal social opportunity in modern America." This interpretation certainly makes sense when applied to an individual like Woodward. There is no evidence that Woodward was associated with the KKK, nor did he demonstrate the kind of religious fanaticism that troubled Wheelwright. He did, however, envision the public schools as a means to improve society, and he believed that such a dream could not be realized if the wealthy segregated themselves from the rest of the population. The ban on private schools, contends Johnson, appealed to a cross-section of working-class and middle-class Portland residents, revealing a deeply seated anti-corporate radicalism and resentment of the Portland political establishment. However, as so many American school reformers have found over time, changes to schooling practices do not address deeper structural inequalities. To Johnson, then, the bill represented a "faux 'liberal' populism," one that was not anti-corporate. What the school bill defenders ended up demanding, he concludes, "was an equal opportunity for all to enter an unequal society through compulsory public education—not the transformation of the hierarchy itself."[111]

Some left-leaning American intellectuals saw other kinds of flaws within Portland's public schools. Upton Sinclair alighted briefly in Portland during his research trip for his book on American schools, *The Goslings*, and he depicted Grout as an administrator who was conservative and malicious. "Mr. Grout is clammy and cold in his personal dealings," wrote Sinclair, who labeled him one of America's "uneducated educators." Sinclair ridiculed Grout's pedagogical "discoveries" and charged that Portland's "textbook-election" system was simply a cover for district-wide graft. Grout was especially fond of bringing all of the city's teachers together in a large assembly once a year "to instruct and inspire them," which to Grout meant offering teachers folksy stories and bits of verse. Because so many of his accounts were drawn from undocumented hearsay and second- or third-hand accounts, it is often difficult to determine the accuracy of Sinclair's revelatory investigations. However, in the case of Portland, Grout made Sinclair's job easier by publishing his literary endeavors in Portland's *School Bulletin*, apparently for the ongoing edification of his teachers.[112] "We do get so tired," confessed one teacher to Sinclair of her experience working in Grout's school system, "we do so crave a little bit of enthusiasm, something to make us think it's worthwhile to go on with the old, dead routine!"[113] Acknowledging Sinclair's severe portrait of Grout, Works Progress Administration historians Powers and Corning attempted to offer some balance in their portrayal of Grout by quoting tributes that praised "the organizing power of his mind, the genius of his pedagogical technique."[114] Nevertheless, this genius was often lost on educators both inside and outside Portland. He was rarely mentioned in national reform circles. When poor health eventually forced Grout to curtail his activities around 1924, Assistant Superintendent Charles Rice began to take on more of Grout's duties. Rice was subsequently chosen as superintendent in 1925 when Grout resigned.

While still an assistant superintendent, Rice had visited a number of cities to investigate their implementation of the "Work-Study-Play" plan created by William Wirt in Gary, Indiana—the plan that had served as the model for Alderman's two-group plan and that Grout had criticized in *The School Bulletin*.[115] Rice was shrewd enough never to refer to the plan as either the two-group plan or the "Gary plan," but he must have been intrigued by its potential when he served under Alderman, for he eventually pursued it on his own initiative in the early 1920s. What Rice ultimately labeled "the platoon school idea" unquestionably served as the guiding philosophy and organizing principle of his twelve-year tenure as superintendent.

PLATOONIZING PROGRESSIVE PORTLAND, 1924–37

"What are the indispensable needs of any school system?" Superintendent Charles Rice asked in 1935. Rice had a ready answer to his own rhetorical question: "a progressive philosophy, adequate teaching ability, homogeneous grouping of pupils, proper selection and arrangement of curricular material, and such attention to the physical environment as to insure the maximum health and comfort of everybody concerned. We find these objectives easier to attain through the enriched curriculum and the specialized instruction inherent in the platoon school organization."[116] By the time Rice took over as superintendent he had essentially been managing the day-to-day operation of the schools for a year, due to Grout's increasing infirmity. Born in Illinois in 1873, Rice had arrived in Portland in 1903, already a seasoned teacher and administrator. By 1904, he had been assigned as a principal to one of Portland's grammar schools, and in 1911 Rice began his service as an assistant superintendent, first under Rigler, then Alderman, and, finally, Grout. Working under all three superintendencies, Rice no doubt learned a good deal about the hazards of district leadership as he observed the successes and failures of each. By way of intellect, Rice seems to have been most akin to Alderman, although by temperament, he appears to have been less impulsive. Rice used his superintendency to pursue his intellectual passions for educational reform; but instead of Alderman's somewhat scattershot approach, Rice consistently organized his educational ideas under a single progressive concept, that of the platoon school. In practice, the platoon school was not radically different from Alderman's original two-group plan.[117]

One of the pivotal events that put Portland in a platoon-school state of mind occurred in 1923 when the school board decided to request yet another survey of the district, its third in ten years. This time the survey was carried out under the auspices of the U.S. Bureau of Education (within the Department of the Interior) and had the expressed purpose of assessing the future school building needs of the city. Although no copy of the final report seems to exist, the survey was conducted by Alice Barrows, who then worked for the Federal Bureau of Education. Barrows was an enthusiastic advocate for platoon schools and recommended their adoption to cities across the country.[118]

As superintendent, Rice rapidly transformed the platoon idea into the district's fundamental organizing principle. Starting with just a handful of platoon schools in 1924, Portland added new platoon programs each year throughout the next decade, eventually boasting nearly fifty schools organized on the plan ten years later. In 1926, Barrows praised the district for its swift improvements. Portland, she said, had developed into "one of the finest and most progressive school systems in the country"; Superintendent Rice was "considered in the East to be one of the best [superintendents] in the country"; and the city's school board had come to be viewed as "one of the best."[119] One need not be a cynic to recognize a consummate promoter in action.

If Horn had noted in his 1917 school survey that Alderman was uninterested in specifics of his own two-group plan, Rice went to the other extreme.

He had a detailed working knowledge of the platoon plan and how it operated in other cities, even serving a term as president of the National Association of Platoon Schools in 1927, by which time there were 760 platoon schools in the United States, representing 125 cities and thirty-four states. Rice's close contact with platoon schools around the country provided him with testimonials about the advantages of the plan. Throughout the mid-1920s, he filled the district's *School Bulletin* with detailed accounts of platoon developments in other urban systems, enumerating the multiple benefits he saw in the plan: platoon schools saved money, they served as a way of strengthening citizenship, they balanced administrative improvements with curricular and pedagogical reforms, and they carved out a place for the academic subject matter that was "a carry-over from the old traditional school."[120]

Whereas most cities that adopted the Gary plan usually implemented it in only a few schools, Rice undertook to spread his adaptation of the program throughout the whole system. Even the Great Depression was not able to stunt the expansion of the city's platoon schools; in 1930, the city had forty-one platoon schools, and by 1935, it boasted forty-eight, thereby allowing Rice to call the plan "the most distinctive feature of the elementary division of the Portland school system."[121]

Platoon schools also offered the means of pursuing other reform initiatives of the era, such as curriculum revision and intelligence testing. The district had established a part-time research department in 1924, placed under the directorship of Burchard Woodson DeBusk, a professor at the University of Oregon, who commuted back and forth between Portland and Eugene. Under DeBusk, the small research department established a psychological clinic and introduced intelligence testing. Group IQ tests were not used as extensively in Portland as they were in many other progressive districts, but they were given to Portland children entering the first grade.[122]

Whether reminding himself or his audience, in 1932, Rice cautioned that, "in the excitement of building programs and the conflict concerning school budgets and tax rates, it is easily possible to overlook the supreme importance of the curriculum in the education of our young people." Rice never became as deeply engaged with curriculum development as did some of his contemporaries, but he firmly believed that platoon schools would lead educators into the process curricular revision. Due to the need to concentrate academic subjects into one part of the day, the platoon schedule inevitably forced educators to separate the curricular "essentials" from the "nonessentials" within the traditional subject matter. This meant, for example, ridding arithmetic of those topics and exercises that were rarely used beyond school and which "had little value as mental training." Likewise, the antiquated spelling list—composed of thousands of words—could be condensed to a shorter list of common words.[123]

Rice was certainly cognizant that curriculum revision taking place in some other districts went well beyond realigned spelling lists. "Practically all cities of the first-class have a special bureau of curriculum revision, adequately staffed and provided with a budget of its own," he said, effectively ensuring modernization of the schools' courses of study. "The Portland Public Schools have been endeavoring to achieve the same results without a special bureau and without any budgetary provision at all," he confessed.[124] Although he had established voluntary committees of principals and teachers to work with the department of research on the revision of the course of study, Rice well knew that assigning teachers extra work in their off-hours, especially when supervised by a part-time research director, would never yield the kind of impressive results achieved in cities like Denver.

By 1937, Rice had served over twenty-five years as a central office administrator, twelve of them as superintendent, and despite his successful navigation of the worst years of the Depression, he became increasingly vulnerable to criticism from both inside and outside the district. Among other complaints, the persistent problem of student failure had become increasingly evident throughout the school system, especially at the high school level. Rice attempted to resolve the problem of low achievement among adolescent pupils by establishing the remedial Better Scholarship High School (later renamed the Edison Six-Year High School) designed to help students who had failed for two consecutive terms. The reported aim of the school was "not to punish but to diagnose and remedy," and its teachers were said to offer training in "habits of study" in order that students might eventually return to their original schools and satisfactorily complete their high school careers.[125] These were the students who educators of the time often dismissed as uneducable, but in offering them an alternative to the traditional program, teachers in the Better Scholarship School stumbled on some unexpected insights, not unlike the teachers of ungraded classrooms earlier in the century.

"The public would probably be surprised to learn that low intelligence is a problem in only a few instances," reported Norman C. Thorne, the assistant superintendent in charge of high schools. "According to tests given every term in the Better Scholarship High School," he said, "70 percent of the students are normal, superior, or very superior in intelligence." The problem with these students was not low intelligence. Rather, Thorne believed, the real "causes of failure are so varied and complex, resulting in so many cases from social and psychological factors, either unknown to or outside the control of the student, that it is unfair as well as unwise either to punish the student or to put him out of the school entirely, which is the policy followed in many other cities."[126]

Thorne explained that the students in the Better Scholarship High School, sometimes "through no lack of intelligence or conscious application, were unable to do intelligent work because of inability to read with comprehension." For these students, Thorne admitted with candor unusual for the era, failure to acquire basic skills was the result of "ineffective teaching." Therefore, if student ability was not the problem, then failure was a condition "subject to correction." The teachers at this high school often found that study and concentration outside the classroom were "rendered impossible" by noise or confusion at home or, sometimes, by financial distress. Other cases at the school included students who suffered from lack of food and clothing or whose families had insufficient money for eyeglasses, tonsillectomies, dental work, carfare, or books. "Illness and physical defects keep many students from doing their full quota of school work," said Thorne; and he steadfastly concluded that "it is an evasion of the problem merely to say that they are lazy or irresponsible."[127]

The revelations of educators like Thorne and other teachers at the school were destined to remain examples of local knowledge, rather than offering a contribution to a national discussion, for as Thorne explained it, the district did not follow up on the school's findings with any kind of "complete scientific program." After 1935, when the school was renamed as the Edison Six-Year School, the instructional focus shifted toward a more practical orientation, and Edison essentially focused on providing its boys with "vocational training in a limited number of trades and academic classes" and its girls with vocational classes in cooking, sewing, weaving, spinning, basket making, art, and piano. How these courses were meant to assist students in returning to their regular high schools was a question often left unexplored, or at least unexplained.[128]

———

This chapter offers several arguments that extend an understanding of district progressivism. Although Oakland and Denver represented cities that ultimately adopted national models of reform, not all cities or school boards were thrilled by the possibility of administrative reorganization, no matter what educators of national prominence might recommend. The particular civic constellation of Portland during the 1910s, and the reluctance of school board members to acquiesce to externally developed reform plans, offers part of the explanation as to why some nationally promoted progressive reforms were unsuccessful locally. For better or worse, Portland's lack of attention to key national initiatives ultimately constrained the ability of the district to acquire outside educational talent and to pursue other related innovations.

Portland school leaders often undertook a different approach to district-wide reform than their contemporaries in either Oakland or Denver. While some districts blended and mingled reforms, Portland swung back and forth between different visions of educational progress, never quite embracing any single approach (until Rice's platoon schools). The school surveys conducted in Portland demonstrated that the surveyors themselves could have contrasting visions of what constituted modern and progressive reform. And the Portland school board showed how it, too, could vacillate between alliances to different reform agendas. The appointment of Grout as superintendent meant a return to a more traditional view of education. During a period of harsh Americanization, Grout aligned the district with very different types of civic actors, such as the Portland Americanization Council and the Daughters of the American Revolution. Although there is no evidence of Grout's involvement with the KKK, the kinds of patriotic and curricular reforms he introduced certainly provided an atmosphere in which suspicion of immigrants could thrive.

Thereafter, Rice's use of the platoon school allowed him to offer something of a stealth version of progressivism. To Rice, the platoon plan served as something of an ideal progressive marriage or, at least, as a protective umbrella for other reforms. Platoon schools included curriculum revision and intelligence testing, provided a path toward improved teaching, focused on the needs of the whole child, offered special subjects such as manual training and physical activity while reducing costs, and presented opportunities for directed play and dramatic performance, while also providing a temporary means of administrative reorganization. In other words, it was not until Rice's tenure that Portland attained full status as a progressive school system.

In Portland, as in some other cities, for all the rhetoric about the needs of children—whether issued from Rigler, Alderman, Grout, or Rice—administrative leaders, school board members, and civic groups often focused predominately on programs that seemed best suited for themselves rather than the intellectual achievement of their pupils. The views that district progressives held about democracy, instruction, and children's abilities had consequences, often significant ones, for the school children of the city, whether manifested through testing, tracking, guidance counseling, or the high school curriculum. Portland offers more evidence of the struggles that urban districts faced in educating students in poverty and shows that district progressives did not respond to clear findings within their own schools demonstrating that "intelligence" was often not the primary problem for students who fell behind.

Seattle, the final case study, also created plans to address the needs of failing students in the 1910s, some of which the superintendent reported to be highly successful. Moreover, Seattle was another school system that resisted calls for administrative reorganization, and yet it developed a reputation as a pedagogically progressive district, one that introduced creative reforms that incorporated both teachers and students. Was it therefore possible to break the mold set by Denver and demonstrate that progressive school districts could flourish in a variety of circumstances?

6

EVOLUTION NOT REVOLUTION IN THE PUBLIC SCHOOLS OF SEATTLE, WASHINGTON

RAISING A MODERN METROPOLIS

By the early 1900s, the vertiginous hills that dominated Seattle's urban landscape had begun to impede the development and expansion of the city, and civic leaders were determined not to have the center of their city consigned to the "bottom of a pit." The steep slopes were no match for Seattle city engineers, who undertook an elaborate endeavor of earthen reconstruction. Between 1904 and 1912, twenty million gallons of water a day were pumped uphill from a lake fed by the Puget Sound. Sixteen million cubic yards of dirt, clay, and boulders were sluiced into flumes and a central tunnel; existing houses were undermined and burned. "By washing nearly as much dirt from the downtown hills as was moved during the digging of the Panama Canal," one longtime resident remembered, "the engineers made it possible for a modern metropolis to be built on the half-drowned mountain that lies between Puget Sound and Lake Washington." At the time, political scientist Charles Zueblin wondered why Portland, Oregon, was able to accommodate itself to its hills and its mountain outlooks, while Seattle felt compelled to flatten theirs. Nevertheless, the story of the hills' decimation stood for years as an illustration of Seattle's dynamic civic vision and its ability to overcome obstacles to progress. In Seattle, they could turn mountains into molehills.[1]

School leaders were equally caught up in the excitement of their own role in building a modern metropolis. At the opening of a new high school in 1910, Seattle superintendent Frank Cooper proclaimed, "This is an hour of congratulation. It is a great thing to live in these times and to be a witness of the . . . almost magical development of this wondrous city." Extolling the expansion and improvement of Seattle that had taken place since his arrival nine years earlier, he continued: "The transformation of our waterfront, the change in the city sky line, the demolition of hills, the surfacing of streets, the extension of utilities, all these appeal to wonder and admiration, but," he added, "none of these changes have been more marked than the building of our high schools." Cooper had reason to be proud. When he had first arrived in 1901, the high school "program" of seven hundred students was housed within another school; less than a decade later, the total high school enrollment had increased to forty-five hundred, and the district had erected three new high school buildings.[2] In the following decade, Superintendent Cole of Seattle captured the continuation of this spirit when he announced in 1928 that "possibly no two of the 2,500 young people who graduate from the Seattle high schools in June will have completed identical courses."[3] Cole viewed this as the promise of educational progressivism realized: complete adaptation to the child.

Fred C. Ayer, the director of research for the Seattle Public Schools, also drew direct links between the city's economy and the strength of the schools in 1924, stating that "publicly controlled education has been recognized by students of social development as the foremost agency of community uplift and civic improvement." Like other district progressives in cities across the country, Ayer maintained a fierce belief that schools played a unique role in securing the commercial health of any city. "Other agencies and organizations will always be of vital importance," Ayer maintained, "but in the long run it is the public school program that will provide the knowledge and civic pride essential for Seattle to become the great seaport and metropolis, culturally and industrially, that it is now openly prophesied by social and historical analysis."[4]

Seattle offers a fourth and final illustration of how city school leaders responded to national reformers and to the innovations implemented by other urban school systems. Like the other three cities in this book, Seattle sought rapid acquisition of urban status, and throughout the era, the school district garnered a national reputation as a progressive school system. Yet Seattle was distinguished by its own unique political context. The city was, for a time, seen as the frontier of insurgent labor politics.[5] Seattle was home to the significant General Strike of 1919 and by 1916 Seattle boasted not just one, but two socialist school board members. One of those socialists was local and national hero, Anna Louise Strong, who after only a year on the board was recalled in a wave of pre–World War I "patriotism." Labor representation on the board did little to stop the district from experiencing a post-strike backlash that directly affected teachers and slashed progressive programs.

Despite turmoil, Seattle gained a reputation as a democratic and pedagogically progressive school system, one that supported a vibrant professional culture of teaching. Female teachers proved instrumental in Seattle's reform efforts and were given new and unique opportunities for career advancement through a cadet-mentoring program and a demonstration school. Although located in a region that was decidedly remote by early twentieth-century standards, Seattle educators sought to prove that they were just as modern as larger cities across the country. And like Oakland and Denver, visitors and experts identified the Seattle city schools as among the most innovative and progressive in the country.

Many districts experienced multiple turnovers in top leadership during the Progressive Era, but Seattle had only three superintendents between 1901 and 1944. One of those superintendents, Frank Cooper, presided over the district for a remarkable twenty-one-year period (1901–22) at a time when other cities experienced political turbulence and transition. Seattle historian Bryce Nelson argues that Frank Cooper was distinguished among reformers of his day because he equated educational progress with improvement in teaching and learning "rather than along corporate and bureaucratic lines." Cooper developed a robust pedagogical and professional culture that came to be known nationally as "the Seattle way." By Nelson's account, Cooper was an exemplary pedagogical progressive whose name should be added to Raymond Callahan's short list of educators considered "unavailing dissenters"— those Progressive Era school leaders, like Denver's Jesse Newlon, who refused to base educational decisions on measures of efficiency. Cooper's independent efforts, says Nelson, meant that Seattle developed unlike patterns in any other city.[6] Was Seattle a progressive outlier?

Evidence from Seattle contributes several insights on district progressivism. Although scholars have treated Seattle's postwar retrenchments as episodes of reactionary conservatism, some of the citizens condemning the district had their own bona fide progressive credentials—indeed, one had been the president of a local suffrage society—raised concerns that contested the core intellectual and democratic nature of Cooper's pedagogically progressive reforms.

THE TEACHERS AND THE TAUGHT, 1901–15

Frank Cooper had already proven himself as a superintendent capable of developing a school system on the frontier when the Seattle school board hired him in 1901. A native of Illinois, Cooper began his teaching career in the Midwest after attending Cornell University for just one year. By the age of twenty-eight, he had been appointed as the school superintendent in the town of Le Mars, Iowa (1883–90). After that, his career moved upward and westward, and at a time when proven experience could trump mere credentials, he served as a professor of pedagogy at the State University of Iowa (1890–91), as superintendent in Des Moines, Iowa (1891–99), and then again as superintendent in Salt Lake City, Utah (1899–1901). His early career was unquestionably marked by a deep and abiding interest in teachers and curriculum, and ambition did not quell these interests. As he moved through new positions, Cooper continued to develop the pedagogical interests that would characterize much of his Seattle superintendency.[7]

By most accounts, Cooper was a teacher's superintendent, for he consistently demonstrated a respect for classroom teachers and an interest in their professional growth. When developing his 1892 curriculum in Des Moines, for example, Cooper wrote that although he had outlined a curricular schedule for the term, he never meant those plans to be so precise or detailed that they left "nothing for the ingenuity of an efficient teacher." During these same years, Portland superintendent Frank Rigler sat in his office devising the details of his fifty-four-unit curriculum, the plan that experts later found had a deadening effect on the whole school system. Meanwhile, Cooper wrote that no curriculum for children should be "so rigid that it leaves unrecognized the varying and individual power of both the teacher and the taught." Even when Cooper proposed specific pedagogical methods, he always intended to leave "a breadth of margin" to the "skill and invention" of the teacher who was most likely to be inspired "without the handicap of too much plan and mechanism." These words were also written at precisely the same time Joseph Rice visited cities across the nation finding classrooms that were overly scripted, mechanical, and inhumane.[8]

Teaching and the "Fires of Enthusiasm"

Cooper saw the district as an organization of educators; its primary purpose was to foster instructional excellence and to develop a robust curriculum. Cooper was unafraid of invoking the notion of efficiency, it should be said, but when he used the term, he consistently linked it to high-quality teaching. "Whatever efficiency comes to mark the work of a school system, whatever progress prevails, the cause must be traced to the zeal, the intelligence and hard work of those who deal directly with the children, the teachers." Throughout his career, Cooper underscored the importance of instruction, and he envisioned the superintendent's duty of selecting new teachers as the "most important, the most responsible, and the most nutritive function in the management of a system of schools."[9] One way he promoted continual professional nourishment among teachers and principals was through district-organized study groups. Among the readings that Cooper gave to his staff to read were the report of the Committee of Ten, Harvard President Charles Eliot's 1892 article on the failures of the school curriculum to improve thinking skills, and articles from the *Forum*, undoubtedly those written by Joseph M. Rice.[10] Few school leaders of the time devoted such concentrated attention to discussing the national reform scene with teachers and principals.

During his first years in Seattle, Cooper held teacher institutes during the school year, inviting outside lecturers to present on educational topics of general interest. However, he soon found—as did Denver's Newlon and Threlkeld some fifteen years later—that these outside lectures "had too little reference to details of work immediately confronting the teachers," and he altered his strategy. Beginning in 1907, Cooper used Seattle's subject supervisors to work with elementary school teachers on the specific goal of improving instruction. Elementary principals met together and then worked with their own teachers. Cooper divided the high school teachers into subject area groups to work on instruction with their department heads and then their principals. Such changes to Seattle institutes, he said, served "to give stimulus and infuse ardor" into the activities of his teachers.[11]

At first glance, these administrative strategies may seem trifling, but as in other cities, the ways in which superintendents approached teaching, learning, and curriculum—and how they pulled and blended teachers into their broader plans—reveals much about how they understood the deeper goals of progressive education. Cooper's early actions also show how a system could generate strategies for widespread teacher growth. Importantly, Cooper's engagement of teachers directly in intellectual activities through the district's reading and study groups also demonstrated a respect that, in turn, led teachers to form their own organizations for continued support and the sharing of ideas. Even though many reformers, at both the national and local level, talked a good deal about improving curriculum and instruction, it was usually the curriculum that received the lion's share of attention. In *Laggards in Our Schools*, for example, Leonard Ayres, like many who followed him, identified curricular change as the primary target, not teaching. Cooper, however, managed to keep an eye fully fixed on instruction.

"Teaching is essentially a spiritual process," Cooper later explained to the Seattle school board when he was asked to justify continued support for his teacher institutes. The daily routine of the classroom tends to "quench the fires of enthusiasm," he said, and they need to be rekindled from time to time. "The problems of the school room are so insistent, so strenuous, and so exhausting," Cooper cautioned, that there was a strong tendency for teachers to become isolated and instructional practices to become stagnant.[12]

Modernizing the Curriculum: Determining Standards

Over the course of Cooper's career, educators across the country shed their faith in the traditional uniform course of study, as we have seen, and all progressive educators agreed the time had come for radical changes to the curriculum. To many reformers, radical meant rapid, not comprehensive. Yet close examination of the four cities studied here reveals some moments of brief local experimentation that emerged sometime between the demise of nineteenth-century uniformity and the establishment of differentiated curricula. Cooper evidenced an experimental bent and an inquisitiveness that characterized only a few of his fellow superintendents. Issuing his first city-wide course of study in 1906, Cooper continued to wonder aloud about the expectations and "fundamentals" of learning that should rest at the heart of the curriculum, and he continued to seek out practitioner input. In 1909, Cooper appointed a committee of principals to study the curriculum to distinguish "essential" and "fundamental" curricular elements from those that were "merely desirable." In other words, Cooper essentially wanted principals to help him develop a core set of common academic objectives, or what would later be called content standards. Once developed, but before the district put these tentative courses of study into operation, Cooper asked principals to submit them to teachers for review and classroom trial, again revealing a rare attention to the professionalism of teachers well before the widespread curriculum revision efforts of the 1920s attempted to do the same.[13]

Cooper maintained a deep interest in what children should be expected to know, and he was equally curious about how children best learned new material. By 1910, Seattle had begun introducing new subjects into both the elementary and high school course of study, and he developed the conviction that the quantity of work required in a number of subjects had to be reduced. Several content areas, Cooper wrote in 1910, contained portions of subject matter "whose chief claim to recognition lies in their having been taught for a long time." This glut of material was especially true of arithmetic and grammar, the two subjects that he felt had "most successfully resisted modernizing." They were the most challenging subjects to fundamentally rethink, in part because of the difficulty of identifying and weeding out unnecessary content.[14]

Learning, Cooper felt, should be more than just knowing "a given number of facts," and he sought ways to incorporate student interests into the curriculum.[15] In part, his concern arose out of Seattle's swelling enrollments.[16] Cooper was gratified by larger numbers of pupils but, just as they did in other cities, some of the new students struggled with traditional schoolwork, prompting Cooper to reconsider his notions of what constituted the "essential" curriculum. "There is a good deal of talk these days," Cooper told school patrons in 1914, "about the high school's failure to prepare all students for their life work."[17] One cause for the mismatch between the high school curriculum and the "life work" was that high schools took far too much of their curricular direction from colleges and universities, a relationship that obliged high schools to closely mimic the traditional disciplines. The unwelcome and patronizing influence of higher education was a common complaint among progressive educators, who found high schools to be one of the most vexing and stubborn institutions of the era. "Probably the most nutritive high school instruction," he noted wryly, "is in those departments where the teachers are least influenced by college standards."[18]

Although Cooper was not enchanted by *college* standards, he was neverthe-less convinced that creating and setting district expectations for all Seattle stu-dents was crucial for both student and teacher success. Once again, he turned to his teachers, asking them to find ways to simplify instruction by looking to the needs of students rather than to the prescription of the colleges or universi-ties. He organized twenty committees of principals and teachers to create new standards for Seattle's courses of study. Cooper acknowledged that curriculum development through committee was a slow process, but he preferred it to a curriculum "made in the Superintendent's office and promulgated immediately by edict." He also recognized it would take several years to complete, given that teachers and principals would need time for deliberation, time for testing new material in classrooms, and then time to discuss results and make adjustments. But it was only through the "free expression of opinion and a candid analysis of divergent views" that good work would be accomplished—or as he framed it, "progressive thought and practice, tempered by experience."[19]

Up until about 1910, Cooper worked somewhat in isolation from develop-ments in other city school systems; his own brief encounters with institutions of higher education meant that he had not developed the academic and intel-lectual ties to networks of other national leaders that were second nature to many other early twentieth-century administrators.[20] But after 1910, Cooper referred more and more to prominent educational journals, he became more visible at the National Education Association, and he visited other cities to examine their school systems. He toured the highly touted progressive schools of Gary, Indiana, but despite his interest in many aspects of the dis-trict's platoon program, he concluded that "the personal touch" was missing in much of the work.[21]

Three brief examples illustrate how Cooper increasingly mingled national innovations with local practices during the 1910s. As Cooper examined other school systems and participated more actively in national reform conversa-tions, he began to modify his basic assumptions.

Comparing Arithmetic Accuracy

"Schools throughout the country frequently are subjected to the criticism," said Cooper in 1914, that they were not securing "adequate returns" from their expenditures on arithmetic. The concern, he explained, was that despite the time and effort spent on the subject, pupils could not "be depended on to add, subtract, multiply or divide with either accuracy or facility." Cooper wanted to find out: Were Seattle students becoming mathematically competent? He was determined to discover how the computational abilities of his pupils compared to those of students in other systems. To do so, he gave arithmetic tests to one-third of the Seattle elementary schools to assess the district's "present methods." The tests he used were those recently devised by S. A. Courtis of Detroit and were the same examinations, Cooper explained, that had been used in a number of other cities to measure the efficiency of school systems.[22] Like other superintendents, Cooper was initially lured into standardized testing by the promise that they would yield new secrets through the powers of comparison.

According to Cooper, much of the test's value lay in the fact that it was given in many different cities under uniform conditions and that the standards in accuracy and rapidity for the eighth graders approximated the types of skills they needed to easily meet the needs of ordinary adult life, thereby giving an indication of students' "life preparedness." The results of the first round of the Courtis arithmetic tests, given in the fall of 1913, demonstrated to Cooper that although Seattle students did not "work as rapidly" as students in Detroit and Boston, they did compare very well in accuracy and reasoning.[23]

The data from the standardized tests had an immediate impact on instruction. Cooper asked his principals to systematically assign short exercises at frequent intervals so that students might practice and improve their test scores. The effort paid off. A second round of tests later in the year showed improved results, prompting Cooper to introduce new "methods of practice" to ensure continued improvement. The tests, felt Cooper, had proven useful as a means of diagnosing the needs of pupils, and he felt that wider use in the future would be wise.[24] Thus, within the space of one year, the use of externally developed tests prompted Cooper to alter district-wide instruction, and he directed his teachers to teach to the test. Although he never stopped working with his teachers to develop powerful instructional practices and sound curricula, the advent of standardized testing signaled a noticeable pivot in Cooper's gaze, from looking within the district for the expertise necessary to improve the system to seeking solutions externally in the rapidly expanding galaxy of educational progressivism.

Other results from the arithmetic assessments puzzled Cooper, ultimately challenging his own conceptions of education. More specifically, he was troubled by the wide disparity in individual scores on the Courtis tests. Some Seattle eighth graders, he reported, had failed to get even a single correct answer on the tests, while pupils at the other end of the scale apparently scored better than the results attained by the actuaries at the New York Life Insurance Company. This dramatic variation of scores from students in the same grade had been reported by all cities, Cooper explained, but it nettled him that it occurred in Seattle, and he deliberated on how his educators might respond.[25]

"Pupils differ greatly in their natural ability to work with numbers," he said; therefore, classroom instruction that might be adequate for one student would be "entirely insufficient" for another. Still, that did not explain the bigger learning issue implicit here: When two students had the same classroom experience, why would one fall far behind while another advanced? The solution, Cooper hypothesized, might be dependent on some form of classroom management that would "make provision for the natural differences of pupils." Cooper committed himself to devoting special attention to the problem over the next year.[26]

Care of the Seattle Student: From Coaching to Classification

The results of the arithmetic tests reinforced some earlier efforts Cooper had made at responding to the differing abilities of students.[27] Cooper pointed to a type of student who particularly troubled him, the group of pupils whom he—in a direct reference to terms used by Ayres and Thorndike—labeled as "backward" or "retarded." Yet Cooper, like some of his contemporaries, did not believe such labels need be permanent. He acknowledged that many of these overage pupils had fallen behind others of their own age "by reason of a delayed start, of illness, frequent change of schools, continued absence, lack of interest in study or slowness of development"—in other words, often due to external circumstances beyond their control, not because of some inherent intellectual weakness. To accommodate these children, Cooper set aside rooms in schools throughout the city in which an "auxiliary teacher" acted as a "coach" to bring each pupil up to grade level.[28] Starting with just three instructors in 1909, the auxiliary teachers helped many students boost their performance, sometimes substantially, and reduced the number of failures and saved precious instructional time for many regular classroom teachers. By 1912 the district had increased the number of auxiliary teachers to forty.

Seattle's auxiliary model, with the goal of returning students to their classroom, was similar to the ungraded-room strategy begun by Vandergaw in Oakland a decade earlier and to those used by Chadsey in Denver and Alderman in Portland during the same period. Like Chadsey, Cooper reported with pride that the auxiliary teacher program seemed to work, but Seattle's success rate was even higher than Denver's. In one special class, said Cooper, 85 percent of the students avoided failure "and were put upon a footing in their classes which gave them hope and courage and assured their future progress."[29]

Cooper felt that other innovations for ensuring the social welfare of children were just as essential as instructional programs designed to return students to grade level. For example, he established a medical program, a dental clinic, and a corps of school nurses; the district created schools for delinquent children and assigned teachers to group homes and to a city hospital; and he established connections between the district psychological clinic and the department of education at the University of Washington. In the years after 1910, Cooper reported regularly on programs for "exceptional" children, and he sent district personnel to visit and observe "schools for the defective" in other cities."[30] For example, the 1915 NEA meeting provided Cooper an opportunity to discuss another innovation he had adopted in Seattle: the intelligence test. Seattle's "child laboratory," Cooper was pleased to report, had the complete apparatus for conducting mental tests. Thus, by 1915, Seattle was on the cutting edge of psychological technology, employing intelligence testing and sorting schemes to improve the functioning of its schools.[31]

Elementary Industrial Centers

In 1915, Cooper introduced "prevocational work" into the schools, calling the innovation "Elementary Industrial Centers." These centers provided Cooper with an institutional mechanism for responding both to local curricular concerns and to nationally advocated initiatives. He explained to readers of his annual report the nature of recent battles between, on the one hand, the National Association of Manufacturers, who had advocated for a completely separate school system, targeting lower-ability students and run by manufacturers, thereby eliminating most of the common curriculum, and on the other hand, those educators who contended that public schools should not abandon vocational training to the "uncertainty" of the special school or agency and instead should provide vocational training alongside a general education.[32] Although the manufacturers' association lost the day, educators continued to discuss how best to introduce vocational training.

Cooper felt that one solution could be found in prevocational education, which he saw as "a medium ground" between educators and manufacturers. He proposed a program tailored to the needs of older elementary students in grades seven and eight "who had found inadequate expression under the older order," clearly meaning pupils who were uninterested, unmotivated, and unsuccessful in school.[33] For students enrolled in prevocational coursework, the school day was divided into two parts: three hours for "academic or book work" and two hours for the industrial work. All students were given the opportunity for what Cooper called the "self discovery of task tendencies and probable abiding interests" as well as guidance in their selection of courses that would lead to a vocation.[34] The students assigned to the prevocational programs were the very students who had troubled Cooper after the results of the Courtis arithmetic test—students who had not succeeded "under the prevailing academic standards"—and he hoped that prevocational coursework might allow them to find "new interest and an enlarged opportunity."[35]

Cooper was aware of the potential contradictions created by the prevocational centers. He sympathized, he said, with the notion that all students should have a general educational background in a common knowledge that would make them "citizens of a common democracy." In a response that blended Deweyan language with a newfound vocational vocabulary, Cooper justified his industrial centers by arguing that this education better suited students' "real needs" much better than if "left to the accident of chance." Moreover, elementary industrial centers, he stated, had been "located in different parts of the city without reference to class or neighborhood distinctions so that all boys and girls who choose to attend may have the benefit of these modified courses."[36] Parceling out these schools equally among the neighborhoods offered Cooper a way to unite democratic education with district-wide adaptation to ability, while avoiding charges that he was determining student futures through the placement of prevocational schools solely in the working-class sections of town. Yet locating industrial centers throughout the city was still not the same thing as providing equal educational opportunity. Though he had once been a fan of Charles Eliot, Cooper's rhetoric on this matter was more tinged with traces of G. Stanley Hall and Fred Hunter than with Eliot's earlier statements on the dangers of predetermining a student's future.

Cooper's Progressivism: Adapting to Tastes and Talents, 1915–22

"Educational progress," Cooper wrote in 1919, "is served rather by evolution than revolution."[37] In his study of Seattle, Nelson uses this notion of evolution to characterize Cooper as a pedagogical progressive who, Nelson says, cautiously developed "an excellent progressive school system" through securing better teachers, methods, curricula, and child welfare services rather than through efficiency-oriented administrative reorganization or the adoption of corporate and bureaucratic values.[38] Yet, Cooper's instructional ideas and practices increasingly became streaked with a gloss of administrative progressivism, as evidenced by his adoption of intelligence testing, new modes of student classification, and vocational education. Here is another progressive paradox—unless, perhaps, Cooper ultimately disavowed efficient, corporate-oriented reforms and developed a system overwhelmingly oriented toward curriculum and instruction, one unfettered by differentiation and reorganization. But that is not what happened.

The evidence suggests that Cooper was a superintendent committed to allowing his teachers instructional freedom, to genuinely including both teachers and administrators in curriculum modernization, and to improving student learning through stronger instruction. Between 1915 and 1922, Cooper continued to embrace the type of pedagogically progressive reforms that characterized some of his earlier approaches with teachers. In his *Seattle School Bulletin*, a publication he inaugurated in 1913 (one similar to those launched in other urban districts), Cooper focused on the themes such as "play and education," proclaiming to teachers that a new emphasis had been placed on "creative play," a notion that had been accepted "in practically all progressive communities" due to its "high educational function."[39] In 1918, the district replaced the traditional school desks, bolted to the floor, with tables and chairs better suited to the atmosphere of a modern classroom for the youngest pupils. "The children," Cooper reported, "are eager, alert, and free from the strain of attempting to adjust themselves to rigid furniture and mechanical discipline."[40] Cooper encouraged teachers to adopt new pedagogical strategies like the project method and "activity learning," and he supplied classrooms with hands-on features such as sand tables, window boxes, and workbenches with tools.[41] Based on these examples, the depiction of Cooper as a pedagogical progressive makes a great deal of sense. Still, school leaders across the country often avidly advertised their instructional innovations, even when these pedagogical reforms did not touch the majority of classrooms.[42]

The flow of progressive ideas had many currents, and Cooper attempted to follow several at the same time, which partially explains his adoption of multiple initiatives, especially those that seem at odds with one another. Cooper was determined not to let Seattle's spot in the corner of the nation's northwest douse its enthusiastic participation in the larger movement for progressive education. "Our extreme location," he told his board in 1917, "makes us, in a way, insular and prevents direct contact with the currents of progression and inspiration." Cooper therefore saw attendance at the NEA annual meetings as essential to his own professional growth as well as to that of the teachers. "I may say that no influence has been so potent in keeping your superintendent alive and keen professionally as the effect of these meetings and the contacts they afford," he told his board.[43]

In 1921, Cooper used the opportunity of the NEA annual meeting in Atlantic City not only to bring a number of teachers and administrators with him but also to sponsor some visitations to other city school systems after the meeting. For example, his director of vocational education visited New York City schools.[44] One of Seattle's high school principals followed a winding path across the country on his return from the annual meeting and studied high school practices in Atlantic City, Pittsburgh, Chicago, Minneapolis, Kansas City, Los Angeles, and Pasadena.[45] A third Seattle administrator visited Rochester, Cincinnati, and Kansas City.[46] Such observations were essential to progressive districts, allowing them to collect fresh ideas, witness a range of school innovations in action, and evaluate other districts against their own in ways the standardized tests never could. Cooper deliberately employed the practice of multiple school and district visitations to great effect both outside and within the district. He recognized that simply identifying promising progressive practices accomplished nothing.

Once Seattle administrators and teachers arrived home from their school scouting trips elsewhere, they were often emboldened to push for progressive change at home, so Cooper sent his practitioners out into the Seattle schools to spark the transmission of exciting innovations. Encouraging "purposeful visitation by principals and teachers in different parts of the system," Cooper explained, helped to foster the "diffusion of ideas and convergence of professional objective."[47] Once teachers and principals had seen new ideas in practice, it was much easier for them to implement those novel methods and approaches.

Cooper's participation in national meetings, along with those of his administrators, ultimately resulted in the accelerated adoption of innovations that built on earlier practices he had introduced into the schools. For example, after his 1913 experiment with standardized math tests whet his appetite for comparative data, Cooper continued to seek out subject-area standardized tests that would measure student skills. On the morning of May 22, 1916, Seattle pupils in grades two through eight were greeted with a surprise spelling test. The results, Cooper was pleased to report, showed that sixty-four out of Seattle's sixty-eight schools were above the average or "standard" of the other eighty-four cities that had administered the test, and he argued for the continued use of testing in Seattle. Standardized assessments—whether in spelling, reading, arithmetic, or handwriting—he said, offered an avenue for the "accurate appraisement of class or school proficiency in elementary essentials. By such means," he explained, "it is possible to set up definite school standards of achievement" and to know how closely Seattle students approached those standards.[48] To the superintendent who had been on a long-term quest to establish standards and minimum essentials, these tests seemed to fulfill some of his goals. At the same time, they marked another step closer to the embrace of social efficiency practices.

Cooper's earlier interest in student classification combined with his new-found fascination of standardized testing led him to introduce district-wide group intelligence testing in early 1921. Seattle had already used early forms of individual IQ testing, and the *group* intelligence test, Cooper explained, was "one of the most interesting and valuable scientific developments" resulting from the Great War. Their successful use by the military and the resulting "economy of money and time," he said, was "now a matter of history," and a number of the "larger cities of the country have already made extensive use of this means of heightening efficiency," including Oakland, among other districts he listed.[49] Testing gave new focus to efforts that were already underway, and the results of the examinations amplified the need for further curricular adjustment. Cooper already had begun to unstitch the notion of the classroom as the primary instructional unit after he had seen the variation in the results of his first standardized test.[50] Now he believed that the teacher's greatest challenges were "to diagnose the individual needs of her pupils" and then to adjust her work accordingly as the best method to promote student growth.[51]

Cooper tinkered with the high school curriculum in an attempt to meet the needs of individual students and conform to national notions of what was modern. By 1917, the high school offered five distinct paths of study, each of which, Cooper said, was "elastic enough to satisfy the inclinations or aptitudes of individual students and a diversity of tastes or talents." By differentiating the high school curriculum and creating courses that met students' abilities, Cooper straddled the line between viewing schooling as a strategy for tracking and as an opportunity to tap into individual proclivities and talents.[52]

Pedagogical Politics and Foiled Plans, 1915–22

The fact that Cooper had such a long tenure, especially during a period when so many superintendents were deposed, can obscure some of the city's political tensions. The mid-1910s were by no means less tumultuous in Seattle than in other cities. One of the most interesting, albeit brief, episodes was the election of Anna Louise Strong to the Seattle school board in 1916. Strong, the daughter of a well-known minister, rapidly gained fame in her own right due to the popular child welfare exhibits she had created for the Children's Bureau in Washington, DC, as well as for the Russell Sage Foundation in New York—where she befriended none other than Leonard Ayres. Strong had earned a PhD in philosophy from the University of Chicago in 1908 and was a fierce child advocate and supporter of pacifist causes. Strong's bid for the school board had been heavily supported by Seattle's women's organizations, many of who passed around petitions on her behalf, demanding that women should have at least one "representative on all educational boards." Strong's victory was therefore a triumph to all women's clubs throughout the city, and they declared her success as momentous because it proved "to Seattle women what may be accomplished when they stand together even though the strong arm of the press is against them."[53]

Strong soon ran up against the grain of Seattle politics, however, in the lead up to the First World War. Despite her popularity, her pacifist views quickly became suspect. Strong maintained public friendships with radicals and anarchists, one of who was indicted under the Espionage Act for circulating anti-conscription pamphlets. After the war began, Strong retained her stalwart anti-war stance and middle-class women's groups, once among her greatest advocates, turned on her. The Seattle Federation of Women's Clubs, the University Women's Club, and the Parent Teacher Association joined with the Seattle Municipal League in demanding her recall. The Recall Committee of the league announced that "the people of Seattle do not want anyone in charge of their schools who is not entirely in accord with America and Americanism." Notwithstanding solid support from labor groups, Strong was recalled in March 1918, barely a year and a half after her initial election.

Although Strong does not appear to have had much of an influence on district policy during her short time on the board, she did not abandon the schools after her departure either. Instead she maintained an avid interest in their activities, writing regular columns in the city's labor newspaper, the *Seattle Union Record*, about innovative dimensions of the system. Not long after the recall, Strong visited some of the city's trade schools, demonstrating she had no intention of hiding from public view. She asked the man in charge of manual arts in the public schools: "What is the latest and more important things" happening in your schools? The head teacher explained their new partnerships with the federal government supported by the 1917 Smith-Hughes Act, which he illustrated by demonstrating their instructional experimentation in the machine shop before touring her through a gas engine auto repair course and a homemaking class for girls. He elaborated on other student coursework, such as math, English, and drawing and explained how instructors tied that material into their lessons on shop problems. Strong commented: "I had a vision of a school which should be an industrial democracy, and an industrial democracy which should be a school—in which jobs that needed doing would be handed over to the departments which could do them, and they would decide whether they were worth doing that way or not—all in a friendly co-operation between intelligent people, without even thinking of profits and costs."[54]

Whether highly optimistic or naive, Strong wrote many other pieces that touted the reforms of the district, with titles such as "Where Stammerers Are Cured" and "Sorting out the Special Classes," in which she featured the work of the Child Study Lab and its use of intelligence tests to classify children. In general, her columns focused to a large extent on the vocational coursework and health benefits of the district, rather than on its scholastic achievements, more so than one might imagine given her academic credentials. She obviously approved of a wide array of coursework available to Seattle schoolchildren, and she celebrated the types of vocational programs that would have pleased Lewis Terman and Ellwood Cubberley. In other words, Strong supported just the kind of administrative progressive programs that observers might have thought labor unions would reject due to an overly narrow curricular focus. But labor leaders did not reject these administrative progressive programs, in Seattle or in many other cities.[55] The era was replete with these fascinating paradoxes; yet to the individuals who expressed their interest in using manual training or intelligence tests to improve the schools, they were not paradoxes.

Within the district, Cooper was about to experience another clash of perspectives. Throughout his tenure, Cooper called on the school board to support his new initiatives, programs, and projects. For his first decade and a half in office, the board was mostly amendable to his recommendations. However, by the mid-1910s, the turbulent period common to many districts, Cooper began to face resistance from the board. In 1916, Cooper proposed that the reorganization of the district's administrative structure was warranted. The school board, he said, was "laboring under the embarrassment of attempting to direct too many distinct working units. All this is time consuming and confusing without the compensation of increased efficiency." Cooper argued that the board concerned itself with too many details of the district's work, a situation he described as "cumbrous, unremunerative, and withal unnecessary." The district should be reorganized, he told the board, with the superintendent repositioned as its executive head.[56]

To support his plan, Cooper provided an extended, five-page quote from Ellwood Cubberley's recently released *Public School Administration*. The selection Cooper chose highlighted Cubberley's arguments in favor of administrative expertise, the separation of legislative and executive functions, and the necessity of adopting professional and business-oriented practices.[57] Despite Cooper's impassioned plea for dispassionate and rational administrative practices—including his apparent faith that he could rely almost completely on Cubberley's testimonial to "wise and intelligent" reorganization—the board rejected the proposal.

One longtime board member, a Seattle businessman with the Victorian moniker of Ebenezer Shorrock, was strongly opposed to the shifting of such duties to the superintendent. "It has recently been suggested in high quarters that the superintendent should be the sole executive, responsible directly to the board, all other officers being subordinate to him," Shorrock explained, in a veiled reference to Cubberley and other elite reformers. But, he said, "while in theory it is good for one individual to bear all the executive responsibility of an organization, the nature of the operations of a school district is so varied that it is too much to expect one man to be capable of supervising intelligently all of them." Shorrock continued: "A superintendent who will, with full satisfactions, handle a large corps of teachers, keep abreast of educational developments in all parts of the country, giving time to discuss them with his assistants and to form a judgment upon them so as to be able to recommend them to his board of directors or otherwise, will have no time to spare for other duties. He should, it is true, keep in touch in a general way with the type of schoolhouses, the general financial policy of the district, etc. but nothing beyond this."[58]

Shorrock was not a critic of all new practices; he was proud of many progressive programs that had been adopted in Seattle during his time on the board, especially the introduction of medical clinics, the addition of vocational guidance, and schools for exceptional students and those with disabilities. But he saw little need for the superintendent to annex the administrative territory that he believed properly belonged to the board. In fact, he turned up at the 1917 NEA meeting to say so.[59]

In 1919, when Cooper submitted a second and similar reorganization proposal to the board, he was not only rebuffed but the board voted to reorganize according to its own management plan: they divided the administrative functions of the district into several departments and made Cooper head of the one division that focused on strict educational matters. The board's action was an unequivocal punishment of Cooper, consequently reducing, rather than expanding, his administrative authority and power.[60]

Cooper's failed attempts to reorganize the district offers some clear insights into several key elements of progressive education at this point in time. The Seattle school board was neither as anxious as Cooper about keeping up with other districts nor as susceptible to the purported logic of educational science. Even though Shorrock himself attended NEA meetings, he gave much less credence to the inner circle of elite educators. In other words, the deference that served as a wedge in other cities did not work in Seattle.

Moreover, board members were hard-pressed to see the explicit advantages of a new administrative arrangement. At the very least, they viewed such change as serving only to decrease their ability to control the system. Nor was there a business coalition pushing for administrative reorganization, as was the case with Oakland and Denver, and therefore little ideological alignment between leaders inside the system and outside. These ingredients were necessary to leverage district reorganization.

A second conclusion about this incident has larger implications for an understanding of educational progressivism in Seattle. Simply put, given the opportunity, Cooper would have fashioned a district structure that looked remarkably similar to the administrative organization of Oakland, precisely the kind of plan based precisely on the same kind of Cubberleyan notions that Cooper now advocated. It is misleading, therefore, to overemphasize Cooper's pedagogical reforms without acknowledging his efforts at adopting these more administratively oriented innovations. Moreover, based on his embrace of quintessential administrative progressive programs, Cooper was not opposed to business values or to elements of social efficiency. Cooper was not alone in this regard; Seattle simply offers further evidence of how district progressives consciously blended different varieties of reforms. Cooper would have quite happily combined creative play with corporate bureaucracy. Seattle serves as a reminder that there were many versions of "business" values and attitudes in these years; scholars should not tag simply one form. In fact, Progressive Era advocates of the commission form of government made just that argument: public business need not be conducted according to only one rational model. Local business leaders, like Shorrock, differed from those with grander corporate organizational visions like Cubberley.

Postwar Progressivism

In the years following the First World War, Seattle experienced a number of social tremors that rattled affluent conservatives: combined political action between suffragists and socialists, socialist agitation, labor unrest, the 1919 General Strike, along with a rapid series of economic peaks and dips. After the war and the General Strike, the tenor of school politics changed even more than it had during the recall of Strong. Although the General Strike had very little direct or immediate effect on schools, its aftermath had a decided influence on teachers, programs, and board politics. Several teachers were fired, not only for political views but also for their pedagogical methods.

One case particularly demonstrated the school board's lack of grasp on effective teaching and its reactionary. Charles Niederhauser was a popular high school social studies teacher, who pushed his students to think critically, often by challenging their views or asking to defend them in class. On one occasion he read his students an article arguing that it would be economically impossible for Germany to repay the full amount of reparations demanded at the Versailles Peace Conference; such a view contradicted the official American position. During another class session, Niederhauser read an editorial declaring that America should adopt a "strong leadership" role in world affairs. However, Niederhauer deliberately substituted the word "Germany" in place of "America." Only after his students expressed indignation at the notion of Germany as a future world leader did Niederhauser reveal the ruse, and a "lively class discussion" ensued.[61] Moreover, Niederhauser was married to the sister of Anna Louise Strong, which did not endear him to the board. And least once, he did not participate in a required flag salute, stating that he did not participate in "ritualist patriotism." The school board seemed to have little understanding of the value of Niederhauser's "discussion method," nor did they appreciate antipatriotic attitudes. Despite very strong student support, the board voted to fire him, arguing that his instructional activities had been seditious. The Central Labor Council responded that the board was "one of the most spineless, jellyfish school boards that ever existed." The board's discharge of Charles Niederhauser, argued the council, demonstrated that school leaders did not really want Seattle students to think for themselves—an argument hard to dispute.[62]

On top of a politically charged atmosphere, the costs of urban expansion began to affect government agencies and the schools. During the first two decades of the century, the Washington state legislature tinkered with its taxation structure and, in 1917, removed the State Tax Commission, which had served as a source of moderation in fiscal deliberations. As a result, state and property taxes increased between 1917 and 1920, and school taxes alone increased by 40 percent. Property taxes shouldered much of the burden for the increasing expenses at both the state and local level, and by 1920, about 70 percent of governmental and public school expenses were paid by property taxes.[63]

At the same time, new civic groups began to appear in Seattle with fresh agendas. One significant organization, created by locals in 1921, was the Voters' Information League, ostensibly set up by Seattle residents to provide nonpartisan political analysis to Seattle citizens. Only later, under investigation by the Federal Trade Commission, was it revealed that the league had been established as a lobbying arm of the privately owned Puget Sound Power and Light company as a means for covertly directing citizen activism in favor of their interests. Nevertheless, at the time the Voters' Information

League chose taxation as one of its core issues and, with little apparent tax relief in sight, the league joined forces with the Seattle Chamber of Commerce to collaborate on several combined goals: reduces taxes, shrink the size of city and county government, and oppose both labor unions and public ownership of utilities. In July 1921, the league brought together a coalition of fifty civic and social organizations to form the Tax Reduction Council (TRC). The TRC's first targets were school expenditures and city employee payrolls.[64]

Cooper's gradually expanding vision of educational progress, linked to national views on reform, had increased expenses. At the same time, some specific school services and curricular programs began to ruffle some community feathers. In 1922, the TRC came to the school board with its demands: reduce school payroll expenses, toss out curricular "fads and frills," and cut many of the district's child welfare programs. The school system, argued the TRC, should adhere to a more narrowly defined educational mission and should transfer some of their social service functions to other, more appropriate, agencies.[65]

The TRC was especially vocal in its criticisms of Cooper and the programs that he had carefully crafted to meet student needs. Tax Reduction Council members complained that "the schools are now running, in addition to the regular academic courses, business colleges, shops, [and] art and music conservatories." They argued for a dramatically reduced set of courses, primarily through curtailing or abolishing the practical and vocational courses. The head of the TRC's high school committee, Mrs. George A. Smith, blasted Cooper for what she characterized as the "breakdown" of the school system.[66]

Among other complaints, Smith objected to Seattle's nonacademic classes, such as manual training and domestic science, arguing that these courses simply served to keep students ignorant. "The autocratic ages long ago discovered," Smith asserted, "that the mind engaged in making fudge, embroidering posies on a piece of cloth, making raffia mats and bird houses, cannot at the same time engage in an analysis of the meaning of the Declaration of Independence, nor contemplation of the tyrannies of empires and kingdoms in comparison with the liberties and happiness of an American Republic."[67]

Mrs. Smith also issued a broader attack on Progressive Era educators. "The American people," she exclaimed, "have allowed the paid educators to dictate the policies of our educational system, with an absolute contempt for the judgment and intelligence of the parents of this country, and they have succeeded so well in throttling the protests of their opponents that they are planning an even more complete and total enslavement through the process of initiative and legislative laws." Although educators had been criticized for their adoption of "fads and frills" since at least the 1890s, postwar sentiments like Smith's gained special traction.[68]

Scholars examining Progressive Era Seattle have depicted Mrs. Smith as member of a postwar reactionary conservative group that sought to dismantle many of the political, social, and educational gains made before the war. However, her surprising backstory reveals more about the complex nature of Progressive Era activism. Smith had been president of the Alki Suffrage Club of Seattle and was especially active in working for women's right to vote until it was achieved in Washington in 1910. In her public appeals to voters, she heralded the democratic foundations of American society, arguing not only that, as citizens and taxpayers, women deserved the right to vote but also that it was an "inalienable right." According to one historian, she often "drew directly from the Declaration of Independence and the U.S. Constitution to bolster her claim of equality with men."[69] As such, her objection to district programs cannot be so easily dismissed as a kneejerk response. Rather, her denunciation could easily be viewed as a thoughtful intellectual critique of Seattle course content.

Smith saw herself as a school reformer, just a different variety of reformer. She worried that schools trained memory at the expense of teaching students to think (overlooking, perhaps, the Niederhauser affair). Despite the hyperbole of her prose, her concerns should be taken seriously, especially those regarding the potential anti-intellectual effects of vocational coursework. In fact, she raises a serious argument that applies to all district progressives and that has been veiled by previous categorizations of superintendents as pedagogical progressives. After all, it was Cooper himself who had spent years worrying over the kinds of substantive academic material that all students should learn, and he had evidenced at least some trepidation over the establishment of Seattle's prevocational schools. Neither Smith's political activity nor her association with postwar tax hawks necessarily means that her critiques of education were unfounded. In fact, the clash of views about the academic nature of the curriculum shows a drawback to affixing labels to progressive education reformers—especially individuals operating at the local level—for they distract scholars from asking certain types of questions. They divert researchers from considering evidence that does not fit the model.

To the community groups, Cooper provided a convenient symbol. The TRC complained that Cooper "seems to be proud of the single fact that he has inaugurated and maintains the most costly system of public school education in the United States. . . . If any city ever needed a business educator at the head of its schools, this city does right now." They desired a frugal educational leader who would stick to basics and fundamentals. The TRC felt that Cooper, at the age of sixty-seven, was ready for retirement, and they called for him to be replaced by a "young, virile Superintendent," arguing that "some able young educator who could take hold of our schools, free from all the entangling alliances, should be chosen to inaugurate a system far less expensive, without materially reducing the efficiency of our schools."[70] Of course, the language smacked of the kind of downtown business elite language circulating through other cities in preceding years, along with an appeal to a certain administrative masculinity.

Cooper did not shrink from attacks on the system he had spent his career building. He argued that the tax cutters were abandoning the children who were most in need. Schooling was a large systematic enterprise, he explained, sounding all the more like Cubberley; while the board could elect to proceed with the cutbacks, he explained, such drastic measures were unthinkable to anyone "deeply interested in the welfare of children and who consider their interests above that of politics or self." Cooper portrayed himself as dedicated to the mass of Seattle citizens, "not for the few."[71] However much each side employed the rhetoric of costs, academic rigor, clear-headedness, or concern for children, by 1922, Cooper had lost many of his battles against Seattle tax cutters, and the school board made substantial reductions to many of his educational programs. Cooper resigned and retired, deeply disappointed to see the system that he had built so substantially altered.

On Cooper's retirement, A. E. Winship reflected on his career in the *Journal of Education*. Under Cooper's administration, Winship said, the Seattle schools had added seven high schools and forty-six elementary schools, established "centres for prevocational work, attended by thousands of boys and girls," organized "special schools for the deaf and mentally deficient," opened twenty-six kindergartens, introduced medical inspections and a medical clinic; and created a corps of auxiliary teachers to work with backward pupils.[72] Winship, a keen observer of local school politics, was no doubt aware that many of these innovations were just the types of reforms that some Seattle citizens sought to curtail. The improvements he tallied proved a testament to the superintendent who had transformed a small collection of frontier schools into the kind of urban school district that most educational leaders would have recognized as progressive and modern.

REFORM OR RETRENCHMENT? SEATTLE SCHOOLS, 1922–30

The school board chose Assistant Superintendent Thomas Cole to replace Cooper. Whether virile or not, Cole was, at the age of forty-one, twenty-six years younger than Cooper and symbolized a new generation of school leadership in Seattle. Cole's path to the superintendency was not dissimilar to Cooper's. He was born in Iowa, attended Upper Iowa University and DePauw University, and became superintendent of schools in Ridgeway, Iowa, at the age of twenty-two. After short terms as superintendent in a couple of Minnesota towns, he served two years as a principal in St. Paul, Minnesota's capitol. In 1911, he arrived in Seattle to become principal of Broadway High School; the board appointed him as assistant superintendent in 1915.

In his study of the Seattle schools, Nelson depicts Cole as an administrative progressive who, preoccupied with efficiency, dismantled many crucial aspects of Cooper's pedagogically oriented system. Other historians of the city have accepted and echoed this sentiment (demonstrating another problem with labels).[73] Yet if Cooper had already introduced intelligence testing, formalized student classification, differentiated the curriculum, and recommended Cubberley's form of administrative reorganization, what among Cole's actions or ideas especially distinguished him as an administrative progressive? Many of the reforms that would characterize Cole as such were in place on his arrival. Analyzing the two men side by side reveals fairly little that would indicate they were at odds with one another. Moreover, Cole labored within a scaled-back school system and under a school board that put a premium on frugality. Indeed, at that point in time, the board continued to be dominated by the miserly banker Ebenezer Shorrock, whom the board secretary later referred to as the "watchdog of the treasury," a title not necessarily intended to be complimentary. It is more accurate to say that evidence on Cole and Cooper further complicates attempts to apply easy analytic labels to Seattle school leaders. They, like Denver's Newlon and Threlkeld, embodied the eclecticism characteristic of district progressives, blending efficiency-oriented practices with innovative, if not original, pedagogical reforms.[74]

One way to understand Seattle's educational developments in the 1920s is to view the balance of power shifting toward the school board and away from the district's top administrators. The 1919 administrative changes the board made as a rebuke to Cooper gave them much more direct decision-making power. Board members kept tight restrictions on new expenses and they introduced reductions in the overall district budget, primarily though stifling teacher salaries. This turn in school affairs had been foreshadowed by the debates between Cooper and the Tax Reduction Council and was characteristic of the general shift in political atmosphere across the country in the 1920s.[75] However, as was the case with Portland, the notion that whole communities retreated into a traditionalist political stupor does not quite fit the facts.

Economy of Administration

At a time when urban superintendents elsewhere launched bold system-building ventures, Cole was constrained from doing the same. He persevered by focusing on incremental administrative refinements that allowed him to pursue other progressivism reforms, somewhat in stealth. Cole's sustained efforts to achieve a progressive vision are clearly evident in the pages of his *Triennial Superintendent Reports*, where he documented the new programs he introduced during his years as superintendent, such as the platoon school, curriculum revision, and expansion of the junior high school.[76]

To keep what programs he could in place, Cole had to convince board members, and vigilant community groups, that neither the district's central administration nor the courses offered by the schools could be considered extravagant. To dispel concerns about costs, Cole published data demonstrating that Seattle's administrative expenses, accounting for 5 percent of the total district budget in 1920, had dropped to just 3.4 percent by 1923, a figure that was also well under the 4.4 percent spent by the average American urban school system. Shrinkage in administrative expenses in turn boosted the percentage of the budget devoted directly to instruction.[77]

Even more dramatically, between 1921 and 1923, per pupil expenditures dropped in the high schools from $149.86 to $125.22 and in the elementary schools from $101.97 to $85.79. District records for these years divulge other budgetary cuts in textbooks, in supplies, and in permanent building improvements. The biggest hit, however, was absorbed by the teachers. Between 1922 and 1923, average grade school teacher annual salaries dropped roughly $141 (or 7.4 percent), while high school salaries dropped $101 (4.6 percent). At the same time, the number of students increased by 1,430, while the total number of teachers in the district *decreased* by ninety-six, due to cost reductions. The budgetary belt tightening resulted in yearly district savings of nearly $340,000 on salaries alone but meant extra burdens for teachers. Yet even while being paid less, teachers were expected to shoulder larger classes and extra duties.[78]

An additional insult to teachers was the board's refusal to allow teachers to work at other jobs during summers or holidays, something the board had forbidden since 1915. All the while, teachers continued to struggle against wartime inflation of 74 percent. These salary disputes, in particular, demonstrated both the disregard with which board members treated their own teachers and the stark class differences between local budget cutters and district employees. The TRC displayed its collective arrogance when it asserted that "surely there is nowhere else in the world so privileged a working class of folk" as teachers.[79] The declines in costs nevertheless pleased the board, and they allowed Cole the kind of breathing space he needed to slowly expand aspects of his progressive program.[80]

Cole found a way to provide cover for future innovations through the introduction of yet another reform: the district research office. Established in 1922 and placed under the direction of Fred C. Ayer, Seattle's Department of Research essentially established a bulwark against community criticisms regarding indulgent expenses. Ayer's department ultimately served as an important, yet unexpected, conduit through which Seattle communicated with other progressive districts. Within three years of taking his post, Ayer had produced two substantial research volumes containing results of a variety of investigations into curriculum supervision, the organization of Seattle high schools, the progress and failure of pupils, and the amount of time allotted to various school subjects in Seattle and forty-nine other urban school districts.

Ayer's two volumes of research findings on Seattle schools were published under the title *Studies in Administrative Research* in 1924. Ayer's investigations also yielded comparative results from forty-four cities, and he displayed his findings through nine organizational charts and some twenty-nine tables of data.

Promotion, Failure, and the Superior Ability of Seattle Students

If cost-conscious board members and community groups voiced concerns about modern curricular innovations, one progressive practice seemed to raise few hackles: the use of intelligence tests to classify Seattle students. In April 1922, the Seattle Principals Association voted unanimously to give citywide intelligence tests to all children in grades three through eight. The following month, the Illinois group intelligence test was administered to over twenty-two thousand children throughout the city. When the results were compiled, Cole triumphantly reported that Seattle schoolchildren had "exceeded the standard score in every grade"—suggesting that Seattle children were more intelligent than students in other American cities.

Such an announcement, however, signaled both a misunderstanding of the purpose of intelligence tests and a misreading of the resulting data. Intelligence test developers would have—or should have—pointed out that intelligence tests were not designed for these kinds of competitive, cross-city comparisons; yet Cole repeatedly claimed that the tests had revealed the "superior ability" of Seattle students, as if the schools were somehow directly responsible for this achievement.[81]

The schools continued to use IQ tests throughout the 1920s and 1930s. Seattle's proclivity for comparing itself to other urban school systems served to reinforce practices also common in other progressive districts, such as homogeneous grouping, standardized testing, or the use of movable furniture in classrooms.[82] The Otis group intelligence test, Seattle administrators explained, had provided the basis for ability grouping in the high schools, making it possible to keep "the rapid student" interested in schoolwork. "There is no dawdling while waiting for the slower part of the class to catch up," claimed Cole, "and the habit of mediocrity is discouraged in those who have better than average power."[83] When justifying the practice of ability grouping, Seattle administrators embraced the language of equal educational opportunity, especially as it applied to programmatic changes based on intelligence tests.

For Seattle schoolchildren, the consequences of Cole's misconstructions of intelligence could be severe. Some students were labeled "motor-minded," thereby requiring "special classes" that focused on "active learning" for younger children and vocational coursework for older ones. Many girls received lessons in dressmaking, in millinery, or in setting up and serving at lunch counters; boys received instruction in basketry, brush making, woodworking, and concrete and sheet metal work. Mrs. Smith's denunciations of these types of classes seemed not to have put a dent in such offerings. That these courses might undermine the authentic democratic goals of progressivism seemed to worry Cole less than the board's potential reaction to the additional costs incurred by such programs. Keenly aware of criticisms leveled at the district regarding seeming extravagances, he explained that special classes were more expensive, "but without them," he said, "there would not be equal school opportunity for all pupils."[84]

By 1924, the district had introduced multiple approaches to classifying and channeling children into various curricular programs and vocational courses. Yet the Seattle schools still contended with significant numbers of children who lingered in the same grade year after year, able to be promoted to the next grade. This problem became an investigative target for Ayer, who reported that, throughout the Seattle schools, 41.9 percent of students in grades one to eight were "overage." Some schools documented even more dramatic findings; although a handful of buildings found that only 20 or 21 percent of their students were overage, others had upwards of 60 percent. Ayer reported that compared to other cities Seattle came out as *second best* in terms of keeping percentages of overage pupils down and was *highest* in terms of the proportion of students whose age rated as "normal" for their grade; Seattle's 47.6 percent "normal" rate was well above Portland's 31 percent or Birmingham's 19 percent.[85]

It had been fifteen years since Leonard Ayres had created a national stir with *Laggards in Our Schools*, and yet school districts like Seattle seemed to be struggling as much as ever with the conundrum of why students were unable to make regular progress. The question remained: Why did some students fail to thrive scholastically? Curriculum differentiation was supposed to help with precisely this problem. Ayer reviewed the relevant research studies that had been conducted to date and cataloged the many causes to which scholars had attributed failure, including truancy, malnutrition, illness, "timidity," irregular attendance, "bad companions," unsatisfactory textbooks, study habits, "poor home life," and, the most common explanation, "low mentality." Ayer also surveyed Seattle's third-, fourth-, and fifth-grade teachers, asking them to report why, in their view, students in their classrooms failed. Teachers believed that "low mentality" accounted for roughly 18.2 percent of the cases of failure; yet other causes did not trail far behind. For example, teachers stated that "school study habits" accounted for 16.5 percent of failures, alongside "previous preparation" (9 percent), "indifference toward school" (8.5 percent), "home environment" (8.3 percent), and "home study habits" (7.8 percent).[86]

Although he quoted Terman's 1919 *The Intelligence of School Children*—and repeated Terman's contention that "the overage child is usually a dull child"—Ayer avoided the common reflex of immediately accepting Terman's argument that academic failure could be attributed to individual intellectual deficiency.[87] Ayer pointed out that Seattle teacher testimonies consistently pointed to a range of explanatory factors, not just one. Moreover, the reasons teachers gave for student failure appeared in essentially the same order "despite the fact that different teachers reported on different pupils in different grades," indicating that his interview data demonstrated consistency. "The fact that each of these so-called problem children has a complex school history, individual traits, and social background which necessitates individual diagnosis and special remedial treatment," Ayer concluded, meant that many of the specific causes of school failure could "be removed by a systematic improvement of the conditions which produce them."[88] In other words, even in the mid-1920s, with IQ tests swirling all around them, Ayer and at least some Seattle teachers could still entertain multiple analytic possibilities regarding the causes of student failure. Perhaps even more important, they could still hold out hope that academic success could be improved by the systematic improvement of the child's environment.

A closer look at Ayer's data, reveals something else about the nature of pupil failure: the total percentage of Seattle students who reportedly failed due to deficient mental capacity was actually quite small. For example, Seattle teachers estimated that the students who failed due to "low mentality" amounted to 18.2 percent of that population, but this figure applied only to those students who *failed* to be promoted in the year of Ayer's study. Therefore, even if relatively large numbers of children were determined to be "overage" for their grades, the total number of students who failed because of low intelligence was a much smaller percentage of Seattle's student population, certainly a proportion of students smaller than the 20 percent of all pupils Terman generally liked to designate as mentally incapable.[89]

Finally, although Ayer mentioned one study that listed "poor teaching" as a reason for student failure (D. C. Bliss's investigation of failure in twenty Indiana cities), teaching was by no means a common explanation for lackluster student performance. Of course, we might expect that teachers, in Seattle and elsewhere, would be hesitant to identify teaching itself as a major cause for student failure, but why did so few researchers probe the potential connections between poor student performance and inadequate instruction? Despite all the attention given to pedagogical methods at the time, the reluctance of researchers to fully examine the strengths and weaknesses of instructional practice in progressive school districts remained a hallmark of the era. Many settled for classification and differentiation.

Yet not all Seattle practitioners saw student classification as a panacea. As in other cities of the period, critical voices of reflection, however muted, intermittently found their way into public discourse. One reappraisal came in the form of a scintillating address given at the 1927 NEA annual meeting by Helen Reynolds, the director of the Seattle department of kindergarten and primary education. She used the opportunity to directly confront classification: "Are we going to become so interested in testing and checking and labeling the little children who come to us, in parceling them into groups and laying out for them schedules to be completed, that we shall ignore their right to enough leisure and opportunity for growing those qualities and abilities which they as individuals possess?" Quoting William Kilpatrick's statement that "not all learning can be assigned," Reynolds asked: "Are we going to ignore the chance of variation which may lead to some creative contribution to the group in which the child lives, in our overemphasis on acquiring the skills of life?"[90]

Not unlike her contemporary in Oakland, Ida Vandergaw, Reynolds demonstrated a sophisticated knowledge of progressive terminology, and she challenged educational experts who proffered "habits lists" as rigid "standards or outcomes which should result from the experiences gained through life activities carried on at home or at school." Far from advocating an obsequious adherence to such externally developed lists, Reynolds called on teachers to be their own best evaluators: "Are we justified unless each day we look backward over the day's happenings and judge them by the standards which in moments of study and reflection we have set up, saying to ourselves, 'This was good, and that was better. These things must be different tomorrow'?" Reynolds's faith in her fellow classroom teachers offered a view of educational practice and research that was essentially Deweyan in its message, situating the teacher as the primary agent of progressive change. "Can we take each day as a problem," she asked in conclusion, "to be freshly solved in the light of all that we have learned from the successes and failures of our effort the day before?"[91]

If Reynolds's spirited commentary showed that practitioner protest was possible, it also reinforced, by its very existence, how rare was open disagreement. Despite statements of concern expressed by Reynolds or any others, Seattle administrators continued to stress how classification and curricular variety offered the kind of equal educational opportunity required in a democracy.

Stealth Curricular and Organizational Expansion

Ayer's research was widely cited by educators in numerous journals, among them the NEA Research Bulletin, which drew heavily on his work for its own publications in 1923–25.[92] Ayer's studies, reported Cole, had also provided a basis for the constructive revision of the Seattle curriculum. Around the same time, the district established a demonstration school, which, alongside curriculum revision, offered avenues for the pursuit of progressive reform. The district's demonstration school—modeled on similar progressive programs in Minneapolis, Cleveland, and "other progressive school systems"— offered potential as a district strategy for improving teacher practice; it built on teaching standards offered by the NEA and centered on presenting "established teaching techniques." It was not an "experimental school," Cole made sure to point out; it sought to disseminate accepted methods rather than generate new ideas or pedagogical innovations.[93]

At the Summit School, the district's primary demonstration site, one could find many of the accouterments of 1920s progressivism: a student-run post office; field trips to the University of Washington museum; lessons titled "Early Seattle—a Puppet Play," "Our School Museum," or "Our Neighborhood Book"; and art classes that fostered "the development of individual talent." Those activities aside, the demonstration school had a serious purpose. Teachers who visited the school to witness the instructional lessons were engaged in serious discussions before and after their classroom observations, and they were asked to consider questions such as: "Was there evidence of careful checking and testing after teaching to see if aims had been realized and for the purpose of directing further work?" Whether Seattle administrators and the teachers who ran the demonstration were able to disseminate these strong instructional practices throughout the district is difficult to ascertain. Nevertheless, it is clear they had learned to become skilled at creating opportunities that would advance teacher professionalization.[94]

The demonstration school and the district's curriculum revision also required thoughtful administrative coordination of the type found in Denver. Ayer's *Studies in Administrative Research* offered another means through which district educators could again raise the topic of administrative reorganization, the effort that Cooper had initiated but that Shorrock and the school board twice shot down. Ayer (no doubt guided by Cole) did not come at reorganization head on but rather through examining "the administrative organization of [instructional] supervision" as carried out in Seattle and elsewhere. Using supervisory practices in other cities as his professed focus, Ayer offered a guarded but sharp critique of the Seattle school board's form of "departmental organization"—the administrative structure that the school board had adopted in 1919 as a rebuff to Cooper's second request for reorganization. "As school systems grow larger," reported an undaunted Ayer, "it becomes necessary to counteract the disintegrating tendencies of independence, diversity, and specialization by the formation of a more unified type of administrative organization."[95]

Ayer's language was just the sort of rhetoric regarding administrative unity and district centralization that Cubberley spent a career deploying so effectively; and whether consciously or not, Ayer borrowed another Cubberley technique, printing two figures that represented, first, the extant organizational setup in Seattle (considered faulty) and, second, a proposed organizational chart of what a redesigned Seattle school district could look like.[96] With the recent budgetary cutbacks in mind, Cole and Ayer no doubt hoped that such a display of administrative efficiency would convince steadfast board members to reconsider reorganization. However, against a school board adverse to significant change, their strategy was patently ineffective. Although Cole was beholden to the business community—especially after its leaders put him on the Seattle Chamber of Commerce—it was the district administrators, rather than the board's businessmen, who argued for corporate-styled reorganization, again illustrating that business organizational models were seen quite differently by alternative types of business professionals.

Undaunted, Cole could be indefatigable in proposing reform, as illustrated by his inclusion of a diagram of Seattle's administrative organization for curriculum revision in his first *Triennial Report* (1921–24). In his final *Triennial Report* (1927–30), he reproduced Ayer's organizational charts of the district's curricular supervision and guidance counseling programs, demonstrating at least symbolic compliance with prevailing norms.[97] Both Cole and Ayer knew that curriculum revision was an innovation that carried clout, and they managed to initiate their own program. However, the program ultimately suffered both from a lack of funding and a reliance on an already overworked teaching corps.[98]

Yellow Administrators

Seattle generally thrived as a growing city in the 1920s and, as in many centers in the urban West, expanding economies often meant escalating prices and expenses. Some rejoiced at the rapid growth, calling Seattle "the largest city of its age," but not all professions kept up with the shifting cost of living, and teaching fared worse than most other occupations. While the salaries of most Seattle workers rose 25 percent between 1919 and 1927, teacher salaries dropped, due to the budget restrictions imposed by the school board. Teachers generally had little in the way of collective bargaining power at this point in time. Most districts had teacher associations, but these were usually unaffiliated with any teacher union, nor were they intended to be. The NEA, controlled by and dedicated to the interests of school administrators, was hardly comparable to an advocacy organization established for the benefit of teachers.[99]

The American Federation of Teachers had been chartered in 1916, and by 1919, it had a total of twelve thousand members scattered among various cities. However, due to pressure from the Red Scare and opposition from the NEA, its membership had dropped to a low of three thousand in 1923. Many unions scaled back their political efforts, yet a number of school boards throughout the country had nevertheless begun to bar the federation or any teacher unionization as a preemptive effort to limit teacher power in local decision making. Seattle was not necessarily the most likely candidate as the federation's western foothold. Despite an active labor movement that ultimately led to the 1919 General Strike, the city experienced several repercussive aftershocks, one of which was a reassertion by the business community of its power. From the perspective of teachers, however, Seattle was a case study in why teachers needed some kind of negotiating clout in asserting their requests for better compensation.[100]

Especially galling to the city's high school teachers was the fact that per pupil costs in the secondary schools had declined from a high of roughly $149 in the early 1920s to $119 in 1927 while class sizes and teacher workloads had only continued to increase. Many teachers felt the situation was dire. "It is impossible for those with dependents to live on our maximum salary of $2,400," the High School Teachers League entreated the board. "The typical high school teacher is not a young woman, living at home and partly supported by her parents as seems to be the popular notion." Teachers had reasons aplenty to be frustrated with the contradictory decisions and mixed messages coming from the school board. The inconsistency could easily be represented by Shorrock who, on the one hand, tried to protect many of the programs that he had seen sprout and grow during his long tenure on the board but, on the other, showed little sympathy for the plight of teachers attempting to get by on low salaries. Worse yet, from the perspective of the financially strapped educators, was the board's resistance to removing the restriction on teachers taking outside work at the same time that board members reminded them that they were paid less than many other salaried workers because they did not have a full twelve-month work year.[101]

When the existing association, the High School Teachers League, was denied in its request for a salary increase in 1927, teachers looked for other means for expressing their grievances. In the middle of that year, Florence Hanson, the American Federation of Teachers' national secretary-treasurer, addressed a group of 350 Seattle high school teachers about establishing a local in their district. Hanson later recalled that the teachers "almost pushed me off the platform in their eagerness to put their signatures on that charter application." The new Local 200 quickly gained a majority of the high school teachers as members and established affiliation with the Seattle Central Labor Council and the Washington State Federation of Labor. With their stature now enhanced, and armed with evidence that Seattle teacher wage scale was the lowest of the thirteen American cities with populations between 250,000 and 500,000, the teachers again went to the school board asking either for an immediate wage hike or for the addition of a millage increase to the ballot in the upcoming March school board 1928 city elections. The board denied both requests. Shorrock sneered that the public was "not competent" to pass judgment on matters such as salary measures, a comment that in turn led the *State Labor News* to respond that "board was at radical variance with democratic principles."[102]

Labor historian Joseph Slater argues that the history of public employee unionization is distinct from that of private employees, in part because of the strike restrictions often placed on public workers. Yet public employees, such as the Seattle teachers, also have available another means of protest: the use of public opinion and the ballot box to dislodge public policy makers. Seattle teachers realized that the fastest approach to redressing their salary problem might come through supporting the opponent to the one incumbent board member, Dr. Caspar Sharples, who was up for reelection in March 1928. One teacher, clearly frustrated with the board's arrogant intransigence, characterized the election as representing "the age-old conflict between democracy and autocracy." Despite the fact that Sharples ultimately beat out his challenger by a narrow margin, the extremely high turnout at the election demonstrated that Seattle's teachers and labor community could still rally significant support. While a usual election turnout averaged around twenty thousand voters, the March 1928 election garnered a total of 84,600 votes, and Sharples won by fewer than seventeen hundred.[103]

Of course, board members were not easily cowed, and for his part, an undeterred Shorrock stated that the board would reject "any movement, either individual or collective, which threatens the efficiency of the schools." In general, Seattle business leaders reacted nervously to any suggestion of worker control, and this was precisely the fear the teachers' Local 200 elicited in 1928 when it argued for "the right and the duty of classroom teachers to direct, in a larger way, the affairs of the schools." That neither the board nor district administrators need be at odds with teachers over determining their appropriate role in a democratic school system could easily have been seen by looking southeast to the example of Denver. At the same time that the Seattle teachers union said it wanted to take "a larger share in management" of the schools and "to assist in determining length, number, and size of classes; in adjusting room conditions; [and] in revising courses of study," Denver administrators Jesse Newlon and A. L. Threlkeld had already delivered those responsibilities to their own teachers as a matter of course for several years.[104]

Seattle was not Denver, of course, and in May 1928, the Seattle school board unanimously passed a resolution that reappointed all high school teachers for the following year but *only* on the condition that they each sign an employment contract with a yellow-dog clause that read: "I hereby declare that I am not a member of the American Federation of Teachers, or any local thereof and will not become a member during the term of this contract." The board announced that Superintendent Cole, along with a number of the district's high school principals, were in agreement with their position. Although the national federation brought a suit against the board, the legal resolution to the issue would ultimately take another two years, finally ending in December 1930 with a Washington Supreme Court decision upholding the union ban. In the meantime, however, the school board endured criticism from inside and outside the city, including a telegram from John Dewey, who wrote that he viewed the yellow-dog rule as "contrary to the American spirit and also highly inexpedient as it will alienate strong and self-respecting teachers from the profession."[105] Alienation was clearly not a concern for this board.

The board held its ground for some time, but in January 1931, just one month after its victory in the state Supreme Court, the board voted unanimously to drop the yellow-dog rule. In the meantime, not only had the Depression become a dominant force, but the school board had also begun to lose its conservative members. Shorrock died in late 1928, and in the 1929 school board elections, two of labor's three candidates were victorious. Although the yellow-dog episode eventually faded from the newspapers and regular district discussions, the Seattle school board had nevertheless shown that Progressive Era power politics could easily overshadow progressive educational innovations.

Whether weary from the union conflict, concerned about a reconstituted school board, or genuinely interested in pursuing an academic career, Superintendent Cole announced his intention to resign in early 1930 in order to accept a position at the University of Washington. Over the objections of its two new, labor-friendly members, the school board selected a Seattle administrator, Worth McClure, to succeed Cole. To labor, and some Seattle progressives, McClure, who had served as an assistant superintendent in the city, represented an uninspired, establishment choice—no "outside man" for Seattle.

———

Frank Cooper obviously had many of the characteristics of the pedagogical progressive but labeling him as such serves to mask some of the many other policies and practices that he introduced into his schools, from IQ testing to differentiation to vocational training. If researchers are to engage in serious analysis of these progressive educators, they should examine the full array of district practices and pay special attention to evidence that does not fit the model. The fact that Cooper followed a number of administrative progressive ideas does not diminish him, but it does force scholars to create and confront fully detailed portraits. In one sense, Cooper does scholars a great service by refusing to act out the two-dimensional labels they have affixed to him.

Seattle educators confronted the challenges presented by children who failed to thrive in early twentieth-century schools. One signal difference that distinguished Seattle was that Frederic Ayer's studies offered a good deal more data than was usually produced within a district. In Seattle, teachers of the 1920s quickly pointed to a range of causes of student failure beyond intellectual ability: school study habits, previous preparation, indifference toward school, home environment, and home study habits. Ayer went so far as to acknowledge that each struggling school child had a complex school history and background and that the causes of failure could "be removed by a systematic improvement of the conditions which produce them."[106] Recall, as well, that the test scores that Ayer used came from assessments administered several years after progressive curricular reforms had already been in place for some time. This might well have provided evidence that the new progressive curricula were not necessarily working as intended. Nevertheless, neither Ayer nor other administrators pushed to inject these kinds of findings into the national arena. We are left wondering why progressives did not ask questions about why their own reforms were not solving the very problems they were designed to address.

Finally, the charges of anti-intellectualism, presented by Mrs. Smith of the TRC should also force reflection about Seattle's coursework. Contemporaries who were predisposed to cherish pedagogical progressive notions rarely were able to respond satisfactorily to critiques that some of the new curricula abandoned rigorous academics, at least outside of the standard platitudes about equal educational opportunity. At best, district progressives were likely to point to the intellectual rigor of the upper-level courses offered to the district's elite children, assuming that all other children were better suited to more general, practical, or vocational curricula. The fact that local discussions about the quality of academic content were so rare points to one of the flaws—or fundamental dilemmas—of both district progressives and to the larger progressive education movement as a whole. How could progressives simultaneously build new schools, promote new programs, monitor schoolchildren's health and well-being, work collaboratively with teachers, design intellectually challenging curricula, and create democratic school system? Was this too much to ask of any single institution?

7

CONCLUSION

DESIGNING THE DEMOCRATIC SCHOOL DISTRICT

254   This book began by asking what it meant to be a progressive urban school district, and having examined the introduction of a wide variety of reforms into four distinct cities, I now return to that question, identifying the conclusions that can be gleaned from side-by-side comparisons of these four school systems. This study's approach of following similar reforms across multiple districts over several decades offers a common foundation for understanding the complexity of instructional and leadership practices in the Progressive Era. The local vantage point also allows for examination of several significant contemporary challenges, a set of concerns that is as rich as it is formidable, including poverty, academic ability and classification, democracy and equal educational opportunity, administrative reorganization and scientific management, curricular and pedagogical change, the proper roles for teachers and school boards in reform, the involvement of labor unions, and the intertwining of municipal and educational politics. Rather than address all these issues simultaneously, this last chapter proceeds by synthesizing some of the book's arguments into four overarching themes: the development of district progressivism; the interplay of educational and municipal reform; the relationship between poverty, differentiation, and intelligence testing; and the articulation of "true" and "false" democracy. Finally, it reflects on how this history of urban school systems matters for educational practice today and suggests some potential lessons that early twentieth-century city school systems might hold for the successful operation of school districts in the early twenty-first.

THE DEVELOPMENT OF DISTRICT PROGRESSIVISM

Looking at educational progressivism from the perspective of the district provides the kind of fine-grained attention to local reform, rhetoric, and practices that yields an alternative version of progressivism, a type that developed at the level of the city school system and was distinct from the analytic streams that historians have stocked with nationally prominent progressive theorists and academics. The traditional categories used to characterize Progressive Era leaders prove conceptually inadequate when used to analyze the activities of local practitioners of the period, specifically those in urban districts. District progressives were unburdened by many of the conceptual divisions that distinguished national leaders and their theories; most district practitioners borrowed from a range of reformist tendencies rather than conforming to any single category.

The appropriative tendencies of local urban educators have been overlooked partly because of the methodological tendency to develop single case studies but also due to an immense fascination with Dewey-inspired reforms, on the one hand, or to outsized attention to the initiatives of scientific management experts, on the other. Some cherished heroes of pedagogical progressivism turned out to have had remarkable administrative savvy, and most district leaders blended all sorts of ideas and practices previously believed to be antagonistic. In other words, this study demonstrates that the penchant for combining seemingly incompatible innovations was a hallmark of district progressives, not an idiosyncratic tic. What at first glance seems an eclectic or iconoclastic approach to adopting progressive innovations was instead a definitive pattern characterizing all four urban districts. In fact, the propensity for amalgamation cut across multiple districts, decades, programmatic trends, and administrative personalities, whether in Seattle under Cooper and Cole, in Denver under Newlon and Threlkeld, in Oakland under Hunter, or in Portland under Alderman in 1910s or Rice in the 1920s and 1930s.[1] Scholars certainly must recognize how pedagogical reforms sometimes required a modicum of social efficiency to grease the rails.

It would be a mistake, however, to interpret this conclusion as indicating that educators previously described as creative innovators, leaders such as Cooper or Newlon, were instead rigid administrationists. Not only did administrative reorganization accompany reforms that were more pedagogically oriented, but progressive leaders also often saw such reorganization—characteristic of Cubberley's plans—as essential to carrying out their instructional and curricular innovations. Where scholars see contradictions among practices, district progressives saw pragmatic programs that helped them reach their goals. District leaders were quite comfortable living with the paradoxes that scholars have argued were endemic both to progressive education and to the larger Progressive Movement; and they were able to accept the compromises necessary (if they even considered them compromises) to conduct school on a day-to-day basis.

Blended progressive practices were much more than simple hybridizations; indeed, they typified a consistent attitude exemplified among district leaders who took the reins of city school systems after 1913. In other words, they mark the very character of district progressivism itself.[2] The tendency to conjoin contradictory practices symbolizes the era. Rather than hybridization, the process might be better understood as something more akin to genetic recombination, whereby the progeny exhibit character traits that did not exist in either parent. The original ideas are altered and what emerges is something new, something remarkably American.

One weakness of the analytic urge to divide educational practitioners into distinct categories, understandable though it may be, is that it masks the *core nature of district progressive practice.* As such, this oversight matters at several levels. Excessive attention to Hunter's district-wide testing schemes and efficiency measures diverts analysis from the multiple efforts in Oakland that might otherwise have been considered more pedagogical in nature, such as William Cooper's intensive attention to improving instructional practice in the social studies. Also overlooked would be central office administrators' exhaustive efforts to visit classrooms throughout the district or Vandergaw's candid remarks about the implementation challenges of progressive practices. Scholarly emphasis on the pedagogical proclivities of Seattle's Frank Cooper has already sidetracked attention from Cooper's delight with standardized testing and his yearning to gain administrative control of his district, the type that school boards in both Oakland and Denver bequeathed to their superintendents around 1917. Moreover, treating Cooper as a rare specimen of imaginative pedagogical leadership slights the attention that his successor, Superintendent Cole—previously characterized as a staunch administrative progressive—gave to establishing Seattle's Demonstration School and to his continued work with teachers after Cooper's departure.

At another level, branding some administrators as pedagogical progressives sidesteps other important debates about the nature of democratic education, such as whether vocational education as implemented by these districts constituted a liberating force or an oppressive damper on future prospects. That Seattle administrators could, at the same time, embrace competing visions of schooling is all too easy to overlook; after all, the diverse array of individuals considered progressive—Anna Louise Strong, Mrs. Smith, and Frank Cooper—differed markedly on the importance that vocational education should play in an industrial democracy. Could progressives be pedagogically progressive while at the same time creating coursework that constrained the futures of students? The answer seems to be yes. While some critics of "progressive education" writ large have long leveled charges of anti-intellectualism and unjust tracking at early twentieth-century educators, the label of pedagogical progressivism has often shielded certain district progressives from some of these complaints, instead deflecting blame onto administrative progressives. Scholars will have to face the awkward possibility that corporate structure may have been a precondition for the active involvement of teachers in building planning and curriculum development. Understanding and embracing the full extent of district progressive proclivities offers a more complete, albeit perplexing, portrait of local educational progressivism. Yet it is also a depiction that is more thought-provoking and stimulating for future inquiry. The inclusiveness of district progressivism could be a weakness, of course. This was especially the case with the harsher forms of Americanization, and district progressivism's lack of a strong philosophical core also meant that it allowed the Ku Klux Klan to claim coherence with broad progressive educational goals, as it did in Oakland and Portland.

What then, in sum, was this new district, this *progressive city school system*? To the district progressives, the most advanced formulation of the new model of the progressive district could be found in those city school systems that refashioned themselves into broad educational service agencies: that new kind of district organized to "provide some form of suitable training for almost every conceivable type of activity" as Denver's Chadsey put it. Moreover, because American cities served as hothouses for the many new types of jobs and opportunities that increasingly characterized the U.S. economy, progressive urban districts could also attract the best talent and resources, even if cities like Portland found that their reluctance to engage in district reorganization meant that it could not attract highly qualified candidates from elsewhere to consider the Portland superintendency.

It is difficult to read the annals of these four districts without astonishment at the sheer multitude of innovations they introduced over the course of fifty years, a list that by the 1920s included programs as diverse as broad new types of curricula, group intelligence testing, standardized achievement testing, domestic science, visual education, vocational schools, vocational guidance, business courses, and massive building programs, among many others. It is little wonder, then, that educators in these districts failed to concentrate their energies on core concerns of education, such as instruction, for they saw pedagogical change as only one road to reform. In the process, the urban school district adopted a new role as the *coordinator* of educational change. At its best, progressivism meant that schools focused on the success of every child: academic, emotional, physical, or civic success. Yet, at its worst, progressivism could confuse student learning with any trivial school undertaking—constructing flytraps, demonstrating patriotism, or passing salesmanship classes—with accomplishment of more meaningful intellectual tasks.

One way to assess district progressivism is to ask whether it ultimately alleviated the specific problems and concerns originally articulated by reformers such as Joseph Rice, Jacob Riis, Leonard Ayres, and Frederic Burk. The evidence here is mixed. Certainly, urban educators made significant physical changes to schools, replacing unsafe, unhealthy, and uninviting buildings with modern, well-outfitted, even grand, structures. Squalid city schools certainly had not disappeared by 1940, but each of the four cities studied here created new educational settings that exemplified a concern not only for students' well-being (through lunchrooms, fire escapes, and new ventilation and lighting) but also for the new kinds of learning experiences that could be offered to them in new gymnasiums, modern science labs, and more spacious classrooms outfitted with movable desks, sand tables, and workshops. To the reformers who focused primarily on these physical upgrades, school was as much an instructional institution as it was a corrective to the social and economic problems of the urban environment.

District progressives often took the more-traveled road of adopting reforms that were tangible, digestible, and easily diagrammed, graphed, or charted; these innovations could be more swiftly implemented and were easier to explain to teachers, parents, and taxpayers. In addition, because each city school system operated as a "unit," whereby interrelated reforms were introduced simultaneously or in quick succession, districts raised their chances for success in implementation of common reforms. Unified operation also meant, however, that negative side effects of new practices could become magnified and more severe. Districts that had reorganized around the principle of student classification, for example, also fused into place a district-wide system of differentiated curricula that would later prove immensely difficult to dismantle. The benefits of unified coordination, the kind represented by the aesthetic of the organizational chart, was therefore accompanied by the burden of predestination, the kind that came with student tracking.

By the late 1920s, Newlon was in the midst of his intellectual transition from superintendent to academic, yet he still emanated the enveloping, unifying glow of the progressive thought that had so distinguished his tenure in Denver. For example, in a 1929 speech, given on the occasion of Dewey's seventieth birthday, Newlon reflected on Dewey's immense impact on the field of education. In so doing, he combined ideas and personalities that this study has shown were frequently woven together by district progressives. "The leading figures in the development of a profession of school administration, such as George D. Strayer," Newlon said, "acknowledge their debt to Dewey." Superintendents such as Ella Flagg Young and academics like Rugg, Bobbitt, and Kilpatrick also had been influenced deeply by Dewey, he added. To Newlon, Dewey's notion of "education as a social process," Strayer's "socialized recitation," and Hunter's "socialized education" were all compatible. As a school leader, Newlon synthesized the ideas and practices that made the most sense from his perspective in the district central office. Indeed, the case of Denver demonstrates how readily local administrators blended ideas as they confronted the many instructional, logistical, and organizational challenges faced by Progressive Era school systems. In choosing school reforms, the main criteria for many local district progressives was less often philosophical coherence than, more simply, utilitarian harmony. "In the broadest sense," Newlon concluded, "there is no conflict between Dewey's philosophy of education and the scientific movement."[3] And there is no better encapsulation of district progressivism than Newlon's 1929 synthesis.

THE INTERPLAY OF EDUCATIONAL AND MUNICIPAL REFORM

The yearning for more systematic approaches to school district governance emerged from the same wellspring as other municipal reform efforts. Charter reforms, urban surveys, the unleashing of civic groups to attack entrenched problems, and the use of new forms of budgeting and management all demanded the attention of a wide range of municipal citizens. One difference distinguishing the schools from other municipal institutions was that districts were often *in* the city but not *of* the city; yet their fiscal independence rarely seemed to matter to taxpayer commissions set on trimming government expenditures across the board. The vision of schools as separate from politics was a mirage. Just as municipal politicians and leaders sought to use their city apparatus to broaden the scope of urban life, urban school district leaders endeavored to use the new progressive school district as the framework around which all new educational activity could take place, to wit, the expansion of school from a relatively small part of young person's life into a vast system that included almost every conceivable activity and experience.

Much like the deliberations of civic reformers as they attempted to reformulate the types of municipal relationships that would allow for more accountability and efficiency—whether through commission governments, city-manager plans, or strong mayors—progressive educational reformers hoped that the reorganization of city school systems would provide the structure for the kind of world they wanted to create.

What makes this era so remarkable it that virtually all actors in the sphere of public municipal business were *simultaneously* rethinking leadership, organizational structure, democratic governance, citizen participation, integrity, and privilege. How should schools and cities be managed in ways that ensure efficiency and accountability? Moreover, the intertwining of municipal reforms, the expansion of new types of civic groups, and the acceleration of educational change were dynamic elements that influenced one another. Portland presents perhaps the best example of the complex interactions between civic and school concerns. At roughly the same time that community taxpayer's group and city elites decided to employ the New York Bureau of Municipal Research to conduct a survey of city governance affairs, citizens requested, through the voice of Richard Montague and others, that a school district survey be carried out as well. However, the dual inquiries on the city and schools by outside evaluators led to a kind of civic cognitive overload, and attention to the schools took a back seat to the multiple painful and pressing issues laid out by the municipal survey. Nevertheless, these interactions were remarkably consequential, not always because of the content of the reports (often too expansive to address in any kind of strategic way) but because of their time-specific and context-dependent nature. In other words, they made conditional the types of reforms that could reasonably be considered at any one point, given the ideology of the external monitoring group. Denver experienced similar political activity in the 1910s to shore up professionalism on the school board, but that initiative derived in part from a desire to squash ongoing board member bickering. Newlon benefited from the changes that took place several years before his tenure, but his administration was not necessarily the target of the original civic group.

During the years that stretched from 1913 to 1923, each city experienced large escalations in taxation, often due to the newer educational practices and programs implemented by districts. Much of the cost can also be explained by the rapid school construction needed to meet skyrocketing enrollments. The same kinds of efforts at modernization and accountability that swept across cities also affected school leaders and architects, meaning more expansive visions were blended with higher standards for building codes: modern, well-outfitted, even grand, structures required additional investments, all related to increasing demands brought about by urbanization. Expansion led districts to capture the attention of civic taxpayer groups, providing new targets for these groups. In Seattle, the TRC, originally organized to address city payrolls, eventually turned its attention to the city school system. This was how progressives participated as local citizens: through civic organizations and social clubs.

THE RELATIONSHIPS BETWEEN POVERTY, DIFFERENTIATION, AND INTELLIGENCE TESTING

Combined records from these school systems yield substantial evidence that urban educators in each of these four districts understood that intellectual ability was not the sole cause for student academic failure. Before the widespread use of intelligence tests, local practitioners not only sought out the reasons for student failure but also experimented with viable approaches to getting pupils back to grade level. As early as 1897, Oakland instructors found that guiding students back to "first principles" in a subject area could help them return to grade level. And again, in 1918, Oakland committees reported a range of explanations for student failure—irregular attendance, class size, lack of clear promotion standards, teachers unfit to teach, poverty, and home environment—they could find no single cause. At the same time, Virgil Dickson asserted that mental testing should be given to kindergarten and first-grade students in order to sort them properly for their scholastic abilities and future careers.[4] In Denver and Seattle, the superintendents detailed promising practices in ungraded rooms around 1911; and in 1916, Alderman reported that Portland's ungraded rooms allowed students who were both behind and advanced to work at their own pace. In many cases, these strategies for helping students catch up academically were remarkably successful. In fact, Cooper reported an 85 percent success rate with his auxiliary teacher program in Seattle.[5]

What this means is that a policy window opened for American schools between the years between 1909 (Ayres's *Laggards in Our Schools*) and 1919 (Terman's *Intelligence of School Children*). It was during this short period that districts devoted efforts to developing alternative instructional approaches, the kind that could address the problem of overage students. Practitioners often had success with inventive methods for assisting students to return to their grade, and they talked of expanding these programs. Although the language of district reports is sometimes opaque, when local educators used phrases like "home conditions," "environmental conditions," truancy, or prolonged illness, among others, these descriptors usually referred to conditions of family poverty (albeit usually mixed with patronizing attitudes on the part of district progressives). Indeed, district records offer clear evidence that student failure disproportionately affected poor children, especially those from immigrant and minority families—dwellers of those "thickly populated sections of the city" that Hunter felt should be targeted for his Americanization programs. However, time and again, awareness of the connections between poverty and student achievement remained articulated primarily at the local level without gaining any national coherence or traction. Even in the districts where practitioners uncovered multiple sources of evidence that poverty and other "environmental conditions" appeared to be major causes of poor academic performance, leaders never turned this connection into a central focus for investigation. Of all the topics that were avidly discussed at NEA annual meetings, this particular conundrum about the nonschool factors that influenced pupil progression through the grades remained remarkably underexplored.

In a 1916 study, Teachers College researcher Charles Elmer Holley began to identify the connections between parental education, socioeconomic status, and children's performance in school, remarking how his findings on these relationships could serve to disrupt the standard thinking on heredity and performance; but little attention was paid to this kind of study, nor to other evidence about the academic effects of poverty. In part, this was because the narrative about the need for differentiated schools had already been established, and even those presented with contradictory evidence managed to ignore or overlook it.[6]

It is worth a momentary reflection about what might have happened in American education had the IQ test never been developed or had it been developed at a later period.

If district leaders had spent more time digging further into the evidence of wide variations in student achievement—or looked more closely at the wildly uneven "retardation" rates across schools—they might have been forced to pause and rethink their assumptions.

Given the slow advance of some of these inquiries, the abrupt new direction that many districts took after Terman's introduction of group intelligence tests is rather remarkable. "Again," he wrote in 1919, "we see that the chief cause of retardation is not irregular attendance, the use of a foreign language in the home, bad teeth, adenoids, malnutrition, etc., but inferior mental endowment. Educational reform may as well abandon, once for all, the effort to bring all children up to grade." In truth, Terman did very little to rule out these other external factors. In part, this was because he had already decided what the research said about American schoolchildren. When he spoke to a large audience of Denver teachers and students in 1916, Terman declared: "We have come to recognize in the last half-dozen years that all children are not born equal, as we have always insisted on believing, and that some children come into the world better provided with mental and physical faculties than others."[7] Terman's confusion of the inherent worth of each child with differences of academic ability surely marked one of the greatest failures of the era. It was Terman's idea, not the student, that was defective.

Various forms of student classification preceded intelligence testing, indicating that the will to sort children into groups, whether by ability, interests, or nationality, was part of turn-of-the-century American ideology. By the mid-1890s, for example, Oakland had already identified differences in the academic ability of children and had begun to seek explanations for these disparities. At the same time, they began to adjust their course offerings to better suit the needs and projected vocations of their students. It was in 1893— some twenty-five years before intelligence tests took hold—that the principal of the Oakland High School matter-of-factly proclaimed that there would always be different classes of students in the high school and that he foresaw a day when Oakland would offer "a system of differentiated schools to its citizens" that would be the pride of the city.[8] These examples indicate an interest and a predilection for tracking that in some ways established the conditions for the differentiation that followed.

Perhaps one belief stands out in stark relief. Many progressives held an abiding assumption that the nation would be led by its intellectual elite.

THE ARTICULATION OF "TRUE DEMOCRACY"

Public deliberations regarding conceptions of *true* and *false* democracy proliferated throughout the first decades of the twentieth century far too widely to be ignored: Nicholas Murray Butler's 1907 call for an "aristocracy of intellect"; Cubberley's insistence to Denver school board members that they were the proper representatives of democracy and therefore should pass executive power to the superintendent; and Hunter and Dickson's reworking of "equal educational opportunity" in Oakland. Why was it so important to these contemporaries that they refine or alter definitions of democracy? And what made conceptions of "false" democracy so insidious?

A dark undercurrent flowed through the Progressive Era, a shifting perception about who counts in a democracy. Underlying the rhetoric of citizen participation, common schooling for all, and statements about democratic opportunity was a deeper question lurking behind the surface of American life, the type that might undermine the social fabric of society. In this case, the concern had to do with intellectual equality. The wide differences in intelligence test scores convinced people like H. H. Goddard that Americans could not possibly all be intellectually equal, and he worried that the intellectual deficiencies inherent in a vast array of the citizenry threatened democracy and placed a grave responsibility on the small minority who possessed the intelligence necessary for leadership.[9] Thorndike articulated a similar view, the notion that democracy worked best when the "masses" allowed themselves to be ruled by the intelligence of others. "What is true in science and government seems to hold good in general for manufacturing, trade, art, law, education, and religion," argued Thorndike. "It seems entirely safe to predict that the world will get better treatment by trusting its fortunes to its 95- or 99-percentile intelligences than it would be by itself. The argument for democracy is not that it gives power to all men without distinction, but that it gives greater freedom for ability and character to attain power."[10]

Unlike Thorndike and Goddard, the practitioners who were closer to the students usually had better insights into the heights children and teachers could reach when given the opportunity. Another vision of democracy was offered by Newlon and, especially, Threlkeld. Newlon's democratic vision can be seen in the ways he included teachers, from the very beginning of his tenure, in salary and building deliberations and decisions, and at very practical level, Newlon demonstrated a tremendous respect when he alleviated them from their daily classroom work to permit them to engage in the equally essential work of curriculum development. Allowing for democratic engagement requires making time for those deliberations.

The optimism of Newlon and Threlkeld offers a sustaining vision, less because it presents a fully developed philosophy of education than that it holds at its core deep assumptions about the fundamental duties of the public school in a democratic society: it must ensure that all children learn and it must find methods for doing so. A democracy suffers if it does not persistently invent novel ways to complete these tasks. Threlkeld's notion of intelligence diverged sharply from Thorndike's and gives a much less individualized conception of intelligence. Threlkeld argued that only through millions of people learning, thinking, and working together could native genius truly reach its greatest achievements. The same applied to all fields of intellectual activity, Threlkeld believed. "Obviously," he concluded, "in a society in which only ten thousand people are questioning, inquiring, arguing, thinking, there is not the possibility for the potential leader of intelligence that there is in a society where ten million or one hundred million people are thinking for themselves."[11]

American society is currently undergoing a major transformation that is not completely dissimilar to the one that occurred roughly a hundred years ago, and schools and districts are once again being asked to respond. Consider the parallels. Americans live in an increasingly diverse society, one that is struggling to understand what immigration, or a halt to immigration, will mean for its future. Poverty and economic inequality portend deep rifts ahead within an already divided nation, one in which the wounds of racism have never healed. The United States is engaged in war overseas, now as then, as it seeks to adjust its role among other nations on the planet. Meanwhile, the country experiences tectonic economic shifts: then it was the transition from an agricultural to a manufacturing economy; now it is from a manufacturing economy to something else (a service economy or, perhaps, a gig economy).

Modern technology has transformed the nature of information and its distribution, leading school reformers to declare that the internet and its attendant devices will revolutionize education, just as previous generations proclaimed that their own innovations (radio, motion pictures, television) would alter the way humans learned. Young people are told to develop the creativity and problem-solving skills required to manage careers in a rapidly changing world, now as then. Thousands of inequitably funded public school systems struggle to properly educate children in even the most basic of tasks, skills, and knowledge. Crusaders once again promise that the right types of organizational restructuring (charter schools, vouchers, online education) will ensure that all children learn.

In sum, Americans of the Progressive Era and the present era face the same kind of core challenges. Many of the decisions made by educators in the 1910s and 1920s established the foundation for the public school system that has persisted for the past century. Progressives offered new forms of schooling that they hoped were more child friendly, but it was an incomplete solution delivered through an inequitable educational system within the context of an unequal world. If Americans still believe, as some clearly do, that the nation will be led by its upper-percent "intelligences," then districts and states will never manage to find the resources or the political will to educate each child to her or his highest potential.[12] One lesson that Americans can certainly take from their past is that bedrock changes in the nature of schooling, once completed, tend to stay in place for remarkably long period.

Only in a democracy in which millions of people are "questioning, inquiring, arguing, thinking," as A. L. Threlkeld explained it almost a century ago—learning and growing together—will the nation truly reach its own full potential. That is a richer understanding of education in a democracy.

LIST OF ARCHIVES, LIBRARIES, AND COLLECTIONS CONSULTED

In conducting my research, I found a rather fine line that formally distinguished an archive from a special collection from a good research library and
even from a bookshelf or a vault tucked away in the school district central
office (or one of its many other buildings). Therefore, I list all libraries, collections, and offices I visited in the course of my investigation.

CALIFORNIA
California Room and General Collection, Oakland Public Library
Cubberley Library, Stanford University School of Education
Oakland Public Schools
Professional Library, Oakland Public Schools
Special Collections, Green Library, Stanford University

COLORADO
Colorado Historical Society
District Central Office, Denver Public Schools
Newlon Papers, Threlkeld Papers, Special Collections, University of Denver
Western History Room and General Collection, Denver Public Library

OREGON
Alderman Papers, Special Collections, University of Oregon, Eugene
Archives/Records Management/Office of Public Information, Portland Public
     Schools District Central Office, Portland Public Schools
Oregon Collection and General Collection, Portland Public Library

WASHINGTON
Library and Special Collections, University of Washington, Seattle
Seattle Public School Archives, Seattle Public Schools

OTHER

Archives and General Collection, Teachers College, Columbia

Boise Public Library

District Central Office, Boise Public Schools

Peabody Library, Vanderbilt University

Pennsylvania State University Libraries

NOTES

INTRODUCTION

1   For examples of influential studies of the 1960s, see Raymond E. Callahan, *Education and the Cult of Efficiency: A Study of the Social Forces That Have Shaped the Administration of the Public Schools* (Chicago: University of Chicago Press, 1962); Michael B. Katz, *The Irony of Early School Reform* (Cambridge, MA: Harvard University Press, 1968); David Rogers, *110 Livingston Street: Politics and Bureaucracy in the New York City Schools* (New York: Random House, 1968). For critiques of the school district in recent decades, see Chester E. Finn Jr., "Beyond the School District," *National Affairs* (Fall 2011), 130–45. For other critiques—and some proposed solutions—regarding school districts, see John E. Chubb and Terry M. Moe, *Politics, Markets, and America's School* (Washington, DC: Brookings Institution, 1990); Paul T. Hill, Christine Campbell, and James Harvey, *It Takes a City: Getting Serious about School Reform* (Washington, DC: Brookings Institution, 2000); Frederick M. Hess, *Spinning Wheels: The Politics of Urban School Reform* (Washington, DC: Brookings Institution Press, 1999); for another approach, see Education Commission of the States, *The New American School District* (Denver: ECS, 1995). For an overview of the literature on school districts, historically conceived, see David A. Gamson and Emily M. Hodge, eds., *The Shifting Landscape of the American School District: Race, Class, Geography, and the Perpetual Reform of Local Control, 1935–2015* (New York: Peter Lang, 2018).

2   For representative critiques, see Peter Schrag, *Village School Downtown: Boston Schools, Boston Politics* (Boston: Beacon Press, 1967); Rogers, *110 Livingston Street: Politics and Bureaucracy in the New York City Schools*; Charles E. Silberman, *Crisis in the Classroom: The Remaking of American Education* (New York: Vintage Books, 1970); Jonathan Kozol, *Death at an Early Age: The Destruction of the Hearts and Minds of Negro Children in the Boston Public Schools* (Boston: Houghton Mifflin, 1967); Colin Greer, *The Great School Legend: A Revisionist Interpretation of American Public Education* (New York: Basic Books, 1972); Clarence J. Karier, Paul Violas, and Joel Spring, *Roots of Crisis: American Education in the Twentieth Century* (Chicago: Rand McNally, 1973).

3   For an excellent study of the state role in education during this same period, see Tracy Steffes, *School, Society, and State: A New Education to Govern Modern American, 1890–1940* (Chicago: University of Chicago Press, 2012).

4   See, e.g., Peter G. Filene, "An Obituary for 'The Progressive Movement,'" *American Quarterly* 22 (Spring 1970): 20–34; Daniel T. Rodgers, "In Search of

Progressivism," *Reviews in American History* 10 (December 1982): 113–32. For a deliberation on a synthesis of the streams of Progressive Era reform, or a lack thereof, see Arthur Link, *American Epoch: A History of the United States since the 1890s* (New York: Knopf, 1955), 68–91; David B. Tyack, *The One Best System: A History of American Urban Education* (Cambridge, MA: Harvard University Press, 1974), 196–97; for additional historiography, see David A. Gamson, "District Progressivism: Rethinking Reform in Urban School Systems, 1900–1928," *Paedagogica Historica* 39, no. 4 (August 2003): 417–34; Lawrence Cremin noted over fifty years ago that no "capsule definition" of progressive education would ever exist, and most scholars agree that the remarkably diverse ideas, reforms, and practices of the era defy tidy synthesis; Cremin, who generally relied on a broad inclusivity in his analysis, nevertheless described individual progressive educational leaders as "scientists," "sentimentalists," or "radicals." Taking a different tack, historian Ellen Condliffe Lagemann captures another division within the larger movement another way, suggesting that, although Edward Thorndike and John Dewey "both spoke and wrote in the 'progressive' idiom, the differences of view that separated them were large and significant." Appreciating the differences between these two men and their ideas is essential, she suggests, because "one cannot understand the history of education in the United States during the twentieth century unless one realizes that Thorndike won and Dewey lost" ("The Plural Worlds of Educational Research," *History of Education Quarterly* 29 [1989]: 185). See also Ellen Condliffe Lagemann, *An Elusive Science: The Troubling History of Education Research* (Chicago: University of Chicago Press, 2000); Lagemann acknowledges that she says this "in part to be perverse." Lawrence A. Cremin, *The Transformation of the School: Progressivism in American Education, 1876–1957* (New York: Vintage, 1961); some researchers have gone further, claiming, e.g., that the phrase "progressive education" was "not only vacuous but mischievous." Consequently, historians have abandoned the effort to be analytically all-inclusive and instead have examined progressivism from sets of more compartmentalized perspectives with carefully bounded parameters. American educational historians have generally treated school reform from one of three standpoints. They have studied innovation from the perspective of national movements and their leaders, they have used the lens of particularly vibrant experimental schools, or they have traced the success or failure of specific educational innovations. The full list is virtually endless. Based on the findings from studies taking the perspectives above, Herbert M. Kliebard, e.g., studying the leaders of national curriculum reform efforts, differentiates among the humanists, the developmentalists, the social efficiency experts, and the social meliorists as a way of contending with the "vague, essentially undefinable, entity called progressive education" (*The Struggle for the American Curriculum, 1893–1958*, 2nd ed. [New York: Routledge, 1995]); see also, e.g., Cremin *Transformation of the School*; Tyack, *One Best System*; Susan F. Semel and Alan R. Sadovnik, eds., *"Schools of Tomorrow," Schools of Today: What Happened to Progressive Education?* (New York: Peter Lang, 1999); Ronald Cohen and Raymond Mohl, *The Paradox of Progressive Education: The Gary Plan and Urban Schooling* (Port Washington, NY: Kennikat Press, 1979); Paul Davis Chapman, *Schools as Sorters: Lewis M. Terman, Applied Psychology, and the Intelligence Testing Movement, 1890–1930* (New York: New York University Press, 1988).

5   I avoid use of the term "educationists," heavily used as a pejorative term by critics of progressivism in the post–World War II era and sometimes employed in

recent years by historians and scholars. By way of terminology, I use the phrase "educational progressives" rather broadly, employing it as a way of referring to the educators between 1890 and 1940 who strove for school reform (rather than arguing for adherence to the status quo). When I wish to differentiate between different types of progressivism, I endeavor to do so clearly in the text.

6 Daniel T. Rodgers, *Atlantic Crossings: Social Politics in a Progressive Age* (Cambridge, MA: Belknap Press of Harvard University Press, 1998); O. M. Plummer, "President's Address," *Journal of Proceedings and Addresses of the National Education Association of the United States* (1915), 1031 (hereafter cited as *NEA Addresses and Proceedings*).

7 Charles A. Beard, "Reconstructing State Government," *New Republic* 4, no. 42 (April 21, 1915): 16.

8 See, e.g., the discussion of this perceived incompatibility between democracy and efficiency in Ronald D. Cohen and Raymond Mohl, *The Paradox of Progressive Education,* 10; on Allen, see Mordecai Lee, "Glimpsing an Alternate Construction of American Public Administration: The Later Life of William Allen, Cofounder of the New York Bureau of Municipal Research," *Administration & Society* 45, no. 5 (October 2013): 522–562; William H. Allen, *Efficient Democracy* (New York: Dodd, Mead & Co., 1907).

9 Cremin, *Transformation of the School,* 277, ix; Rugg was identifying progressive activities between 1875 and the 1930s. For his list, see Harold Rugg, *Foundations for American Education* (Yonkers-on-Hudson, NY: World Book Co., 1947), 569–70. For an excellent discussion of the challenges facing historians of education attempting to define progressivism, including some cautions regarding interpretive pitfalls, see Kliebard, *Struggle for the American Curriculum,* 231–51. While some historians, such as Larry Cuban or Arthur Zilversmit, have developed keen case studies of single or multiple districts, they often do so to trace the implementation of specific types of reforms, not packages of district-wide agendas. Cuban and Zilversmit both argue that they were rather rare. See Arthur Zilversmit, *Changing Schools: Progressive Education Theory and Practice, 1930–1960* (Chicago: University of Chicago Press, 1993); Larry Cuban, *How Teachers Taught: Constancy and Change in American Classrooms, 1890–1990,* 2nd ed. (New York: Teachers College Press, 1993).

10 For cautions on the pitfalls of western exceptionalism, see Robert D. Johnston, "Beyond 'The West': Regionalism, Liberalism, and the Evasion of Politics in the New Western History," *Rethinking History* 2, no. 2 (1998): 239–77, and "There's No 'There' There: Reflections on Western Political Historiography," *Western Historical Quarterly* 42, no. 3 (Autumn 2011), 331–37.

11 I thank Ralph Rodriguez for the suggestion of the phrase "cumulative case studies." In other words, readers might approach each individual case study on its own, as a way of exploring reform in a particular city, or they might read the chapters progressively, as it were, thereby seeing how larger themes emerge and become linked across the four districts.

12 Jane Addams, *The Second Twenty Years at Hull-House* (New York: Macmillan, 1930), 192.

13 Arthur S. Link, "What Happened to the Progressive Movement in the 1920s," *American Historical Review* 44 (1959): 845. Other discussions of 1920s progressivism include Lynn Dumenil, "'The Insatiable Maw of Bureaucracy': Antistatism and Education Reform in the 1920s," *Journal of American History* 77

(1990): 499–524; Paul W. Glad, "Progressives and the Business Culture of the 1920s," *Journal of American History* 53 (1966): 75–89.

14   For examples and discussions of these perspectives, see Rodgers, "In Search of Progressivism"; Zilversmit, *Changing Schools*; Michael Katz, *Reconstructing American Education* (Cambridge, MA: Harvard University Press, 1987); Cremin, *Transformation of the School*; Tyack, *One Best System*; Robert D. Johnston, *The Radical Middleclass: Populist Democracy and the Question of Capitalism in Progressive Era Portland, Oregon* (Princeton, NJ: Princeton University Press, 2003).

15   Since Bernard Bailyn's *Education in the Forming of American Society* (New York: Vintage, 1960), educational historians have been regularly admonished to ensure that their analyses of educational change are properly embedded within the larger social, cultural, political, and economic context. For the most part, the strongest scholars in the field have always done so. I absolutely agree that in order to fully comprehend the changes in these cities during this period, it is important to appropriately balance urban social history with more focused inquiries into the history of schooling. However, a reverse of that conventional equation is also true: it is equally important that, in documenting the history of schooling, historians accurately interpret educational change. Doing so also requires that historians consciously develop a deep understanding of some of the fundamentals of American public education, the importance of good instruction, the nature of sound curriculum, and the kinds of policies that foster strong teaching, whether in the past or present.

16   For an excellent discussion of the historiography of the Ku Klux Klan and the "New Historiography of Second Klan," see Johnston, *The Radical Middle Class*, 234–38.

17   In a review essay examining several monographs on urban schooling, Wayne Urban points out the tendency of some city-school scholarship to use as a starting point the question, "How and why did urban public schools go from among the best school systems in the country, to among the worst in the nation today?" This question not only implies a presentist approach to the history of American education, argues Urban, but it also betrays a certain golden age nostalgia for an assumed era of educational excellence. See Wayne Urban, "Portraits of Failure," *Journal of Urban History* (November 1996): 113–19.

18   Diane Ravitch, *Left Back: A Century of Failed School Reforms* (New York: Simon & Schuster, 2000), 95–100, 461.

CHAPTER 1

1   The first line of this paragraph draws on the phrase used by President Bill Clinton in his first inaugural address: "There is nothing wrong with America that cannot be cured by what is right with America." William J. Clinton, "Inaugural Address" (January 20, 1993), Online by Gerhard Peters and John T. Woolley, The American Presidency Project (website), https://www.presidency.ucsb.edu/documents/inaugural-address-51.

2   Ellwood P. Cubberley, "Organization of Public Education," *NEA Addresses and Proceedings* (1915), 95; Ellwood P. Cubberley, "State and County School Administration," in *School Administration Progress of Twenty-five Years* (Milwaukee: Bruce Publishing Co., 1916), 5.

3   Charles A. Beard, *American City Government: A Survey of Newer Tendencies* (New York: Century Co., 1912), 312. See, e.g., Ellwood P. Cubberley, *Public School Administration* (Boston: Houghton Mifflin, 1916), esp. chap. 19; Scott Nearing, *The New Education* (Chicago: Row, Peterson, & Company, 1915); Randolph S. Bourne, *The Gary Schools* (Cambridge, MA: MIT Press, 1970).

4   Daniel T. Rodgers, *Atlantic Crossings: Social Politics in a Progressive Age* (Cambridge, MA: Harvard University Press, 1998), 112.

5   O. M. Plummer, "President's Address," *NEA Addresses and Proceedings* (1915), 1031.

6   *Oregonian*, January 1, 1917.

7   Bradford Luckingham, "The Urban Dimension of Western History," in *Historians and the American West*, ed. Michael P. Malone (Lincoln: University of Nebraska Press, 1983), 334–35.

8   Bradley Robert Rice, *Progressive Cities: The Commission Government Movement in America, 1901–1920* (Austin: University of Texas Press, 1977), 63–67.

9   Fred C. Ayer, *Studies in Administrative Research*, 2 vols. (Seattle: Seattle Public Schools, 1924), 1:46–47.

10   John L. Davie, "Address of Welcome," *NEA Addresses and Proceedings* (1923), 140.

11   Walter Nugent, *Into the West: The Story of Its People* (New York: Alfred A. Knopf, 1999), 131–32. The peak year for homesteading was 1913, with 59,363 final homestead entries comprising almost eleven million acres of land transferred from federal to private ownership; after that year, farms and farm populations stopped expanding, then held steady until the late 1930s, when rural America then began its slow demographic decline into the end of the twentieth century.

12   For accounts of the urban West, see Carl Abbott, *How Cities Won the West: Four Centuries of Urban Change in Western North America* (Albuquerque: University of New Mexico Press, 2008); Gerald D. Nash and Richard W. Etulain, eds., *The Twentieth-Century West: Historical Interpretations* (Albuquerque: University of New Mexico Press, 1989); Patricia Nelson Limerick, Clyde A. Milner II, and Charles E. Rankin, ed., *Trails: Toward a New Western History* (Lawrence: University Press of Kansas, 1991); Richard White, *"It's Your Misfortune and None of My Own": A History of the American West* (Norman: University of Oklahoma Press, 1991); Gerald D. Nash, *Creating the West: Historical Interpretations, 1890–1990* (Albuquerque: University of New Mexico Press, 1991); Clyde A. Milner II, *A New Significance: Re-envisioning the History of the American West* (Oxford: Oxford University Press, 1996); Richard W. Etulain, "Research Opportunities in Twentieth-Century Western Cultural History," in *Researching Western History: Topics in the Twentieth Century*, ed. Gerald D. Nash and Richard W. Etulain (Albuquerque: University of New Mexico Press, 1997); Patricia Nelson Limerick, "The Case of Premature Departure: The Trans-Mississippi West and American History Textbooks," *Journal of American History* 78 (March 1992): 1380–94. For studies focused on western educational history, see Kathleen Weiler, *Country Schoolwomen: Teaching in Rural California, 1850–1950* (Stanford, CA: Stanford University Press, 1998); David B. Tyack, *One Best System: A History of American Urban Education* ([Cambridge, MA: Harvard University Press, 1974]— Tyack offers examples of the development of urban schooling in Oregon and California); Polly Welts Kaufman, *Women Teachers on the Frontier* (New Haven, CT: Yale University Press, 1984); Judith Raftery, *Land of Fair Promise: Politics*

and Reform in Los Angeles Schools, 1885–1941 (Stanford, CA: Stanford University Press, 1992). On early demands of the African American community for equal rights to education, see A. Odell Thurman, *The Negro in California before 1890* (San Francisco: R and E Assoc., 1973); and Delores Nason McBroome, *Parallel Communities: African-Americans in California's East Bay, 1850–1963* (New York: Garland, 1993).

13 "Symposium—a Western Association," *Sierra Educational News* 8, no. 4 (April 1912): 243–54. I have found little evidence, however, to indicate any kind of western exceptionalism; western schools did not develop in a significantly different form than those in the East. Scholars who have studied nineteenth-century schooling, point out the remarkable similarities in schools and school practices across the country, especially striking considering the lack of any centralized agency directing reform and the absence of any mandates or inducements to do so. Just as common schooling was an institution-building social movement, progressive education was an institution-changing social movement, albeit with a variety of new mechanisms for spreading the progressive gospel. However, westerners did have reason to see some differences from their eastern colleagues aside from the great distances that separated them. For example, immigration took on a distinct character in the West, western schools often had the luxury of space and less crowding from other buildings, and their populations expanded at a rate unparalleled in the East or Midwest.

14 Ibid.

15 A. E. Winship, quoted in Portland Public Schools, *School Bulletin* (May 16, 1914).

16 See Richard White, *"It's Your Misfortune and None of My Own": A New History of the American West* (Norman: University of Oklahoma Press, 1991), 313. Also see Harvey Kantor, *Learning to Earn: School, Work, and Vocational Reform in California, 1880–1930* (Madison: University of Wisconsin Press, 1988).

17 Leonard P. Ayres, *An Index System for State School Systems* (New York: Russell Sage Foundation, 1920).

18 Frederic C. Howe, *The City: The Hope of Democracy* (New York: Scribner's, 1906), 9.

19 William Munro, *The Government of American Cities* (New York: MacMillan, 1917), 51. On these points, see also Paul Boyer, *Urban Masses and the Moral Order in America, 1820–1920* (Cambridge, MA: Harvard University Press, 1978).

20 Boyer, *Urban Masses and the Moral Order in America*, 190.

21 Lincoln Steffens, *The Autobiography of Lincoln Steffens* (New York: Harcourt, Brace, & World, 1931), 645.

22 William Howard Taft, "A National Standard of Education," *NEA Addresses and Proceedings* (1915), 375–77.

23 Charles A. Beard, introduction to J. B. Bury, *The Idea of Progress: An Inquiry into Its Origin and Growth* (New York: MacMillan, 1932), xl.

24 Daniel Burnham, quoted in Beth Bagwell, *Oakland: The Story of a City* (Novato, CA: Presidio Press, 1982), 172.

25 Lawrence A. Cremin, "The Curriculum Maker and His Critics: A Persistent American Problem," *Teachers College Record* 54 (February 1953): 234.

26 Jesse H. Newlon, *Twentieth Annual Report of School District Number One in the City and County of Denver and State of Colorado* (Denver: Denver School Press, 1923).

27 D. E. Phillips and Jesse H. Newlon, *The New Social Civics* (Chicago: Rand McNally, 1926), 289. Newlon was superintendent of the Denver public schools and Phillips was a professor of psychology at Denver University who had spent years on the Denver school board.

28 Jesse B. Sears and Adin D. Henderson, *Cubberley of Stanford and His Contribution to American Education* (Stanford, CA: Stanford University Press, 1957), 101; on this point, also see Tyack, *One Best System.*

29 Charles Zueblin, *American Municipal Progress* (New York: MacMillan, 1916), xi.

30 Munro, *Government of American Cities*, 51.

31 Compare William J. Reese, *The Power and Promise of School Reform: Grassroots Movements during the Progressive Era* (Boston: Routledge & Kegan Paul, 1986).

32 G. Stanley Hall, "The Contents of Children's Minds," *Princeton Review* 11 (May 1883): 255. It would be some time before scholars challenged their definitions of "normality," and many urban educators agreed with Hall that city children seemed differently bred.

33 Hall, "Contents of Children's Minds," 253, 255. Hall's methods would hardly be seen as robust by the research requirements of today's psychologists. For example, because families still sent their children to school at a variety of ages, Hall's subjects ranged in age from four to eight years of age—a large developmental spread. Nevertheless, it is hardly fair to judge him by the standards of a field that he had helped to create some 125 years ago; his was among the very first of American empirical psychological studies.

34 Ibid.

35 Ibid., 253, 255.

36 Ibid., 272.

37 Henry Turner Bailey, "Outwitting the City," *Progressive Education* 4, no. 3 (July–August–September 1927), 169–74.

38 Ibid., 171.

39 Zueblin, *American Municipal Progress*, 1.

40 Ibid., 2.

41 Phillips and Newlon, *New Social Civics*, 273.

42 Howe, *The City*, 23.

43 For additional discussion of this development, see David A. Gamson, "From Progressivism to Federalism: The Pursuit of Equal Educational Opportunity, 1915–1965," in *To Educate a Nation: Federal and National Strategies for School Reform*, ed. Carl F. Kaestle and Alyssa Lodewick (Lawrence: University Press of Kansas, 2007): 177–201.

44 National Education Association, "A Handbook of Major Educational Issues," *NEA Research Bulletin* 4 (September 1926): 210–11.

45 Ibid.

46 Frederic C. Howe, *Confessions of a Reformer* (New York: Charles Scribner's Sons, 1925), 113–14, quoted in Rodgers, *Atlantic Crossings*, 160.

47 For example, see the discussion of the Denver survey in chap. 4.

48 David S. Snedden and William H. Allen, *School Reports and School Efficiency* (New York: MacMillan, 1908), 19, 4–6. For a discussion of the early uses of educational research, see also Ellen Condliffe Lagemann, *An Elusive Science: The Troubling History of Education Research* (Chicago: University of Chicago Press, 2000).

49 For discussions of the complaints of common school leaders, see: Carl F. Kaestle, *Pillars of the Republic: Common Schools and American Society, 1780–1860* (New

York: Hill and Wang, 1982); Lawrence Cremin, ed., *The Republic and the School*: *Horace Mann on the Education of Free Men* (New York: Teachers College Press, 1957).

50 Joseph M. Rice, *The Public-School System of the United States* (New York: Century Co., 1893), 20.

51 Ibid., 31–32.

52 Ibid., 95.

53 Ibid., 171, 175, 57.

54 Ibid., 39.

55 The Author of the "Preston Papers" [L. A. Yendes], "The Critic at Sea: A Review of *The Public School System of the United States*," *Education* 15 (November 1894): 150, 154–55.

56 Henry G. Schneider, "Dr. Rice and American Public Schools," *Education* 13 (1893): 356–57.

57 Ibid.; for other critiques of Rice's *Forum* articles, see Cremin, *Transformation of the School*, 6–8.

58 Robert H. Wiebe, *The Search for Order, 1877–1920* (New York: Hill and Wang, 1967), 44, 167. Tyack documents other aspects of the shift from village school to urban system in *One Best System*.

59 See Michael B. Katz, *Reconstructing American Education* (Cambridge, MA: Harvard University Press, 1987), chap. 2.

60 Jacob Riis, *A Ten Years' War* (1900), reprinted in *Jacob Riis Revisited: Poverty and the Slum in Another Era*, ed. Francesco Cordasco (Garden City: Doubleday, 1968), 382.

61 Jacob Riis, *The Children of the Poor* (1892), reprinted in *Jacob Riis Revisited*, ed. Cordasco, 204.

62 Riis, *A Ten Years' War*, 381.

63 Ibid, 381, 384.

64 John Spargo, *The Bitter Cry of the Children* (New York: MacMillan, 1906), 63.

65 Ibid., 64.

66 Ibid., 58. Spargo complained that "the modern public school, with its splendid equipment devised to promote the mental and physical development of future citizens, is based on motives and instincts of self-preservation as distinct and clearly defined as those underlying our systems of naval and military defences against armed invasion. . . . We are proud, and justly so, of the admirable machinery of instruction which we have created, the fine buildings, laboratories, curricula, highly trained teachers, and so on, but there is a growing conviction that all this represents only so much mechanical, rather than human, progress" (59).

67 Ibid., 77, 79.

68 Adele Marie Shaw, "The True Character of New York Public Schools," *World's Work* 7 (1903–4): 4210, 4213, 4211.

69 Helen M. Todd, "Why Children Work: The Children's Answer," *McClure's Magazine* 40 (April 1913), 76; for additional discussion of Helen Todd's encounters with Chicago children, see Tyack, *One Best System*.

70 Adele Marie Shaw, "From Country School to University," *World's Work* 8 (1904): 4795.

71 The proceedings for the 1897 NEA Department of Superintendence record that this meeting took place, but, in a rather unusual omission, no minutes, statements, or responses were reported.

72 Leonard P. Ayres, "Measuring Educational Processes through Educational Results," *School Review* 20 (March 19, 1912): 300.

73 Ibid.

74 See Edgar B. Wesley, *NEA: The First Hundred Years* (New York: Harpers & Brothers, 1957), chap. 23; Herbert M. Kliebard, *Struggle for the American Curriculum, 1893–1958*, 2nd ed. (New York: Routledge, 1993), chap. 1.

75 David C. Berliner, "The 100-Year Journey of Educational Psychology," in *Exploring Applied Psychology: Origins and Critical Analyses*, ed. Thomas K. Fagan and Gary R. VandenBos (Washington, DC: American Psychological Association, 1993), 46; Wesley, *NEA*, 271; Joseph M. Rice, *Scientific Management in Education* (New York: Hinds, Noble & Eldredge, 1913).

76 See Kliebard, *Struggle for the American Curriculum*, chap. 4.

77 Paul Chapman has argued that progressive educators had an abundance of solutions that were in search of problems; while that might accurately describe the period after World War I, we hardly find a shortage of problems between 1890 and 1917. See Paul Chapman, *Schools as Sorters: Lewis M. Terman, Applied Psychology, and the Intelligence Testing Movement, 1890–1930* (New York: New York University Press, 1988).

78 Although Cremin, in *Transformation of the School*, argued that enrollment drove reform, it may well have been the problem of "retardation" that truly ignited the flame of reform.

79 Leonard P. Ayres, *Laggards in Our Schools: A Study of Retardation and Elimination in City School Systems* (New York: Survey Associates, Inc. & Russell Sage Foundation, 1909).

80 Ibid. Just a year before, Thorndike had published a report: Edward L. Thorndike, *The Elimination of Pupils from School*, U.S. Bureau of Education Bulletin no. 4 (Washington, DC: Government Printing Office, 1908). Ayres drew on his findings. Thorndike's study, however, was assiduously assailed, due in part to the critical attitude it took toward school systems. One reviewer said that "the particular results stated in the text were wormwood and gall to the school superintendents of those cities whose systems appeared in an unfavorable light." See Ronald F. Falkner, "Elimination of Pupils from School: A Review of Recent Investigations," *Psychological Clinic* 2 (February 15, 1909): 258; and Geraldine Jonçich Clifford, *The San Positivist: A Biography of Edward L. Thorndike* (Middletown, CT: Wesleyan University Press, 1984), 301.

81 Ayres, *Laggards in Our Schools*, 4. Two points deserve attention: first, clearly the situation that Ayres and Thorndike had identified was a significant national problem not endemic to any particular region, and second, these problems were concentrated in city schools.

82 Ayres, *Laggards in Our Schools*, 8; Thorndike, *The Elimination of Pupils from School*.

83 Ibid., 1, 4, 197.

84 Ibid., 4–5.

85 Ibid., 45.

86 Ibid., 47–48.

87 See Vivian Trow Thayer, *The Passing of the Recitation* (Boston: D. C. Heath & Co., 1928), chaps. 6 and 7.

88 Frederic Burk, *Lock-Step Schooling and a Remedy*, State Normal School at San Francisco, Monograph Series A (Sacramento, CA: F. W. Richardson, Superintendent of State Printing, 1913), 4, 8.

89   Ibid., 8, emphasis in original.

90   Ibid., 5.

91   Burk's best-known student was Carleton Washburne, who became superintendent of the highly touted progressive schools of Winnetka, Illinois. See Arthur
Zilversmit, *Changing Schools: Progressive Education Theory and Practice, 1930–
1960* (Chicago: University of Chicago Press, 1993).

92   National Center for Education Statistics, "Table 38: Historical Summary of
Public Elementary and Secondary School Statistics: 1869–70 to 1993–94," *Digest
of Education Statistics* (Washington, DC: U.S. Department of Health, Education,
and Welfare, Education Division, National Center for Education Statistics 1996).
Also available at http://nces.ed.gov/programs/digest/d96/D96T038.asp.

93   Even as late as 1915, we can find expressions of a nineteenth-century sentiment
among some educators; one state superintendent argued that the state could create and enforce uniform standards of citizenship, intelligence, and morality; see
Francis G. Blair, "The Determination of the School District," NEA *Addresses and
Proceedings* (1915), 427–30.

94   William H. Maxwell, "City School Systems," *NEA Addresses and Proceedings*
(1890), 448.

95   See, e.g., Michael Schudson, *The Good Citizen: A History of American Civic Life*
(Cambridge, MA: Harvard University Press, 1998).

96   Maxwell, "City School Systems," 452–53.

97   These comments, and others following Maxwell's presentation, are all included
in "Discussion," *NEA Addresses and Proceedings* (1890), 460–68.

98   Maxwell, "City School Systems," 461, 464–65.

99   Ibid.

100   Charles Meek, "Developing a School System," *NEA Addresses and Proceedings*
(1913), 172–78.

101   Nearing, *New Education*, 31, 125.

102   Joseph M. Gwinn, "Twentieth-Century Developments in City School Administration," in *School Administration in the Twentieth Century*, ed. Jesse B. Sears
(Stanford, CA: Stanford University Press, 1934), 19.

103   Frank J. Goodnow, *City Government in the United States* (New York: Century
Co., 1910), 19.

104   Zueblin, *American Municipal Progress*, 11.

105   Ellwood P. Cubberley, *Public Education in the United States: A Study and Interpretation of American Educational History* (Boston: Houghton Mifflin, 1934), 719.

106   Zueblin, *American Municipal Progress*, 2, 5.

CHAPTER 2

1   "Is it possible for all educators to meet on a common ground and together lay
out definite plans of action?" asked a frustrated Joseph Rice just before the turn
of the century in an 1896 *Forum* essay. Although Rice's concerns may have characterized the 1890s, by 1912, when his second collection of essays was published
under the title *Scientific Management in Education*, his concern did not quite
fit the tenor of the times; by then many educators felt they were on their way
toward designing specific programs for educational improvement. Rice, *Scientific Management* (New York: Hinds, Noble & Eldredge, 1913), 21.

2   "Editorial," *American School Board Journal* 46 (June 1913): 28. For further discussion on this period of rapid superintendent turnover, see Raymond E. Callahan, *Education and the Cult of Efficiency: A Study of the Social Forces That Have Shaped the Administration of the Public Schools* (Chicago: University of Chicago Press, 1962).

3   As noted in chap. 1, Walter Nugent also pinpoints the year 1913 as significant; thereafter, the expansion of the western population shifted away from the farms and into the cities, a swing that unleashed new possibilities and conflicts alike; Walter Nugent, *Into the West: The Story of Its People* (New York: Alfred A. Knopf, 1999).

4   For example, Patricia Albjerg Graham's study of the Progressive Education Association bookends her study around 1919 (*Progressive Education: From Arcady to Academe* [New York: Teachers College Press, 1967]). Michael McGerr, *A Fierce Discontent: The Rise and Fall of the Progressive Movement* (New York: Free Press, 2003), covers the period 1870–1920.

5   Henry F. May, *The End of American Innocence: A Study of the First Years of Our Time, 1912–1917* (1959; repr., New York: Columbia University Press, 1992).

6   Ibid., xxiii.

7   Some reformers, such as G. Stanley Hall and John Dewey, recognized deeper sources for contemporary agitation and understood how powerful the currents of industrialization and urbanization were. Unlike Hall, who perceived only rain in the dark clouds of urban expansion, Dewey astutely perceived that there might be resulting advantages as well as disadvantages. In his 1899 lecture, "The School and Social Progress," Dewey argued not for a constricted approach to schooling the city-bred child but for a more expansive, creative view of education, one energized by the innate excitement, spontaneity, and curiosity of the child (in John Dewey, *"The School and Society" and "The Child and the Curriculum"* [1900; repr., Chicago: University of Chicago, 1990], 12–13.) But the great challenge for educators of the twentieth century was, of course, how to turn ideas like these into workable school practices.

8   Paul H. Hanus, "Improving School Systems by Scientific Management," *NEA Addresses and Proceedings* (1913), 252.

9   W. S. Deffenbaugh's list of the characteristics of the ideal progressive urban district also included: a superintendent who had been given more responsibility was then held accountable for results; better-trained teachers; updated and reorganized curricula; and "a cosmopolitan high school centrally located and elementary schools out near the people" ("City Schools of Tomorrow," in *School Administration Progress of Twenty-five Years* [Milwaukee: Bruce Publishing Co., 1916], 69–79).

10 Elmer Ellsworth Brown, "Educational Progress of the Past Fifteen Years," *NEA Addresses and Proceedings* (1915), 48–54.

11 Ellwood P. Cubberley, "State and County School Administration," in *School Administration Progress of Twenty-five Years* (Milwaukee: Bruce Publishing Co., 1916), 5.

12 The Progressive Era gave birth to such a diverse array of educational initiatives that one could easily spend a fruitful lifetime identifying, analyzing, and tracing these reforms. Nevertheless, the purpose of my study is to examine a few of these reforms in the context of four cities. Therefore, my summary of reforms throughout this chapter is, by necessity, incomplete.

13   Franklin Bobbitt, "The Supervision of City Schools," *Twelfth Yearbook of the National Society for the Study of Education*, pt. 1 (Bloomington, IL: Public School Publishing Co., 1913).

14   The U.S. House of Representatives, e.g., issued its *Report of the Commission on National Aid to Vocational Education* (1914), a prelude to the Smith-Hughes Act of 1917, which provided districts with federal vocational education funding. The *Fourteenth Yearbook of National Society for the Study of Education* (Bloomington, IL: Public School Publishing, 1919) contained the influential 1915 report of the Committee of the National Council of Education on Economy of Time in Education titled "Minimum Essentials in Elementary-School Subjects." And the NEA published another significant commission report a few years later, this one from the Commission on the Reorganization of Secondary Education: the 1918 *Cardinal Principles of Secondary Education* (Department of the Interior, Bureau of Education, Bulletin no. 35 [Washington: Government Printing Office, 1918]).

15   Each of the four cities examined here offer examples of deliberate implementation.

16   See, e.g., Graham, *Progressive Education*; David B. Tyack, *One Best System: A History of American Urban Education* (Cambridge, MA: Harvard University Press, 1974); Daniel T. Rodgers, "In Search of Progressivism," *Reviews in American History* 10 (December 1982): 113–32.

17   On this point, see Lawrence A. Cremin, *The Transformation of the School: Progressivism in American Education, 1876–1957* (New York: Vintage, 1961); and Robert B. Westbrook, *John Dewey and American Democracy* (Ithaca, NY: Cornell University Press, 1991).

18   Charles H. Judd, "The Curriculum: A Paramount Issue" in *NEA Addresses and Proceedings* (1925), 806–7. See also David C. Berliner, "The 100 Year Journey of Educational Psychology," in *Exploring Applied Psychology: Origins and Critical Analyses*, ed. Thomas K. Fagan and Gary R. VandenBos (Washington, DC: American Psychological Association, 1993), 46–47.

19   See Daniel T. Rodgers, *Atlantic Crossings: Social Politics in a Progressive Age* (Cambridge, MA: Belknap Press of Harvard University Press, 1998).

20   See, e.g., Harry E. Bard, *The City School District: Statutory Provisions for Organization and Fiscal Affairs* (New York: Teachers College, 1909); Robert C. Wood with Vladimir V. Almendinger, *1400 Governments: The Political Economy of the New York Metropolitan Region* (Cambridge, MA: Harvard University Press, 1961).

21   This ideal is in part what David Tyack has characterized as the "one best system" of educational organization, the blueprint that prominent "educational elite" proposed as the type of system that all school districts should adopt; see Tyack, *One Best System*. This one best system incorporated a great number of administrative changes as well as programmatic innovations.

22   To some progressives "student needs" required the use of new child-centered pedagogical methods, such as activity projects and individualized instructional programs; but to others it implied the use of intelligence testing to determine the unique and specific "abilities" of the child and the creation of curricular tracks. For all progressives, it meant crafting more welcoming, nurturing environments for students through a deemphasis on the traditional curriculum. For example, as Jacob Riis put it in one of his more upbeat appraisals of educational progressivism, "The cram and jam are being crowded out as common-sense teaching steps in and takes their place, and the 'three H's,' the head, the heart, and the hand—a whole boy—are taking the place too long monopolized by the 'three R's.'" Riis, *A*

Ten Years' War (1900), reprinted in *Jacob Riis Revisited: Poverty and the Slum in Another Era*, ed. Francesco Cordasco (Garden City: Doubleday, 1968), 392.

23 John Dewey, *Democracy and Education* (New York: Free Press, 1916), 194. Even Cubberley, who devoted more attention to things administrative than curricular, said that the construction and adaptation of the courses of instruction would be "the real measure of [superintendent] competence" (Ellwood P. Cubberley, *Public School Administration* [Boston: Houghton Mifflin, 1916], 274).

24 Modern curricula, went the argument, necessitated the creation of new types of school spaces, such as gymnasiums, playgrounds, swimming pools, science labs, manual training facilities, domestic science rooms, and gardens—things that the one-room schoolhouse could never have offered.

25 Herbert S. Weet, "Some Ideals and Accomplishments of the Rochester School System," *NEA Addresses and Proceedings* (1921), 703.

26 Jesse H. Newlon, *Educational Administration as Social Policy* (New York: Charles Scribner's Sons, 1934), 93–94.

27 David Tyack and Elisabeth Hansot have argued that these social engineers of school reform were quite clear about their assessment of social and educational needs, but that "they were less clear about the philosophical premises of their values or the political process by which priorities should be set" (David Tyack and Elisabeth Hansot, *Managers of Virtue: Public School Leadership in America, 1820–1980* [New York: Basic Books, 1982], 156).

28 Jesse B. Sears and Adin D. Henderson, *Cubberley of Stanford and His Contribution to American Education* (Stanford, CA: Stanford University Press, 1957), 133; JoAnne Brown argues that educational psychologists of the period sought to emulate scientific methods because they believed that that the path of science led to consensus, whereas traditional philosophical methods too often led to conflict or dissension (*The Definition of a Profession: The Authority of Metaphor in the History of Intelligence Testing, 1890–1930* [Princeton, NJ: Princeton University Press, 1992]).

29 Karl Pearson, *The Grammar of Science* (1892; repr., New York: Meridian Books, Inc., 1957), 19. Also see Brown, *Definition of a Profession*, 127. For more on these points, see Ellen Condliffe Lagemann, *An Elusive Science: The Troubling History of Education Research* (Chicago: University of Chicago Press, 2000), chap. 3.

30 Watson quoted in Clarence J. Karier, *The Individual, Society, and Education*, 2nd ed. (Urbana: University of Illinois Press, 1986), 177.

31 Thorndike quoted in Geraldine Jonçich Clifford, *The San Positivist: A Biography of Edward L. Thorndike* (Middletown, CT: Wesleyan University Press, 1984), 3.

32 Guy M. Whipple, "The Intelligence Testing Program and Its Objectors— Conscientious and Otherwise," *School and Society* 17, no. 440 (June 2, 1923): 601. Whipple's article is divided into two issues (nos. 439 and 440): 561–68, 596–604.

33 Nicholas Murray Butler, *True and False Democracy* (New York: MacMillan, 1907), 5, 16, 15.

34 There is a long tradition within the historiography of analyzing those dual fears of Americans about their own democracy—elite power versus mass rule. Two of the best recent works are Michael Schudson, *The Good Citizen: A History of American Civic Life* (Cambridge, MA: Harvard University Press, 1998); and Sean Willentz, *The Rise of American Democracy: Jefferson to Lincoln* (New York: W. W. Norton, 2005).

35 Ellwood P. Cubberley, *Changing Conceptions of Education* (Cambridge, MA: Houghton Mifflin, 1909), 65, 64.

36 Henry H. Goddard, *Human Efficiency and Levels of Intelligence* (Princeton, NJ: Princeton University, 1920), 97.

37 See, e.g., Carl F. Kaestle, *Pillars of the Republic: Common Schools and American Society, 1780–1860* (New York: Hill and Wang, 1982).

38 Horace Mann quoted in Lawrence Cremin, ed., *The Republic and the School: Horace Mann on the Education of Free Men* (New York: Teachers College Press, 1957), 77, 87.

39 See, e.g., Dewey, *Democracy and Education*, 87.

40 See Westbrook, *John Dewey and American Democracy*, 508; Herbert M. Kliebard, *The Struggle for the American Curriculum, 1893–1958*, 2nd ed. (New York: Routledge, 1995); for a series of recent discussions on Dewey, see the special thematic issue commemorating the hundredth anniversary of the publication of *Democracy and Education*: "Re-assessing John Dewey's 1916 Publication *Democracy and Education*," special issue, *Journal of the Gilded Age and Progressive Era*, vol. 16, no. 4 (2017).

41 Diane Ravitch, *Left Back: A Century of Failed School Reforms* (New York: Simon & Schuster, 2000), 95–100, 461. Tensions continue to exist within the historiography on the question of how "democratic" were the progressives. See also Diane Ravitch, *The Troubled Crusade: American Education, 1945–1980* (New York: Basic Books, 1983), and *The Revisionists Revised: A Critique of the Radical Attack on the Schools* (New York: Basic Books, 1978). On the revisionist reinterpretation, see also Daniel T. Rodgers, "In Search of Progressivism," *Reviews in American History* 10 (December 1982): 120. For examples of various viewpoints in the historiography, see Richard Hofstadter, *Anti-intellectualism in American Life* (New York: Knopf, 1970); Clarence J. Karier, Paul Violas, and Joel Spring, *Roots of Crisis: American Education in the Twentieth Century* (Chicago: Rand McNally, 1973); Joel Spring, *Education and the Rise of the Corporate State* (Boston: Beacon, 1972); Michael B. Katz, *The Irony of Early School Reform* (Cambridge, MA: Harvard University Press, 1968), and *Class, Bureaucracy, and the Schools* (New York: Praeger, 1975); Samuel Bowles and Herbert Gintis, "Capitalism and Education in the United States," *Socialist Revolution* 5 (1975): 101–38; Ronald D. Cohen and Raymond Mohl, *The Paradox of Progressive Education: The Gary Plan and Urban Schooling* (Port Washington, NY: Kennikat Press, 1979), 10; Julia Wrigley, *Class Politics and Public Schools: Chicago 1900–1950* (New Brunswick, NJ: Rutgers University Press, 1982); Harvey A. Kantor, *Learning to Earn: School, Work, and Vocational Reform in California, 1880–1930* (Madison: University of Wisconsin Press, 1988); Ira Katznelson and Margaret Weir, *Schooling for All: Class, Race, and the Decline of the American Ideal* (New York: Basic Books, 1985); David L. Angus and Jeffrey E. Mirel, *The Failed Promise of the American High School* (New York: Teachers College Press, 1999), 198; William Graebner, *The Engineering of Consent: Democracy and Authority in Twentieth Century America* (Madison: University of Wisconsin Press, 1987); Schudson, *The Good Citizen*.

42 See esp. Graebner, *Engineering of Consent*; Schudson, *The Good Citizen*.

43 Joseph Gwinn, "Twentieth-Century Developments in City School Administration," in *School Administration in the Twentieth Century*, ed. Jesse B. Sears (Stanford, CA: Stanford University Press, 1934), 20–21.

44 Cubberley, *Changing Conceptions of Education*, 56–57.

45 Ibid.

46 John Dewey, quoted in Westbrook, *John Dewey and American Democracy*, 178.

47 John Dewey, *The School and Society* (Chicago: University of Chicago Press, 1900), 38.

48 Dewey, *Democracy and Education*, 119–20.

49 Westbrook, *John Dewey and American Democracy*, 179.

50 John Dewey, *Democracy and Education*, 87, and "Learning to Earn: The Place of Education in a Comprehensive Scheme of Public Education," *School and Society* 5, no. 117 (March 24, 1917): 334.

51 Charles Zueblin, *American Municipal Progress*, rev. ed. (New York: MacMillan, 1916), 3.

52 Julie A. Rueben, "Beyond Politics: Community Civics and the Redefinition of Citizenship in the Progressive Era," *History of Education Quarterly* 37 (Winter 1997): 399–420. Reuben's insightful discussion is perhaps a more subtle interpretation than some of the sharper critiques of progressive notions of democracy, such as that made by Graebner, *The Engineering of Consent*.

53 Frederick Elmer Bolton, Thomas Raymond Cole, and John Hunnicut Jessup, *The Beginning Superintendent* (New York: Macmillan Co., 1937), 1.

54 Edward L. Thorndike, "Intelligence and Its Uses," *Harpers* 140 (December 1919– May 1920): 235. For additional discussion of Thorndike's views, see Clarence J. Karier, *The Individual, Society, and Education: A History of American Educational Ideas*, 2nd ed. (Urbana: University of Illinois Press, 1986), 174.

55 Henry Herbert Goddard, *Human Efficiency and Levels of Intelligence* (Princeton, NJ: Princeton University Press, 1920), 101. This volume is a collection of talks Goddard delivered as the featured speaker at Princeton's prestigious Louis Clark Vanuxem Lectures on April 7, 8, 10, and 11, 1919.

56 Goddard, *Human Efficiency and Levels of Intelligence*, 95.

57 Leila Zenderland, *Measuring Minds: Henry Herbert Goddard and the Origins of American Intelligence Testing* (New York: Cambridge University Press, 1998), 296.

58 Ibid., 237; Goddard's paternalistic view of democracy emerged out of the belief that society could be scientifically divided; such divisions, he said, demonstrated that "the people who are now doing the drudgery are, as a rule, in their proper places" (Henry Herbert Goddard, *Psychology of the Normal and Subnormal* [New York: Dodd, Mead, and Co., 1919], 246).

59 Ibid., 237. For an enlightening discussion of Goddard and other devotees of intelligence testing, see Stephen Jay Gould, *The Mismeasure of Man* (New York: W. W. Norton and Co., 1996), 191.

60 Nearly a decade later, Goddard recanted some of his more extreme proclamations about "scientific" labels he himself had popularized, arguing instead that "morons" and the "feebleminded" were much more educable that he had acknowledged. Nevertheless, his earlier comments were deeply influential, coming as they did at the very moment when educators began to accept intelligence tests into the schools.

61 A. F. Weber, *The Growth of Cities in the Nineteenth Century* (New York: Published for Columbia University by the Macmillan Co., 1899), 442.

62 Committee on City School Systems, "School Superintendence in Cities," *NEA Addresses and Proceedings* (1890), 309.

63 D. E. Phillips and Jesse H. Newlon, *New Social Civics* (Chicago: Rand McNally, 1926), 288.

64 Edward L. Thorndike, *The Elimination of Pupils from School*, U.S. Bureau of Education Bulletin no. 4 (Washington, DC: Government Printing Office, 1908).

65 Bolton, Cole, and Jessup, *Beginning Superintendent*, 14.

66 Lewis Terman, *The Intelligence of School Children* (Boston: Houghton Mifflin, 1919), 17.

67 Ibid., 73.

68 Daniel Calhoun, *The Intelligence of a People* (Princeton, NJ: Princeton University Press, 1973), 70–78, 71; Stanley J. Zehm, "Educational Misfits: A Study of Poor Performers in the English Class, 1825–1925" (PhD diss., Stanford University, 1973). On the early efforts at ability grouping, see also Tyack, *One Best System*, 201–2.

69 Terman, *Intelligence of School Children*, 17, 73.

70 Gould, *Mismeasure of Man*, 56.

71 Scholars have described how schools functioned as the societal sorters of children and have explored the classifying and categorizing tendencies of educators at all levels of the system. See, e.g., Paul D. Chapman, *Schools as Sorters: Lewis M. Terman, Applied Psychology, and the Intelligence Testing Movement, 1890–1930* (New York: New York University Press, 1988); Jeannie Oakes, *Keeping Track: How Schools Structure Inequality* (New Haven, CT: Yale University Press, 1985); Hamilton Cravens, *The Triumph of Evolution: The Heredity-Environment Controversy, 1900–1941* (Baltimore, MD: Johns Hopkins University Press, 1988).

72 Lewis M. Terman, *Mental and Physical Traits of a Thousand Gifted Children* (Stanford, CA: Stanford University Press, 1925).

73 Jesse Newlon and A. L. Threlkeld, "The Denver Curriculum-Revision Program," in *The Twenty-Sixth Yearbook of the National Society for the Study of Education*, pt. 1 (Bloomington, IL: Public School Publishing Co., 1926), 229.

74 John Dewey and Evelyn Dewey, *Schools of Tomorrow* (New York: E. P. Dutton & Co., 1915). Several years later, Evelyn Dewey published another book, celebrating the Porter School; see Evelyn Dewey, *New Schools for Old: The Regeneration of the Porter School* (New York: E. P. Dutton & Co., 1919).

75 Carleton Washburne and Myron M. Stearns, *Better Schools: A Survey of Progressive Education in American Public Schools* (New York: John Day Co., 1928), 47, 65.

76 Newlon and Threlkeld, "Denver Curriculum-Revision Program."

77 Cubberley, *Public School Administration*, 433, 436; Scott Nearing, *The New Education* (Chicago: Row, Peterson, & Company, 1915).

78 Charles Hughes Johnston, Jesse H. Newlon, and Frank G. Pickell, *Junior-Senior High School Administration* (New York: Charles Scribner's Sons, 1922), 24.

79 Despite the uniformity that some historians have attributed to these reforms or the isomorphism that some sociologists believe explains the diffusion of these innovations across school systems, the three reforms examined here were rarely adopted and implemented in the same ways, at the same times, or through the same processes.

80 Committee on City School Systems, "Report of the Committee on City School Systems," *NEA Addresses and Proceedings* (1890), 310.

81 Bobbitt, "The Supervision of City Schools," 7. See esp., Callahan, *Education and the Cult of Efficiency*.

82 Cubberley, *Public School Administration*, 174–75, 172–73, 170–71.

83 Scholars have offered a variety of explanations for the diffusion of Progressive Era educational innovations. Lawrence A. Cremin noted the role of state
departments of education and the U.S. Office of Education in disseminating
information through research bulletins and leaflets. In *Transformation of the
School*, Cremin lists a variety of mechanisms through which progressive ideas
and innovations diffused, stating that "schools generally began to be visibly
affected." He later modified this view, writing, "as frequently occurs with reform
movements, the language of education probably changed more rapidly than
the practice of education, and small, specific, concrete changes in practice
tended to be adopted more rapidly than larger, more general ones" (*American
Education: The Metropolitan Experience, 1876–1980* [New York: Harper & Row,
1988], 239). Raymond Callahan traced the dissemination of business values
throughout school systems to certification programs and schools of education.
Callahan argues that school superintendents and other educational leaders were
disproportionately dazzled by "efficiency experts" and notions of "scientific
management." Callahan characterized the urban school district as fertile ground
for Taylorite business practices advocated by reformers like Frank Spaulding
and Franklin Bobbitt, in part because of the "vulnerability" of schoolmen to
"public criticism and pressure" (*Education and the Cult of Efficiency*, viii). David
Tyack and Elizabeth Hansot (*Managers of Virtue*) have discussed how ideas
were carried by an "interlocking directorate" of administrative progressives and
a national network of reformers. Edgar B. Wesley has enumerated the topics
that gained most attention at the annual meetings of the NEA (*NEA: The First
Hundred Years, The Building of the Teaching Profession* [New York: Harper &
Brothers, 1957], chap. 5). Patricia Graham (*From Arcady to Academe*) and Diane
Ravitch (*Troubled Crusade*) each explored the role of the Progressive Education
Association in transmitting pedagogically progressive practices, while Jeffrey
Mirel has highlighted the importance of reform discourse in spreading new ideas
("Progressive School Reform in Comparative Perspective," in *Southern Cities,
Southern Schools: Public Education in the Urban South*, David N. Plank and Rick
Ginsberg eds. [New York: Greenwood Press, 1990], 151–74). In addition to expla-
nations offered by historians about the dissemination of educational reforms,
sociologists have developed theoretical tools for analyzing diffusion. Specifically, institutional theorists have been intrigued by the diffusion of innovations
and have offered explanations for how and why organizations tend to become
more and more similar. Relevant to this study are notions developed by David
Strang and John Meyer on the "theorization" of innovation. Strang and Meyer
argue that the characteristics of certain types of reforms aid in their diffusion
potential. For example, innovations that can be easily reduced to models, charts,
and diagrams are more easily spread among members of an organizational field.
Paul J. DiMaggio and Walter W. Powell, "The Iron Cage Revisited: Institutional
Isomorphism and Collective Rationality in Organizational Fields," in *Institu-
tionalism in Organizational Analysis*, ed. Walter W. Powell and Paul J. DiMaggio
(Chicago: University of Chicago Press, 1991); David Strang and John W. Meyer,
"Institutional Conditions for Diffusion," *Theory and Society* 22 (1993): 487–511.

84 "A Diagram of the Commission-Manager Plan as Recommended by the National
Municipal League, 1914," *American City* 12, no. 6 (June 1915): 514; this image is
shown in fig. 2.7.

85 Cubberley, *Public School Administration*, 175.

86 For corollaries with municipal government reforms, see Bradley Robert Rice, *Progressive Cities: The Commission Government Movement in America, 1901-1920* (Austin: University of Texas Press, 1977); see also Samuel P. Hays, introduction to *Building the Organizational Society: Essays on Associational Activities in Modern America*, ed. Jerry Israel (New York: Free Press, 1972); Tyack, *One Best System*.

87 See, e.g., James Weinstein, *The Corporate Ideal in the Liberal State, 1900-1918* (Boston: Beacon Press, 1968); Spring, *Education and the Rise of the Corporate State*; Robert H. Wiebe, *The Search for Order, 1877-1920* (New York: Hill and Wang, 1967); Callahan, *Education and the Cult of Efficiency*.

88 See Hollis L. Caswell, *City School Surveys: An Interpretation and Appraisal* (New York: Teachers College, 1929).

89 For a good example, see Fred Newton Scott, "Efficiency for Efficiency's Sake," *School Review* 23, no. 1 (January 1915): 34-42.

90 Dewey, quoted in Westbrook, *John Dewey and American Democracy*, 107.

91 Ella Flagg Young, "Grading and Classification," *NEA Addresses and Proceedings* (1894), 85.

92 Like many "scientific" innovations of the era, child study labs were often established by university faculty who combined good intentions with a rather naive, and often misguided, faith in the potential of expertise to solve the problems of human society. Almost as quickly as educational scientists could invent new terminology and detect previously unknown learning problems, they began to quantify, measure, and categorize students according to their traits and capacities. Child study labs often coordinated their efforts with nearby school districts; see, e.g., "Studies on Children," *Annual Report of the Public Schools of the City of Oakland for the Year Ending June 30, 1893* (Oakland, CA: Board of Education, 1893), 23-44, hereafter cited as *Oakland Annual Report* with year of publication.

93 Psychologist Anne Anastasi remarked that, by the 1950s, the notion of IQ had become so deeply embedded in the public mind that is was difficult to remove: "as much a part of our culture—and as difficult to dislodge—as singing commercials and Howdy Doody" ("The Measurement of Abilities" *Journal of Counseling Psychology* 1, no. 3 [October 1954]: 164-68).

94 Terman, *Intelligence of School Children*, esp. chap. 4.

95 Lewis M. Terman, *Intelligence Tests and School Reorganization* (Yonkers-on-Hudson, NY: World Book Co., 1922), 3.

96 Cubberley, *Public School Administration*, 293-97.

97 National Education Association, *Report of the Committee on Secondary School Studies* (Washington, DC: Government Printing Office, 1893), 17. In quoting the report some years later, Charles W. Eliot himself emphasized the italicized words ("The Fundamental Assumptions in the Report of the Committee of Ten [1893]," *Educational Review* 30 [November 1905]: 328).

98 G. Stanley Hall, *Adolescence: Its Psychology and Its Relation to Physiology, Anthropology, Sociology, Sex, Crime, Religion, and Education*, vol. 2 (New York: D. Appleton and Co., 1904), 512, 510.

99 Charles W. Eliot, "Fundamental Assumptions in the Report of the Committee of Ten," 331-32, and "Shortening and Enriching the Grammar School Course," *NEA Addresses and Proceedings* (1892), 620.

100 Eliot, "The Fundamental Assumptions in the Report of the Committee of Ten," 330-31.

101 Frank Parsons, *Choosing a Vocation* (Boston: Houghton Mifflin, 1909), 3 (my emphasis).

102 See e.g., National Education Association, *Cardinal Principles of Secondary Education: A Report of the Commission on the Reorganization of Secondary Education* (Washington, DC: Government Printing Office, 1918); Oakland Public Schools, *Oakland Annual Report* (Oakland, CA: Oakland Public Schools, 1917–18).

103 National Education Association of the United States, Commission on the Reorganization of Secondary Education, *Vocational Guidance in Secondary Education: A Report of the Commission on the Reorganization of Secondary Education*, Bulletin 1918, no. 19 (Washington, DC: Government Printing Office, 1918), 16; Dewey, *Democracy and Education*, 130. See also Dewey, *The School and Society*, 35.

104 NEA, "Keeping Pace with the Advancing Curriculum," *Research Bulletin of the NEA* 3, nos. 4–5 (September–November 1925): 109, 113.

105 See Kliebard, *Struggle for the American Curriculum*.

106 Judd, "The Curriculum," 806, 808.

107 Quoted in Adele Marie Shaw, "How Successful Are the Public Schools?" *World's Work* 9 (1904): 5485.

108 Eliot, "Fundamental Assumptions in the Report of the Committee of Ten," 326.

109 Eliot, "Shortening and Enriching the Grammar School Course," 621.

110 Scholars interested in curricular change have tended to gravitate toward the years between 1915 and 1940 because of the burst of curricular reform energy that took place across the country during that twenty-five-year period. Historians have seen the publication of Franklin Bobbitt's 1918 book, *The Curriculum*, as initiating the rise of the "curriculum expert," if not the emergence of a whole new field—curriculum making. The advocates of this new vocation believed that it offered an approach to curriculum development more systematic than anything Dewey had yet presented. See, e.g., Ravitch, *Troubled Crusade*, 49.

111 I employ the term "fidelity" here as it's used by David B. Tyack and Larry Cuban, *Tinkering Toward Utopia* (Cambridge, MA: Harvard University Press, 1995)

112 NEA, "Keeping Pace with the Advancing Curriculum," 119–24.

113 On curriculum revision, see Ravitch, *Left Back*, 188–90; in much of her work Ravitch is sharply critical of progressive education.

114 For a good description of both contemporary conflicts and historiographical differences, see Kliebard, *Struggle for the American Curriculum*; Jonathan Zimmerman, *Whose America? Culture Wars in the Public Schools* (Cambridge, MA: Harvard University Press, 2002).

115 Rice, *Progressive Cities*; Harold A. Stone, Don K. Price, and Kathryn H. Stone, *City Manager Government in the United States: A Review after Twenty-Five Years* (Chicago: Public Administration Service, 1940); Frank Mann Stewart, *A Half Century of Municipal Reform: The History of the National Municipal League* (Berkeley: University of California, 1950); Ariane Mary Aphrodite Liazos, "The Movement for 'Good City Government': Municipal Leagues, Political Science, and the Contested Meaning of Progressive Democracy, 1880–1930" (PhD diss., Harvard University, 2007).

116 Rice, *Progressive Cities*.

117 William Munro, *The Government of American Cities* (New York: MacMillan, 1916), 388.

118 Eliot quoted in Rice, *Progressive Cities*, 60.

CHAPTER 3

1   A. A. Dennison, "The City of Oakland," in *Greater Oakland, 1911: A Volume Dealing with the Big Metropolis on the Shores of San Francisco Bay*, ed. Evarts I. Blake (Oakland, CA: Pacific Publishing, 1911), 9–16; see also Beth Bagwell, *Oakland: The Story of a City* (Novato, CA: Presidio Press, 1982), 170.

2   Charles Zueblin, *American Municipal Progress* (New York: MacMillan, 1916), 22.

3   John L. Davie, "Address of Welcome," *NEA Addresses and Proceedings* (1923), 140; Bagwell, *Oakland*. Western progressives felt they had a unique opportunity to mold their new cities in ways that the older, more "crowded" and "congested" eastern cities did not. Oakland had qualities characteristic of the quintessential progressive western city, such as its role in trade and industry, its civic dynamism, and its pursuit of municipal reform; see Bradford Luckingham, "The Urban Dimension of Western History," in *Historians and the American West*, ed. Michael P. Malone (Lincoln: University of Nebraska Press, 1983), 323–43.

4   The "needs of the present," A. C. Barker explained, resulted from national changes afoot. "The passing of the frontier, the growth of cities, and the increase of specialization in every department of human endeavor have rendered changes inevitable" ("Addresses of Welcome," *NEA Addresses and Proceedings* [1915], 35).

5   Davie, "Address of Welcome," 140.

6   Quoted in Marta Gutman, *A City for Children: Women, Architecture, and the Charitable Landscapes of Oakland, 1850–1950* (Chicago: University of Chicago, 2014), 213.

7   *World* quoted in Chris Rhomberg, *No There There: Race, Class, and Political Community in Oakland* (Berkeley: University of California Press, 2004), 42.

8   Rhomberg, *No There There*.

9   Edgar J. Hinkel and William E. McCann, eds., *Oakland, 1852–1938: Some Phases of the Social, Political and Economic History of Oakland, California*, 2 vols. (Oakland, CA: Oakland Public Library and the Works Progress Administration, 1939).

10 "Oakland Studies Given Eastern Praise," *Oakland Post-Enquirer*, May 7, 1932; "Oakland School Courses Lauded," *San Francisco Chronicle*, May 15, 1932.

11 Paul Davis Chapman, *Schools as Sorters: Lewis M. Terman, Applied Psychology, and the Intelligence Testing Movement, 1890–1930* (New York: New York University Press, 1988), 64. Oakland's connections to Lewis Terman at Stanford University led to a district-wide experiment that was one of the most comprehensive uses of mental tests before the First World War, and, as such, Oakland provided something of a model for other districts to follow. Other historians have noted Oakland's adoption of the prevailing "scientific" language of ability as well as the district's program of curricular tracking, which was an outgrowth of its testing program. See, e.g., David B. Tyack, *One Best System: A History of American Urban Education* (Cambridge, MA: Harvard University Press, 1974), 209; Paula S. Fass, *Outside In: Minorities and the Transformation of American Education* (New York: Oxford University Press, 1989), 68; Irving J. Hendrick, "California's Response to the 'New Education' in the 1930's," *California Historical Quarterly* 53 (Spring 1974): 27. According to Diane Ravitch, school districts like Oakland provide evidence that Progressive Era educators failed in their responsibility to foster the intellectual development of American schoolchildren; the fact that in the 1930s Oakland high school students could take courses in "leisure activities" or

"personal management" strikes her as evidence of Oakland's disparaging attitude toward solid intellectual values; see Ravitch, *Troubled Crusade*, 63.

12 See, e.g., Kitty Kelly Epstein, *A Different View of Urban Schools: Civil Rights, Critical Race Theory, and Unexplored Realities* (New York: Peter Lang, 2006), 13.

13 Rhomberg, *No There There*, 60–61.

14 Quoted in Richard White, *"It's Your Misfortune and None of My Own": A New History of the American West* (Norman: University of Oklahoma Press, 1991), 313.

15 Oakland Public Schools, *Oakland Annual Report* (Oakland, CA: Oakland Public Schools, 1893), 17. (Hereafter in this chapter referred to simply as *Oakland Annual Report*, plus the year.)

16 On the nineteenth-century curriculum, see Carl F. Kaestle, *Pillars of the Republic: Common Schools and American Society, 1780–1860* (New York: Hill and Wang, 1982); Tyack, *One Best System*; *Oakland Annual Report* (1891).

17 *Oakland Annual Report* (1893), 23–44.

18 Ibid., 8.

19 Ibid., 61–62.

20 *Oakland Annual Report* (1900), 18–26. Some schools in the East and Midwest had already established ungraded rooms, but these were most often described as rooms for the "unfit"; see e.g., Robert L. Osgood, "Undermining the Common School Ideal: Intermediate Schools and Ungraded Classes in Boston, 1838–1900," *History of Education Quarterly* 37, no. 4 (Winter 1997): 375–98.

21 *Oakland Annual Report* (1900), 18–26.

22 Ibid.

23 *Oakland Annual Report* (1900), 19.

24 Total enrollment in 1890: 9,565; in 1900–1901: 11,792; in 1910–11: 22,589; in 1918: 36,595; in 1929: approximately 45,000; in 1939: approximately 50,000; author's compilation from *Oakland Annual Reports*.

25 *Oakland Annual Report* (1910).

26 Ibid., 7.

27 *Oakland Annual Report* (1911); *Oakland Annual Report* (1912). For a discussion of testing and tracking in Oakland, see Chapman, *Schools as Sorters*, 55–64.

28 See M. Kliebard, *The Struggle for the American Curriculum, 1893–1958*, 2nd ed. (New York: Routledge, 1993); Diane Ravitch, *Left Back*, esp. chap. 5.

29 No longer would children all to be educated together; instead, students should be educated separately and designated as "retarded," "ordinary," or "above average." What worked for the elementary schools should also be applied to the high schools. The city's high schools, of course, had already been experimenting with organization and curricular reorganization since the 1890s, and by the close of the century's first decade, Oakland high school students could choose among three alternative curricula: one for those interested in "University of California preparation," a second for "general" education, or a third "Two Year Commercial Course." *Oakland Annual Report* (1913).

30 Ibid.

31 Department of Public Instruction, Oakland, California, *A General Report by the City Superintendent of Schools, 1913–1917* (Oakland, CA: Board of Education, 1917), 11 (hereafter cited as *Oakland Superintendent's Report* [1913–1917]); the "perfect storm" comment is an allusion back to Raymond E. Callahan, *Education and the Cult of Efficiency: A Study of the Social Forces That Have Shaped*

the *Administration of the Public Schools* (Chicago: University of Chicago Press, 1962).

32 Barker, "Addresses of Welcome," 35.

33 Compare Ellen Condliffe Lagemann, "The Plural Worlds of Educational Research," *History of Education Quarterly* 29 (1989): 185.

34 Hinkel and McCann, eds., *Oakland*, 468.

35 *Oakland Superintendent's Report* (1913–17), 5.

36 For a contemporary overview of the literature, see Aubrey Augustus Douglass, "The Junior High School," *Fifteenth Yearbook of the National Society for the Study of Education*, pt. 3 (Bloomington, IL: Public School Publishing Co., 1916).

37 See Oakland Public Schools, "The Intermediate School Situation in Oakland California," pt. 2 of *Oakland Superintendent's Report* (1913–17), 8. Barker characterized the junior high as "an attempt to carry out the recommendations of the Committee of Ten," whose report still carried weight with some educators. The junior high, he said, "retains the traditional studies of the elementary school, often with a reduced time allotment, and endeavors to teach [students] more effectively by the departmental method with better trained teachers." (The "departmental method," at the time popular in some cities, sought to replicate the specialized teaching of secondary schooling in the junior high or upper elementary grades.) The junior high school thereby allowed for the introduction of discipline-based subject matter—history, science, and modern languages—into the seventh- and eighth-grade courses of study. Barker also pointed to variations on and customizations to the junior high in several other cities, courses given titles such as "commercial," "cosmopolitan," "boys' industrial or prevocational," and "girls' trade or home economics." A. C. Barker, "The Intermediate School or Junior High School," *NEA Addresses and Proceedings* (1917), 266.

38 For an example of contemporary treatment of the Committee of Ten, see Frank Spaulding's commentary in Ellwood P. Cubberley, Fletcher B. Dresslar, Edward C. Elliot, J. H. Francis, Frank E. Spaulding, Lewis M. Terman, and William R. Tanner, *The Portland Survey: A Textbook on City School Administration Based on a Concrete Study* (Yonkers-on-Hudson, NY: World Book Co., 1915), 194; Oakland Public Schools, "The Intermediate School Situation in Oakland California," 16.

39 Barker was deeply curious about how different cities adapted the junior high plan in their own school systems, in part because the innovation became controversial in some of the cities into which it was introduced. Therefore, he had his director of research conduct a survey of other cities across the country implementing the junior high school. The fifty-three replies Oakland received gave a unique glimpse of the reform activity at the time. "Cities generally throughout the United States," testified Barker after reviewing the results, "are doing just about what Oakland is doing with respect to the junior high school problem; namely, experimenting." Oakland "ranked high," he reported, betraying a competitive tone, with other cities that had introduced different variations of the junior high school. Barker noted, e.g., that Oakland developed one junior high as a version of the platoon school of Gary, Indiana. Oakland Public Schools, "The Intermediate School Situation," 38, 22.

40 Ibid., 38.

41 See, e.g., the report of Barker's own director of research, Wilfred Talbert, in *Oakland Superintendent's Report* (1913–17); see also Ellen Condliffe Lagemann,

An Elusive Science: The Troubling History of Education Research (Chicago: University of Chicago Press, 2000).

42 We would be mistaken to assume that superintendents like McClymonds and Barker were truly the chief decision makers of their schools systems. They *were* the head administrators for one strand of the district, usually called the "education department" and, as such, they were responsible for working with teachers and principals. They also held authority for the development of "the course of study," the standard term for the nineteenth- and early twentieth-century curricular frameworks that each superintendent wrote, adapted, or customized and then printed in annual reports. Most other responsibilities, however, were retained by the school board, primarily through board committees that could conduct business virtually independently. These divisions often meant that separate contracts were awarded to local businessmen, often as a form of political favoritism. Under McClymonds and Barker, district responsibilities had been distributed between board committees, the secretary of the board, the district purchasing agent, the superintendent of buildings and grounds, and the superintendent of schools, as represented in fig. 3.1. The "perfect storm" of city school system conflicts reported by the *(American) School Board Journal* in 1913 was in part a result of the clashes that ensued between different worldviews and different conceptions of how public schools should be run. It was also a reflection of local politics ("Editorial: Superintendency Changes," *School Board Journal* 46, no. 6 [June 1913]: 28).

43 Steven Jay Blutza, "Oakland's Commission and the Council-Manager Plans" (PhD diss., University of California Berkley, 1978), 210.

44 Ellwood P. Cubberley, *Report of a Survey of the Organization, Scope, and Finances of the Public School System of Oakland California* (Oakland, CA: Oakland School Board, 1915), 3 (hereafter cited as *Oakland Survey*).

45 On Cubberley's popularity as a surveyor, see Tyack, *One Best System*, 137.

46 Cubberley et al., *The Portland Survey*, 28; Cubberley, *Public School Administration* (Boston: Houghton Mifflin, 1916), chap. 12.

47 Cubberley, *Oakland Survey*, 10, 29, 17–26.

48 With utter certainty in the soundness of his prescriptions, Cubberley backed up his arguments about cost savings and efficiency not with evidence from reforms undertaken in other cities but by advocating his reforms as "progressive" and as commonplace in the business world (*Oakland Survey*, 10, 21, 46).

49 "Berkeley Will Be Experted," *Oakland Tribune*, October 14, 1913.

50 *Oakland Superintendent's Report* (1913–17); A. C. Barker, "Address of Welcome," *NEA Addresses and Proceedings* (1923), 35.

51 Lewis B. Avery, "The Future High School," *NEA Addresses and Proceedings* (1915), 750–51.

52 "Educators May Split on Charges," *Oakland Tribune*, January 18, 1917.

53 "Barker Not to Seek Office," *Oakland Tribune*, January 19, 1917.

54 "Citizens to Pick Man for Barker's Job," *Oakland Tribune*, January 21, 1917; "Choice of School Head Is Puzzle," *Oakland Tribune*, January 23, 1917.

55 "Citizens to Pick Man for Barker's Job," *Oakland Tribune*, January 21, 1917.

56 "'Free Selves from Pull,' Advice of Expert to School Board," *Oakland Tribune*, April 2, 1917.

57 Frank E. Spaulding, *School Superintendent in Action in Five Cities* (Rindge, NH: Richard R. Smith, 1955), 537–38.

58 Ibid.; "Choice of Hunter Is Confirmed," *Oakland Tribune*, April 17, 1917.
59 "Fred M. Hunter Is Named New School Superintendent," *Oakland Tribune*, April 10, 1917.
60 "Barker Issues Statement; Denies Intention to Resign," *Oakland Tribune*, April 3, 1917.
61 William A. Spooner, "Protect the Schools from Political Intrigue," *Tri-City Labor Review*, April 6, 1917.
62 "Educators Report on School Head: Endorse Plan to Install New School Officer," *Oakland Tribune*, April 14, 1917.
63 Ibid. Capwell was also president of Security Bank and Trust and, later, a vice president of the Athens Athletic Club (Oakland's elite social organization).
64 Tyack, *One Best System*.
65 Davie, "Address of Welcome," 140.
66 As Paul Davis Chapman notes in his study of the intelligence testing movement, Oakland's connections to Lewis Terman at Stanford University led to a district-wide experiment that was one of the most comprehensive uses of mental tests before the First World War and, as such, Oakland provided a model for other districts to follow (*Schools as Sorters*, 64). Other historians have noted Oakland's adoption of the prevailing "scientific" language regarding ability as well as the district's program of curricular tracking that was an outgrowth of its testing program; see Tyack, *One Best System*, 209; and Paula S. Fass, *Outside In: Minorities and the Transformation of American Education* (New York, Oxford University Press, 1989), 68.
67 Hunter elaborated on these ideas in several places, see Fred M. Hunter, "Leadership in Education," *NEA Addresses and Proceedings* (1918), 622, "Earmarks of an Efficient School System," *NEA Addresses and Proceedings* (1917), 822–23; *Oakland Annual Report* (1917–18), 19–20, and "The Most Important Thing in American Education," *NEA Addresses and Proceedings* (1921), 274–81.
68 *Report of the Superintendent of Schools, 1915–1916* (Lincoln: Board of Education, Lincoln, Nebraska), 5–6 (hereafter cited as *Lincoln Annual Report*).
69 "Fred M. Hunter Is Named New School Superintendent," *Oakland Tribune*, April 10, 1917. However, a review of Hunter's doctoral thesis gives the distinct impression that Hunter was a rather weak scholar; see Frederick Maurice Hunter, "Teacher Tenure Legislation in the United States" (PhD Diss., University of California, 1924); the study is primarily a compilation of teacher tenure laws with virtually no analysis.
70 "Fred M. Hunter Is Named New School Superintendent."
71 On the Cleveland Conference, see Tyack and Hansot, *Managers of Virtue*, 131–33; Geraldine Clifford, unpublished manuscript (used by permission of the author).
72 "Fred M. Hunter Is Named New School Superintendent."
73 *Oakland Annual Report* (1917–18), 294.
74 *Lincoln Annual Report*, 5–6.
75 *Oakland Annual Report* (1917–18), 311.
76 Ibid.
77 See *Lincoln Annual Report*.
78 In crafting a newly conceived annual report for Oakland, Hunter appeared to follow the advice of reformers such as David Snedden and William H. Allen, who had argued in their 1908 book *School Reports and School Efficiency* that any "superintendent aiming to secure public support of a progressive school policy

will advance that policy by insisting upon a general circulation of his report"
([New York: MacMillan, 1908], 176).

79 The collection of school district annual reports in Cubberley Education Library
at the Stanford University School of Education attests to the widespread circulation of these reports. Cubberley regularly requested that districts send him
reports, while city superintendents sent their reports to other districts with
requests for reciprocation.

80 *Oakland Annual Report* (1917–18), 17.

81 Ibid., 26.

82 Ibid., 27.

83 Ibid., 19–20; Hunter, "Most Important Thing in American Education," 274–81.

84 See, e.g., Jane Addams, "Socialized Education," chap. 18 in *Twenty Years at
Hull-House* (New York: Macmillan, 1910), and *Democracy and Social Ethics* (New
York: Macmillan, 1902). For further discussion, see Lawrence A. Cremin, *Trans-
formation of the School: Progressivism in American Education, 1876–1957* (New
York: Vintage, 1961), chap. 3.

85 See, e.g., William T. Whitney, *The Socialized Recitation* (New York: A. S. Barnes
Co., 1915); Charles L. Robbins, *The Socialized Recitation* (Boston: Allyn &
Bacon, 1920).

86 Hunter, "Leadership in Education," 622, and "Earmarks of an Efficient System,"
822–23; John Dewey, *The Way Out of Educational Confusion* (Westport, CT:
Greenwood Press, 1931), 31.

87 William John Cooper, "The Public Schools Social Studies Report," in *Addendum
to the Superintendent's Annual Report, 1917–1918* (Oakland, CA: Oakland Public
Schools, 1918), 140.

88 Ibid.; W.W. Kemp, "Leadership Exemplified," *Phi Delta Kappan* 18, no. 3 (1935):
74–75.

89 *Oakland Annual Report* (1917–18), 48; George Drayton Strayer and Naomi
Norsworthy, *How To Teach* (New York: Macmillan, 1917).

90 Hunter's views can be seen as part of the broader "social efficiency" movement,
and the roots of his ideas also have elements in common with Herbert Spencer's
notion of the "social organism." Furthermore, his expressed interest in developing students' natural abilities could echo the *statements* of John Dewey, even
as they had closer affinity to the *ideas* of Lewis Terman and Frank Parsons. See
Cremin, *Transformation of the School*, chap. 4; Kliebard, *Struggle for the American Curriculum*, chap. 4.

91 Hunter, "Most Important Thing in American Education," 279.

92 Hunter, "Earmarks of an Efficient School System," 822, 823 (my emphasis).

93 See, e.g., "Vocational Guidance and Child Accounting," *Oakland Annual Report*
(1917–18), 155–168; for a derisive view of the educational goal of "holding power,"
see Ravitch, *Left Back*, esp. chap. 5.

94 "Vocational Guidance and Child Accounting," *Oakland Annual Report* (1917–
18), 155.

95 "Reprint from 'Our Public Schools': Failure and Retardation Cost Oakland
$120,000 Per Year," *Oakland Annual Report* (1917–18), 27.

96 "Report of Committee on Junior High Schools," *Oakland Annual Report* (1917–
18), 55–63. The committee suggested modeling these on the very successful junior
highs of cities like Rochester, New York, a district that had demonstrated the
ability to send large percentages of students on to high school.

97 Ibid., 60.

98 Ibid., 60, 61.

99 E. Morris Cox, "Survey of Nationalities," *Oakland Annual Report* (1917–18), 34–38.

100 A number of educators worried about the potential hazards posed by "Bolshevism." Among them was H. H. Goddard; see Leila Zenderland, *Measuring Minds: Henry Herbert Goddard and the Origins of American Intelligence Testing* (New York: Cambridge University Press, 1998), 297.

101 Hunter, "Most Important Thing in American Education," 275–76; see also *Oakland Annual Report* (1917–18), 30–32.

102 Hunter, "Most Important Thing in American Education," 276; *Oakland Annual Report* (1917–18), 256.

103 *Oakland Annual Report* (1917–18), 20.

104 "Report of the Committee on Neighborhood Schools and Americanization," *Oakland Annual Report* (1917–18), 66–67.

105 Hunter, "Earmarks of an Efficient School System," 825, 826.

106 *Oakland Annual Report* (1917–18), 33.

107 Ibid., 78.

108 See, e.g., Stephen Jay Gould, *The Mismeasure of Man* (New York: W. W. Norton and Co., 1996).

109 Hunter, "Earmarks of an Efficient School System," 823; *Oakland Annual Report* (1917–18).

110 Virgil E. Dickson, "Report of the Department of Research," *Oakland Annual Report* (1917–18), 173–247.

111 Virgil E. Dickson, "The Relation of Mental Testing to School Administration" (PhD diss., Stanford University, 1919), 95.

112 Compared to Chicago, e.g., Oakland's implementation of intelligence testing was uneventful; see Julia Wrigley, *Class, Politics, and Public Schools: Chicago 1900–1950* (New Brunswick, NJ: Rutgers University Press, 1982), 170–74.

113 *Oakland Annual Report* (1917–18), 173; "University Offers Opportunities," *Superintendent's Bulletin*, August 25, 1925.

114 Virgil Dickson, "Classification of School Children According to Mental Ability," in Lewis M. Terman et al., *Intelligence Tests and School Reorganization* (Yonkers-on-Hudson, NY: World Book Co., 1922), 33.

115 Ibid., 33–34.

116 Lewis Terman, "The Problem," in Terman et al., *Intelligence Tests and School Reorganization*, iii, 32.

117 *Oakland Annual Report* (1917–18), 173.

118 Dickson, "Classification of School Children," 35.

119 William C. Bagley, "Educational Determinism; or Democracy and the I.Q.," *School and Society* 15 (April 8, 1922): 381.

120 Lewis Terman, "The Psychological Determinist; or Democracy and the I.Q.," *Journal of Educational Research* 6 (June–December 1922): 62, 58–59.

121 Virgil E. Dickson, *Mental Tests and the Classroom Teacher* (Yonkers-on-Hudson, NY: World Book Co., 1923), 171.

122 Dickson, "Classification of Students," 52.

123 Dickson, *Mental Tests and the Classroom Teacher*, 171.

124 Ibid., 223, 226.

125 Rhomberg, *No There There*, 57.

126 KKK flyer quoted in Rhomberg, *No There There*, 59.

127 "Election Results," *Oakland Tribune*, April 18, 1923.

128 "Fifty Thousand See Richmond's Patriotic March," *Oakland Tribune*, July 4, 1924.

129 "Oriental Butchers Menace White Labor," *Union Labor Record*, April 2, 1920.

130 "Eureka Market Sells Chinese Handled Meat," *Union Labor Record*, February 27, 1920; "'For Ways That Are Dark and Tricks That Are Vain, the Heathen Chinee [*sic*] Is Peculiar,'" *Union Labor Record*, February 13, 1920; "Butchers Carry on Oriental Campaign," *Union Labor Record*, June 18, 1924.

131 "Students Strike on Parents Call in Race Dispute at Swett School," *Oakland Tribune*, September 27, 1926.

132 "School Race War Still Continues," *Oakland Tribune*, October 5, 1926.

133 "P-TA. Passes Petitions Bar Chinese," *Oakland Tribune*, October 9, 1926; "Strike over Chinese at School Ends," *Oakland Tribune*, October 12, 1926; "Oakland P.T.A. Indorses Hunter's Chinese Stand," *Oakland Tribune*, October 19, 1926.

134 *Map of Central Terrace*, Mutual Realty Company, Oakland, California, 1915 quoted in Rhomberg, *No There There*, 52.

135 "Negro Fights Piedmont Ouster," *Oakland Post-Enquirer*, May 20, 1924.

136 E. A. Daly, "Alameda County Political Leader and Journalist," an oral history conducted in 1971, *in Perspectives on the Alameda District Attorney's Office*, Regional Oral History Office, Bancroft Library, University of California, Berkeley, 1972, p. 10, quoted in Rhomberg, *No There There*, 52–53.

137 Einar Jacobsen, "A Study of How a City School System Keeps the Tax Payer Informed about the Aims, Purposes and Accomplishments of the Schools" (MA thesis, University of California, Berkeley, 1922), 18–24.

138 Ibid., 17.

139 Ida Vandergaw and Elizabeth Madison, "Improvement of Teaching by Means of a Permanent Exhibit and Project Library," *Superintendent's Bulletin: Special Edition* (January 1926), 9.

140 Ibid.

141 Fred Hunter to Jesse Newlon, January 8, 1928, Jesse H. Newlon Papers, Special Collections and Archives, University of Denver.

142 *The Oakland Public Schools: Superintendent's Bulletin* 9, no. 2 (August 16, 1928): 3; "Organization of Administration and Supervision of the Oakland Public Schools" *The Oakland Public Schools: Superintendent's Bulletin*, Supplement, 10, no. 14, November 7, 1929; Willard E. Givens, "The Reminiscences of Dr. Willard E. Givens," typescript, transcription of a tape-recorded interview conducted by Paul Hopper with Givens in Washington, DC, March 21, 1968, Oral History Research Office, Columbia University.

CHAPTER 4

1 Lincoln Steffens, *The Autobiography of Lincoln Steffens* (New York: Harcourt, Brace, & World, 1931), 651, 653. For his part, Steffens said he had gone along on the 1911 European trip, "to see if there was any muck to rake and any reforms to copy" (647).

2 Steffens, *Autobiography*, 653; Robert Speer, quoted in Lyle W. Dorsett, *The Queen City: A History of Denver* (Boulder, CO: Pruett Publishing Co., 1977), 138.

3 Charles A. Johnson, *Denver's Mayor Speer* (Denver: Bighorn Press, 1969), xix.

4   Speer, quoted in Stephen J. Leonard and Thomas J. Noel, *Denver: Mining Camp to Metropolis* (Niwot: University Press of Colorado, 1990), 140; Dorsett, *Queen City*, 142.

5   William Gilpin, *The Mission of the North American People: Geographical, Social and Political,* 2nd ed. (Philadelphia: J. B. Lippincott & Co., 1874), 127; see discussion of Gilpin in Carl Abbott, *How Cities Won the West: Four Centuries of Urban Change in Western North America* (Albuquerque: University of New Mexico Press, 2008), 1–4.

6   A. E. Winship, "Personality of Denver," *Journal of Education* 103 (June 24, 1926): 696; cf. Larry Cuban, *How Teachers Taught: Constancy and Change in American Classrooms, 1890–1990,* 2nd ed. (New York: Teachers College Press, 1993).

7   Denver Public Schools, *The Denver Program of Curriculum Revision*, Monograph No. 12 (Denver: Board of Education, 1927), 17; A. L. Threlkeld, "Curriculum Revision: How a Particular City May Attack the Problem," *Elementary School Journal* 25 (April 1925): 573.

8   Gary L. Peltier, "Jesse H. Newlon as Superintendent of the Denver Public Schools, 1920–1927" (PhD diss., University of Denver, 1965), 192.

9   Denver offers the student of educational reform a unique perspective on how one district coordinated efforts, worked with teachers, drew on external expertise, and publicized its activities in ways that, by all accounts, were remarkably successful. Historians have noted that individual schools often adopted the reforms advocated by pedagogical progressives more quickly than larger public school systems, in part because single schools could be more flexible and receptive to innovation. See Arthur Zilversmit, *Changing Schools: Progressive Education Theory and Practice, 1930–1960* (Chicago: University of Chicago Press, 1993), 37.

10   Scholars have sought to explain how Denver's strategies differed from those of districts less successful in their efforts at progressive reform. According to Lawrence A. Cremin, the great strength of Newlon's approach was his success at moving teachers to the very center of the business of curriculum making. Denver's reforms, said Cremin, were "quickly taken up by school systems across the country as a kind of prototypical example of progressive innovation at its best" (*Transformation of the School: Progressivism in American Education, 1876–1957* [New York: Vintage, 1961], 299–302). In studying the extent of Denver's pedagogical progressivism, Larry Cuban argues that Newlon and Threlkeld "blended administrative progressivism with clear pedagogical views on the pivotal role of the teacher in instructional and curricular decisionmaking and on the importance of flexible, activity-centered schools that linked daily life to what students learned" (*How Teachers Taught*, 78). I agree with Cuban's assessment of this aspect of Newlon and Threlkeld's approach, and I seek to build on his and other scholars' discussions of the school system by examining in more detail the "administrative" side of Denver's progressive practices.

11   "Superintendents of Denver," n.d., Superintendent's Clipping File, Western History Room, Denver Public Library,

12   On Gove's bid for the New York position, see Diane Ravitch, *The Great School Wars: New York City, 1805–1973* (New York: Basic Books, 1974), 161.

13   Aaron Gove, "City School Systems," *NEA Addresses and Proceedings* (1890), 463–64.

14   Ibid.

15 Patricia Ann Shikes, "Three Denver Public School Superintendents: A Historical Study of Educational Leadership" (PhD diss., University of Denver, 1987),
68. Upton Sinclair, writing well after Gove's tenure, decried the corporate control
that he felt had corrupted Denver school elections and spending and characterized
Gove as an "efficient superintendent," meaning "that he served his masters, by
keeping out of the system all revolutionary and dangerous new ideas, such as kindergartens, manual training and directed play." Sinclair believed that Gove's post-
superintendent position as a lobbyist for the Great Western Sugar Company—
owned by one of the city's industrial barons—was proof of the cozy relationship
between Denver corporations and the city school system; Upton Sinclair, *The
Goslings: A Study of American Schools* (Pasadena, CA: Upton Sinclair, 1924), 155.

16 Aaron Gove, "Discussion," *NEA Addresses and Proceedings* (1901), 488–89, 364,
488. On mental discipline, see Walter Bernard Kolesnik, *Mental Discipline in
Modern Education* (Madison: University of Wisconsin Press, 1958).

17 Margaret Haley, "Why Teachers Should Organize," *NEA Addresses and Proceedings* (1904), 145–52.

18 Aaron Gove, "Limitations of the Superintendent's Authority and of the Teacher's
Independence," *NEA Addresses and Proceedings* (1904), 152.

19 Ibid., 153.

20 Gove's assistant superintendent, Lewis Greenlee, took the reins of the superintendency after Gove's resignation, but he made few alterations to the district in
his three years as superintendent.

21 Denver Public Schools, *Eighth Annual Report of School District Number One in
the City and County of Denver, Colorado* (Denver: Board of Education, September 30, 1911), 15 (hereafter cited as *Denver Annual Report*, plus the year).

22 Ibid., 13–20.

23 "Superintendents of Denver."

24 Historians David Tyack and Elisabeth Hansot describe Chadsey as part of the
"Educational Trust," one of the policy elite, who later became a charter member
of the exclusive Cleveland Conference. Tyack and Hansot, *Managers of Virtue:
Public School Leadership in America, 1820–1980* (New York: Basic Books, 1982),
131, 141; Jeffrey Mirel, *The Rise and Fall of an Urban School System: Detroit, 1907–
81* (Ann Arbor: University of Michigan Press, 1993), 17.

25 New York's William Maxwell might serve as another example of a superintendent who anticipated how new social conditions would affect the character of
American education.

26 *Denver Annual Report* (1909–10), 12.

27 *Denver Annual Report* (1910–11), 13.

28 Ibid., 13–16.

29 Ibid., 13.

30 *Denver Annual Report* (1909–10), 13, 12.

31 *Denver Annual Report* (1908–9), 11–15.

32 Ibid., 13–14. Chadsey did not cite specific examples of the cities he had in mind,
though it is quite possible that Oakland was one of those cities.

33 *Denver Annual Report* (1909–10), 14.

34 *Denver Annual Report* (1910–11), 16; *Denver Annual Report* (1909–10), 15.

35 Larry Cuban asserted that Denver was politically quiet during this period
(*How Teachers Taught*). See also Bradley Robert Rice, *Progressive Cities: The*

Commission Government Movement in America, 1901–1920 (Austin: University of Texas Press, 1977), chap. 5.

36 Denver Chamber of Commerce, *Reports of the Special Committee on Commission Form of Government*, September 30, 1911, quoted in Rice, *Progressive Cities*, 67.

37 J. Paul Mitchell, "Boss Speer and the City Functional: Boosters and Businessmen versus Commission Government in Denver," *Pacific Northwest Quarterly* 63, no. 4 (October 1972): 155–64, 162.

38 Ibid., 163.

39 Ibid.

40 Bureau of Municipal Research, New York, *City and County of Denver: Report on a Survey of Certain Departments . . . Prepared for the Colorado Tax Payers Protective League* (Denver: Great Western Printing and Publishing Co., 1914).

41 Johnson, *Denver's Mayor Speer*, 195–200.

42 *Denver Times*, quoted in H. S. Gilbertson, "Denver Goes Back," *American City* 14, no. 6 (June 1916): 578; see also Rice, *Progressive Cities*, 91.

43 Minutes of the School Board of Denver, Colorado, January 27, 1915.

44 Cited in Shikes, "Three Denver Public School Superintendents," 144.

45 The *Denver Post* and *Rocky Mountain News* carried accounts of the survey in January and February 1916; see "Citizen's Review School Trouble," *Rocky Mountain News*, February 18, 1916; Carleton Washburne and Myron M. Stearns, *Better Schools: A Survey of Progressive Education in American Public Schools* (New York: John Day Co., 1928), 74–82. See also "Superintendents of Denver."

46 Franklin Bobbitt et al., *Report of the School Survey of School District Number One in the City and County of Denver* (Denver: School Survey Committee), hereafter cited as *Denver School Survey*.

47 Franklin Bobbitt, "General Organization," in *Denver School Survey*, 106, 128.

48 Franklin Bobbitt, "General Organization and Management," pt. 1 of *Denver School Survey*, 111.

49 Lewis M. Terman was not one for vague critique or generalized recommendations, and he was as data driven in his investigation of Denver's school buildings as he was in his assessment of intelligence. He even quantified the regularity with which floors should be swept, mopped, and waxed to insure that they were "neither unsightly nor slippery" ("The Building Situation and Medical Inspection," pt. 5 of *Denver School Survey*, 6, 39–42).

50 "Educational Writings," *Elementary School Journal* 17, no. 4 (December 1916): 222–24.

51 Bobbitt, "General Organization," 105–10; Ellwood P. Cubberley, "Supplemental Report on the Organization and Administration of School District Number One in the City and County of Denver," in *Denver School Survey*, 18.

52 Ibid., 18–20.

53 Ibid., 15, 12.

54 Ibid., 16.

55 "Jones and Guyer Are Defeated in Fight upon New School Laws," *Denver Post*, January 27, 1916; "School By-Laws Will Be Adopted by Board Members," *Denver Post*, June 14, 1916.

56 "Citizens Review School Trouble."

57 Ibid.; "School By-Laws Will Be Adopted by Board Members."

58 Minutes of the School Board of Denver, Colorado, March 26, 1917. The *Colorado School Journal* later recalled of Cole: "He came when the educational interests were in the greatest danger and it was chiefly through his efforts that great misfortunes did not come to the entire system. His earliest act was the reinstatement of over 150 teachers who had summarily and with no assigned reasons been dismissed from the Denver system. This endeared Mr. Cole to the entire teaching force and gave notice to all that injustice in Denver school administration would not be tolerated" ("Carlos M. Cole," *Colorado School Journal* 36, no. 1 [September 1920]: 16).

59 I draw upon Shikes, "Three Denver Public School Superintendents," for much of this discussion. See also Washburne and Stearns, *Better Schools.*

60 Shikes, "Three Denver Public School Superintendents."

61 Herbert M. Kliebard found "no clear ideological direction" in Newlon's work as a superintendent, and Larry Cuban argues that Newlon blended administrative and pedagogical progressive approaches. Historian Raymond E. Callahan, who dismissed most Progressive Era superintendents as the puppets of businessmen, identified Newlon as a "true educator," one of the few intellectual heroes who raised dissenting voices against the excesses of the drive toward school efficiency. Yet, Callahan focused more on Newlon's writings during his tenure at Teachers College, leaving his actions as Denver's superintendent relatively unexamined; this is unfortunate, for Newlon offers a somewhat more complicated picture of the ways in which administrative efficiency and progressive pedagogical reform sometimes intersected. Kliebard, *The Struggle for the American Curriculum, 1893–1958,* 2nd ed. (New York: Routledge, 1993), 182; Cuban, *How Teachers Taught,* 78; Callahan, *Education and the Cult of Efficiency: A Study of the Social Forces That Have Shaped the Administration of the Public Schools* (Chicago: University of Chicago Press, 1962), 203.

62 Newlon correspondence from Fred Hunter, August 4, 1920 and Newlon to Fred Englehart, August 23, 1920, quoted in Shikes, "Three Denver Public School Superintendents," 145–46.

63 By 1923, as he reviewed his first three years in the district, Newlon reported that "progress has been made in improving curricula and methods of instruction, but, because of the condition[s] which existed, it has been necessary, during this period, to put the emphasis upon the more material phases of administration" (Jesse H. Newlon, *Twentieth Annual Report of School District Number One in the City and County of Denver and State of Colorado* [Denver: Denver School Press, 1923], 7).

64 Gary Peltier, in his study of Newlon's superintendency, argues that the 1916 survey report provided the "logical starting point" for Newlon's overhaul of the system ("Jesse H. Newlon," 116).

65 Newlon, *Denver Annual Report* (1923), 8–9.

66 The older systems of classifying students, such as age grading, Newlon said, had "proved inadequate in many respects" because students did not all progress through the schools at the same rate (ibid., 23).

67 Lincoln Public Schools, *Report of the Superintendent of Schools, 1917–1919* (Lincoln: Board of Education, 1920), hereafter cited as *Lincoln Superintendent's Report,* plus year.

68 Jesse Newlon to Fred Hunter, January 7, 1937, Jesse H. Newlon Papers, Special Collections and Archives, University of Denver.

69 Ibid.; *Lincoln Superintendent's Report* (1915–17); Thomas Fallace and Victoria Fantozzi have cautioned scholars about the imprecision of the term "social efficiency"; I continue to use the phrase, in part, because my argument about district progressivism supports their point. See Fallace and Fantozzi, "Was There Really a Social Efficiency Doctrine? The Uses and Abuses of an Idea in Educational History," *Educational Researcher* 42, no. 3 (April 2013): 142–50.

70   Fred Hunter telegram to Jesse Newlon, July 31, 1920, Newlon Papers.

71   Fred Hunter to Jesse Newlon, August 4, 1920, Newlon Papers; see also correspondence quoted in Shikes, "Three Denver Public School Superintendents," 145–46; stipulations of Newlon's contract come from Denver school board minutes for July 27, 1920, and August 11, 1920, also cited in Shikes, "Three Denver Public School Superintendents," 146–47. Newlon had also written to Hunter: "I shall want to talk my problems over with you frequently during the next year or two, and shall count on you for advice."

72   See, e.g., Jesse H. Newlon, "The Need of a Scientific Curriculum Policy for Junior and Senior High Schools," *Educational Administration and Supervision* 3 (May 1917): 267.

73   Ibid., 265.

74   See Robert B. Westbrook, *John Dewey and American Democracy* (Ithaca, NY: Cornell University Press, 1991).

75   Ibid., 264, 266.

76   "New School Men for Denver," *Colorado School Journal* 36 (September 1921): 22.

77   Peltier, "Jesse H. Newlon," 131.

78   For example, Newlon was one of the leaders to support NEA reorganization in 1920, rather harshly silencing Margaret Haley's opposition to the plan (A. E. Winship, "The Great Event," *Journal of Education* 42 [August 19, 1920]: 118–20; Sinclair, *The Goslings*).

79   I am indebted to Patricia Ann Shikes for her careful study of the Newlon era in Denver. My sections on the single-salary schedule and the building program draw on her careful research ("Three Denver Public School Superintendents").

80   Ibid., 161–64.

81   Ibid.

82   Ibid.

83   Denver Public Schools, *The Denver School Building Program*, Monograph No. 13 (Denver: Denver Public Schools, 1928), 5, 31–32; Shikes, "Three Denver Public School Superintendents," 165–67.

84   Newlon, "Need of a Scientific Curriculum Policy," 267.

85   Newlon, "Need of a Scientific Curriculum Policy," 267, 266. At no time did Hunter or Strayer grant such power to teachers; rather, these two men viewed teaching as more of a series of steps to be followed, a set of directions to be given from above and followed below. In 1917, Strayer explained to teachers how to follow the steps of a "drill lesson" or an "induction lesson" in his book, *How to Teach*, while Hunter cautioned teachers always to adhere to the specific recitation standards that had been established by the district. In that same year, Newlon sounded a different tone. George D. Strayer and Naomi Norsworthy, *How to Teach* (New York: Macmillan Co., 1918), chap. 13; Fred M. Hunter, "Earmarks of an Efficient School System," *NEA Addresses and Proceedings* (1917), 822.

86   Wilson left little documentation behind detailing his efforts, but according to Newlon, Wilson's experimentation had demonstrated that "the best 'courses' were those that were the results of the cooperative efforts of teachers and executive officers" (Newlon, "The Need of a Scientific Curriculum Policy," 266–67).

87 Cuban, *How Teachers Taught*; Diane Ravitch, *Troubled Crusade: American Education, 1945–1980* (New York: Basic Books, 1983).

88 A. L. Threlkeld, "What Denver Has Done in Two Years to Remake Its Course of Study," *Teachers Journal and Abstract* 1 (January 1926): 37.

89 Peltier, "Jesse H. Newlon," 126.

90 Denver Public Schools, *The Denver Program of Curriculum Revision*, 11.

91 Ibid., 12.

92 For an example of how school critics successfully used "fads and frills" to undermine a superintendency during the same period, see chap. 6 on Seattle.

93 Threlkeld, "What Denver Has Done," 39.

94 Threlkeld, "Curriculum Revision," 573; Denver Public Schools, *Denver Program of Curriculum Revision*, 12.

95 See, e.g., Cremin, *Transformation of the School*, 299.

96 Threlkeld, "Curriculum Revision," 576.

97 Ibid., 574.

98 Threlkeld, "What Denver Has Done," 38.

99 Jesse H. Newlon and A. L. Threlkeld, "The Denver Curriculum Revision Program," in *Twenty-Sixth Yearbook of the National Society for the Study of Education*, pt. 1 (Bloomington, IL: Public School Publishing Co., 1927), 238.

100 Threlkeld, "Curriculum Revision: How a Particular City May Attack the Problem," 576.

101 Ibid., 577.

102 Denver Public Schools, *Denver Program of Curriculum Revision*, 14.

103 Threlkeld explained that this plan allowed the committees from each level of the system to work out their course of study as best they saw fit, but that the curriculum specialist might call joint meetings of all three committees when appropriate ("Curriculum Revision," 577).

104 Ibid., 578.

105 Ibid., 579; I further discuss Denver's use of achievement tests later in this chapter.

106 As a consequence, there was no need for the outside specialist to "sell" himself; teachers had already identified the need for external expert advice (ibid., 579–80).

107 Denver Public Schools, *The Denver Program of Curriculum Revision*, 28.

108 Threlkeld, "What Denver Has Done," 38.

109 Marie D. Murphy, "Teacher Participation in Curriculum Revision in the Denver Schools," *Colorado School Journal* 40 (October 1924): 16.

110 "Teacher Participation in Curriculum Revision," 19–20.

111 Anna P. McArthur, quoted in Peltier, "Jesse H. Newlon," 243.

112 A. E. Winship of the *Journal of Education* reported that at the 1922 NEA annual meeting Newlon "brought with him one of the best city delegations in the country" ("Eminent City Superintendents," *Journal of Education* 96 [July 20, 1922]: 65).

113 "Should Overaged Students Receive Special Promotion?" *Denver Public Schools Bulletin* 1, no. 5 (February 1928): 8; "The Denver Schools Rate High," *Denver Public Schools Bulletin* 1, no. 4 (January 1928): 2–4; "The Appraisal Testing Program," *Denver Public Schools Bulletin* 2, no. 2 (October 1928): 7–9.

114 The test results were reported through two publications: the *Denver Public Schools Bulletin*, intended for teachers and administrators employed in the district, and the [Denver] *School Review*, subtitled the "Official Publication of the Denver Public Schools," for a broader public audience. See, e.g., "Test Results Show Value of Denver's School Program," [Denver] *School Review* 11, no. 1 (March 1929): 8. More detailed results of the district's internal evaluations were reported in *Denver Public Schools Bulletin* (vol. 2) throughout the 1928–29 academic year.

115 "The Appraisal Testing Program," *Denver Public Schools Bulletin* 2, no. 2 (October 1928): 7–9; see also Peltier, "Jesse H. Newlon," 172–78.

116 A. K. Loomis, "Recent Developments in Curriculum-making in Denver," *Progressive Education* (September 1929), 262.

117 Denver Public Schools, *Courses of Study in Arithmetic and Reading for the Slow-Learning: Elementary School Grades One, Two, Three, Four, Five, and Six*, Course of Study Monograph no. 29 (Denver: Denver Public Schools, 1930).

118 Peltier, "Jesse H. Newlon," 181.

119 V. T. Thayer, "The Denver Course of Study in Secondary Education," *Educational Research Bulletin* 6, no. 1 (January 5, 1927): 19 (this journal was published by the Bureau of Educational Research, College of Education, Ohio State University).

120 NEA, "Keeping Pace with the Advancing Curriculum," *NEA Research Bulletin* 3, nos. 4–5 (September–November 1925): 121, 182–83.

121 Harold Rugg and George S. Counts, "A Critical Appraisal of Current Methods of Curriculum Making," *Twenty-Sixth Yearbook of the National Society for the Study of Education* (Bloomington, IL: Public School Publishing Co., 1927), 425; A. Gayle Waldrop, "Denver Is Pioneer in New School Curriculum Adapted to Individual Intelligence," *Dallas Morning News*, May 2, 1926.

122 Jesse H. Newlon and A. L. Threlkeld, "The Denver Curriculum-Revision Program," in *Twenty-Sixth Yearbook of the National Society for the Study of Education*, pt. 1 (Bloomington, IL: Public School Publishing Co., 1927), 239.

123 Ibid., 239–40.

124 Denver Public Schools, *The Denver Program of Curriculum Revision*, 18.

125 Threlkeld, "What Denver Has Done," 38.

126 Newlon and Threlkeld, "The Denver Curriculum Revision Program," 240.

127 Denver Public Schools, *The Denver Program of Curriculum Revision*, 18.

128 Ibid., 18–19.

129 Peltier, "Jesse H. Newlon," 168–69.

130 Cuban, *How Teachers Taught*, 86–91.

131 By January 1928, the Denver Research Department had grown to house a staff of nine.

132 A. L. Threlkeld, "Changing Conceptions of Curriculum Making," 13, address given at the Fifth Annual Educational Conference, Lexington, Kentucky, October 26, 1928, Threlkeld Papers, Penrose Library, University of Denver.

133 For Dickson's use of Edison to point out the futility of elevating the quality of education, see Virgil E. Dickson, *Mental Tests and the Classroom Teacher* (Yonkers-on-Hudson, NY: World Book Co., 1923), 223.

134 Threlkeld, "Changing Conceptions of Curriculum Making," 14.

135 Charles E. Greene, "Anent Classification," *Denver Public Schools Bulletin* 5, no. 1 (October 1931): 2–4.

136 Ibid. See also Percival M. Symonds, "Homogeneous Grouping," *Teachers College Record* 32, no. 6 (March 1931): 501–17.

137 Guy Fox, "City-Wide Norms for 6A and 9A Mental Tests," *Denver Public Schools Bulletin* 5, no. 6 (May 1932): 8.

138 "Testing Service from the Department of Research in 1931–1932," *Denver Public Schools Bulletin* 5, no. 6 (May 1932): 2.

139 Symonds, "Homogeneous Grouping," 505; Greene, "Anent Classification," 4.

CHAPTER 5

1 Carl Abbott, *Portland: Planning, Politics, and Growth in a Twentieth-Century City* (Lincoln: University of Nebraska Press, 1983), 33–35.

2 Recent scholarship has challenged the notion that Portland was especially conservative; see, e.g., Robert D. Johnston, *The Radical Middle Class: Populist Democracy and the Question of Capitalism in Progressive Era Portland, Oregon* (Princeton, NJ: Princeton University Press, 2003).

3 See also David B. Tyack, "The Perils of Pluralism: The Background of the Pierce Case," *American Historical Review* 74, no. 1 (October 1968): 74–98.

4 A. E. Winship, "Looking About: Portland, Oregon," *Journal of Education* 81, no. 8 (February 25, 1915): 199–201.

5 David Tyack has written about the development of the Portland school system up to 1913 in "Bureaucracy and the Common School: The Example of Portland Oregon, 1851–1913," *American Quarterly* 29 (Fall 1967): 475–98; see also *The One Best System: A History of American Urban Education* (Cambridge, MA: Harvard University Press, 1974).

6 Alfred Powers and Howard McKinley Corning, eds., *History of Education in Portland* (n.p.: Works Progress Administration Adult Education Project under the Sponsorship of the General Extension Division, [Oregon] State System of Higher Education, 1937), 333.

7 Lee A. Dillon, quoted in ibid., 185.

8 Frank Rigler, *Portland Annual Report* (1896), quoted in Tyack, "Bureaucracy and the Common School," 493. One of Rigler's predecessors, Superintendent Ella Sabin (1888–91), had been known for her experiments in bringing teaching methods under "the enlivening influence of the 'new education.'" Not coincidentally, Rigler chose to leave Portland during her three-year tenure.

9 Portland Public Schools, *Thirty-fifth Annual Report of School District No. One, Multnomah County, Oregon, Including the City of Portland* (Portland, OR: Board of Directors, 1908), hereafter cited as *Portland Annual Report* with publication date.

10 *Portland Annual Report* (1910), 118; Ella Flagg Young, "Grading and Classification," *NEA Addresses and Proceedings* (1894), 85.

11 Ibid.

12 William T. Harris, quoted in Powers and Corning, eds., *History of Education in Portland*, 176.

13 Ellwood P. Cubberley, *Public School Administration* (Boston: Houghton Mifflin, 1916), 305.

14 Powers and Corning, eds., *History of Education in Portland*, 184.

15 Cubberley, *Public School Administration*, 174–75.

16 E. H. Whitney, quoted in Powers and Corning, eds., *History of Education in Portland*, 184.

17 Powers and Corning, eds., *History of Education in Portland*, 336.

18 Ellwood P. Cubberley, Fletcher B. Dresslar, Edward C. Elliot, J. H. Francis, Frank E. Spaulding, Lewis M. Terman, and William R. Tanner, *The Portland Survey: A Textbook on City School Administration Based on a Concrete Study*

(Yonkers-on-Hudson, NY: World Book Co., 1915), 428; hereafter cited as *The Portland Survey* (1915).

19 Portland School Board Minutes, January 22 1913.

20 E. Kimbark MacColl with Harry H. Stein, *Merchants, Money, and Power: The Portland Establishment, 1843–1913* (Portland, OR: Georgian Press, 1988), 446–47.

21 Cubberley et al., *The Portland Survey* (1915); David Tyack also discusses some aspects of the background to the survey; see Tyack, *One Best System*, 191–93.

22 Cubberley et al., *The Portland Survey* (1915), 154–55.

23 Ibid., 127.

24 Ibid., 173–74, 194.

25 Ibid., 24, 23–24.

26 Ibid., 35.

27 Ibid., 365–71. In his discussion of special classes for "Truants, Incorrigibles and Misfits," Terman advocated adoption of the system of his co-surveyor Los Angeles Superintendent Francis: "No mistake would be made," Terman insisted, "if the Los Angeles method of dealing with this problem were copied in detail by Portland."

28 Correspondence to the survey committee is archived in the Oregon Historical Society; David Tyack generously offered me his copies of these letters, which he had collected at an earlier date.

29 Ibid.

30 Cubberley et al., *The Portland Survey* (1915), 12, 25–33; these images were then reproduced in Cubberley, *Public School Administration*, 174–75, 172–73.

31 Ibid., 217–19 (my emphasis).

32 Ibid., 220.

33 Portland Public Schools Board of Education, Minutes of the Portland School Board, May 1, 1913, Portland Public Schools central office.

34 Cubberley et al., *The Portland Survey* (1915), 258–59.

35 Jesse B. Sears and Adin D. Henderson, *Cubberley of Stanford and His Contribution to American Education* (Stanford, CA: Stanford University Press, 1957), 173–74.

36 Randolph Silliman Bourne, *Education and Living* (New York: Century, 1917), 84–90.

37 George Strayer, review of *The Portland Survey*, by Ellwood P. Cubberley et al., *Educational Review* 52 (December 1916): 519–20.

38 Cubberley et al., *The Portland Survey* (1915), 124.

39 Bureau of Municipal Research, *Organization and Business Methods of the City Government of Portland, Oregon: Report by Bureau of Municipal Research, New York City* (New York: Bureau of Municipal Research, 1913), 74, 72.

40 Tyack, "Bureaucracy and the Common School," 493.

41 Lewis Raymond Alderman, "Happy Is the Man: An Autobiography," rev. and ed. (Mrs. Lewis) Lola Lake Alderman, unpublished manuscript, n.d., Alderman Papers, Special Collections and University Archives, University of Oregon.

42 For a brief biographical sketch of Alderman, see Powers and Corning, eds., *History of Education in Portland*, 174.

43 A. E. Winship, quoted in "Portland, Oregon," Portland Public Schools, *School Bulletin* 1, no. 16 (May 16, 1914): 1.

44 Oregon Civic League, *Digest of Survey of Portland Public Schools* (Portland, OR: Schwab Printing Co.), 1914.

45 Cubberley, *Public School Administration*, 174–75.

46 "School Head Will Fight for Position," *Portland Oregonian*, July 14, 1918.

47 *Portland Annual Report* (1914), 33–34.

48 Ibid.

49 "Portland's Public School System Is of Highest Rank," *Portland Oregonian*, January 1, 1917.

50 Alderman, "Happy Is the Man."

51 *Portland Annual Report* (1916), 23–24.

52 *Portland Annual Report* (1915), 28.

53 Portland Public Schools, *School Bulletin* (April 25, 1914); *Portland Annual Report* (1915), 29. L.R. Alderman explains the school credit program in more detail in *School Credit for Home Work* (Boston: Houghton Mifflin, 1915).

54 *Portland Annual Report* (1915), 29–30.

55 "Inland Empire Teachers' Association," Portland Public Schools, *School Bulletin*, vol. 1, no. 13 (April 25, 1914).

56 Portland Public Schools, *School Bulletin* (January 28, 1916).

57 Alderman, "Happy Is the Man," 86.

58 O. M. Plummer, "President's Address," *NEA Addresses and Proceedings* (1915), 1031.

59 "Portland's Public School System Is of Highest Rank," *Portland Oregonian*, January 1, 1917.

60 *Portland Annual Report* (1917), 26.

61 This sentiment was not unlike that expressed the following year by John Dewey and his daughter, Evelyn, in their book, *Schools of To-morrow* (New York: E. P. Dutton Co., 1915).

62 *Portland Annual Report* (1917), 26–27.

63 L. R. Alderman, "The Two-Group Plan," *NEA Addresses and Proceedings* (1917), 801.

64 Ibid., 802.

65 Grace DeGraff, "Tenure of Office," *NEA Addresses and Proceedings* (1915), 1052–53. DeGraff was also the subject of resounding endorsement by Winship for the census of Portland school children she had recently conducted.

66 Alderman, "The Two-Group Plan," 801–2.

67 *Portland Annual Report* (1916), 22.

68 Alderman, "The Two-Group Plan," 802–3.

69 Ibid., 803.

70 Ibid., 802; *Portland Annual Report* (1917), 20–21.

71 "Portland Public School System of Highest Rank," *Portland Oregonian*, January 1, 1918.

72 Ronald D. Cohen and Raymond Mohl, *The Paradox of Progressive Education: The Gary Plan and Urban Schooling* (Port Washington, NY: Kennikat Press, 1979), 10.

73 Alderman, "The Two-Group Plan," 802.

74 Frank A. Fitzpatrick, review of *The Gary Schools*, by Randolph S. Bourne, *Educational Review* 52 (December 1916): 524–27.

75 "Test Results Disappointing," *Portland Telegram*, March 2, 1916; "Test Disappoints Alderman Camp," *Portland Telegram*, March 6, 1916; "Why Not Fair Play?" *Portland Oregonian*, March 7, 1916.

76 *Portland Telegram*, March 20, 1916; "Costs of Schools Mount out of Proportion to Student Increase," *Portland Telegram*, June 17, 1916.

77 P. W. Horn, *Report of Supplementary Survey of Portland Public Schools* (Portland, OR: Portland Public Schools, 1917), 5.

78 Ibid., 14.

79 Ibid., 24–25.

80 Ibid.

81 Ibid., 30.

82 Ibid., 24–25.

83 Ibid., 59–62.

84 On the establishment of the earliest departments of research, see John M. Brewer, *History of Vocational Guidance: Origins and Early Development* (New York: Harper & Brothers, 1942).

85 "L. R. Alderman Is Deposed by Board," *Portland Oregonian*, July 6, 1918; "School Head Will Fight for Position," *Portland Oregonian*, July 14, 1918; *Portland Oregonian*, August 2, 1918.

86 Powers and Corning, eds., *History of Education in Portland*, 335–36.

87 Abbott, *Portland*, 66.

88 E. Kimbark MacColl, *Growth of a City: Power and Politics in Portland, Oregon, 1915 to 1950* (Portland, OR: Georgian Press, 1979), 8.

89 "Editorial," *Oregon Journal*, quoted in Powers and Corning, eds., *History of Education in Portland*, 337.

90 "School Head Will Fight for Position," *Portland Oregonian*, July 14, 1918.

91 "Naming of School Head Is Problem," *Portland Telegram*, February 8, 1919.

92 Ibid.

93 "School Director," *Oregon Voter* 13, no. 9 (June 1, 1918): 24.

94 "Rotten Mess," *Oregon Voter* 14, no. 2 (July 13, 1918): 20; "Better School System Is Aim of Committee," *Portland Telegram*, April 4, 1919.

95 Charles A. Rice, "Daniel A. Grout: A Tribute," *Oregon Education Journal* 3 (May 1929): 15.

96 "Wear a Mask and You May You Save Your Life," Portland Public Schools, *School Bulletin* (January 18, 1918).

97 Stuart A. Courtis, "The Gary Public Schools: Measurement of Classroom Products," quoted in Portland Public Schools, *School Bulletin*, vol. 7, no. 15 (January 10, 1920).

98 For a brief discussion of the creation of the Research Department in the Portland Public Schools, see Henry David Sheldon, ed., *De Busk Memorial Essays* (Eugene: University of Oregon, 1937).

99 John Higham, *Strangers in the Land: Patterns of American Nativism 1860–1925* (1955; repr., New York: Atheneum, 1966), 234–63.

100 *Portland Telegram*, February 2, 1918.

101 Higham, *Strangers in the Land*, 237; *Portland Annual Report* (1923), 44.

102 "Americanization in the Schools," Portland Public Schools, *School Bulletin*, vol. 6, no 25 (April 26, 1918).

103 Portland Public Schools, *School Bulletin* (January 20, 1923).

104 *Portland Telegram*, February 2, 1918.

105 "Instruction in American Ideals," *School Bulletin*, vol. 6, no. 25 (April 26, 1918); and see "To Fight German Teaching: American Defense Society Starts Propaganda in Schools," *New York Times*, December 31, 1918.

106 The *Oregon Voter* carried the full transcripts of the addresses given by William F.

Woodward and William D. Wheelwright—see "Debate on the School Bill," *Oregon Voter* 31, no. 1 (October 7, 1922): 14–22.

107 Ibid.

108 Ibid.

109 "$1,000,000 More Taxes," Oregon Voter 31, no. 1 (October 7, 1922): 16–17; Johnston, *The Radical Middle Class*, 231; David B. Tyack, "The Perils of Pluralism: The Background of the Pierce Case," *American Historical Review* 74, no. 1 (October 1968): 74–98.

110 Higham, *Strangers in the Land*, 260.

111 Johnston, *The Radical Middle Class*, 222.

112 "One Old Negro's Philosophy," Portland Public Schools, *School Bulletin*, vol. 7, no. 3 (September 13, 1919).

113 Sinclair, *Goslings*, 131.

114 Charles A. Rice, "Daniel A. Grout: A Tribute."

115 On the 1924 trip, Rice visited Gary, Detroit, Akron, Youngstown, Pittsburgh, Washington, DC, and Kansas City, MO.

116 Charles A. Rice, "Representative School Systems: Portland, Oregon," *Journal of Education* 118 (December 2, 1935): 526.

117 For background on Rice, see Powers and Corning, eds., *History of Education in Portland*, 339.

118 See, e.g., Alice Barrows, *School Building Survey and Program for Warwick, Rhode Island*, U.S. Department of the Interior, Office of Education, Bulletin (1930), No. 33 (Washington, DC: Government Printing Office, 1931). On Barrows, see Raymond A. Mohl, "Alice Barrows: Crusader for the Platoon School, 1920–40," *Elementary School Journal* 77, no. 5 (May 1977): 351–57.

119 "Report of Miss Alice Barrows, Federal Bureau of Investigation, Washington, DC, to the City Club," *Portland City Club Bulletin*, May 7, 1926 quoted in Mac-Coll, *The Growth of a City*, 284.

120 Powers and Corning, eds., *History of Education in Portland*, 235; Charles A. Rice, *Portland's Platoon Schools* (Portland, OR: Multnomah County Library, n.d.), 14; Rice reported on his visits to other school districts that were implementing platoon schools over several installments of the *School Bulletin*; see Charles A. Rice, "A Report on the Platoon Plan as Operated in Several Eastern Cities," the *School Bulletin* for May 3, 1924, May 10, 1924, May 24, 1924, May 9, 1925, December 19, 1925, and December 17, 1926.

121 Rice, "Representative School Systems: Portland," 525.

122 Max Barr, "Dr. Burchard Woodson DeBusk and the Research Department of the Portland Public Schools, 1924–1931," in *De Busk Memorial Essays*, ed. Henry Davidson Sheldon, 17–20; "Intelligence Tests Need Intelligent Application," Portland Public Schools, *School Bulletin*, vol. 10, no. 13 (January 13, 1923).

123 *Portland Annual Report* (1932), 52; Rice, *Portland's Platoon Schools*, 14. Rice said platoon schools brought about an "overhauling of the course of study."

124 *Portland Annual Report* (1932), 53.

125 Ibid., 66–67.

126 Ibid.

127 Ibid.

128 Ibid., 240–41.

CHAPTER 6

1   Murray Morgan, *Skid Road: An Informal Portrait of Seattle* (New York: Viking Press, 1951), 3; Roger Sale, *Seattle: Past to Present* (Seattle: University of Washington Press, 1976), 74; see also, Matthew Klingle, *Emerald City: An Environmental History of Seattle* (New Haven, CT: Yale University Press, 2009), 5.

2   Seattle Public Schools, *Annual Report of the Board of Directors of Seattle School District No. 1, City of Seattle* (Seattle: The District, 1910), 23, 32 (hereafter cited as *Seattle Annual Report*, with year of publication).

3   "Educational Guidance Second Only to Teaching," *Educational Bulletin* 4, no. 8 (May 1928).

4   Fred C. Ayer, *Studies in Administrative Research*, 2 vols. (Seattle: Department of Research, Seattle Public Schools, 1924), 1:46.

5   See John C. Putnam, *Class and Gender Politics in Progressive-Era Seattle* (Reno: University of Nevada Press, 2008); and Elizabeth S. Clemens, *The People's Lobby: Organizational Innovation and the Rise of Interest Group Politics in the United States, 1890–1925* (Chicago: University of Chicago Press, 1997).

6   Bryce Eugene Nelson, *Good Schools: The Seattle Public School System, 1901–1930* (Seattle: University of Washington Press, 1988), 62, 172. I am indebted to Nelson's careful and detailed study of the development of the Seattle schools during Cooper's tenure. Although this chapter overlaps with the years of Nelson's book, I develop an analysis that differs from his.

7   West Des Moines Public Schools, *Biennial Report of the Public Schools of West Des Moines, Iowa, 1890–1892* (Des Moines, IA: West Des Moines Public Schools, 1892), hereafter cited as *Des Moines Annual Report*, with year of publication; Nelson, *Good Schools*, also provides some background on Cooper.

8   West Des Moines Public Schools, *Biennial Report*, 19.

9   Ibid.

10 *Des Moines Annual Report* (1894), 23–24.

11 *Seattle Annual Report* (1910), 31.

12 "Why a Teachers' Institute?" Seattle Public Schools, *Seattle School Bulletin: For the Promotion of Increased Co-operation between Home and School*, vol. 2, no. 2 (November 1915), hereafter cited as *Seattle School Bulletin*.

13 *Seattle Annual Report* (1910), 23.

14 Ibid.

15 *Seattle Annual Report* (1913), 29.

16 "School Attendance: A Reason for Compulsory School Laws," *Seattle School Bulletin*, vol. 1, no. 5 (March 27, 1914).

17 "High School Courses. An Explanation," *Seattle School Bulletin*, vol. 1, no. 3 (January 15, 1914).

18 *Seattle Annual Report* (1910), 33.

19 *Seattle Annual Report* (1911), 20.

20 Cooper's brief encounters with institutions of higher education meant that he had not developed the customary ties to networks of other leaders that were second nature to many early twentieth-century educators. Indeed, his unique reliance on his teachers and administrators as resources in thinking through curricular improvements might have been a result of his professional independence.

21 Ibid., 34.

22 *Seattle Annual Report* (1914), 47.

23 Ibid.

24 Ibid., 48, 51.

25 Ibid., 50.

26 Ibid., 51.

27 *Seattle Annual Report* (1910), 26.

28 *Seattle Annual Report* (1912), 27.

29 *Seattle Annual Report* (1910), 27.

30 Frank Cooper, "The Mentally Defective Pupil," *NEA Addresses and Proceedings* (1915), 447.

31 NEA Roundtable of Superintendents of Cities with a Population of from 25,000 to 250,000, "Current Methods of Dealing with the Exceptional Pupil," *NEA Addresses and Proceedings* (1915), 445–66; Cooper, "Mentally Defective Pupil," 448.

32 *Seattle Annual Report* (1915), 62.

33 Ibid.

34 Ibid., 62, 63.

35 Ibid., 62–63.

36 Ibid.

37 Frank Cooper, quoted in Bryce E. Nelson, "Frank B. Cooper: Seattle's Progressive School Superintendent, 1901–1922," *Pacific Northwest Quarterly* 74 (October 1983): 167. A few years earlier, Ellwood Cubberley made much the same remark about educational progress being evolutionary rather than revolutionary in his comments regarding Bobbitt's Denver school survey. Nelson comments that Cooper's attitude about the evolutionary nature of progress characterized Cooper's tenure in Seattle; while I agree that Cooper took an evolutionary approach, rather than a revolutionary one, my conclusions about the results of Cooper's superintendency obviously differ from Nelson's.

38 Nelson, "Frank B. Cooper: Seattle's Progressive School Superintendent, 1901–1922," 167.

39 "Play and Education," *Seattle School Bulletin*, vol. 3, no. 5 (April 1916). Using Rousseauian language, Cooper continued: "Play, the spontaneous expression of childhood, is nature's way of preparing the body and mind of the youth for the adult of tomorrow."

40 "A Modern Primary Room," *Seattle School Bulletin*, vol. 6, no. 3 (June 1919).

41 Cooper's descriptions as well as those of his supervisors and principals testify to the types of innovations introduced into schools; e.g., see *Seattle Annual Report* (1913), 34–36, 38–40, 41–54; I also draw here on Nelson's descriptions of Seattle's progressive characteristics in "Frank B. Cooper," 168–69.

42 Larry Cuban, *How Teachers Taught: Constancy and Change in American Classrooms, 1890–1990*, 2nd ed. (New York: Teachers College Press, 1993), 46–114.

43 Frank Cooper, Memorandum to School Board, January 3, 1917, Seattle School Archives, Seattle Public Schools; also see Nelson, *Good Schools*, 62.

44 "Reports of Visits to Eastern Schools: Schools Adapted to Community Needs," *Seattle School Bulletin*, vol. 9, no. 3 (March 1921).

45 Ibid.

46 "Observation on Elementary Schools," *Seattle School Bulletin*, vol. 9, no. 3 (March 1921).

47   Frank B. Cooper, "The Ideals and Accomplishments of the Seattle School System," *NEA Addresses and Proceedings* (1921), 715.

48   *Seattle Annual Report* (1916), 61, 60.

49   "Intelligence Tests," *Seattle School Bulletin*, vol. 9, no. 3 (March 1921).

50   *Seattle Annual Report* (1914), 62.

51   *Seattle Annual Report* (1916), 70.

52   *Seattle School Bulletin* (January 1917).

53   Quoted in Putnam, *Class and Gender Politics in Progressive-Era Seattle*, 192.

54   Anna Louise Strong, "Glimpses in Seattle's Schools: Trade Training with Government Help," *Seattle Union Record* (June 13, 1918).

55   Ibid.

56   Frank Cooper, Memorandum to the Seattle School Board, December 30, 1916, Superintendent's Office Administrative Working Files, Box 1, Folder "Administration," Seattle School Archives, Seattle Public Schools.

57   Ibid.

58   E. Shorrock, "Some Unsolved Problems in School Administration," *NEA Addresses and Proceedings* (1917), 356–57.

59   Ibid.

60   On this development, see Nelson, *Good Schools*, 137.

61   Keith A. Murray, "The Charles Niederhauser Case: Patriotism in the Seattle Schools, 1919," *Pacific Northwest Quarterly* 74, no. 1 (January 1983): 14, 11-17.

62   Ibid., 12.

63   Richard C. Berner, *Seattle, 1921–1940: From Boom to Bust* (Seattle: Charles Press, 1992), 37, 41, 55–57.

64   Ibid.; Nelson, *Good Schools*.

65   Mrs. George A. Smith, "Letter to President and Members of the School Board, Seattle, Washington," March 31, 1922, Seattle School Archives, Superintendent Files, "Tax Reduction Council"; I also draw on the discussion of these events in Nelson, *Good Schools*, 146–65; and in Berner, *Seattle, 1921–1940*, 55–57.

66   Smith, "Letter to President and Members of the School Board."

67   Ibid.

68   Ibid. As early as 1893, e.g., the *Chicago Tribune* published more than thirty editorials attacking educational "fads and frills," and throughout this period, newspapers across the country continued to do so; see Charles R. Foster, *Editorial Treatment of Education in the American Press*, Harvard Bulletins in Education, no. 21 (Cambridge, MA: Harvard University Press, 1938).

69   Putnam, *Class and Gender Politics in Progressive-Era*, 101–2.

70   Smith, "Letter to President and Members of the School Board."

71   Smith, "Letter to President and Members of the School Board." Cooper specifically singled out one new board member, E. F. Taylor, an ally of cost-cutting community groups, labeling him an elitist. "Mr. Taylor stands for the one in forty," Cooper asserted, adding: "I stand for the forty rather than for the one" (see Nelson, *Good Schools*, 164).

72   A. E. Winship, "Cooper Resigns," *Journal of Education* 45 (April 13, 1922): 395–96.

73   See Nelson, *Good Schools*; Dominic W. Moreo, *Schools in the Great Depression* (New York: Garland, 1996), 85.

74   Rueben Jones, "On the Board," Manuscript by the Secretary to the School Board, Seattle Public School Archives, 8.

75 See, e.g., Paul W. Glad, "Progressives and the Business Culture of the 1920s," *Journal of American History* 53, no. 1 (June 1966): 75–89; David B. Tyack, "The Perils of Pluralism: The Background of the Pierce Case," *American Historical Review* 74, no. 1 (October 1968): 74–98.

76 As a cost-cutting measure, the district reduced the annual printing and distribution of district's annual reports by combining multiple years into a single report.

77 *Triennial Report of the Public Schools, Seattle, Washington, 1921–1924* (Seattle: Board of Directors, Seattle Public Schools, 1924), 35–38; *Triennial Report of the Public Schools, Seattle, Washington, 1927–1930* (Seattle: Board of Directors, Seattle Public Schools, 1930), hereafter cited as *Seattle Triennial Report*, with years of publication.

78 *Seattle Triennial Report* (1921–24), 137.

79 Tax Reduction Council quoted in Doris Hinson Pieroth, *Seattle's Women Teachers of the Interwar Years: Shapers of a Livable City* (Seattle: University of Washington Press, 2004), 164; Nelson, *Good Schools*, 159.

80 *Seattle Triennial Report* (1921–24), 137.

81 Actually, Cole's enthusiasm was doubly unwarranted. Not only did Cole's pronouncements exemplify an erroneous view of intelligence test results, but also, because Seattle administrators had reported the scores according to the "mental age" scale (rather than using the intelligent quotient whereby mental age was divided by chronological age), concentrations of students who were above-age for their grade, would have been likely to boost scores. Despite (or perhaps because of) misconceptions about this relatively new psychometric technology, Seattle school leaders continued to employ the tests throughout the 1920s and 1930s as a basis for the "better classification" of schoolchildren (*Seattle Triennial Report* [1921–24], 5–7). For a discussion of these and similar misinterpretations, see J. McVicker Hunt, *Intelligence and Experience* (New York: Ronald Press, 1961); and Stephen Jay Gould, *The Mismeasure of Man* (New York: W. W. Norton and Co., 1996).

82 *Seattle Triennial Report* (1921–24), 61–62, 60. In terms of the intermediate, or junior high, schools, Cole reported that "the practice of grouping is in accord with that generally adopted by American cities, according to 'City School Leaflet No. 22,' U.S. Bureau of Education, December, 1922" (*Seattle Triennial Report* [1924–27], 23).

83 *Seattle Triennial Report* (1921–1924), 80.

84 "The Opportunity of the Special Classes," *Seattle School Bulletin* (March 1925), 1–4.

85 *Seattle Triennial Report* (1921–24), 56–58; Fred C. Ayer, *Studies in Administrative Research*, 2 vols. ([Seattle]: Board of [School] Directors, 1924–25), 1:94–117, 2:107–26. Ayer stated that the districts he used were comparable in the methods they used to collect age-grade data.

86 In his review of the literature, Ayer cited studies by Cubberley, Terman, Ayres, Rugg, and Oakland's Virgil Dickson (*Studies in Administrative Research*, 2:116–19).

87 Terman quoted by Ayer, *Studies in Administrative Research*, 2:115.

88 Ibid., 119.

89 Ibid. 117; Ayer provides no bibliographic information on the Bliss study he mentions.

90 Helen Reynolds, "Judging the Worth of Activities," *NEA Addresses and Proceedings* (1927), 469–70.

91 Ibid.

92   See, e.g., National Education Association, "Facts on the Public School Curriculum," *NEA Research Bulletin* 1, no. 5 (November 1923): 326–29, and "Keeping Pace with the Advancing Curriculum," *NEA Research Bulletin* 3, nos. 4–5
(September–November 1925): 126–59.

93   "Demonstration Is Begun at Summit," *Seattle Educational Bulletin* 3, no. 3
(December 1926); *Seattle Triennial Report* (1924–27), 57–65; *Seattle Triennial
Report* (1927–30), 15–25. In 1925, Cole relaunched the regular bulletin from the
superintendent's office and renamed it the *Seattle Educational Bulletin*.

94   "Demonstration at Summit Explained," *Seattle Educational Bulletin* 4, no. 2
(November 1927); also see Pieroth, *Seattle's Women Teachers of the Interwar
Years*, 87-101.

95   Ayer, *Studies in Administrative Research*, 2:55.

96   Ibid., 56, 68, 71, 73.

97   *Seattle Triennial Report* (1921–24), 53; *Seattle Triennial Report* (1927–30), 9, 44.
On Seattle's continued use of comparisons and efforts to seek outside advice
regarding features such as upper-grade organization, see *Seattle Triennial Report*
(1921–24), 54.

98   On curriculum revision efforts in Seattle, see Frank E. Willard, "Revising the
Elementary School Curriculum," *Seattle Educational Bulletin*, vol. 1, no. 1 (Janu-
ary 1925); S. E. Fleming, "High School Curriculum Study," *Seattle Educational
Bulletin*, vol. 1, no. 1 (January 1925); F. E. Willard, "Curriculum Groups Show
Good Progress," *Seattle Educational Bulletin*, vol. 2, no. 8 (May 1926); and S. E.
Fleming, "Year Proves Worth of Curricula Shifts," *Seattle Educational Bulletin*,
vol. 2, no. 8 (May 1926); and *Seattle Triennial Report* (1924–27), 49–57.

99   Helen Mary Reynolds, "Problems Involved in Curriculum Revision in the
Elementary Schools of Seattle," *Progressive Education* 6 (1926): 242; Joseph E.
Slater, *Public Workers: Government Employee Unions, the Law, and the State,
1900–1962* (Ithaca, NY: IRL Press/Cornell University Press, 2004).

100   Slater, *Public Workers*; Moreo, *Schools in the Great Depression*.

101   Quoted in Moreo, *Schools in the Great Depression*, 84.

102   Slater, *Public Workers*, 43.

103   Quoted in ibid., 44.

104   Ibid.; for my earlier discussion of Denver school leaders, see chap. 4.

105   Slater, *Public Workers*, 48.

106   Ibid., 119.

CHAPTER 7

1   As I explain, this eclecticism is not exactly the kind of hybridized practice
described by Larry Cuban in *How Teachers Taught: Constancy and Change in
American Classrooms, 1890–1990*, 2nd ed. (New York: Teachers College Press,
1993), and I suggest that we find a pattern here that was more widespread.

2   Again, see Cuban (ibid.). Also in Cuban, see deliberations on "social efficiency"
and "scientific management," 76–91.

3   Jesse H. Newlon, "John Dewey's Influence in the Schools," *School and Society* 30
(November 23, 1929): 698.

4   Dickson did include the following statement. "WARNING: Lest the reader misun-
derstand our attitude toward the use of the mental tests, let us give this warning

statement. We do not believe that a mental test should be taken as the *sole* basis for grading or promoting or segregating children. What we do believe is that the mental test furnishes very important facts to be included as *one* factor, together with such other factors as health, attitude, behavior, training, environment, and heredity, in the making of the decision of what should be done for each individual child." Oakland Public Schools, *Oakland Annual Report* (Oakland, CA: Oakland Public Schools, 1917–18), 223.

5   Note that, in the *Oakland Report* for 1911–12, Superintendent McClymonds calls for ungraded rooms as a form of differentiation.

6   See, e.g., Arthur G. Powell, Eleanor Farrar, and David K. Cohen, *The Shopping Mall High School* (Boston: Houghton Mifflin, 1985); see especially Cohen's notes to chap. 5, where he identifies the contrast between evidence and interpretation.

7   "Superstudents' Schools Needed," *Rocky Mountain News*, February 19, 1916.

8   The historiography of early twentieth-century democracy has also, at times, tended to emphasize the themes of social control and industrial democracy in describing the motivations of the elite in spreading democratic practice. Although these analyses have much to offer—and, indeed, describe remarkably well the view that superintendents such as Aaron Gove took of his teachers as workers in a shoe factory—an overreliance on these concepts distracts us from some of the nuances of progressive thinking on the nature of American society. See, e.g., William Graebner, *The Engineering of Consent: Democracy and Authority in Twentieth Century America* (Madison: University of Wisconsin Press, 1987); and Herbert M. Kliebard, *Struggle for the American Curriculum, 1893–1958*, 2nd ed. (New York: Routledge, 1993). Kliebard, for one, makes a great deal of the social control stance of Edward Ross. Yet I found not one reference to Ross's writings among the many comments of district progressives, whether at national professional meetings, in personal letters, or in local documents or reports. Most of these men were not bashful about making a variety of claims or dropping names to back their arguments, so one would expect to see them discuss Ross if they drew on his work. This is not to say Ross was not influential, but the local evidence does not offer evidence of his widespread influence.

9   Leila Zenderland, *Measuring Minds: Henry Herbert Goddard and the Origins of American Intelligence Testing* (New York: Cambridge University Press, 1998), 296.

10 Edward L. Thorndike, "Intelligence and Its Uses," *Harpers* 140 (December 1919– May 1920): 235.

11 A. L. Threlkeld, "Changing Conceptions of Curriculum Making," 13-14, address given at the Fifth Annual Educational Conference, Lexington, Kentucky, October 26, 1928, Threlkeld Papers, Penrose Library, University of Denver.

12 Tom Clynes, "How to Raise a Genius," *Nature* 537 (September 8, 2016): 152–55.

INDEX

ability to learn, 67–71, 80, 85, 129, 138, 145–47, 171, 189, 215–17
Addams, Jane, 7, 113, 119, 208
administrative progressivism, 3, 65, 75, 78, 115, 156
administrative reorganization: Bobbitt on, 75, 151; Cubberley on, 75–78, 151–53, 181, 193, 241; curriculum reform and, 86; defined, 74–79; in Denver, 151–58, 181; depicted in organizational charts, 76, 77, 152, 153, 156; Dewey troubled by, 79; efficiency and, 78, 229; as foundation for other reforms, 115; intelligence testing and, 129; municipal reformers and, 76, 77, 93, 94, 95, 138, 259; in Oakland, 108, 111–12, 114, 115, 181; offers superintendents executive power, 59, 193, 203, 248; pedagogical progressivism and, 255; political powers and, 138; as progressive reform, 6, 23; proposed in Seattle, 230, 234–36, 241, 248; recommended in Portland, 191, 193, 203; requires relinquishment of school board authority, 115, 193; resistance to, 218, 248; student classification and, 86, 129; unsuccessful in Portland, 216–17, 257; unsuccessful in Seattle, 218, 234–36
African Americans, 42, 83, 134, 273–74n12
Alderman, Lewis R., 192–202, 204–5, 207–9, 212–13, 217, 227, 255, 261
Alki Suffrage Club (Seattle), 239
Allen, William H., 4, 31, 118, 149
American Commonwealth, The (Bryce), 46
American Council of Education, 57
American Defense Society, 209
American Federation of Labor, 160
American Federation of Teachers, 249–51
Americanization, 25, 257, 261; in Oakland, 113, 117, 119, 122–25, 132, 138; in Portland, 207–9, 211, 217

American Municipal Progress (Zueblin), 24
annual reports, 33; in Denver, 146, 156, 158, 160, 174; in Oakland, 104, 114, 118, 126–27; in Portland, 194, 200, 207; in Seattle, 228
Asians, 132–34
assessment. *See* testing
Athens Athletic Club (Oakland), 106
attendance, 40–41, 43, 45, 54, 69–70, 86, 261–62; in Denver, 147; in Oakland, 106, 117, 126, 138; in Portland, 184–85, 202; in Seattle, 245
Avery, Lewis, 109, 135
Ayer, Fred, 16, 19, 220, 243
Ayres, Leonard: on curriculum, 42, 223, 233; on differences between schools, 42, 43; as director of education and statistics at Russell Sage Foundation, 19, 40, 41; on efficiency of state school systems, 19, 20; on explanations for student failure, 41–42, 69; influence on district progressives and policy, 101–2, 122, 146, 188, 227, 245, 261; as investigator of student failure and overageness, 41, 43, 79, 245; lack of attention to racial disparities and, 42; *Laggards in Our Schools* and, 41; on Los Angeles, 43; on New York City schools, 41, 42; on Portland, 43; on Joseph Rice and assessment, 39; Strong and, 232; on student failure as an urban problem, 41, 43, 258, 261, 277n81; on student inability to learn, 42; on western states, 19

Bagley, William C., 23, 130
Bailey, Henry Turner, 27
Baltimore, MD, 33
Barker, Albert C., 97, 103–6, 109–13, 115, 193
Barrows, Alice, 213
Barzee, Lloyd, 135